D1544809

THE MAKING OF MODERN ISRAEL

Also by Leslie Stein

The Hope Fulfilled: The Rise of Modern Israel

THE MAKING OF MODERN ISRAEL

1948–1967

LESLIE STEIN

polity

First published in 2009 by Polity Press
Reprinted in 2009

Polity Press
65 Bridge Street
Cambridge CB2 1UR, UK

Polity Press
350 Main Street
Malden, MA 02148, USA

ISBN-13: 978-0-7456-4466-0

A catalogue record for this book is available from the British Library.

Typeset in 10.75 on 14 pt Adobe Janson
by Servis Filmsetting Ltd, Stockport, Cheshire
Printed and bound in the United States by Maple-Vail Book Manufacturing Group

For further information on Polity, visit our website: www.politybooks.com

To Clara with love

CONTENTS

List of Illustrations

Tables

ACKNOWLEDGMENT

All photographs in the body of this book are derived with permission from the Israel Government Press Office.

PREFACE

This book aims to provide a succinct overview of one of the most critical periods in Israel's short history, during which the country's nature and character were molded. Within a time frame of only 19 years, Israel fought three separate wars. In two of them its very existence was at stake. On the home front, it absorbed a deluge of migrants from a diverse number of countries causing its population to double within four years. From its inception, the state had been confronted with acute economic difficulties, intra-Jewish ethnic tensions, a problematic Arab minority and a secular–religious divide. Apart from defense issues, Israel faced a generally hostile or, at best, indifferent international community. Unlike its Arab neighbors, it was hard pressed to secure great-power patronage or even official sympathy and understanding.

Based mainly on secondary sources, this book is grounded in a wide study of the received literature, both in Hebrew and English. Hopefully, its strength lies in a judicious synthesis of the published material yielding the reader a reliable and novel account of Israel's fateful and turbulent infancy. Although unashamedly sympathetic to Israel's general plight, I have not stinted in reporting the country's blemishes and occasional misdeeds. The educated lay reader as well as the student pursuing Israeli studies can therefore rest assured that the text presents a balanced and, as far as humanely possible, fair rendition of Israel's early years.

In an effort to ensure accuracy, I was able to secure the assistance of the following eminent Israel historians: Mordechai Bar-On, Yoav Gelber, Efraim Karsh, Michael Oren, and Anita Shapira. They each scrutinized various chapters and proffered advice. Where any defects remain, the fault is purely mine. Warm thanks are due to Andrea Drugan, Polity's editor, for her enthusiasm, encouragement, and wise counsel. My wife Clara and son Mark gave useful advice relating to stylistic matters whereas Helen Boneham and Debbie Jeffrey, both of Macquarie University, assisted me respectively with the construction of maps and the backup of files. As usual, the staff members of my university's inter-library loan department were extraordinarily forthcoming. To all of the above, I wish to express my gratitude.

Finally, I would like to single out my wife Clara for her constant support, understanding, and patience while I was engaged in the writing process. It is to her that this book is dedicated.

Leslie Stein
Macquarie University,
Sydney, Australia

INTRODUCTION

By the late nineteenth century, the Jews, who had been in exile for almost two thousand years, found their ancestral homeland in Palestine largely occupied by Arabs and governed by the Turks. Considering that they were then dispersed throughout the world as a weak and vulnerable minority, their ascendancy to statehood some decades later, in May 1948, constituted an extraordinary historic landmark. Many likened the rebirth of Israel to a modern miracle. Even distinguished savants, who could not bring themselves to believe in miracles, were awed by Israel's re-emergence. Included among them was Arthur Koestler who wrote: "If a golf ball were suddenly to start off towards the hole without being hit, this would not constitute a miracle but merely what is called a statistically highly improbable event. In the same way the rebirth of Israel is not a miracle, but it is, there is no getting around it, a statistically highly improbable event."[1]

Israel's re-emergence resulted from the interplay of actions undertaken by Jews and non-Jews alike. As the Jews strove for statehood by dint of hard work and sacrifice, external variables were critical in either promoting or retarding their venture.

Essentially, Koestler's golf ball began to get rolling in 1881 when the Russian Czar, Alexander II, was assassinated. Because a woman who had played a secondary role in Alexander II's demise was identified as being

Jewish, the Russian press inferred that the Jews were generally culpable. A month later, that is, in mid-April and about the time of the Russian Orthodox Easter, when the Passover blood libel was usually circulated, a series of pogroms (anti-Jewish riots) erupted, encompassing more than a hundred different localities,

There seemed little doubt that the pogroms were pre-planned and, if not government-organized, then at least government-inspired. The general populace reveled in the outrages and, to the dismay of the Jews, the revolutionary and liberal establishment either endorsed the violence or stood aloof in stony silence. Not surprisingly, most Jews concluded that they had no future in Russia. Increasingly, they set their sights on migrating to more enlightened western countries. Nonetheless, a tiny minority determined that, no matter where they went, they would always be strangers in strange lands and that their only salvation lay in returning to and redeeming the land of Israel. By the end of 1882, acting on such convictions, some seven thousand Russian Jews settled in Palestine.

Palestine at that time was an Ottoman Empire backwater. It was populated by less than half a million Arabs who overwhelmingly were subsistence farmers subject to wretched housing and sanitary conditions. Most were illiterate and, plagued by malaria, typhus, typhoid and cholera, they had very low life expectancies. Large tracts of land were desolate and swamp-ridden and transport and communication facilities were few and far between. In a letter from Palestine dated July 29, 1882, Leib Bienstock wrote that

> to this day there are no roads, not only from village to village but also from the city of one region to another. The road between Jaffa and Jerusalem is riddled with ridges and potholes even though the coachmen pay excessive taxes. Throughout the entire length of the road, you will not find a single stone that has been laid properly.[2]

The Jaffa to Jerusalem road was only laid in 1869 to commemorate the official visit of the Austrian Kaiser Franz Joseph. Up to then wagons were a sight unseen, with all transport being undertaken on pack animals.

Among the Arabs were some 25,000 pious Jews who had over the centuries gravitated to Palestine to engage in prayer and contemplation. Not being in the least bit Zionistic (see *Zionism* in glossary), they resented the arrival of those bent on farming. Furthermore, dismayed by what they regarded as the lax religious observance by the newcomers, their rabbis, in 1883, proclaimed that Palestine was incapable of sustaining mass immigration and that the settlers were "not walking in the road of the Torah and the fear of God and, far from drawing redemption near, they were delaying it, God forbid!"[3]

Upon their arrival in Palestine, Jewish aspiring farmers purchased derelict and malaria-infested land along the coastal plain and in parts of the Galilee which they began to cultivate. Most of the newcomers were family men, drawn from the ranks of the lower middle class. To their dismay, a combination of inexperience, the harsh physical environment, and bureaucratic obstructionism rapidly caused their scant savings to be depleted. Hovering on the verge of bankruptcy, they were rescued by Baron Edmond de Rothschild who not only provided them with capital and technical expertise but also attended to their consumer and social needs. By 1904, in no small part through Rothschild's seemingly boundless munificence, the Jewish population in Palestine (known in Hebrew as the "Yishuv") had reached a total of 55,000.

At the close of the nineteenth century, a modern political Zionist movement emerged. The inception of political Zionism (see glossary) was largely the outcome of the single-handed efforts of its founder, Theodor Herzl. In 1891, Herzl, who was born into a reform Jewish-Hungarian family, became the Paris correspondent of the Vienna based *Neue Freie Presse*. During the course of his journalistic assignments, he became increasingly troubled by manifestations of rabid anti-Semitism. Having become obsessed with the "Jewish problem," he eventually concluded that the primary cause of his people's tribulations lay in their statelessness. In 1896, he published his famous booklet in which he argued the case for the formation of a Jewish state. This resulted in a flurry of well-wishers and offers of support. Matters rapidly gathered momentum and, by August 1897, Herzl presided over the founding congress of the World Zionist Organization, held at Basel, Switzerland. Over two hundred delegates from twenty different countries attended. Their goals, encapsulated into what became known as the Basel Program, were expressed in terms of their seeking "to secure the creation of a home for the Jewish people in Palestine secured by public law."

Even beforehand, Herzl had made overtures to various personages and heads of state in his quest for an internationally recognized charter to facilitate Jewish settlement in Palestine. While none of his efforts bore fruit, the new Zionist movement established valuable economic institutions, such as the Jewish National Fund and the Jewish Colonial Bank for Palestine. When, in the period 1904 to 1914, a second migratory wave of Jewish migrants streamed into Palestine, a locally based office of the World Zionist Organization was able to afford them a modest amount of practical assistance.

Like the initial migratory wave (*aliyah*) that preceded it, the second one was the product of endemic Russian-Jewish persecution. In the years immediately prior to the 1905 Russian revolution and in the period shortly thereafter, as reactionary forces regrouped to undermine the democratic reforms, the Jews were once again bedeviled by pogroms. The first one took place in April 1903 in Kishinev. Later, in September of the same year, violence broke out in Homel. Then in October 1905, at the height of the revolutionary fervor, approximately 690 separate pogroms, mainly in the Ukraine, were recorded. All told, a total of 876 Jews were slaughtered.

Traumatized by such events, socialist Zionist youth hastened to Palestine, where they devised a doctrine of the "conquest of labor," entailing the transformation of Jews from occupations in commerce (where they were unduly represented) to those involving manual labor. They upheld that the "normalization" of the structure of the Jewish work force resting on a solid working-class base was an essential prerequisite for the formation of a viable and self-reliant Jewish society. True to their beliefs, they sought employment as unskilled farm hands. This put them on a collision course with the now established farmers of the first *aliyah* whose Zionist ardor had already waned and who preferred hiring cheaper and more compliant Arabs. As a result, the process of obtaining work was often a humiliating one. One youngster by the name of Eliyahu Even-Tov remembered standing on the threshold of a farmer's abode while the farmer and his family ate their evening meal. While partaking of his food and drink, the farmer fixed his gaze on him. Eventually, speaking in Yiddish, the farmer grunted "You idiots. This is the land of the Ishmaelites [Arabs] and not the land of Israel. If fellows like you would only go to America where you would make a fortune, then even here things would not be so bad." As Even-Tov later wrote, "twenty-five years have passed since then and still within my heart, there lingers the painful image of my standing alongside that door."[4]

Being paid a pittance, the youngsters dwelled in decrepit shacks where they made do with discarded boxes for furniture. To sustain themselves, they entered into makeshift communes, pooling their meager earnings and arranging for women comrades to cook for them. At the end of a day's grinding toil, they were able to derive some sense of solidarity and comfort from dancing the *hora* (a circle dance). Given such conditions, the turnover rate was high but in 1910, some, among the more stout-hearted, managed to establish the first kibbutz, Degania.

David Ben-Gurion, Israel's first prime minister, was among such youth. Arriving in Palestine from Poland in 1906 at the age of twenty, he first worked as a farm hand before moving full-time into the political arena by joining the newly formed Poalei Zion (Workers of Zion) party. Along with Moshe Sharett, who migrated with his family to Palestine in 1906 at the age of twelve, Ben-Gurion spent a couple of years in Istanbul studying law and acquiring a working knowledge of Turkish. Sharett, by virtue of his father first settling in a remote Arab village, had already attained fluency in Arabic. During the First World War, Ben-Gurion found himself in America where he joined the (British) Jewish Legion to return to Palestine in uniform. After the war, he was among the founders of the Histadrut (Jewish Labor Federation) and for many years served as its secretary general. Subsequently, both he and Sharett occupied key posts in the Jewish Agency, which, from 1923, represented and administered the Jewish community. Although physically short in stature, Ben-Gurion towered above all others and was the main driving force in declaring Israel's independence.

The youthful Jewish farm laborers were not the only ones then breaking new ground. Middle-class immigrants living in Jaffa, a port city dominated by Arabs, assumed the initiative in establishing Tel Aviv. They were driven to do so by Jaffa's general lack of sanitation and by its all pervading filth and malodor. Running water was unavailable and the wells from which it was drawn were frequently contaminated, giving rise to repetitive outbreaks of typhoid. There were no shops selling fresh food, which could only be secured in an oriental-style bazaar or in open air markets. For good measure, a shortage of accommodation led to high rental costs.

In 1907, some sixty Jewish Jaffa residents formed a housing estate association and, with finance supplied by the Jewish National Fund, they were by 1910 able to move into their new homes on sand dunes acquired just north of Jaffa. In accordance with their stated aims, the houses were built "in an orderly manner, with wide and attractive streets, to include, in as much as possible, sanitary installations, such as sewage drains, water pipes and so on, and to set an exemplary standard for the general development of urban Jewish settlement."[5] Soon other housing associations were formed and by 1914 Tel Aviv (still officially part of Jaffa) contained 139 private dwellings housing 1,419 people.[6] The Palestine Office of the World Zionist Organization relocated there, as did a number of workshops. Under the mayoralty of Meir Dizengoff, Tel Aviv began to assume the role of the center of the Yishuv. As Arthur Ruppin, the World Zionist Organization's emissary, enthused: "You will find in the Jewish neighborhood [Tel Aviv] an effervescent Jewish life that possibly has no counterpart anywhere else in the world."[7]

Two other and possibly linked pre-World War One events bear mentioning. On account of the early Jewish settlements being subject to the depredations of marauding Arab bands, in 1909 members of Poalei Zion founded a Jewish defense organization called Hashomer (the Guard). Adherents of Hashomer had a romantic and heroic aura about them. They tended to dress in Arabic garments, complete with *keffiyas* (headscarves) held in place by thick woollen bands. With their dazzling moustaches, their bandoliers and large riding boots, they cut dashing figures as they mounted their caparisoned horses. All were armed, some sporting rifles and revolvers and some even brandishing swords. Their presence in the settlements that hired them provided farmers with a measure of security.

During the same period, aspects of an Arab nationalism began to emerge. In Palestine, this was expressed through petitions to Turkish authorities requesting the prohibition of both further Jewish immigration and land sales to Jews. While almost all articulate Arabs were opposed to the Zionist enterprise, some writers were not oblivious to the merit of the Zionists' case. For example, in his book, *The Awakening of the Arab Nation in Turkish Asia*, published in 1905, Neguib Azoury wrote: "Two important phenomena, *with the same characteristics* but which are diametrically opposed to each other, and which have so far not attracted notice, are appearing in Turkish Asia. They are the Arab national awakening and the latent efforts of Jews to re-establish, on a grand scale, their ancient kingdom of Israel."[8] Even earlier, in 1899, in a letter to Rabbi Zadok Kahn, the chief rabbi of Paris, Yusuf al-Khalidi, a prominent Jerusalem Arab, wrote: "Who can challenge the rights of the Jews to Palestine? *Good lord, historically it is really your country.*"[9] But he hastened to add that the native population would not countenance Zionism. Nevertheless, such opposition did not manifest itself in any serious or generally violent way until after the First World War when the masses were whipped up by the Muslim clergy.

It was the First World War itself that initially posed a serious challenge to the continuity of the Yishuv. Since almost all Jews who settled in Palestine retained the citizenship of their countries of origin, Russian-Jewish nationals were deemed to be enemy aliens (Turkey had allied itself with Germany). In December 1914, 7,000 were summarily expelled followed, during the next year, by another 4,000. Those that remained had to contend with unbearable hardships. Palestine was ravished by a locust plague and, after being cut off from trading with the outside world, a chronic and severe food shortage unfolded causing widespread hunger and malnutrition.

The Jews were not simply passive spectators. In March 1915, throwing in their lot with the Allied Forces, some 500 exiled members of the Yishuv enlisted in the British army's Zion Mule Corps to serve as muleteers in Gallipoli under the command of Colonel John Patterson. Their senior Zionist officer was Captain Joseph Trumpeldor who, as a Jewish-Russian soldier in 1904, lost his left arm in the Russian–Japanese War. Despite his physical handicap, Trumpeldor not only served in the corps with due dispatch but just prior to that he was farming in Palestine. After the war, he supervised the defense of the Jewish settlement of Tel Hai, where he was fatally shot. As a doctor attended to him, he murmured: "It doesn't matter. It is good to die for our country." Both his words and deeds inspired generations of pioneers to ride out the seemingly endless struggles that culminated in Israel's independence.

The Zion Mule Corps was wound down in December 1915 at the

end of the Gallipoli campaign, to be replaced, in 1918, by the formation of the British Jewish Legion, also commanded by Colonel Patterson. Some of the 5,000 Jewish Legionnaires saw action in Palestine just before the war ended. Finally, a small group within the Yishuv banded together to spy on behalf of Britain. Their ring, which they called Nili, supplied the British with vital information relating to the strength and deployment of Turkish forces. It was uncovered when one of its carrier pigeons landed among the chief of police's own birds. The group was soon rounded up and badly manhandled. Their leader, Sara Aaronson, was subject to agonizing torture. At one point she was escorted back to her house for a change of clothing and, while alone in her bathroom, she reached for a pistol secreted behind a panel and shot herself. She died three days later.

In September 1918, the British, who had captured Jerusalem the previous December, completed their conquest of Palestine. Turkish rule, which dated from 1517, had finally been brought to an end and the country was now in the hands of a benevolent world power. More significantly, that power had recently committed itself to "the establishment in Palestine of a national home for the Jewish people." The commitment was conveyed in a letter to Lord Rothschild issued on November 2, 1917, by Arthur Balfour, the British Foreign Secretary. It soon became known as the Balfour Declaration and essentially it represented the charter that had so eluded Herzl.

A lion's share of the credit for the issuing of the Balfour Declaration can be attributed to Dr Chaim Weizmann, who became Israel's first president. Born in Russia in 1874, Weizmann studied biochemistry in both Switzerland and Germany. In 1904, he took up a lectureship in chemistry at Manchester University. On account of his groundbreaking research into a fermentation process which could facilitate the production of acetone, needed for explosives, Weizmann was appointed as an adviser to the Ministry of Munitions and the Admiralty, both overseen by Lloyd George. At the same time, he was a fully fledged Zionist, holding the co-vice presidency of the British Zionist Federation. Being an urbane and cosmopolitan intellectual, Weizmann used his charm to prevent British cabinet ministers from deviating from their chosen path of issuing a proclamation in favor of a Jewish homeland in Palestine. Although they were primarily interested in securing the backing of

American Jewry for the war effort, they were also motivated by a religious sense of fair play.

Armed with a League of Nations mandate to administer Palestine in accordance with the objectives of the Balfour Declaration, Britain assumed full responsibility for the running of the country. Between 1919 and 1923, 35,000 Jews immigrated to Palestine. Then in the period 1924–6, another 62,000 arrived. The first group consisted of young pioneers fleeing from a wave of persecution sweeping through the Ukraine and White Russia where, between 1915 and 1921, perhaps a quarter of a million Jews "were slain or allowed to starve to death."[10] The second group was made up of mature-aged middle-class migrants leaving Poland on account of legislation that undermined Jewish economic life.

The young pioneers provided welcome support to the budding kibbutz movement by creating new collective settlements on stretches of land in the Jezreel Valley purchased by the Jewish National Fund. The land in question, which had been neglected over many generations, was for the most part barren. It was strewn with rocks, covered with weeds and thistles, remote and swarming with snakes and scorpions. The lower parts were swamp-ridden and infested with malaria-bearing mosquitoes. During the day, there were few, if any, trees to provide shade and at night the sound of howling jackals and the constant expectation of attacks from roving Bedouin provided an uneasy rest for the settlers. When draining the swamps, the settlers stood waist-deep in water, digging channels and laying grids of clearance pipes. Some of them succumbed to malaria, others were chronically enervated.

With the government allocating large sums of money for public works, partly to provide jobs for unemployed migrants, pioneers organized temporary labor brigades to secure subcontracts for the construction of various sections of a highway. Like the kibbutzim (plural of kibbutz), the labor brigades were organized on a collective and equitable basis. Sleeping in camps and rising at dawn, members would set to work dynamiting large boulders that would then be piled next to the road in the making. Sitting astride each pile, young women would pound the rocks into small gravel stones, which after being laid, were compressed by steamrollers. The road workers were subject to the searing Palestinian heat waves that invariably occur each summer and which were exacerbated by the nature of the materials which they had to handle. In winter, torrential rains loosened their tent pegs, allowing strong gusts of wind to sweep away their canvas covers. Food on hand was barely edible and dysentery was rife.

Rallying to such workers were Golda Meir and Levi Eshkol, both of whom were destined to become Israeli prime ministers. Born in Kiev in 1896, Meir along with her parents migrated to the USA in 1903. But by 1921, she and her husband Morris Meyerson, a sign painter, went to Palestine where they were accepted as members of Kibbutz Merhavia situated in the Jezreel Valley. In 1924, Meir left the kibbutz to become a labor Zionist functionary, occupying various posts in the Histadrut and then in the Jewish Agency. Levi Eshkol, a year older than Meir, was born in a village not far from Kiev. Unlike Meir, he went to Palestine in 1914 and joined the Jewish Legion after British forces had occupied much of the country. But at the war's end, he too became a kibbutz member (of Kibbutz Degania Beth) and, like Meir, he ultimately abandoned kibbutz farming to embroil himself in labor affairs, being (among other things) a founding member of the Histadrut and then a leading light in its agricultural center.

Throughout most of the 1920s, Palestine enjoyed relative tranquility but, both at the beginning and end of the decade, there were serious anti-Jewish disturbances. In response, the Jews established an underground defense militia known as the Haganah that superseded Hashomer and which had a more serious military orientation. The initial outburst of unrest in 1921 was quickly contained yet, by 1929, incited by Haj Amin al-Husseini, the Mufti of Jerusalem, attacks upon Jews resumed with an even greater degree of venom. That 67 pious non-Zionist Jews in Hebron and 45 in Safad were massacred suggests that the assailants were motivated by Islamic anti-Semitism.

Al-Husseini was in essence handed the post of Mufti of Jerusalem by Sir Herbert Samuel, the country's first high commissioner. Being himself a Jew, Samuel was anxious to demonstrate to the Arabs that he was even-handed. That led to him being easily persuaded to promote al-Husseini, an outright anti-Semite and opponent of the British administration whose clerical accreditations were, to boot, minimal. Compounding his poor judgment, Samuel also appointed al-Husseini as president of the newly formed Supreme Muslim Council. The Council, which had a large non-audited government financed budget, had been accredited with official control of all Muslim religious trusts and courts. By assuming its presidency, al-Husseini not only became the recognized head of the country's Muslim community, but also the most powerful political force within the Arab-Palestinian movement.[11]

During the 1930s, the Jewish population increased significantly. Between 1930 and 1939, when Central and Eastern Europe was gripped by an exceedingly virulent strain of racist Jewish hatred, more than 270,000 sought refuge in Palestine bringing the Yishuv's numbers to 475,000, or slightly more than 30 percent of the entire population. A large proportion of the Jewish immigrants emanated from Nazi Germany and Austria. Many were members of the free professions while others were scientists and entrepreneurs, au fait with commerce and industry and with a flair for sound organization and order. Mobilizing its enriched human resources, as well as large quantities of imported capital, the Yishuv made significant economic headway. It also widened its cultural life. In 1936 under the leadership of the world famous violinist, Bronislaw Huberman, the Palestine Symphony Orchestra was formed. Its first conductor was Arturo Toscanini.

Meanwhile, the Arabs began to be increasingly alarmed at the accelerating pace of Jewish immigration. Had it continued, they would most certainly have become a minority. Matters reached a climax in April 1936 with the outbreak of a general Arab uprising, entailing volunteers from neighboring countries. The main thrust of the rebels' enmity was directed against the British seen as the Yishuv's official sponsors and protectors. The scale of the fighting was both ferocious and extensive. At one point the rebels captured Hebron, Beersheba, and the Old City of Jerusalem, while in Nablus they strutted about armed to the teeth without let or hindrance. With the government's resources being stretched to the limit, the cooperation of the Yishuv was elicited. A special mandatory auxiliary police force, manned by Jewish volunteers, almost all of whom were members of the Haganah, was commissioned. By the spring of 1939 that force numbered close to 21,000 men.[12] In addition, the Hanagah openly organized its own mobile units, some of which received guidance and instruction from Orde Wingate, a sympathetic British officer. By the end of 1939, after the arrival of British reinforcements under the command of General

Bernard Montgomery (later famous for defeating the Nazis in the battle of El Alamein) and after applying torture, arbitrary executions in the field and the imposition of collective punishment,[13] the government ultimately prevailed.

The Arab uprising had the perverse effect of enabling the Yishuv to emerge with an enhanced degree of self-confidence in its ability to fend for itself. Indeed, had it not been for the Arab rebellion, which compelled the Jews to realign and reorganize their own paramilitary apparatus, it is highly unlikely that they would have withstood the combined Arab offensive arraigned against them some ten years later. With that aspect of the revolt rebounding to their benefit, there was yet another outcome that was very much to their detriment. As war clouds in Europe gathered momentum, Britain became increasingly anxious to pacify the Arabs. To secure Arab support or, at a minimum, to ensure Arab neutrality, it officially reneged on its commitment to the Zionists. Over a five-year period, commencing in May 1939, a ceiling of only 75,000 additional Jews were to be allowed into Palestine. Thereafter, further inflows were to be contingent upon Arab consent. Given that there was absolutely no chance of such consent being forthcoming, the British volte-face threatened to terminate the entire Zionist venture.

With the Royal Navy undertaking to intercept unauthorized boats bearing Jewish refugees to Palestine, the Haganah planned to sabotage British naval installations. But once Britain, on September 3, 1939 declared war on Germany, the Yishuv offered His Majesty's Government its full cooperation and encouraged its members to enlist in the British armed forces. Some 26,000 did so, including members of the British Jewish Brigade that in the closing months of the war fought in Italy under a banner bearing the Star of David. The Yishuv also rendered the British military assistance in its campaign to subdue Vichy forces in Lebanon. It was while aiding the British in Lebanon that Moshe Dayan, Israel's future chief of staff and defense minister, lost his left eye. Born in 1915 in Degania and raised in the farming village of Nahalal, Dayan's disability did not prevent him from serving in the War of Independence and in subsequent wars. He was an intrepid but wayward warrior.

While the Yishuv pulled its weight in helping to defeat Nazi Germany, the Arabs, despite being wooed by Britain with its newfound anti-Zionist policy, tended to side with the enemy. During the war the

Palestinian's unchallenged leader, Haj Amin al-Husseini, was ensconced in Germany organizing Arab and Muslim volunteers to fight alongside the Germans and broadcasting Nazi propaganda to the Middle East and North Africa. Despite the British–Egyptian Treaty stipulating that Egypt was to come to Britain's aid in time of war, Egypt declared itself a non-belligerent ally. In Iraq, the British army had to unseat Rashid Ali al Gailani, who, in 1941, after a successful coup, strove to place the Mosul oil fields at Hitler's disposal.

Immediately after the war and in the wake of Haj Amin al-Husseini's shameful collaboration with Hitler, involving an appeal to the Nazis to include Palestinian Jews in the Holocaust, the Yishuv anticipated that Britain would revert to its previously held pro-Zionist position. When the British Labour Party was swept to power in July 1945, the Zionists were ecstatic, for its platform included an unequivocal commitment to their cause. The British Labour Party, in a conference held in December 1944, adopted a position that even the most statist of mainstream Zionists hesitated to take. Not only did it favor Palestine in its entirety becoming the Jewish National Home, in which the Jewish Agency would have full freedom to determine the country's immigration and economic policies but it even suggested that "the Arabs be encouraged to move out as the Jews move in."[14] As Weizmann emphasized, he and his colleagues "had never contemplated the removal of the Arabs."[15]

However, on assuming office, the new Labour government, now subject to the anti-Jewish bias of top-ranking foreign affairs officials, had a change of heart. It began to fear for the security of its oil imports and for its standing among Middle Eastern states. Accordingly, it reverted to the anti-Zionist policy of the previous administration. Notwithstanding the intercession of the Americans for an immediate transfer to Palestine of 100,000 displaced Jewish refugees, Britain now set immigration quotas at no more than 1,500 per month.

In despair, the Yishuv took up arms. Key bridges were sabotaged, direct attacks on army and police installations were undertaken, and a wing of the King David Hotel in Jerusalem, which housed the British military headquarters, was demolished. Three Yishuv organizations took part: the Haganah (representing the bulk of the Yishuv), the Irgun, and the Lehi. The Irgun was a relatively small minority-supported body under the command of Menahem Begin. Born in 1913 in Brest (then part of Poland), Begin, after graduating in law at the University of Warsaw, became the leading light in Betar, a youth movement dedicated to the establishment via the barrel of a gun of a Jewish state on both sides of the River Jordan. In the early stages of the war he was imprisoned by the Soviets and then, when Germany invaded Russia, he was released and joined the Polish army. Not believing his luck, he was included in a detachment that was sent to Palestine. Once there, friends arranged for his discharge, thereby enabling him to assume control of the Irgun, which was based on Betar principles. In 1977, Begin became prime minister of Israel. He had a solid classical education and was a superb orator and skilled linguist. As to Lehi, an even smaller deviant fighting force than the Irgun, it was far less restrained. Its leader Avraham Stern had a penchant for robbing banks as a means of financing it.

The British sought to quash the Yishuv's uprising by detaining leading Zionists, placing cities and settlements under curfew, and conducting sweeping searches for weapons. Fortunately for the Jews, Britain desisted from applying even more stringent measures so as not to alienate the US, its exclusive economic benefactor. Finally, in February 1947, faced with limited freedom of action and burdened by the growing cost of its involvement in Palestine, Britain reluctantly referred all matters relating to Palestine to the United Nations.

After conducting a thorough investigation, a Special UN Commission recommended that Palestine be partitioned into a Jewish and an Arab state with Jerusalem to be placed under international supervision. In part, the Commission was influenced by the submission of a high-ranking Syrian official who candidly admitted that under an Arab-Palestinian regime all Jews would be expelled. This led the Commission to conclude that the Jews could not reasonably be entrusted to Arab domination and that awarding them a state of their own made both ethical and political sense. In the area of Palestine that the Commission outlined for a Jewish state, the Jews not only constituted a majority but they had also carved out a state in the making. That budding state had its own self-contained economy, a system of democratic self-government, a defense force (albeit an underground one), comprehensive health and educational institutions, its own language (Hebrew), and a vibrant cultural life.

As it happens, there was one other factor that persuaded the UN Commission of the strength of the Jewish case and that was the saga

of the *Exodus*. In July 1947, an old Chesapeake Bay ferryboat, originally named *President Garfield* and then *Exodus*, left Port de Bouc, near
Marseilles, France, with 4,500 Jewish Holocaust survivors. Bound for
Palestine, it was soon tracked and escorted across the Mediterranean
by the British navy which then attacked it, killing three Jews on board.
The badly damaged *Exodus* was then taken to the Palestine port of Haifa
where the British forced the refugees to return to Port de Bouc in three
other vessels. In France, the passengers refused point blank to disem-
bark and, for their part, the French were not prepared to compel them
to do so. The ships were then ordered to proceed to Hamburg where the
refugees were dragged, kicking and screaming, into a detention camp in
the heartland of Germany. All this made a deep impression on the UN
Special Commission, convincing it of the immediate need to allow Jews
entry into Palestine.

On November 29, 1947, the Commission's recommendations were
adopted by a two-thirds majority of the UN General Assembly. The
voting pattern was remarkable; contrary to expectations, the Soviet
Union sided with America. Both states had their own reasons for favoring partition, Russia because it provided an opportunity to eject Britain
from Palestine, the US because it seemed the decent thing to do.

While the Jews were more than satisfied with the UN decision, the
Arabs, who were not prepared to yield as much as an inch of the country,
resolutely opposed it. They immediately expressed their opposition by
attacking the Yishuv. In the course of the next few months, as Britain
gradually relinquished its responsibility to administer the country and
to maintain an elementary degree of law and order, the Yishuv found
itself at the receiving end of Arab fury. Its access to settlements in the
Galilee and the Negev, and more importantly, to Jerusalem, was under
constant threat. At first, not wishing to clash with British forces, the
Yishuv maintained a relatively passive stance. But by April 1948, when
the British evacuation from Palestine was in full swing, the Haganah
went on the offensive. Supply convoys reached besieged Jerusalem and
in the second half of the month the Yishuv wrested control of Tiberius,
Haifa, Safad, and Jaffa.

On May 14, 1948, on the eve of the date set by Britain for the termination of its mandate and with the area that the UN had allotted to the
Jews being firmly in their hands, the state of Israel was finally declared.

Its inauguration was announced by David Ben-Gurion at a small gathering that assembled in the main hall of the Tel Aviv Art Museum. (Israel then had only 650,000 Jews.) As the proceedings concluded, strains of the Israeli national anthem, "Hatikvah," played by the Palestine Symphony Orchestra (now the Israel Philharmonic Orchestra) wafted from the floor above. The hope expressed in the anthem's final verse: "the hope of two thousand years, to be a free nation in our homeland, the land of Zion and Jerusalem," was, after many years of blood, sweat and tears, finally realized.

The very next day, the fledgling state was invaded by the Arab armies of Syria, Iraq, Transjordan, and Egypt, plus a small contingent from Saudi Arabia. The Arab League's objective, as articulated by its secretary general, Abdul Rahman Azzam Pasha, was to ensure that the UN partition demarcations would "be nothing but a line [sic] of fire and blood."[16]

Map 0.1   *Palestine on the eve of the War of Independence*

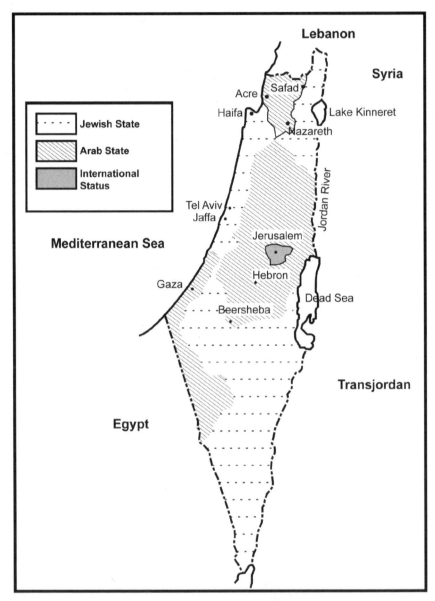

Map 0.2 *United Nations General Assembly Partition Plan*

1

THE WAR OF INDEPENDENCE

At first light on May 15, 1948, Egyptian planes heralded the pan-Arab invasion by bombing Tel Aviv. Thereafter three broad fronts more or less opened simultaneously. The Syrians, with some Lebanese assistance, threatened Israel's north, Iraq and Transjordan its center, and Egypt its south.

As the warring parties faced off one another, there was a near balance in the number of opposing troops along most of the *broad* fronts, except that, within specific arenas, isolated kibbutzim were vastly outnumbered. Of the 30,000 men and women enlisted in the Haganah and its offshoot the Palmah, about 25,000 were posted at the frontlines, matching the 24,000 soldiers that the Arabs had mustered.[1] Even though there appeared to be some parity in numbers, unlike the invaders, who were starting *de novo*, Israel's troops were fatigued. They had just undergone five and a half months of combating local Palestinian as well as bands of foreign volunteers and in the process lost 753 soldiers, including many seasoned officers. What is more, the arms at Israel's immediate disposal were vastly inferior to those of the Arabs in terms of both quantity and quality. Apart from a limited stock of mortars and PIATs (projector infantry anti-tank weapons, a type of crude bazooka), the Israelis had no field guns to speak of and, barring some Hispano Suiza guns, virtually no anti-aircraft weapons. Their armor consisted of a handful of iron-plated vehicles and two Cromwell tanks acquired from a couple of British deserters. Having no fighter planes, their air force merely included a few Piper Cubs and Austers, two transport planes and three improvised "bombers." Rifles and machine guns lacked standardization, coming as they did from a variety of sources. Only 60 percent of Israeli soldiers bore arms.[2] Ammunition was in such short supply that merely 50 bullets per rifle and 700 per machine gun were available.[3]

The writers Luttwak and Horowitz claimed that the Arabs by contrast had 152 field guns, 140–159 armored cars, 20–40 tanks and 55–9 fighter aircraft.[4] While these figures may somewhat overstate the military hardware readily available to the Arabs,[5] in the early stages of the war, with the disposition of arms nevertheless decisively in their favor, the Arabs stood a rather good chance of overwhelming the Yishuv. Certainly that was the opinion of Yigal Yadin, the director of Israel's military operations.[6] Three days before the Arab invasion, on being asked by Ben-Gurion, Israel's prime minister and minister of defense, to provide an assessment of the prospects of Israel prevailing, Yadin hedged his reply. He thought that the odds at best stood at 50 percent but more realistically the Arab advantage was greater.[7] Yadin's dismal appraisal seemed credible. That same day Kibbutz Kfar Etzion, situated south of Bethlehem, was stormed by the British-drilled troops of the Arab Legion in conjunction with thousands of armed local Arabs. One hundred and twenty settlers, including twenty-one women, were slaughtered. Only four survived by escaping.[8] As the historian Benny Morris noted, the battle for Gush Etzion in which Kibbutz Kfar Etzion was one of four Jewish settlements, represented "the first time a large Haganah contingent and settlement bloc had confronted a regular Arab army – and the result had been swift and disastrous."[9]

The Northern front

Within a few hours of the Egyptian air attack, the Syrians, with three infantry battalions, a battalion of armored cars, a company of tanks and an artillery regiment entered the Jordan valley immediately south of Lake Kinneret (the Sea of Galilee). Advancing toward Samakh (now Zemah) lying along the southern shores of the lake, the Syrians entrenched themselves on the outskirts of the village as a prelude to

Map 1.1 *Arab invasion, May–June 1948*

seizing it. Their incursion into the Jordan valley caught the Israelis off guard because they were anticipating it further north. All they had on hand was a battalion of 400 Israeli soldiers of the Haganah's Golani Brigade plus scores of armed farmers.[10]

Reading the writing on the wall, settlers from Degania A, situated slightly west of Samakh, sent a three-man delegation to Tel Aviv. There they met with Ben-Gurion. On hearing their plea for urgent assistance, Ben-Gurion informed them; "there are not enough guns, not enough planes; men are lacking on all fronts. The situation is very severe in the Negev, is difficult in Jerusalem, in Upper Galilee. The whole country is a front line. We cannot send reinforcements."[11] At that point Ben-Zion Yisraeli, a Degania A veteran, broke down and cried. Many years later Ben-Gurion recalled that he was shocked by Yisraeli's outburst and by the fact that he was unable to console him.[12] The delegation's leader, Joseph Baratz, a founding member of Degania A, then turned to Yadin, who provided him with even less solace. Yadin explained that there was no alternative other than to allow the Arabs to approach within twenty or thirty meters of their kibbutz and then to fight them and their armor in close combat. In answer to Baratz's question as to whether they should seriously take such a risk, Yadin insisted: "Yes, there is no other way; it is indeed a grievous risk, but it is the only way."[13]

In the interim, the two kibbutzim of Degania A and B tried to create the impression that they were being amply reinforced. At night, they repetitively drove their vehicles up the slopes of the mountains west of the Jordan valley with their lights extinguished to return with them on. In addition, tractor engines were ignited in the hope that they would mimic the sound of tanks.[14]

Such ploys did not faze the Syrians. In the early hours of the morning of May 18, Samakh was pounded by a concentration of artillery. Improvised trenches were far too shallow to afford adequate protection and the surviving Jewish defenders were forced to flee. The Israelis then tried to hold the Syrians at bay from a nearby police station but superior Syrian firepower told against them.[15] At the same time, two other neighboring settlements, Shaar Hagolan and Masada, were abandoned.

Two days later at daybreak the two Deganias, under the command of Moshe Dayan, faced their moment of truth. Degania A's seventy defenders confronted a cluster of armored cars, five Renault tanks, and an

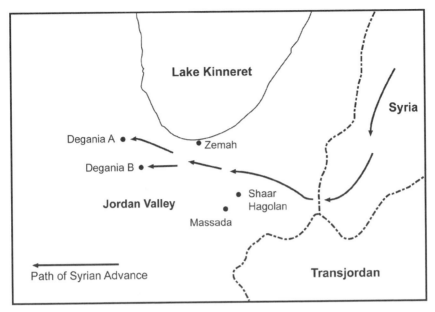

Map 1.2 *Battle of the Deganias*

infantry company that followed in their wake. After smashing the kib-butz's pillboxes and concrete bunkers, the tanks pierced its outer fence. Two armored vehicles were disabled by a 20-mm gun but one tank was able to draw near to the inner fence. From a ten-meter distance, a youth hurled a Molotov cocktail at the tank, setting it ablaze and killing its two-man crew. Other vehicles were destroyed by three-inch mortar, more Molotov cocktails, and by one of three PIATs that Dayan had brought in from Tel Aviv. By chance, a gap emerged between the enemy's armor and its infantry, allowing the Israelis to machine-gun the latter. With six of their armored vehicles put out of action, the Syrians withdrew. In Degania B, two successive tank and infantry assaults, coming within thirty meters of the defenders' positions, were similarly rebuffed.

As the day progressed, the battle for the Deganias was ultimately resolved. Four antiquated field guns of pre-World War One vintage, just off an incoming boat, were rushed to the area. Ben-Gurion at first insisted that the guns be consigned to the Jerusalem front. But after being subjected to Yadin's incessant importuning, Ben-Gurion acqui-esced. The field guns were to be positioned in the north for no more than 24 hours.[16] Nicknamed "Napoleonchiks," they lacked sights and their crews knew only vaguely how to operate them. Once they were positioned on an elevation overlooking the Jordan Valley, the gunners practiced firing into Lake Kinneret. As they attained some basic level of proficiency, they trained their weapons on enemy armor located between Samakh and the Deganias. One of the rusty guns malfunctioned but the other three discharged about 500 shells, killing some thirty Syrians.[17] Working on an assumption that only they possessed heavy guns – an assumption that was valid up to that point in time – and not realizing that Israel's entire stock amounted to only four, the Syrians retreated but not before razing Shaar Hagolan and Masada.

On the day that Syria entered the Jordan valley, the Palmah's Yiftah Brigade seized the Arab village of Malikiya to prevent it from becoming a gateway into the Galilee. But before the Israelis could dig in, they were showered with mortar, prompting them to withdraw. A subsequent Israeli recapture of the village on May 28 hardly fared better. By June 6, the Israelis had been outclassed by a joint force of Syrians, Lebanese, and the mainly foreign volunteer Arab Liberation Army (ALA) led by Fawzi al-Qawuqji, a Lebanese-born Arab with pro-Nazi sympathies who had been in Germany during World War Two. Consequently, al-Qawuqji's men were able to pour into the Central Galilee, still in Arab hands. Although al-Qawuqji was the ALA's field commander, the organization was founded and controlled by the Military Committee of the Arab League directed by Isma'il Safwat, a retired Iraqi general. Even before May 1948, the ALA had been active in Palestine, having infiltrated the country between January and March before temporarily withdrawing on the eve of the termination of the British mandate. What rankled Safwat was that only 800 of the 5,000 volunteers recruited by the ALA emanated from Palestine and that most of them deserted shortly after being trained.[18]

Meanwhile, the Syrians, with two infantry battalions supported by artillery and tanks, assailed the farming settlement of Mishmar Hayarden north of Lake Kinneret and west of the River Jordan. At first they made little headway but by June 10, after revving up their forces to a two-brigade level, they overpowered the settlement. Two other settlements facing similar threats were more resilient. Kibbutz Ein Gev on the east coast of Lake Kinneret thwarted a three-pronged Syrian offensive while Sejera (now known as Ilania) routed al-Qawuqji's irregulars.

By June 13 when fighting was suspended in terms of a UN sponsored truce (that officially commenced on June 11), Israel had held in check the bulk of its northern invaders. The Lebanese moved no further than Malikiya, al-Qawuqji was beaten at Sejera and the only Syrian gain of any consequence was at Mishmar Hayarden.

The Central front

On May 15, the Iraqis crossed the River Jordan to attack Kibbutz Gesher roughly twelve kilometers south of Lake Kinneret. Meeting with no success, they redeployed to Samaria from where they advanced toward the coastal plain to contest the settlement of Geulim. While so engaged they were abruptly summoned to the West Bank town of Jenin where the Haganah had just entered. The Israelis were dislodged but the intensity of the fighting there caused the Iraqis to lose all appetite for further military ventures. Subsequently, they remained inactive until the war's end.

Of all the armies arraigned against Israel, Transjordan's Arab Legion was the most efficient and the most professional. It was trained, supplied, and largely officered by the British under the command of John Bagot Glubb (Glubb Pasha) appointed in April 1939. Of the six million pounds incurred in its war against Israel, nearly five and a half million was financed by Britain.[19] Such a state of affairs, whereby a permanent member of the UN Security Council was actively supportive of a member state intent on violating the peace, constituted a travesty of international justice. In fact, even before the British had left Palestine, Arab Legion units were encamped there. After the Jews had objected, they and the Americans were reassured that the units in question would return to Transjordan. But such reassurances counted for nought. On May 13, additional Arab Legion units stationed east of the River Jordan were ordered to cross over into Palestine. They began arriving via the Allenby Bridge on May 14, brimming with confidence that they would defeat the Jews within a fortnight.

King Abdullah of Transjordan coveted land designated by the UN as part and parcel of a Palestinian state. Although he may have had some initial reservations about conquering Jerusalem, as a devout Muslim, the city meant much to him. At the heart of Jerusalem stood the Old

City immured by thick stone walls housing seven impregnable portals. Within its precepts were the four distinct Jewish, Muslim, Christian and Armenian Quarters, each containing venerable sites. For the Jews there was the second Temple Mount and the Western Wall and for the Muslims the Dome of the Rock (on the Temple Mount) from which Mohammed is reputed to have ascended to heaven. Outside the Old City were relatively new neighborhoods. Jewish ones were largely in the west and Arab ones in the east.

Apart from the historic and religious allure of Jerusalem, control of the city would have yielded either protagonist with a valuable strategic asset. In Glubb Pasha's opinion, "if the Jews captured the whole of Jerusalem, they could drive down the main road to Jericho, and the whole position in Palestine would be turned. If the Jews could seize Allenby Bridge, the Arab Legion in Palestine would be cut off from its base, and would suffer a military disaster."[20] On the other hand Ben-Gurion feared that, if Jerusalem fell, the blow to the Israelis' morale would have been so catastrophic that they would have lacked the resolve to defend Tel Aviv and Haifa.[21]

In the early morning of May 19, after a sweeping artillery and mortar bombardment, the Arab Legion wrested the northerly Jerusalem Arab district of Sheikh Jarrah. As a result, the Israeli enclave at Mount Scopus that housed the Hebrew University and the Hadasah Hospital was put out on a limb. The League then proceeded to the Old City via the Damascus Gate to link up with two of its infantry companies that two days earlier had arrived from Jericho to reinforce armed Palestinians. Since May 16 the latter had already begun encroaching upon the Jewish quarter, which was then cut off from the rest of Jewish Jerusalem. The Arabs would breach the wall of a Jewish house, toss a grenade through it, and then crawl through to the next room or residence. (All houses sat cheek by jowl with one another.) As they closed in, hand-to-hand fighting ensued. Soon the Israelis found themselves defending a steadily contracting area in which most of their field commanders were either killed or wounded.[22] By May 26–7, the Legionnaires, who had replaced the Palestinians, captured and needlessly blew up the Hurva Synagogue, the Old City's largest and most hallowed Jewish house of worship.[23] Finally on May 28, after ten days of fighting and with the small remnant of Jewish defenders being sleep-deprived, hungry and just about

out of ammunition, a delegation of rabbis negotiated a surrender. All Jewish soldiers were to be taken prisoner but civilians and those seriously wounded were to be transported to West Jerusalem. The fall of the Jewish quarter was a grievous loss not only to Israel but to the entire Jewish nation.

For the Arab Legion the capture of the Jewish quarter constituted but one aspect of the battle for Jerusalem. On May 22, as fighting raged in the Old City, an armored Transjordanian column led by Bill Newman, an Australian, sought to enter Jaffa Street, the modern city's main thoroughfare. As it approached the Notre Dame Monastery, the column's forward carrier was immobilized by a Molotov cocktail, lobbed by a sixteen-year old boy from one of the monastery's upper levels.[24] Burning furiously, the carrier inadvertently obstructed the rest of the column, forcing the Legionnaires to withdraw. The next day Legionnaires made it to the monastery's ground floor. But after an intensive hand-to-hand battle in which the Arabs suffered many casualties and were beaten back, Newman decided to call it quits.[25]

On May 21, a few kilometers south of Jerusalem, the Muslim Brothers (who were incorporated into the Egyptian army) challenged Kibbutz Ramat Rahel with the assistance of a company of regular Arab Legion forces as well as irregular (local) Legion volunteers. The offensive opened with an artillery barrage that climaxed the following day in an infantry charge leading to the settlement's fall. Later that night, while the Arabs were preoccupied with looting, the Israelis returned. They briefly regained the upper hand only to lose it the next afternoon. Then on May 24, a battalion of the Etzioni Brigade reoccupied the kibbutz and entrusted its defense to two small detachments. But they were no match against a third Arab assault which began the same day and which involved a far larger number of infantry assisted by armored vehicles and half-tracks. The Arabs secured the eastern section of the settlement and, just as they were about to topple the rest of it, Israeli reinforcements arrived. Fighting continued throughout the night and the following day. By the next evening (May 25) the Arab force was spent. After changing hands on four separate occasions, Ramat Rachel was firmly and securely under Israeli control.

No further ground assaults either in the Holy City or within its immediate outskirts were initiated. But until June 11 the Arab Legion fired over 10,500 shells into West Jerusalem, causing the deaths of 316 Jews and the wounding of 1,422 others, almost all of whom were civilians.[26] Walter Eytan reported that "there is scarcely a single home that has not been shelled, scarcely a family that has not suffered some loss in dead or wounded."[27] With no meaningful Israeli supply convoys having entered Jerusalem since April 20, food stocks were dwindling to an intolerably low level. Individual daily rations were reduced to two pieces of bread, thin soup, and some canned vegetables. Piped water ceased to flow and the little water available was distributed by horse-driven carriages. Domestic fuel was non-existent. People coped by pruning city trees, gathering deadwood and ripping off the doors of deserted Arab homes.[28] Not having electricity, the inhabitants "learnt to live in darkness, covered in soot from the cooking fires and surrounded by the foul stench of toilets that had not been flushed for weeks."[29] In brief, living conditions were wretched. Short of the Haganah expeditiously relieving the beleaguered Jews, they would not have been able to endure much longer.

In that light, importance was attached to the Arab village of Latrun overlooking the Tel Aviv–Jerusalem highway. For the Israelis, possession of it was an indispensable condition for accessing Jerusalem. By May 15, Latrun was under the control of al-Qawuqji's Arab Liberation Army but a day later it suddenly pulled out before awaiting replacements. During the next two days, Latrun was, by default, held by the Haganah. Then on May 18, when the General High Command, in anticipation of an Egyptian northerly advance, ordered all available troops to assist in occupying Arab villages near Rehovot, the village was abandoned. Almost instantly, the vacuum was filled by the Arab Legion, putting Jerusalem once more beyond the Yishuv's grasp.

The first Israeli attempt to recapture Latrun took place on May 24. Latrun was well fortified. It contained a British-built police stronghold, bolstered by artillery on the crest of a hill 1,300 feet high called Gun Hill. It was also well provisioned with trenches and defense posts in the estate of a neighboring Trappist monastery and in surrounding villages. Yadin, sensing that a premature frontal attack on Latrun would be suicidal, requested far more time than the 24 hours allotted him to make all the necessary arrangements. However, Ben-Gurion, having just learnt from Haim Herzog (the Haganah's intelligence officer and future Israeli president) that Jerusalem's bread stocks were almost depleted, brooked no further delay.[30] Israel was to go on the offensive forthwith come what may.

Responsibility for the mission was vested in both the 2nd Battalion of the Alexandroni Brigade (one of the Haganah's most competent battalions)[31] and the 72nd Battalion of the new 7th Brigade. The latter was manned by a handful of hardened troops, 500 fresh Yishuv recruits and about 140 recently arrived immigrants,[32] of whom some had seen combat in the Russian and Polish Armies.[33] At about ten at night (of May 24) members of the two battalions boarded buses at Kibbutz Hulda to be taken to the front. Instead of leaving there and then, the men needlessly sat around for close to five hours. As they waited in vain for both additional manpower and an artillery unit, their senior officers were involved in a heated dispute regarding the appropriateness of the operation.[34] By three in the morning of May 25, they finally departed. The Alexandroni Battalion was meant to attack Latrun, while the 7th Brigade battalion was to place itself on Alexandroni's right flank. Due to their late start, the men took to the field of battle at daybreak. They had forsaken the opportunity of enjoying the cover of darkness and although at first they were hidden in fog this soon lifted. Within next to no time, withering machine gun and artillery fire rained down on the exposed Israelis, forcing them to retire.

Two platoons from the Alexandroni Brigade were particularly hard pressed. They were riveted to a small wadi by gunfire arising from the whole spectrum of the enemy's arsenal. One of the platoons, commanded by 20-year-old Ariel Scheinerman, who later became known as Ariel (Arik) Sharon, was exceptionally vulnerable. Armed local Arabs in search of booty were closing in on it. At one point, having been pinned to the ground, Sharon raised himself to get the lay of the land, only to absorb a bullet fired from above that entered his stomach and exited through his thigh. The shock of it all compelled him to exclaim "ima" (mother). Fearing that all his remaining men would be slaughtered ("almost half the platoon was dead and most of the others wounded, some critically"),[35] Sharon advised them to retreat as best as they could. He then crawled on his hands and knees, striving to make his way over a series of terraces. Before setting out Sharon was forced to abandon Simha Pinhasi, a youngster from his adjacent home village who was wounded in both legs. No one was fit enough to carry him. "With a look and a quick nod Pinhasi indicated that he would cover the withdrawal."[36] By the time that Sharon negotiated the second terrace wall, his strength gave out. Sixteen-year-old Ya'akov Bugin, whose "jaw had been shot up leaving a mass of gore" came to his assistance.[37] Bugin kept moving, pushing and propping him over the terrace wall. Eventually, Moshik Lanzet, a deputy company commander, who too was wounded, helped Sharon to his feet and by supporting him from under his shoulders the two limped for several kilometers through smoke and fire. As they eventually came across an Israeli half-track loading survivors, Sharon lost consciousness.[38] It took the best part of a day to extract all the dead and wounded. Apart from the heavy casualties directly inflicted by the enemy, a scorching heat wave had taken its toll. Many of the new immigrants, who were not yet acclimatized and who were not issued with sufficient water bottles, collapsed from dehydration. A total of 71 men perished,[39] of whom two thirds were members of the Alexandroni Brigade.[40] Only 16 new immigrants were killed, not scores or even hundreds as was (and even still is) popularly believed.[41] Had the battle taken place at night, the casualty rate would have been far lower.

The failed operation is now widely regarded as having been ill conceived. The Israelis did not assure themselves of superiority in both manpower and heavy weaponry, essential ingredients in overcoming a near-invincible position. They might have been able to compensate for such shortcomings through an element of surprise but, since they were slow in getting off the mark, their clumsy lumbering toward the front was readily detected. Israeli intelligence was poor. Neither the operational planners nor the field commanders had any inkling of the forces that they were up against.[42] Nonetheless, although the Israelis failed to capture Latrun, their attempt to do so persuaded the Arab Legion to garrison at least a third of its men there. This had the effect of considerably reducing the Legion's direct pressure on Jerusalem and in assisting the Haganah in retaining its possession of Kibbutz Ramat Rahel.

With Jerusalem still beyond Israeli reach, another attack on Latrun was authorized. In preparation for it, David Marcus, a volunteer whose *nom de guerre* was Mickey Stone,[43] was appointed on May 28 as the overall commander of all Israeli forces operating in Jerusalem and the Jerusalem Corridor. Colonel Marcus, a committed Jew, was a West

Point Graduate and one time member of General Eisenhower's staff in Europe.

The second offensive against Latrun took place on May 30. It too ended in failure. In the dead of night, Israeli armored vehicles, commanded by Haim Laskov, stole into the Latrun police fortress courtyard but the Israeli infantry that were to follow through did not do so. Left to their own devices, Israeli sappers in the fortress compound began to blow up the fortress wall. As they were about to set their charges, two wooden buildings next to the fortress became engulfed in flames. With the entire area illuminated the sappers took to their heels. Unbeknown to them, the Arabs had all the while forgotten to lock the fortress's front door.[44]

As before, the Israelis returned to base with nothing to show for the sacrifices incurred. The anonymous authors of the Israel Army's official history were convinced that, had the infantry performed as planned, Latrun would have been taken.[45] Marcus scathingly described the infantry's action as "disgraceful."[46]

The Arab Legion's hold over Latrun remained intact, yet the problem of conveying goods to Jerusalem was basically solved by means of the construction of what became known as the "Burma Road." On account of previous brushes, the 7th Brigade found itself holding a continuous strip of land from Hulda through Deir Muhezin, then through a dirt track, bypassing Beit Susin to within a stone's throw west of the Sha'ar Hagai–Hartuv Road. East of that road, the Harel Brigade held the continuation of the same dirt track that proceeded to the village of Saris where it joined the sealed road to Jerusalem (see Map 1.3). It was soon discovered that, save for a few hundred meters east of Beit Susin, the entire track could be negotiated by motor vehicles. The impassable stretch entailed a precipitous slope of rocky terrain that was at first bridged by the use of porters and mules. Goods were offloaded from motor convoys arriving from Tel Aviv to be reloaded on trucks further along the way. Since that arrangement was suboptimal, hundreds of workers were engaged to alter the contours of that troublesome sector. Laboring mostly by night and sheltered by a ridge of hills from observation by the Arab Legion further north, they rendered the entire track roadworthy. Similarly, the Israelis laid a new water pipe stretching from Rosh Ha'ayin to Jerusalem.

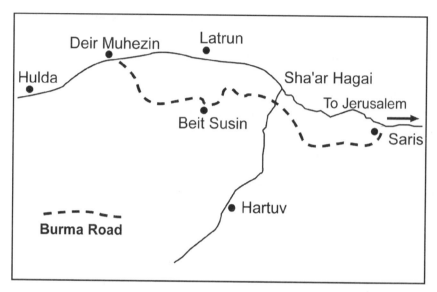

Map 1.3   *The Burma Road*

With the "Burma Road" now in use, a third attempt at capturing Latrun was initiated, lest the Arab Legion use it as a springboard to frustrate the movement of convoys to Jerusalem. Like the operations that preceded it, the third one gave rise to one bungle after another. Commencing on the evening of June 9, ground gained that night was forfeited the next day. On the following night, an Israeli battalion mistakenly captured the wrong outpost, leaving the designated one intact. Later, as a second battalion approached the outpost that the first was supposed to have taken, it incorrectly assumed that the outpost was in friendly hands. In short, the third assault was no more successful than the previous ones.

On June 11, as the first truce took effect, hostilities on the Transjordanian front were suspended. Just then General Marcus was tragically killed. Hours before daybreak, experiencing an upset stomach, he had wandered away from the perimeter of his headquarters at Abu Gosh, draped in a blanket. On returning he was challenged by a sentry. Answering in English, Marcus kept approaching. Since English was used in the Arab Legion, the sentry mistook him for an Arab. He first fired into the air and as Marcus drew nearer, he fatally shot him in the chest. On discovering the identity of his victim, the distraught sentry attempted suicide.

The Southern front

At the outbreak of the war, there were 27 Jewish settlements in the Negev, of which only five had more than thirty defenders.[47] Two battalions of the Negev Brigade, consisting of approximately 800 lightly armed men, were stationed in the general area. Between the Jerusalem Corridor and the Negev, and referred to at the time as the "south," stood the 2,750 strong Givati Brigade.

On May 15 the Egyptian army, under the overall command of General Ahmad al-Mu'awi, crossed the international frontier in two prongs. One advanced along the coastal road in the direction of Tel Aviv, while the other, under Abd-al-Aziz, made for Beersheba, Hebron, Bethlehem, and the outskirts of Jerusalem.

The near-border settlements of Kfar Darom and Nirim offered the Egyptians such a spirited resistance that they decided to give them a wide berth. While the Egyptians could momentarily refrain from capturing Kfar Darom and Nirim, Kibbutz Yad Mordehai, situated next to the main coastal highway, had of necessity to be reckoned with. On May 19, hundreds of Egyptians pitted themselves against 133 Israelis, of whom only 66 were armed.[48] To erode Yad Mordehai's fighting ability, the kibbutz was subject to extensive aerial and artillery bombardments that ignited its wooden buildings. After the softening-up process, the Egyptians entered the kibbutz's compound but were staved off by means of hand-to-hand combat. The next day Yad Mordehai encountered four separate incursions, each of which was repelled but at considerable cost. Weather conditions were atrocious. A hot wind blew sand into everything, including, guns, throats, nostrils, and eyes. Above all, it carried the smell of death.[49] Due to a lack of medical facilities, the injured were inadequately treated and, as a result, the seriously wounded died painfully.

Throughout the next two days, Yad Mordehai was subjected to incessant shelling. Then on May 23, the Egyptians using armored cars re-entered the settlement. By then the defenders were in dire straits. Their machine guns were out of action and their ammunition was running low. They radioed to regional staff headquarters that they were exhausted and feared that, like the members of Kibbutz Kfar Etzion, they too would be slaughtered. Another communication read "our positions and trenches have been destroyed, there is no place for the wounded, there is no water, we lack the means to continue defending the settlement."[50] During the night of May 23–24, an attempt was made to reinforce Yad Mordehai but in the end the rescuing party could only evacuate the wounded. To their fortune, the remaining settlers slipped through the Egyptian lines. All told, 26 Israelis were killed and 40 were wounded.[51] The resolve shown by Yad Mordehai did at least provide the Haganah with a few more days in which to ready itself for a further Egyptian northerly advance.

By May 29 an Egyptian column consisting of around two hundred vehicles converged on Isdud (now named Ashdod).[52] Fortuitously, on that very same day, four Messerschmitt fighter planes, the first to arrive in Israel from Czechoslovakia, were assembled and then flown south-ward to strafe the oncoming column. Ezer Weizman (later president of Israel) recalled that, due to the perilous nature of the Southern front, "there was no time to consider trifles, such as the fact that these planes had never taken off, or even been tested in flight, their parts had not been checked, no one knew whether their systems functioned or if their machine-guns fired. No one was sure that their bombs *would* drop – or that their wings *wouldn't*."[53] In the ensuing melee, one of the planes was hit and its pilot, Eddy Cohen, a South African volunteer, was killed. The air attack, plus the use of the 65-mm guns that the Israelis had just acquired, resulted in the Egyptians arresting their advance some twelve kilometers south of Rehovot. On the night of June 2, in Operation Pleshet, the Israelis extended their counterattack. The engagement, which involved the largest concentration of Israeli troops thus far assembled, did not yield a favorable outcome but it did at least reinforce a new cautionary approach on the part of the enemy. What may have been intended to be a merely temporary lull in the Egyptian thrust turned out to be the ultimate extent of its northerly progression. In any case, it is now generally believed that al-Mu'awi had from the start set himself the more modest objective of proceeding no further north than the Arab village of Yibneh.[54] That did not of course tie his hands elsewhere.

Somewhat to the south, on June 2, the Egyptians attacked Kibbutz Negba with a battery of howitzers and one 3.7-inch guns while also bombing it from the air. As the cannonade peaked, shells saturated the kibbutz at a rate of 600 per hour.[55] Step by step the invaders, who

Plate 1.1   *Kibbutz Negba after attack*

numbered 1,000, intruded upon the 140 embattled defenders.[56] With an Egyptian victory seemingly imminent, a settler succeeded in throwing a Molotov cocktail at an oncoming tank, thereby disabling it. That – plus the sudden appearance of jeeps of the Negev Brigade, taken to be the brigade's vanguard – turned the tide in Negba's favor.

Kibbutz Nitzanim, not far from Negba but situated closer to the coastal highway, fared far worse. Although it fought tenaciously, it could not withstand the large armored force and air strikes that were brought to bear against it. In the late afternoon of June 7, having lost 33 of their comrades and after having being restricted to only one building, the defenders surrendered. Unfortunately, not all survivors were taken into safe custody. Shula Dorchin, attending to the wounds of two isolated immobile youngsters, was bayoneted and disemboweled. She was found with her entrails trailing behind her as she writhed in agony on the ground. The two injured youths were stabbed to death and on the next day, in a nearby village, the heads of two other women from Nitzanim who had strayed from the group were paraded on pikes.[57] To add insult to injury, the kibbutz was later singled out for public opprobrium as if it had prematurely caved in. The charges were completely unwarranted. Nitzanim was not supplied with sufficient weapons, its radio had malfunctioned, and its fortifications were inadequate.[58]

By June 11, all fighting on the Southern front had ceased. By then, Tel Aviv had been bombed on sixteen occasions, Rehovot four times and Rishon Letzion twice. On one day alone, 41 civilians were killed in an aerial bombardment of Tel Aviv's central bus station.[59] While the Egyptians had failed to enter the coastal area originally allotted to the Jewish state, they had overrun two kibbutzim and, of no less moment, were poised to block Israel's pathway to the Negev.

The first truce

Moshe Carmel, the commander of the Carmeli Brigade, likened the truce to dew from heaven.[60] It afforded a welcome respite to the state's tired and overstretched forces. In the course of the fighting, a large proportion of the Haganah's junior officer corps had fallen and there was an urgent need to provide suitable replacements. Above all, the truce allowed Jerusalem to be refurbished with food, medicine, and ammunition.

Against the spirit of the truce, Israel also took advantage of the cease-fire to take delivery of weapons previously ordered. By contrast, the Arabs, who had already expended a large amount of their ammunition, were unable to do likewise because of the UN arms embargo. Unlike the Israelis, they neither had in place an effective network of contacts nor had the general wherewithal to circumvent the embargo.

On June 18, Ben-Gurion, in his capacity as minister of defense, met with Israel's brigade commanders. To his dismay he learnt that morale among the rank and file had reached a low ebb. Officers recounted incidents of desertion, lack of discipline, shortages of clothing and water flasks and, in a case relating to the battle for Sejera, of criminals within the army burgling Jewish homes.[61] A major cause of desertion was a lack of means of support for soldiers' families.[62] In the breathing space that the truce provided, most of the above issues were addressed.

Before the first truce took effect – that is, while Israel was still engaged in active warfare – the Haganah was transformed into Israel's official defense force. This was promulgated on May 28 by the provisional government's Israel Defense Force (IDF) Establishment Order. The order explicitly precluded the existence of any other armed force not under state control. Lehi (see glossary) had already ceased to exist but, on June 2, the Irgun (see glossary) which had continued as an independent body deferred to the government decree in a written undertaking, signed by its leader, Menahem Begin. The agreement explicitly required of the Irgun that it place all of its men and weapons at the IDF's disposal.

During the truce two episodes took place whose outcomes had some bearing on the nature of the Jewish state. The first averted potential anarchy and the second cast a pall over the army's judicial administration.

At the beginning of June, a ship by the name of *Altalena* left a port in southern France for Israel carrying 900 men, 5,000 rifles, 270 light machine guns and large quantities of anti-tank weapons.[63] It was commissioned by the Irgun and, on being instructed to surrender the boat and its contents to the government, the Irgun refused, insisting that it be party to decisions involving the cargo's distribution. The Irgun wished to provide a fifth of the arms to its men in Jerusalem, where the Irgun still existed since Jerusalem had not yet been declared part of Israel. The rest was to be shared among IDF units in which ex-Irgun members were dominant, as well as among other army units.[64] As Begin rationalized, "it was our duty to see to it that the units we sent into the army should receive adequate and efficient weapons."[65] In a post-crisis radio address, he argued "how could we not give it [the weapons] to *our* fighters in the army? How could we refrain from making sure that *our* men get it first?"[66] But that clearly violated the agreement that Begin had just entered. With its authority being undermined, the government categorically rejected the Irgun's demands.

On June 20, the *Altalena* dropped anchor off Kfar Vitkin, about ten kilometers north of Netanya. As Irgun members sought to offload the ship's freight, they were prevented from doing so by an IDF unit led by Uri Bar-On. In a violent clash, two IDF soldiers and six Irgun members were killed. Then before midnight the *Altalena* sailed for Tel Aviv to take up a position opposite the beach promenade. An exchange of fire developed between fighters of the Irgun and those of the IDF's Palmah unit under Yigal Allon's direct command. During the skirmish, a shell, supposedly intended as a warning shot, struck the vessel and set it alight. Those on board jumped into the water to be rescued by the Irgun and Palmah alike. At the end of the day the Irgun had 14 dead and 69 wounded, whereas the IDF suffered two mortalities and six casualties. All in all (both at Kfar Vitkin and Tel Aviv), 24 lives were lost.

The affair did at least purge the state of non-government militia having a quasi-independent status. Many within the Yishuv had cast a leery eye on the Irgun. They suspected that, given half a chance, at least some of its members would have used any enhanced military capability that came their way to subvert the government. Ben-Gurion in particular was convinced that the Irgun's intransigence endangered the state's very existence. His assessment might not have been all that far-fetched. As the *Altalena* saga was being played out, Amihai Faglin, Begin's assistant, casually suggested to an Irgun official, Bezalel Stolitzky, that they round up their men and head off to assume power.[67]

Nine days after the *Altalena* debacle, that is, on June 29, Meir Tubiansky, an IDF captain, was arrested and tried for treason in a kangaroo court, held at Beit Jiz, near the present kibbutz of Nahshon.[68] The charge originated when Tubiansky's colleague, Aharon Cohen, overheard him conversing with Michael Bryant, a British citizen who was his senior at the Jerusalem Electricity Corporation. Cohen incorrectly surmised that Tubiansky was handing over classified material detailing strategic positions in Jerusalem and duly appraised Benjamin Givli of the army's intelligence section who immediately believed that he had a spy on his hands. It was mainly through Givli that the field trial was held. No hard and fast evidence was presented, there were no witnesses, and the accused had no legal representation. After half an hour's duration, the "court" found Tubiansky guilty and sentenced him to death. He was shot later in the day by a hastily improvised firing squad. The cavalier manner in which the proceedings were conducted led the historian Teveth to conclude that the two leading prosecutors, Givli and Isser Be'eri (head of military intelligence), were driven by blind ambition, hoping that their "scoop" would enhance their careers.[69] Alerted by Tubiansky's widow, Ben-Gurion ordered an inquiry into the incident. In July 1949 Tubiansky was posthumously rehabilitated and buried with full military honors at Mount Herzl in Jerusalem. Be'eri alone was tried for manslaughter and sentenced to one day in prison, from sunrise to sunset. After his death in 1958, he too received a posthumous pardon.[70]

Turning to other developments, Count Bernadotte, the newly appointed UN mediator, lost little time in drafting proposals that, though nominally aimed at paving the way for a final settlement, were in fact tailored to satisfy the Arabs whom he regarded as the aggrieved party. (Bernadotte had originally disapproved of the UN November 1947 Palestine partition resolution.) In terms of his plan, Israel's independence was to be considerably circumscribed. The country would merely retain the right to unlimited immigration for two years, all Arab refugees were to be permitted to return to their former homes, and Jerusalem and the Negev were to be allocated to Transjordan. (Israel in turn was to get all of the Galilee.) Faced with Bernadotte's blatantly biased proposals, Abba Eban, Israel's representative to the UN, wrote that that the effrontery of it all left him and his colleagues quite breathless.[71]

It was ultimately revealed that Britain was banking on Transjordan obtaining the Negev as a means of enhancing its own influence and presence (through army bases) in the region. The Israeli Foreign Ministry obtained documentary evidence proving that the notion of handing over the Negev to Transjordan was indeed implanted in Bernadotte's mind by the British.[72] This was confirmed by James McDonald, America's first ambassador to Israel, who affirmed that Bernadotte's plan "was substantially that of His Majesty's Government, as was Bernadotte's suggestion that Jerusalem be given to the Arabs."[73] In the final analysis, neither the Arabs, who continued to reject any form of Jewish self-government, nor the Jews accepted Bernadotte's recommendations.

Throughout the truce Egypt showed no compunction in firing on UN authorized convoys conveying supplies to Israeli settlements in the Negev. It also continued to harass Kibbutz Kfar Darom. On the night of July 7–8, the settlers slipped through enemy lines to awaiting trucks. Carrying their wounded and their two Torah scrolls and destroying whatever was immovable, they bid farewell to their home. Their evacuation was timely for, by the following day, the deserted kibbutz was battered by heavy artillery and assaulted by a combined force of infantry and armor.

With the truce drawing to a close, Bernadotte tried to arrange for a 30-day extension. Israel responded positively but the Arabs rejected the notion outright. The Egyptian press, like those of other Arab newspapers, had fed its readers with glowing accounts of Arab victories and of an imminent occupation of Tel Aviv. Given the widespread dissemination of such fantasies, the Egyptian government was taken to task for agreeing to the truce in the first place. To muffle its critics, Egypt insisted on continuing the war. Fighting resumed at 6 a.m. on July 9.

Ten days of warfare

In Israel's north, the Syrians had retained their hold on Mishmar Hayarden. To displace them, Israel had first to capture the "Custom House" on the east bank of the Jordan. Moving in that direction, IDF troops forded the river to await heavy equipment that was to be delivered over an improvised pontoon bridge. For some reason, the bridge failed to materialize. This left the Israelis in Syrian territory, isolated and exposed. After holding out for two days, they returned to the west of the Jordan where they attacked positions on the perimeters of an area that Syria commanded. With the battles being indecisive, a stalemate ensued with both sides more or less returning to square one. From that point on, the Syrians effectively remained quiescent, making only the occasional armored car foray against one Israeli-held hilltop or another.

In the Western Galilee, the IDF gained a resounding victory against al-Qawuqji's Arab Liberation Army. Al-Qawuqji, having staked his reputation on taking Sejera, deployed most of his forces against that settlement. (Sejera overlooked a vital crossroad through which the ALA forwarded goods from Lebanon to Nazareth.) For eight continuous days Sejera was set upon but the second battalion of the Golani Brigade defending the settlement was far too formidable. While the bulk of al-Qawuqji's men were pinned down in a fruitless exercise, trying to topple Sejera, the IDF was able to operate in other sections of the Galilee. On July 16, in an operation named Dekel (Palm Tree) and under the overall command of Haim Laskov, Nazareth succumbed without offering any serious resistance. The fall of Nazareth paved the way for the IDF to acquire most of the Lower Galiliee.

Within the Central front, Operation Dani[74] commanded by Allon, was set in motion to relieve the Arab Legion of its presence in a region embracing Lydda (Lod), Ramlah, Latrun and Ramallah. Lying ever so close to the southwest of Tel Aviv, Lydda and Ramlah in the Legion's hands seemed to place Israel's largest city in grave jeopardy.

The campaign commenced on July 10 with the seizure of a number of small villages to the west of Lydda and Ramlah, followed by the taking of Lydda airport. In turn, a lightly armed mobile unit of jeeps with mounted machine guns and led by Dayan formed into a single column. At its head was a captured Arab Legion armored car with a two-pounder cannon nicknamed "the terrible tiger." Placing himself in the foremost jeep, Dayan ordered the unit to move from Ben Shemen in the direction of Lydda. About a kilometer from their destination, they were subject to a heavy fusillade. The "terrible tiger" paused to respond in kind while the rest of the unit kept going. Finding that the main road was effectively sealed off, the column veered south along a narrow sidetrack toward Ramlah. On entering the town, the Israelis raced through its streets randomly discharging their weapons. They in turn drew a torrent of fire that tore into their vehicles, puncturing tyres, smashing radiators, severing brakes and, in one instance, divesting a jeep of its bonnet. As Dayan later recalled, their stay there "was exceedingly brief."[75] Gathering their nine dead and seventeen wounded, they returned to Ben Shemen.

No enemy position was taken but the temerity of the raiders unnerved the Arabs, so much so that by nightfall Lydda was swiftly disposed of by a small battalion of the Yiftah Brigade. On the understanding that Lydda's residents would surrender their arms, they were granted permission to remain in their homes. However, the next day, buoyed by the approach of an Arab Legion patrol, they resumed firing, inflicting casualties on the occupying Israelis and mutilating their bodies. After the Arab Legion patrol was overcome, the IDF wrought swift retribution upon the town, killing approximately 250 of its inhabitants.[76] According to the historian Anita Shapira, while the soldiers of the Yiftah Brigade recognized the necessity of defending themselves, they were anything but proud of the way events unfolded. The slaughter emanated from panic that gripped the heavily outnumbered Israelis who lacked confidence and experience in subduing a large hostile civilian population.[77] This, as Tal wrote, meant that they "shot at any suspected source of fire, regardless of who, or where, he was [sic]."[78] About a thousand Lydda residents bore arms and among them were 700 Palestinian militia men belonging to the pro-Husseini fighting force Jihad al-Muqaddas. Also in the town were a company of Legionnaires stationed in the local police station and a few hundred armed tribesmen from Transjordan.[79] For violating the terms of their surrender, almost all of Lydda's remaining population were expelled. On July 12, after Ramlah was quelled, its populace was given the choice of either staying or leaving. Fearing for their wellbeing, the overwhelming majority chose to go.

By that stage, the Israeli High Command would have liked to have gone on to Ramallah. But with a second truce pending, it was decided instead to concentrate on routing Latrun. On the night of July 15, soldiers of the Harel Brigade occupied a ridge to its east. Meeting with exceptionally large Arab Legion forces and not being assisted as expected by a second company, they withdrew at sunrise. Three of the critically wounded could not be evacuated and, contrary to orders, David Miller, a medical orderly, remained behind to care for them. All four were killed.[80] Later in the day (July 16), Latrun was attacked directly. Leading the assault were a number of half-tracks and two Cromwell tanks from a newly formed armored brigade commanded by Yitzak Sadeh. Suddenly, a shell jammed in the barrel of one of the tanks. The tank in question then turned around to rectify the problem and the second tank's driver refused to continue without it. With the rest of the attacking force withdrawing along with the tanks, the final attack on Latrun was aborted.[81] In all of the four battles for its possession, Israel lost a total of 168 soldiers.[82]

Further to the east on July 10, members of the Gadna (a youth battalion consisting of young fighters in the 16–17-year age group) sallied from Jerusalem to storm an Arab village that nestled on the slopes of what is now Har Herzl. They then completed their mission by taking three other villages, including Ein Kerem, all of which were ultimately incorporated into Jerusalem. Finally, on the night of July 16, there was a forlorn attempt to retake the Jewish quarter of the Old City. However, explosives intended to demolish a section of the Old City wall near the Jaffa Gate barely scratched its surface.

On the Southern front, on July 12, a fierce battle once again raged at Kibbutz Negba. Surrounded on all sides, the settlement was subject to a heavy artillery and aerial bombardment, followed by a forward movement of armored vehicles, accompanied by three infantry battalions. Four thousand shells were propelled into the kibbutz whose defenders numbered about one hundred and fifty. They resisted stoically, meeting wave after wave of the advancing enemy with deadly fire. Fighting from sunrise to sunset, without food and with limited water, they lived to see the back of the invaders.

Similarly on July 15, in a surprise attack on Kibbutz Be'erot Yitzhak, the Egyptians penetrated the heart of the settlement to occupy buildings just over thirty yards from its fortified center. Damage to a water tower resulted in the flooding of trenches, which in turn caused a large quantity of ammunition to be spoilt. Reduced to the sole use of hand grenades, the kibbutz radioed that its situation was untenable. Then, at what appeared to be the final hour, the Egyptians paused to realign themselves. That was their undoing, for it allowed sufficient time for an artillery battery of the Negev Brigade to arrive and to play havoc with the attackers' tanks and half-track vehicles, compelling the Egyptians to disengage.

The second truce

The second truce came into force on July 18. Unlike the first one, the second was imposed by the UN Security Council, which used the threat of sanctions against any non-complier. No time limit for the truce's duration was set. It was hoped that the second truce would continue until the UN mediator could arrange for a peaceful resolution of the conflict.

Israel used the lulls in fighting to the best of its advantage. During the first truce, its military manpower increased to almost 60,000. By October 1948, it rose to a level in excess of 90,000.[83] Apart from local sources, recruits were drawn from volunteers mainly from western countries and from newly arrived immigrants. The former, known by the Hebrew acronym Mahal (Mitnadvim Me'Hutz L'Aretz – Volunteers from Abroad) numbered 2,400. Although they were but a small proportion of the IDF, they played a pivotal role in providing it with critically needed skills, especially in aviation where ultimately 171 of Israel's 193 pilots were foreign volunteers.[84] Mahal also furnished the navy with its chief of staff, Paul Shulman (from the US), and a number of its ships' commanders. Many members of the IDF's medical corps were volunteers from abroad, among whom was Dr Stanley Levin from South Africa, noted for performing 28 successive operations within 36 hours.[85] One of the problems of integrating overseas volunteers into the IDF was their lack of knowledge of Hebrew. This not only led to Colonel David Marcus's premature death but also to some lighter moments. In the course of an air attack on an armed column in the region of Tulkarem, an Israeli Messerschmitt was hit. The pilot, an American Jew, guided his faltering plane over the Mediterranean and then parachuted into the sea. On swimming ashore he was confronted by members of a nearby Jewish settlement running toward him. Being of a somewhat swarthy complexion, he could readily have been taken for an Arab. To forestall such an eventuality he kept shouting "gefilte fish" (a popular Jewish delicacy).[86]

Conscripts from new migrants arriving after the state had been proclaimed were known as Gahal (Giyus Me'Hutz L'Aretz – Conscripts from Abroad). Numbering close to 25,000, they hailed from North Africa, Eastern Europe, post-World War Displaced Persons Camps, or from British detention centers in Cyprus. [87] Those from Europe were mainly holocaust survivors. Some had military experience but most were callow recruits.

The Jews were not alone in mobilizing foreign volunteers. Some five hundred Yugoslavs plus a number of Germans, Poles, and over fifty Britons fought on the Palestinian behalf.[88] In addition, thousands of non-Palestinian Arabs served in the Arab Liberation Army, commanded by al-Qawuqj, which saw action in the Galilee. Realistically, one could of course regard the entire four-Arab-state invading force as constituting foreign volunteers since they all supposedly acted on behalf of the Palestinians in territory that was extraneous to them.

Shortly after the start of the second truce, a huge airlift of war material from Czechoslovakia to Israel was set in train. (At Russia's bidding, the Czechs supplied Israel with arms to undermine Britain's influence in the Middle East.) Items included were Messerschmitts, aeronautical spare parts, and large quantities of assorted armaments. Anti-aircraft guns were also obtained from Switzerland and Italy. A sprinkling of surplus US and British Sherman tanks were bought on the open arms market whereas air fuel and a variety of vehicles, including 50 jeeps, were sourced from Holland.

Equipment from the USA was difficult to procure on account of the US arms embargo enforced on 14 December 1947. This was implemented partly as a gesture to the Arabs and partly to avoid an uncontrollable Middle East arms race. By May 29, 1948, the UN Security Council also imposed a general arms embargo. Nonetheless, by means of unauthorized channels, Israel purchased a few US Flying Fortresses and a small consignment of US machine guns and rifles. Israel employed various ruses to circumvent the UN embargo. In Britain, after Israeli agents furtively acquired a few British bombers, they established a film company to shoot a war scene involving the mass take-off of "New Zealand" piloted Beaufighters.[89] As the planes receded into the distance all traces of the company evanesced.

Where Israel had constantly to tread warily was within the UN. On September 16, Count Bernadotte finally submitted a report suggesting that the Negev be awarded to Transjordan. (The report no longer recommended the curtailment of Jewish immigration and the handing of Jerusalem over to the Arabs.) A day later, Bernadotte was assassinated in Jerusalem by three men thought to be members of Lehi. His murder acutely embarrassed the Israeli government, leading Ben-Gurion to apprise the American ambassador that he intended to "outlaw any organization which uses murder or terrorist methods as a means of political or any other action."[90] Without further ado all Irgun and Lehi units still operating in Jerusalem were suppressed.[91]

Given that Bernadotte's report had been officially tabled, Ben-Gurion was convinced that unless Israel assumed complete and indisputable possession of the Negev, it would be deprived of that territory. Britain, with strong support from the US State Department, pressed the UN General Assembly to adopt Bernadotte's report. As Ernest Bevin, the British foreign minister, told the House of Commons, "it is our hope that the United Nations will lose no time in throwing the full weight of their authority behind Bernadotte's proposals."[92] In like vein, on September 21, George Marshall, the US Secretary of State, urged the UN General Assembly to accept the plan in its entirety,[93] describing it as "a generally fair basis for the settlement of the Palestinian issues."[94] Much to Israel's relief, on October 25, when President Truman announced that he would not compel Israel to cede the Negev, the Bernadotte plan was stillborn.

Operation Yoav

During the early months of the second truce, Israel, having been illegally denied access to its Negev settlements, decided to confront the Egyptians with force. By October 15, on the assumption that quiet would continue on all other fronts, it inaugurated Operation Yoav.[95] The UN Truce Supervision Authorities were informed that Israel was intent on asserting its right of free and unhindered passage to the Negev. Conventional wisdom has it that, as an Israeli convoy came within a stone's throw of Egyptian positions, it was attacked. One vehicle went up in flames and the rest withdrew. This might well have been the case but in his memoirs Yitzhak Rabin wrote: "The Egyptians did not open fire. Nerves were stretched. The pretext for action was predicated on us being blocked. Eventually something occurred and there is no need to go into details. There was fire from here and fire from there. A pretext arose."[96] Robert Lovett, the acting US Secretary of State, also believed that the incident was contrived[97] whereas the American author Kurzman wrote that "it was not clear that it was *Egyptian* explosive power that caused the damage."[98] Whatever the case, an Egyptian violation of the cease-fire was officially noted. By sunset, in a surprise move, the Israeli air force appeared over the Egyptian Sinai base at El Arish where it destroyed a large number of grounded aircraft, thus ensuring Israel temporary mastery of the skies.

There were two components to Operation Yoav. The first involved units of the Yiftah Brigade that set out from Kibbutz Nir Am in the direction of Beit Hanun in what is now the Gaza Strip. They were charged with sealing the coastal road to box off Egyptian forces situated to the north but the ingenuity of Egyptian army engineers outwitted them. Using wire netting, logs and boards, the engineers conducted their troops over the sand dunes and coastal beaches, enabling those that were stationed in Isdud (Ashdod) to relocate between Gaza and Rafah.

The second component, entailing the main brunt of Operation Yoav, took place further to the east. It commenced at dawn on October 16 with the aim of overwhelming Iraq-el-Manshie, situated on the Majdal (now Ashkelon)–Hebron Road (see Map 1.4). To accomplish their task, the Israelis had first to command a hill with an overall view of the general terrain. An infantry company of the 7th Brigade, led by Uzi Narkiss, approached such an elevation with the expectation of being fully covered by an armored corps. However, four of the twelve light tanks available were knocked out and only one of the two heavy tanks functioned properly. This exposed the infantry to devastating fire from a battery of guns stationed in Faluja (to their west). Within minutes, a third of the company was wiped out. Those that pulled through gathered at nearby Kastina where they spent the night around a campfire. In a melancholy refrain, they began to intone what were normally stirring Palmah songs. As the night wore on, they regained their composure and their spirits began to soar. By the following day, with the arrival of reinforcements, they were once again battle-ready.[99]

The fiasco at Iraq-el-Manshie shifted the IDF's focus to the Faluja junction (see Map 1.4). The operation began on the night of October 17 and the following day the junction fell to the Israelis. What then stood between the IDF and the Negev were six strategic heights at Huleikat, where the Egyptians were well entrenched and surrounded by barbed-wire enclosures and minefields. A platoon of the Givati Brigade punctured the defenses in one of them. But by then most of its men were either dead or wounded.[100] However, a more favorable resolution was attained at the next position where, after a bayonet charge and

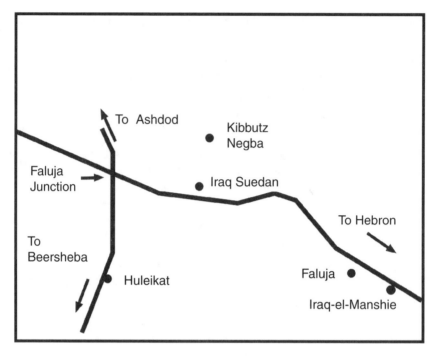

Map 1.4 *The Faluja Junction*

close-knit fighting involving biting, the Israelis disposed of all opposition.[101] They then came across 30 Vickers machine guns which they
learnt to operate from a captured Saudi Arabian sergeant. These having
been put to good use, all remaining Egyptian strongholds folded,
affording Israel an open road to the Negev.

Not being cognizant of the nature of the battles to his north,
Beersheba's Egyptian commander failed to place his men on full alert.
In the early hours of October 21, he was both surprised and mortified
when the Israelis simply sauntered almost unopposed into his biblical
township. A French-speaking unit composed of undisciplined North
African Jews led the advance. With its penchant for callousness, the unit
rounded up a dozen Arabs that were cowering in a sewage ditch. The
Arabs were forced to a wall and then shot in cold blood.[102]

At Duwaima, west of Hebron, Arab civilians, that is, women, children
and the elderly, were massacred after their village yielded to an IDF
mobile unit of mainly ex-Lehi fighters. The number killed is not known

precisely. Gelber, an Israeli historian, suggests that it was 22 (in addition to the 80 Arab soldiers felled in battle). Morris provides an estimate of 80–100 whereas Ben-Gurion recorded a range of 70–80.[103] Some of the confusion relates to the fact that heavy casualties were imposed on the villagers in the normal course of battle. The post-battle slaughter came to light after a platoon commander confessed that he had ordered it. A court martial was not instituted for lack of witnesses willing to testify against him. Sadeh, the supreme commander of the unit in question, showed no contrition and refused to appear before Isser Be'eri, who investigated the carnage.[104]

On October 22, a UN-ordained cease-fire came into effect, followed by a UN Security Council demand that all parties return to positions held prior to the latest round of fighting. Paying no heed, Israel went on to claim Isdud and repossess the ruined kibbutzim of Nitzanim and Yad Mordehai. The next day, that is, on the 23rd, the IDF appeared at Sdom at the southern end of the Dead Sea.

Despite being subject to inordinate pressure to obey the UN withdrawal injunction, Israel refused to do so. It reminded the Security Council that the Egyptians had invaded territory assigned to Israel and, were it to comply, it would in fact be sanctioning a violation of a previous UN resolution.[105] By way of compromise, it offered to remove its mobile forces while keeping its fixed ones in place. This was accepted by the UN's acting mediator and the matter was settled.

Although Operation Yoav had achieved its major objective (clearing the way to the Negev), the Egyptians still remained in the Gaza Strip, in a short line radiating westward from Auja, in a small enclosure in the Faluja region (known as the Faluja Pocket), and to a limited degree in the Hebron Hills.

The Faluja Pocket, which was manned by a sizable brigade, contained Iraq-el-Manshie, Faluja, the village Iraq Suedan, and its fortress. With the latter in close proximity to the road leading to the Negev, the IDF sought to neutralize it. Contrary to standard practice and in the interest of achieving maximum precision, the Israelis chose to fight in broad daylight. The assault began on November 9 at 2.00 p.m with a deafening barrage emitted by a large battery of 75-mm guns. Two hours later, with the late afternoon sun adversely affecting the defenders' field of vision, there was a final thrust from the west. Remnants of the barbed-wire enclosure were cleared and sappers approached and blew open the fortress wall. Just as Israeli troops were about to storm the fortress, the Egyptians debouched from it with their hands in the air. Although some casualties were incurred in a diversionary attack, the fortress itself was subdued without a single Israeli loss.

The rest of the Faluja Pocket remained under siege. This caused the Egyptians to suffer from shortages of food and medicine. Meals were restricted to two per day and surgical operations had to be performed with a razor blade.[106] Despite such deprivations, Sayid Taha, the brigade's commander, known as the "Black Wolf" on account of his dark Sudanese complexion, refused to capitulate. He did however agree to meet with Allon, the commander of the IDF's Southern front. At their meeting, held at Kibbutz Gat, Allon paid tribute to the gallantry and fighting spirit of the Egyptians and implored Taha to consider the lives of his remaining men. As an inducement, he offered to accept a surrender that, far from being degrading, would have entailed full military honors. Taha, conceding that he was in a bind, declared that while he could not necessarily save the lives of his men, he was duty-bound to preserve the good name of the Egyptian army and therefore he chose to fight "to the last bullet or to the last man."[107]

In a move to further reduce the extent of the Faluja Pocket, a battalion of the Alexandroni Brigade was ordered to attack Iraq-el-Manshie. During the early hours of December 28, three companies entered the village's precincts. Company C went on ahead in an attempt to capture a dominant hill. After failing to do so and finding itself cut off from the other two companies, it took cover behind the mud walls of a village courtyard. By dawn Egyptian artillery had dispensed with all its men. The death toll exceeding 90 was Israel's highest arising from a single engagement.[108] From then on, the Faluja Pocket, where among others Abdel Nasser (Egypt's future president) languished, was no longer disputed.

Operation Hiram

On the Central and Northern fronts, there was general compliance with the terms of the second truce, the exception being al-Qawuqji of the PLA who reasoned that, since he was not a member of the United Nations, the truce did not apply to him. On October 22, he captured the hill of Sheik Abd overlooking the settlement of Manara situated three miles from the nearest Jewish hamlet. To avert its downfall, the IDF decided to expunge the Arab enemy from within the entire Galilee. Accordingly, on the night of October 28, the IDF commenced Operation Hiram (named after the king of Tyre, one-time ally of King David and Solomon). It concluded within 60 hours with the complete collapse of al-Qawuqji's army and of all other Arab opposition, leaving Israel in full possession of the Galilee, bar the Syrian bridgehead at Mishmar Hayarden. Furthermore, a handful of Lebanese border villages were taken.

As a sequel to the IDF's sweeping success, some outrages, including rape, were inflicted on Arab civilians.[109] In Ilabun, 13 villagers were slaughtered, almost certainly in revenge for the previous decapitation of two Israelis and the parading of their heads in the village's streets.[110] In Safsaf and Saliha, dozens of civilians were killed in cold blood despite having raised white flags.[111] In addition to such atrocities, the looting of Arab property was commonplace. Anything of value such as carpets, radios, coffee grinders, vehicles, tools, and farm animals was pilfered. Much to his sorrow, Ben-Gurion listed in his diary the "moral defects within us, defects that I never even suspected existed. I am referring to the mass depredation [of Arab property] in which all sections of the Jewish community have participated."[112] Ben-Gurion demanded stern punishment for those responsible for the general pillage.[113] On November 7, the cabinet took stock of the issue. During the session, Aharon Cizling, the minister for agriculture, regretted that "now Jews too have behaved like Nazis."[114] On November 17, acting on a government ruling, Allon warned his men not to harm captured Arab soldiers or civilians. Enemy prisoners were to be treated humanely and courteously and unjustified killings of civilians were to be regarded as acts of murder. To drive the point home, Allon insisted that all his officers append their signatures to his order.[115]

The demise of the Palmah

On May 15, 1941, the Haganah, under Sadeh's drive, established military units known by the Hebrew acronym Palmah (from Plugot Mahatz – Shock Companies). During the final years of the British mandate,

the Palmah financed its ability to become a standing force by billet-
ing its fighters in kibbutzim where they divided their time between
agricultural work and military training. By virtue of its lifestyle, the
Palmah developed its own unique *esprit de corps*. Though the Palmah
was an offshoot of the Haganah, it maintained its own central command which continued to function during the War of Independence.
Occasionally, on being issued with a directive by the General Staff, a
Palmah unit refused to execute it unless or until it was confirmed by
Palmah headquarters.

Having dismantled the Irgun and Lehi and having absorbed its men
into the IDF's general ranks, Ben-Gurion regarded the continued quasi-
autonomy of the Palmah as an anomaly. On October 7, the Palmah was
formally required to place its three brigades (Negev, Yiftah, and Harel)
under the direct control of the IDF's GHQ. Allon, the Palmah's commander, appealed against the decision on the grounds that the Palmah
embodied attributes not shared by the rest of the IDF. These included
its skills as a commando force, its reputation for daring exploits, and the
inclusion within its ranks of members of pioneering youth movements.
Ben-Gurion responded that, as he favored instilling a pioneering ethos
into the army as a whole, there was no reason to distinguish between
Palmah and non-Palmah units. He went on to assert that "with all due
respect to its glorious past, the Palmah is now part of the Israeli Defense
Forces and must share the same status as other Army units."[116] In that
light, November 7 was determined as the Palmah's final day.

In retrospect, the official demise of the Palmah was necessary in the
interests of consistency and of ensuring that the IDF functioned as a
fully integrated body. But Ben-Gurion was also accused of having been
motivated by party political considerations. It was no secret that the
Palmah was controlled and mainly manned by members of the Mapam
party that were far to the left of Ben-Gurion's party, Mapai. (60 of the
Palmah's 64 commanders were Mapam members.)[117] Mapam's leaders
had openly stated that they regarded the Palmah as representing one
of the country's few ironclad bulwarks against the rise of fascism and
proudly pointed to its role in the *Altalena* affair. Such statements suggested the possibility that the Palmah might in the future further secular
class interests as interpreted by its radical command. Although the likelihood of that happening was rather remote (for in practice the Palmah

Plate 1.2 *Some senior Palmah staff: second from left, Yitzhak Rabin; fifth from left, Yigal Allon*

hierarchy accepted Ben-Gurion's verdict), it nevertheless presented itself as a theoretical danger.

Even had the Palmah been a Mapai-dominated organization, it is almost certain that Ben-Gurion would not have acted otherwise for he was wary of the Palmah for one other reason. He had a much higher regard for officers who had served within the British and other regular armies and regarded the Palmahniks, whose fortitude he nonetheless much admired, as amateurs. As far back as April 1943, Ben-Gurion, on addressing a Palmah unit in Ashdot-Ya'akov, startled his listeners by indicating that he hoped to see them all serving within the framework of the British army.[118] In essence, Ben-Gurion wished to transform the IDF into an army compatible in nature and organization with western ones.

Operation Horev

As already mentioned, although it had strengthened its hold on an expanded area of the Negev, the IDF had yet to dominate all of it. To that end Operation Horev was activated. On December 22, Israel informed the UN that it considered itself entitled to renew hostilities since, contrary to a Security Council resolution of November 16, Egypt had refused to enter into negotiations for an armistice agreement.

Because most of the Egyptian army was concentrated along the coastal road between Rafah and Gaza, where it was embedded in strongly defended fortifications, the IDF chose first to eliminate the enemy's more fragile positions further east. That necessitated the conquest of Auja, in the vicinity of the Negev–Sinai border. Straddling the length of the sealed and sole road leading to Auja were a number of Egyptian detachments that constituted a buffer against any Israeli advance. But, thanks to Yadin's archaeological knowledge, the possibility of rapidly constructing an alternative route came to mind. Yadin identified the existence of remnants of an ancient Roman highway that lay in a straight line from Beersheba to Auja. With appropriate modifications, the disused track could be made serviceable.

To carry out the roadworks with a modicum of secrecy, a massive assault was orchestrated along the Rafah–Gaza front to serve as a feint. For good measure, the Israelis hoped to drive a wedge into the Egyptian lines roughly halfway between Rafah and Gaza. For that purpose the

IDF was to capture Hill 86. During the night of December 22, after a heavy bombardment involving 75-mm guns over the entire front, a battalion of the Golani Brigade made for and took the hill. The battalion then dug in to await the delivery of heavy equipment. But a freak rainstorm that flooded the surrounding wadis made them impassable. The next day, the Egyptians counterattacked. Tanks and half-tracks equipped with flame-throwers gave cover to their advancing infantry. Soldiers of the Golani Battalion fought bravely but their limited supply of ammunition soon ran out and, in any case, the heavy onset of rain and mud caused most of their light arms to jam.[119] By 3 p.m. they had abandoned the hill, deserting some of their wounded. The battle for Hill 86 did at least convince the Egyptians that the Israelis were bent on hurling them into the sea. Kamel Ismael El Sharif attested that they arrived at that conviction after finding plans to that effect on the body of an Israeli officer.[120]

All the while IDF engineers labored frenetically to make good the old Roman track but progress on it turned out to be tardy. In order to attack Auja within a reasonable time frame, plans to utilize the entire Roman road were jettisoned. Having traversed a large part of it, an armored column (of Sadeh's 8th Brigade) brazenly entered the existing highway. Much to its astonishment, all the Egyptian roadside positions had been abandoned. The battle for Auja then began. The first offensive was rebuffed by a combination of Egyptian fighter planes and land forces. But the second one, moving unexpectedly from a westerly position, punched through the Egyptian lines and on December 27 Auja was subdued.

The following day, an Israeli column consisting of tanks, armored vehicles, and motorized infantry ventured from Auja. Within minutes, it crossed the international frontier to enter Egypt. Then by daybreak on December 29, Abu Ageila fell. (The Egyptian area commander suffered a nervous breakdown and had to be relieved of his duties.)[121] Hours later, an Israeli raiding party consisting of a tank and commando battalion proceeded in the direction of El Arish, claiming on the way Bir Lahfan as well as a nearby airstrip. But for want of sufficient infantry capable of manning all their newly gained positions, the Israelis returned to Abu Ageila.

Alarmed by their sudden reversal of fortune, the Egyptians urgently appealed to Transjordan and Iraq to open additional fronts so as to ease the pressure put upon them but their Arab "allies" turned a deaf ear to such entreaties. As far as Transjordan was concerned, the defeat of Egypt would have strengthened its position both with the Palestinians and the Arab world in general.[122] However, on December 29, the Egyptians were rescued by non-Arabs. The UN Security Council demanded an immediate cease-fire and a return of Israeli and Egyptian forces to positions held prior to the current round of fighting. Concurrently Britain invoked the 1936 Anglo-Egyptian Treaty (which, as it happened, Egypt wished to abrogate) and issued Israel with an ultimatum that, unless Israel withdrew from Egypt without delay, Britain would intercede. Ben-Gurion in turn declared that Britain had no legal or moral authority to arrogate to itself the right to enforce Security Council decisions. He did however assure the US government, through whom the ultimatum was delivered, that the Israeli incursion into Egypt was merely a tactical maneuver and that the IDF would evacuate the Sinai Peninsula by January 2.

What Ben-Gurion did not divulge was that the IDF had designs on capturing Rafah. Had it done so, it would have boxed in the Egyptian army in an area that corresponds to the present-day Gaza Strip. For that purpose, prodigious efforts were expended on claiming a series of strongholds within Rafah's reach. The results were inconclusive but sufficient progress had been made for a successful onslaught against Rafah to be undertaken. On January 7, just as Israel was about to administer the *coup de grâce*, it was compelled to abide by a newly imposed cease-fire. Egypt had finally agreed to enter into negotiations for an armistice agreement. During that same day, four British Spitfires, on a reconnaissance mission over battle zones in the Rafah region, were downed. Menacingly reinforcing its garrison at Aqaba, Britain demanded of Israel both an explanation and compensation. Heartened by such a stance, Egypt then announced that it would after all not negotiate with Israel unless Israel withdrew from strongholds lying within its territory south of Rafah. With Israel acceding to such demands, the way was clear for the commencement of armistice talks.

The armistice agreements

The armistice negotiations with Egypt, which opened on January 13, 1949, took place at the Hotel of Roses in Rhodes. In the first session, the Egyptians insisted that Israel return to positions held before the commencement of Operation Yoav. But in the end they relented and, on February 24, they accepted an armistice agreement that allowed for the evacuation of their besieged brigade at Faluja. Further concessions obtained entailed the demilitarization of Auja and its immediate environs and the stationing there of the Mixed Armistice Commission's Headquarters. For its part, Egypt no longer laid claim to any component of the Negev.

Once an armistice with Egypt was concluded, Israel entered into negotiations with Lebanon at Rosh Hanikra, and with Transjordan in both Transjordan itself, where the substance of the talks was held, and in Rhodes. Agreement with Lebanon, which involved the return to Lebanon of 14 villages captured during Operation Hiram, was reached on March 23, 1949. The (British) mandatory boundary was accepted as the armistice border and Lebanon agreed to remove Syrian units from its territory.

In preliminary discussions with Transjordan, Israel was given to understand that, because Transjordan retained control of the southern half of the Negev (where there had been no fighting), it ought to be attached to its kingdom. Such an assertion was unacceptable to Israel. For one, the UN had awarded the bulk of the Negev to the Jewish state and, for another, possession of the Red Sea town of Eilat along the Gulf of Aqaba was essential to Israel for it to trade with East African and Asian countries. Accordingly, units of the Negev and Golani Brigades, in the context of Operation Uvdah (Fact), were requisitioned to close in on Eilat. Troops of the Negev Brigade were to cross the center of the Negev while those of the Golani Brigade were to skirt the international border with Transjordan. The operation began on March 5, 1949, when a relatively small convoy of the Negev Brigade left Beersheba. It passed through Mahtesh Ramon (a large crater) and continued southward to a preliminary destination some 50 kilometers north of Eilat. The going was tough. The terrain was strewn with stones and boulders, which periodically had to be dynamited. At times, drivers had to negotiate passes no wider than their vehicles. By their journey's end, the Israelis had constructed a crude runway so that transport planes could land, ferrying additional men and equipment. Operation Uvdah climaxed on March 10 with both units arriving at Eilat at more or less the same time. (The Negev Brigade preceded the Golani one by only two hours.) Eilat, known in Arabic as Umm Rashrash, was deserted. It consisted of a tiny police station and a small batch of mud huts with thatched roofs. En route, the Golani Brigade drew fire from an Arab Legion company. Rather than replying, the Israelis bypassed it. As it happened, the company unilaterally withdrew. In all probability King Abdullah wished to avoid a pointless confrontation with Israel over mainly desert territory.[123] Also within the context of Operation Uvdah, the Alexandroni Brigade took Ein Gedi on the western shore of the Dead Sea as well as nearby parcels of land, including Masada.

Talks with Transjordan were complicated by Iraq which, despite holding a small section of Palestine, refused to negotiate with Israel. Instead, it repatriated all its forces while handing over the territory it had occupied to the Arab Legion. Since Israel viewed such developments as conferring a military advantage to Transjordan, it successfully bargained for a stretch of land to the west of Jenin, including Wadi Arah, which gave it direct passage between Hadera and Afula. In return, Israel conceded a small area on the western and southern slopes of the Hebron Mountains. On April 3, 1949, an armistice agreement was concluded and signed in Rhodes. A special committee was established to resolve outstanding issues. These included Israel's use of the Hebrew University and Hadasah Hospital on Mount Scopus, unfettered passage through the main highway between Jerusalem and Tel Aviv, access to the holy places and the cemetery on the Mount of Olives, as well as the renewal of traffic along the Jerusalem railroad. Ultimately, the agreement was only honored in respect to the railway.

On April 5, 1949 Syrian–Israeli talks were convened in a tent near Mahanayim (west of the Jordan River). Then on July 20, 1949, after bitter wrangling, an armistice agreement was signed, bringing the War of Independence officially to an end. Syria undertook to remove all its troops stationed in territory that the UN had allocated to Israel on condition that there be a demilitarized zone between the international boundary and the line which Syria had held.

Ostensibly the Arabs invaded Israel in furtherance of Palestinian independence. But in practice, all the Arab states were in one way or another totally self-serving. In 1937, at the first Pan-Arab Convention on the Palestine problem, the Syrian delegate called for the return of

Palestine to its "mother country," Syria.[124] At a *minimum*, the Syrians wished to annex the Eastern Galilee containing the headwaters of the Jordan River. Iraq would have liked to possess Haifa, where the oil pipeline from Mosul terminated, and if possible to stifle the entire Jewish state. King Abdullah of Jordan wished to add most of Palestine to his kingdom. Above all, he was mindful of foiling the ambitions of his rival, Haj Amin al-Husseini, the Mufti of Jerusalem, whose strident Palestinian nationalism offended him. In principle, he was not opposed to a Jewish state though he would have preferred it to be subordinate to his authority. It has been suggested that he intended to limit his incursion into Palestine to the areas nominated by the UN for the Palestinians.[125] But it is difficult to escape the conclusion that had his forces been capable of overwhelming the Israelis, they would have done so. The historian David Tal indicates that Abdullah certainly did not exclude that possibility.[126] On April 26, in addressing parliament, he explicitly foreshadowed occupying Palestine. By calling upon the Jews to accept his rule, it was clear that he had every intention of entering Israeli-designated territory.[127] Then in mid-May, after the Arab Legion had swiftly occupied the bulk of the West Bank without encountering any Israeli opposition, Abdullah toyed with seizing both Jerusalem and Tel Aviv.[128] However, when it came to the crunch, recognizing the cost that Israel would have imposed on his forces, Abdullah decided that he would simply settle for the West Bank (including East Jerusalem).[129]

As for Egypt, it became entangled in Palestine mainly to maintain its leadership of the Arab League and above all to act as a counterweight to Abdullah's expansionism. Internal pressures were also instrumental, for King Farouk was warned (or should one say goaded?) by the British embassy that unless Egypt participated in the Arab invasion, its government would fall.[130] In practice such advice was sound. Against a backdrop of public concern for the growing number of Palestinian refugees (before the state of Israel was even declared), leading Egyptian Muslim clerics decreed that the liberation of Palestine was beholden upon all Muslims.[131] A Muslim motif pervaded the thoughts of the Arab combatants, particularly among the Muslim Brothers who ultimately inspired the formation of Hamas. The following Hadith from the Koran was frequently invoked: "The day of resurrection does not come until

Muslims fight against Jews, until the Jews hide behind trees and stones and until the trees and stones shout out 'O Muslim, there is a Jew behind me, come and kill him.'"[132]

Had the Arab armies succeeded, a Palestinian state would not have arisen. The victors would simply have claimed the territories they conquered, just as in April 1950 Transjordan had annexed the West Bank and as Egypt retained exclusive control of the Gaza Strip. Throughout the war and during its immediate aftermath, the plight of Palestinian refugees was viewed primarily as a humanitarian issue. No Arab regime recognized the Palestinians as a distinct national group.[133] When for instance on June 12, 1948 Azzam Pasha, the secretary of the Arab League, suggested that Haj Amin al-Husseini, the leading figure in the Palestinian Arab Higher Committee (AHC), be seated at an Arab League meeting, his recommendation was rejected on the grounds that the forum was one of heads of state and foreign ministers of which Husseini was neither.[134] Although the Arabs tended to pay lip service to the Palestinian cause by purporting to further Palestinian claims to either autonomy or independence, their proposals were often as not designed to further their own agenda. For example, Egyptian support in September 1948 for an All-Palestine Government located in Gaza was simply a ploy to counter Abdullah's desire to seize Palestinian territory. Recognizing that, the following October Abdullah convened a Congress of Palestinians in Amman which denounced the All-Palestine Government and which favored union with Transjordan.[135] Much to their misfortune, the Palestinians lost a golden opportunity to attain statehood in 1948 by virtue of their stubborn refusal to come to terms with the rise of Israel. Their intransigence, in Glubb Pasha's view, led to their undoing.[136]

It is worth noting that, while Britain stood behind the Arab world and viewed its setbacks as its own,[137] it was no hard and fast friend of the Palestinians. Essentially, Britain sought an outcome whereby its protégé Abdullah in partnership with Egypt would assume possession of at least the Negev. When peace feelers were first mooted between Israel and Transjordan and it became clear that Abdullah was prepared to renounce all claims to the Negev, Sir Hugh Dow, acting consul-general, was horrified. He argued that Britain should not "allow" King Abdullah to proceed in that direction.[138] As for a Palestinian state, Ernest Bevin, the UK foreign secretary, opined that it would be too small and weak to maintain itself.[139]

Tentative peace negotiations

A United Nations Palestine Conciliation Commission induced the parties to the conflict to gather in Lausanne to negotiate a final peace settlement. The talks, which at Arab insistence were indirect ones (that is, the parties did not meet face to face), began in the summer of 1949 and by September had ended in failure. As one Israeli participant observed, the unwillingness of the Arabs to negotiate directly certainly did not suggest a genuine willingness to negotiate in any other way.[140] The Arabs refused to discuss substantive issues unless Israel agreed to re-admit all the Palestinian refugees, a pre-condition that Israel adamantly rejected. On being subject to American pressure, Israel partially relented by offering to accept 100,000 refugees in the context of a peace agreement but that gesture failed to satisfy the Arabs.

During the period 1949–51, King Abdullah was genuinely interested in securing a separate peace treaty with Israel. By December 1949, both sides were willing to sign a document clarifying general points of agreement. These included the provision to Transjordan of an outlet to the Mediterranean, transit rights from Hebron to Gaza via Beersheba, the demilitarization of the Jerusalem corridor, and a guarantee that the Anglo-Transjordanian Treaty would not apply to that area.[141] As the talks progressed, Abdullah was even prepared to make concessions in Jerusalem such as ceding to Israel both Mount Scopus and the Jewish quarter in the Old City. The negotiations appeared to be coming to a head in February 1950 when the parties were on the threshold of initialing a five-year peace treaty (as a prelude to a permanent one). It was then that inter-Arab pressures railroaded the whole process.[142] Transjordan was threatened with expulsion from the Arab League which would have resulted in closed borders with its neighboring Arab countries. As Glubb Pasha explained the matter: "The mere fact that King Abdullah admitted his desire for peace was enough to impel the Arab League to declare that talk of peace was treason to the Arab cause."[143] Appreciating Abdullah's dilemma, Israel offered additional incentives entailing the handing over of a small amount of territory near Jenin.

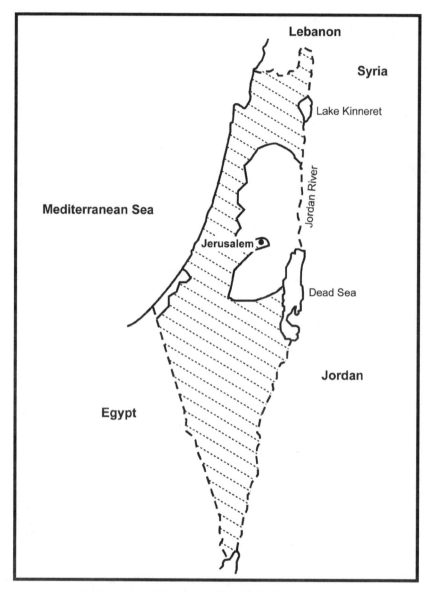

Map 1.5   *Israel in 1949*

However, by the end of May, Britain, France, and the USA issued their Tripartite Declaration undertaking to prevent, either with or without UN cooperation, Middle East frontiers from being altered by force. That declaration, which effectively accorded international acceptance of the armistice frontiers as permanent ones, satisfied Israel's primary objectives. As for Abdullah, while he still wished to forge peaceful relations with Israel, few of his key politicians were willing to stand by him. By May (when Transjordan was renamed Jordan), not only was the entire Jordanian cabinet opposed to negotiating with Israel but so were at least 44 of the country's 50 members of parliament.[144] On Friday, July 22, 1951, Abdullah was assassinated at point-blank range by an agent of Haj Amin al-Husseini while making his way to prayer in East Jerusalem's el-Aksa Mosque. With Abdullah's demise, all faint remaining hopes of concluding a peace treaty were extinguished. Abdullah was succeeded by his eldest son Talal. Being afflicted with mental illness, Talal was forced to abdicate in August 1952 in favor of his son, Hussein. Because Hussein at 17 years old was still a minor, he was not crowned until April 1953.

Peace overtures were also forthcoming from Syria. In April 1949, Syrian delegates to the Armistice Conference had met directly with their Israeli counterparts and had explicitly offered to sue for peace in return for control over half of Lake Kinneret.[145] It seems that both the Syrian president Husni al-Za'im (who was a Kurd) and the premier Husni Barazi were willing to normalize relations with Israel. Ben-Gurion did not run with the Syrian offer, partly because he had doubts relating to the Syrian leaders' staying power. (They had seized the reins of government in a coup engineered in March 1949.) His misgivings were soon borne out. In August 1949, al-Zai'im and Bazari were deposed and murdered in the context of yet another military putsch led by uncompromising anti-Zionists. Any agreement with al-Za'im that Israel might have concluded would have been both ephemeral and at the expense of some Israeli territory.

A deplorable aspect of the Arab invasion is that the UN did little to counter it. In his memoirs, Trygve Lie, who was the UN's first secretary general, wrote: "The invasion of Palestine by the Arab States was the first armed aggression that the world had seen since the end of the war. The United Nations could not permit that aggression to succeed and at the same time survive as an influential force for peaceful settlement, collective security, and meaningful international law."[146] Yet instead of acting to deter the Arabs, either by imposing sanctions or threatening them with the use of force, the UN behaved as if it had to maintain a position of even-handedness vis-à-vis all the protagonists. For this to have happened, Britain could claim a lion's share of the credit. When on May 17, 1948 at a UN Security Council session the United States proposed that, in view of the fact that the peace had been violated, the Council should demand an immediate cease-fire, Sir Alexander Cadogan, the UK delegate, vetoed the proposal. With a straight face, he expressed doubt as to whether aggression had actually occurred.[147] As the pro-Zionist British officer Richard Meinertzhagen caustically pointed out "surely invasion [of Palestine] is the essence and proof of aggression."[148] Participating in the Security Council debate, Vasily Tarasenko of the Ukraine reminded the forum that "according to the rules of the international community each government has the right to restore order only in its own country. None of the Arab states whose troops had entered Palestine could claim that Palestine formed part of its territory."[149]

Conclusion

On the eve of the war, King Abdullah was, at his own request, appointed commander-in-chief of the Arab High Command while Nur al-Din Mahmoud was made chief of staff. In practice, both positions were merely honorary ones with each Arab army performing as an independent entity so that their overall push lacked cohesion. Having only committed themselves to a war against Israel some time in April 1948, they acted without sufficient preparation and planning.[150] In fact Egypt had not committed itself wholeheartedly until as late as May 12 and, although part of the Arab coalition, Lebanon refrained from actually invading Israel. Arab opening gambits were dictated as much by political rivalries as by military considerations.[151] Had the Arabs acted in unison in the early phases of the war, they might well have emerged victoriously.

In failing to press their initial advantages, the Arabs provided the IDF with the opportunity to consolidate and strengthen itself. By the war's end, Israel emerged with a defense capability that far surpassed its rivals. On account of an unusually high proportion of young people in the Yishuv, over 100,000 conscripts were finally drafted. This ultimately allowed the IDF to man 12 mobile brigades, supported by artillery, armor, an air force, and a navy.

Thanks to Ben-Gurion's foresight (which was not at the time widely shared by other Yishuv leaders), when the war commenced over 80 percent of Israel's military ordnance was already ordered and largely paid for. Finance was not a problem since donations from world Jewry more than covered Israel's military expenditures.[152] This meant that as soon as secure transport shipments were arranged, Israel's accretion of armaments proceeded apace. By contrast, the Arab Legion was plagued by acute budgetary problems (notwithstanding Britain's assistance) that not only compounded its ability to finance new initiatives but also its ability to sustain ongoing expenditures. The Arabs' armament advantage steadily declined, not only because Israel began to acquire weapons from Czechoslovakia and other sources but also because Britain, by virtue of the UN arms embargo, was unable to resupply them. Not anticipating the embargo, the Arabs failed to stockpile large quantities of weapons and ammunition.[153]

A number of other factors contributed to the failure of the invading forces. Israel benefited from having short internal lines for its logistic and communication requirements. It enjoyed great flexibility in adjusting to changing circumstances and, once its forces increased in scope, it could allow for the rapid redeployment of units from one front to another.[154] Moreover, various social and organizational factors worked to the Arabs' disadvantage.[155] Within the Egyptian army all operational initiatives were in the hands of the High Command and it would never have dawned on junior officers to seek permission to assume individual responsibility for the engagements in which they participated. Even though the Egyptian soldiers fought doggedly as exemplified by their stand at the Faluja Pocket, their military training was less than perfect, especially in terms of night fighting. After the first truce, almost all the Arab forces tended to rely on static defense, foregoing mobility and sudden raids. This allowed the Israelis to determine which fronts to activate. As Ben-Gurion put it, Israel won the war "not because our army performed miracles but because the Arab army [sic] was rotten."[156]

For Israel the war ended triumphantly. The country withstood the combined assault of four regular armies and went on to incorporate significantly more territory than the UN had originally apportioned it.[157] Had the Arabs accepted the UN partition resolution, the Israelis would have made do with their allotted share. Shortly after November

29, 1947 when the UN Partition Resolution was adopted, Ben-Gurion, cautioning against irredentist notions in a seminal and well-publicized speech, advocated the preservation of the UN recommended borders.[158] But once the Arabs strove to extirpate the Jewish state, the Israelis felt entitled to expand their frontiers. Had it confined itself to its allocated area, it would simply have permitted foreign invaders, such as Transjordan and Egypt, to extend their presence in regions in which they had no legitimate claim. There were some Israelis who would have liked to have seized the day to acquire even more land but they were restrained by both international and internal considerations. Moshe Sharett, Israel's foreign minister, for one, stressed the prime importance of ensuring that Israel's Jewish majority was firmly anchored. Addressing his compatriots, he pronounced: "We have to approach the problems with a demographic rather than a territorial scalpel."[159]

Israel's achievements arising from its War of Independence came at a heavy price. Between November 1947 when irregular warfare first erupted and January 1949, the nascent state lost close to 6,000 citizens, amounting to nearly 1 percent of its population. The fatalities incurred were over-represented in specific age groups. If one examines the cohort ranging from 17 to 20 years of age, one discovers that its death rate amounted to 6 percent.[160] Allowing for the small size of Israel's population, the writer Van Creveld estimates that "the blood bath was more intense than that undergone by either Britain or Germany in 1914–1918."[161] The toll in the War of Independence approached a third of all Israelis killed in action between November 1947 and the end of the twentieth century. No other Israeli war matched it.

The memory of those who gave of their lives so that the Jewish nation might have a small sovereign patch of land is indelibly etched in Israeli minds. Monuments to the war dead are strewn throughout the country. On the Jerusalem–Tel Aviv Highway, rust-proofed shells of vehicles destroyed in efforts to convey food and supplies to embattled Jerusalem serve as a graphic reminder of the fact that Israel was born in bloodshed and sacrifice. Unfortunately, all the travails sustained were merely the first of endless rounds of violence and enmity. The defeat suffered by the Arabs at the hands of the Jews whom they loathed and detested was too bitter a pill for them to swallow. Instead of simply putting the past behind them, they became obsessed with the magnitude of their humiliating setback. Due to a mixture of religious zeal, intolerance, cynical political manipulation, and general xenophobia, hatred of Israel and a burning passion for revenge became an article of faith of the highest magnitude. Surrounded by such foes, Israel's continued existence after the War of Independence could never be taken for granted.

2

THE ARAB REFUGEES

The War of Independence left in its wake an exodus of hundreds of thousands of Palestinians who found themselves homeless and destitute. Typically, refugees took flight at a moment's notice without having time to wind down their affairs and to ensure a smooth transfer of their property. The country's roads were strewn with fleeing families carrying, in bundles, their meager possessions. In Haifa there was a wild scramble to the port to ensure places on board boats departing for Lebanon. On arrival in the surrounding Arab territories, the refugees found that the host authorities were ill-equipped in receiving them. The regimes were not budgeted for such an eventuality and, at best, could only provide makeshift assistance. This meant that for the most part, refugees who were not at first accepted into camps, no matter how rudimentary, found themselves sleeping in the open. Bread doled out to them was insufficient to sustain them in good health and as a result hunger was rife as were a multitude of infectious diseases. Eventually, some order evolved from the surrounding chaos. The refugees' needs were beginning to be met, at least at a very basic level, in December 1949 when the UN Relief and Works Agency for Palestinian Refugees (UNRWA) was formed and assumed responsibility for their care.

Although no one could possibly deny the suffering and misery experienced by those unfortunate people, serious divergences of opinion as to the dimension and causes of the Palestinian refugee problem remain. Official Israeli sources place the number of Arab refugees at 630,000.[1] By contrast, the Arabs claim that there were over a million. But such claims are almost certainly excessive, for UNRWA has conceded that invalid refugee identity cards were issued in abundance.[2] In all probability, the true figure is close to 726,000, derived by deducting the number of Arabs that remained, that is, 133,000, from the 859,000 that were present prior to hostilities in all of the territory that Israel ultimately held.[3] Even that figure would have been lower had not the UN uniquely tailored the definition of Palestinian refugees. According to the UN, all Arabs who had dwelled in Palestine between June 1946 and May 1948 and who had lost both their homes and means of livelihood as a result of the 1948 Arab–Israeli war are deemed to be Palestinian refugees.[4] For no other refugee category throughout the entire world did the UN specify a *minimum* period of residence in one's homeland to qualify for refugee status. It is therefore not unreasonable to assume that there must have been a significant number of Arabs who were not born in Palestine. Otherwise, why would such a clause have been inserted? In this regard one might note US president Franklin Roosevelt's claim, made in 1939, that "Arab immigration into Palestine since 1921 vastly exceeded the total Jewish immigration during the whole period."[5] Granted that there is a degree of uncertainty regarding the precise magnitude of Arab migration, the fact that Arab migration actually occurred is beyond question.

With respect to the ultimate source of the refugee problem, it essentially arose as a by-product of the Arab–Jewish conflict culminating on May 15, 1948, with the invasion of Israel by four regular Arab armies. As Jacob Malek, the Soviet delegate to the UN, put it; "the existence of Arab refugees in the Middle East is the result of attempts to scuttle the UN General Assembly's decision regarding Palestine. Those implicated bear direct responsibility for the refugees' plight."[6]

Rather than facing reality, the Arabs have turned history inside out by leveling the *entire* blame for the refugee problem against the Jews. Among other things, they point to the slaughter in April 1948 of over one hundred men, women, and children in the village of Deir Yassin. That massacre (which was brought about by dissident Zionist forces and which was roundly condemned by the Yishuv's leadership) certainly instilled fear amongst the Palestinians. But there is no way of knowing just how many fled as a consequence. In any case, it occurred in the course of a battle in which civilians and combatants were intermingled. The attackers had no prior intention of harming civilians and even took the trouble to bring a loudspeaker with them to warn the Arabs off. Unfortunately the vehicle to which the speaker was attached tumbled into a ditch.

Above all, the Israelis have been accused of resorting to Plan Dalet (D) of the Haganah as a device for ridding themselves of the Arabs and, of late, Ilan Pappe has assumed the leading role in propagating such a charge. Because his book, *The Ethnic Cleansing of Palestine*, is widely perceived as containing definitive proof of Israel's prior intentions to banish the entire Arab population, it is necessary to divert briefly from our historical discourse to examine the essence of Pappe's thesis.

Throughout his text, Pappe repeats ad nauseam that Plan Dalet constituted *the* master plan for clearing out the Arabs by spelling "out clearly and unambiguously: the Palestinians had to go."[7] Pappe leans on Plan Dalet to such an extraordinary extent that if one were to remove it from the equation he would be left with an empty box. But even with Plan Dalet remaining in place, Pappe's case disintegrates the moment its full contents are revealed. Rather than doing so directly, Pappe draws on others to substantiate the plan's sinister designs. For example, he quotes Simha Flapan as having written: "The military campaign against the Arabs, including the 'conquest and destruction of the rural areas,' was set forth in the Hagana's Plan Dalet." From this Pappe concludes that "the aim of the plan was in fact the destruction of both the rural and urban areas of Palestine."[8] What the reader is not told is that on the very page from which Pappe quotes, Flapan proceeds to explain that "the tenets of the plan were clear and unequivocal: The Haganah must carry out 'activities against enemy settlements which are situated within or near to our Haganah installations, with the aim of preventing their use by active [Arab] armed forces.'"[9] In fact, Flapan emphasizes that Plan Dalet was none other than an operational military document to secure the nascent Jewish state. (Readers can examine Plan Dalet for themselves in an English version available in *The Journal of Palestine Studies*, Autumn 1988.)

In discussing the Haganah's approach to Arab villages that it wished to subjugate, Plan Dalet recommended that in the event of a village offering resistance, its armed forces ought to be destroyed and the population expelled beyond Israel's borders. *But* if no resistance is offered "bodies will be appointed consisting of people from the village to administer the internal affairs of the village."[10] As any open-minded person would readily appreciate, such a clause is totally at variance with a document that is purported to provide guidelines for cleansing Palestine of its Arabs. Pappe's thesis is pure fable. In practice, Plan Dalet, which was merely carried out in the second half of April,[11] was only effectively applied in the Upper Galilee and had no appreciable bearing on the Arab flight.[12] Many of the Arab villages that were stormed by the Haganah were found to be empty.[13] The occupants had fled in anticipation of imminent hostilities.

Pappe's credibility as a reliable chronicler is further undermined by his loose or at best careless use of quotations and sources. Drawing upon Ben-Gurion to demonstrate that from March 1948, it was Zionist policy "to ethnically cleanse the country as a whole,"[14] he quotes him as having said that the Haganah "captured many Arab positions and liberated Tiberias and Haifa, Jaffa, and Safad . . . so on the day of destiny, that part of Palestine where the Haganah could operate was almost clear of Arabs."[15] From this quotation the uninformed reader might well conclude (as no doubt Pappe would like him or her to do) that the Jews drove the Arabs out of the above listed towns. But the quotation in question contains an ellipsis. In the original source the words omitted between "Safad" and "so" are as follows: "The first town to fall to the Haganah was Tiberias. That was on April 18. We told the Arabs there that they might stay, if they gave up their arms and fought no more. They chose to go, encouraged by the British, who took them away in trucks to Syria. The same thing happened elsewhere."[16] In Pappe's deft hands, a statement disowning responsibility for an Arab flight is transformed into an admission of culpability.

In relation to the battle for Haifa, Pappe alleges that Mordechai Maklef, a senior Haganah officer, "orchestrated the cleansing campaign, and the orders he issued to his troops were plain and simple: 'Kill any Arab you encounter; torch all inflammable objects and force doors open with explosives.'"[17] The author admits to having felt rather unsettled by such a claim, for in life anything is possible. But on acquiring a copy of the document cited by Pappe as his source for Maklef's order,[18] his unease turned into confusion, for the document in question simply conveyed the Haganah's terms for an Arab surrender.

At one point, Pappe described how on arriving in Haifa shortly after the battle, Golda Meir found "cooked food still on the tables, children had left toys and books on the floor, and life appeared to have frozen in an instant."[19] Then without any apparent reason Pappe assumed that the scene left "no lasting mark on her or her associates' determination to continue with the ethnic cleansing of Palestine."[20] However, a few days later, on May 6, Meir explained to the Jewish Agency Executive that "our behaviour should be such that if, because of it, they [the Arabs who had left Haifa] come back, [then] let them come back."[21]

The bottom line is that Pappe is at a loss to show that the Israelis acted on the basis of a master plan to banish the Arabs. Simha Flapan, a sharp critic of Israeli policies and on whom Pappe relied, was adamant that the Palestinians were not driven out as a matter of general policy. He contended that "it must be understood that official Jewish decision making bodies – the provisional government, the National Council, and the Jewish Agency Executive – neither discussed nor approved a design for expulsion, and *any proposal of the sort would have been opposed and probably rejected.*"[22] No documentation or testimony has come to light that either Ben-Gurion or IDF heads issued any *general* injunction to expel or otherwise harm Arab civilians.[23] On the contrary, when, for instance, Nazareth was conquered on July 16, 1948, all of its Arab inhabitants stayed put, even though Moshe Carmel, an IDF commander, would have liked to eject them. He was prevented from doing so by an urgent message from Ben-Gurion forbidding their expulsion.[24] Similarly, after it was learnt that the Harel Brigade had evacuated the residents of Abu Gosh, a friendly Arab village, the General Staff insisted that they be allowed to return. To this day, Abu Gosh remains intact as a viable Arab township. Finally, in anticipation of an IDF conquest and occupation of Gaza, Ben-Gurion decreed that the Arab inhabitants were to be permitted to "stay in their places."[25]

Events surrounding the mass exodus from Haifa (the total of which included nearly 10 percent of the Palestinian refugees) add credence to the view that the Jews had no plans to evict the Arabs. At a meeting in Haifa between Jews and local Arab dignitaries, held immediately after the battle for the city (April 22, 1948), the Arabs were promised full and equal residency rights.[26] On receiving the Jewish offer, the Arabs requested a brief adjournment to contact the Arab states for advice. Hours later they announced to everyone's amazement, including Major-General Stockwell, a senior British officer who acted as an observer, that rather than live under Jewish control, they would leave for Lebanon. In conclusion they stated "we do not recognize you and we shall return when you are no longer here." Stockwell, who was utterly astounded, asked them whether they had taken leave of their senses.[27] In vain, the Jewish mayor, Shabetai Levy, implored them to reconsider their decision. (Confirmation of Jewish efforts to persuade the Arabs not to flee has been provided by both American diplomats and British officials.)[28] On May 1, after visiting Haifa, Ben-Gurion insisted that "the remaining Arabs (five to six thousand) should be treated on the basis of human and civil equality."[29] Years later the Palestine Liberation Organization (PLO) claimed that the Haifa Arabs were banished but the Haifa Arab dignitaries had in writing confirmed to Stockwell that their exodus was indeed voluntary.[30] In a memorandum issued in 1950 and addressed to the heads of the Arab states, the Arab National Committee of Haifa boasted that "the Arab delegation proudly asked for the evacuation of the Arabs and their removal to neighboring Arab countries."[31]

The Haifa debacle precipitated additional flights both from within the immediate area and from other places such as Jaffa and Safad.[32] As already suggested, in Tiberias all Arabs remaining in the city after it had fallen to the Haganah accepted a British offer to evacuate them. A similar offer was conveyed to the Jews of Safad but, notwithstanding their precarious circumstances, they rejected it.[33] Meanwhile in a cable to ALA regional headquarters al-Hassan Kam al-Maz, Safad's Arab section's military commander, assured his superiors that "morale is very strong, the young are enthusiastic, we will slaughter them [the Jews]."[34] Al-Maz's statement highlights the irony that if anyone was seeking the ethnic cleansing of Palestine, it was the Arabs. In March 1948, Haj Amin al-Husseini, the de facto leader of the Palestinian Arab Higher Command, informed an interviewer in a Jaffa newspaper, *Al Sarah*, that the Arabs "would continue fighting until the Zionists were annihilated and the whole of Palestine became a purely Arab state."[35] For Husseini such a stark declaration was not one banded about in the normal course of Arab hyperbole: it was entirely consistent with his collaboration with the Nazis during the Second World War and with his request to them to extend their solution to the Jewish problem to Palestine.[36] Haj Amin's relative, Abdel Qader al-Husseini, who headed the Palestinian militia in the Jerusalem region, was also a firm believer in ethnically cleansing the country of Jews. In his way of thinking, "the Palestine problem will only be solved by the sword; all Jews must leave Palestine."[37]

Whenever Arab forces overran Jewish settlements such as those of the Kfar Etzion bloc, Kfar Darom, Yad Mordehai, Nitzanim, Masada, Shaar Hagolan, and so on, they had no compunction in razing them to the ground. That their numbers were relatively small is due solely to the fact that the Arabs did not succeed in vanquishing more. Amos Oz had felicitously summarized the difference between Israel and its foes by noting that

> the Arabs implemented a more complete "ethnic cleansing" in the ter-
> ritories they conquered than the Jews did. Hundreds of thousands of
> Arabs fled or were driven out from the territory of the State of Israel
> in the war, but a hundred thousand remained. Whereas there were no
> Jews at all in the West Bank (including the Jewish quarter of the Old
> City of Jerusalem) or the Gaza Strip under Jordanian and Egyptian
> rule. Not one.[38]

By May 14, when Israel was established and about to be invaded by regular Arab armies, some 300,000 refugees had already fled.[39] That is, while the British still ruled Palestine, large numbers of Arabs from Haifa, Safad, Tiberis, and Jaffa vacated Jewish-controlled areas. Even as early as the end of January 1948, just two months after the UN partition resolution, 30–40,000 Arabs had sought refuge in neighboring countries.[40] The first Palestinian refugees to depart were Arab notables and their families who may have recalled previous temporary migrations such as occurred during the First World War and during the 1936–9 Arab rebellion, when 40,000 Arabs left the country.[41] On those occasions, fleeing Palestinians were able to return once quiet had been restored. Between December 1947 and March 1948, the number of upper-strata Arabs leaving Palestine reached 75,000.[42] Ironically, during that period the Arabs distinctly had the military upper hand. So much so, that George Marshall, the US Secretary of State, fearing that the Yishuv stood on the brink of destruction, believed that the Palestine Partition scheme ought to have been suspended. The full extent of the exodus of the Arab elite can be inferred from Majid Al-Haj, an Arab–Israeli academic, who reported that after the war, "*nearly all* members of the Palestinian Arab middle and upper classes – the urban landowning mercantile, professional and religious elite – were no longer present in Israel."[43] In fact by the end of March 1948 not a single member of the Arab Higher Committee, the Palestinian's leading authority, remained in the country.[44] Whatever factors drove them, the Arab elite set a standard of desertion that was readily emulated by the broad uneducated masses.[45]

The Arab elite's growing absence led to the closure of schools, hospitals, and business enterprises. General municipal and social services, which had previously been delivered by the British bureaucracy, collapsed. Unlike the Jews, the Palestinians failed to create a self-contained state in the making and were unable to take over as the British withdrew. This resulted in increased unemployment and welfare losses, all of which had a demoralizing effect.[46] The worsening social situation was also exacerbated by the unruly behavior of extraneous Arab militias. As one leading Arab citizen in Haifa recalled, "robber gangs terrorized the residents. Food prices became inflated. A panic exodus began."[47] Haj Mahmad Nimar El-Hitiv, after highlighting the fear implanted by Arab thieves in Haifa, went on to bemoan the fact that in Jaffa foreign Arabs sexually molested the local women, causing many to leave the city.[48] The situation was so intolerable that "the population became more afraid of their defenders than of the Jews."[49] This was confirmed by Nimr al Khatib who complained that as a result of the actions of members of the Arab Liberation Army "people's lives became worthless and women's honour was defiled."[50]

The large spontaneous Arab exodus baffled the Yishuv. On May 18, 1948, Ben-Gurion recorded in his diary: "I visited Jaffa. The city was almost empty. Only here and there were a few Arabs wearing tarbooshes. The port was deserted but the warehouses were full . . . I could not understand why Jaffa's inhabitants left the city".[51] (In point of fact about four thousand Arabs remained in Jaffa.)[52] Many Israelis thought that the Palestinian Arab High Committee (AHC) encouraged the Arab outflow to involve the Arab League in its conflict against the Jews. But Morris counters that viewpoint by attesting that from April 1948 onward he "found no evidence to show that the AHC issued blanket instructions, by radio or otherwise, to Palestine's Arabs to flee."[53] This still begs the question as to whether there were locally based calls or whether there were any emanating from the AHC that applied to specific localities or situations. In this regard, Morris himself reported that "during April–May (1948), more than 20 Arab villages were largely or completely evacuated because of orders by local Arab commanders, by Arab governments or by the AHC, mostly for pre-invasion military reasons."[54] Some Arab leaders have indeed claimed that Arab governments summoned the Palestinians to leave. Such was the view of Khalid al-Azm, Syria's prime minister during the War of Independence.[55] Others have found fault with Arab regimes for creating the very atmosphere that fostered the Arab flight. The secretary of the Arab League stated that "the wholesale exodus was partly due to the belief of the Arabs, encouraged by the boasting of the unrealistic Arab press and the irresponsible utterances of some of the Arab leaders, that it would be only a matter of weeks before the Jews were defeated by the armies of the Arab states."[56]

Although the Israelis did not precipitate the Arab refugee flight, they eventually resorted to the expulsion of numerous villagers, in some cases rather ruthlessly. But the number of people involved was far less than half of the total Arab outflow and the incidences were mainly determined in the heat of battle and by the need to deny strategic positions to the enemy.[57] On March 23, *after more than 100,000 Arabs had already fled*, Safwat, the overall commander of the Arab Liberation Army, noted to his astonishment that the Jews "have not attacked a single Arab village unless provoked by it."[58] Some of such villages were those that had been taken over by the Arab Liberation Army for use as operational bases.[59] In other instances, villages were emptied of their Arab inhabitants because the Israelis felt that they could not adequately cope with the invasion of regular Arab armies with a hostile local population at their immediate rear.[60] Flapan also affirmed that the military benefits of razing *certain* Arab villages "were so evident that liberal and socialist commanders and their troops were able to overcome any qualms."[61] Such actions resulted in at least 350 Arab villages and townships being completely wiped out.[62] Israel simply did not have enough personnel to garrison each captured village and, had they been left intact, there was always the chance that they could be reoccupied by enemy forces. The Israelis did not feel that the expulsion of various Palestinian villagers was morally reprehensible, considering that the Palestinians sought Israel's destruction. Certainly their presence near the borders and expected invasion routes, not to mention along critical roadways, made Israel vulnerable.[63] On May 8, 1948, no less a person than Sir Allan Cunningham, the British high commissioner in Palestine, agreed that "the Jews for their part can hardly be blamed if in the face of past Arab irregular action and the continued threat of interference by Arab regular forces, they take time by the forelock and consolidate their positions while they can."[64] Even Azzam, the Arab League secretary general, appreciated the strategic merit from Israel's point of view in expelling specific Arab villagers. He lamented that by "driving out the inhabitants [from areas] on or near roads by which regular forces could enter the country," the Jews were providing the Arab armies with the "greatest difficulty in even entering Palestine after May 15."[65]

The largest IDF expulsions of Arab civilians occurred at Lydda and Ramlah, involving in excess of 30,000 people. There, as mentioned in the previous chapter, the expulsion orders arose as a result of the exigencies of combat. The two towns were captured by the Israelis in mid-July 1948. Days later when Arab Legion armored cars approached the area, Lydda's civilian population (which had formally surrendered) rose up against the IDF. Once the Arab Legion was repelled and the uprising quelled, Lydda's inhabitants were "invited" to leave. As is universally the case, the expulsion was painful and traumatic. Gutman, a senior IDF officer, witnessed soldiers indicating the direction in which the residents of Lydda were to go.

A multitude of people filed out. Women trudged along loaded with parcels and bags on their heads. Mothers dragged their children after them. The elderly and the young, women and infants, all marched off. Wagons filled to the brim were drawn by mules, while some were pulled by people . . . At one point a woman knelt down in the middle of the road writhing in the agony of labour . . . A strange silence crept over [the town's] streets. Doors of shops and houses were left open and within each building everything was in disarray.[66]

What particularly raised the ire of the Israeli commanders was that, despite an appeal to the Arab population to surrender their arms, not a single rifle was forthcoming.[67] As opposed to the Arabs of Lydda, those of Ramlah left "voluntarily." They were provided with buses to escort them to the Transjordanian front. Nevertheless, in both towns, a few hundred Arabs were adamant that they were not going to budge and to this day they and their descendants remain there. Ben-Gurion had in fact issued a directive that the Arabs should be allowed to remain in place provided they assumed responsibility for their own food consumption. He stressed that "by no means should women, children, sick and elderly people be forced to depart."[68] Unfortunately, Ben-Gurion's instructions were delivered too late. Allon initiated the evacuation, fearing that the Arab Legion was on the verge of opening up a large offensive pivoted around Lydda and that it would therefore be to Israel's strategic disadvantage not to relieve itself of Lydda's Arab population.[69] It is worth bearing in mind that most of Lydda's and Ramlah's residents who had suffered the trauma of an internecine battle, who felt abandoned by the Arab Legion and whose food and medical supplies were running low needed little prodding in seeking refuge in Arab-held territory.[70]

Even shortly after the War of Independence, some Arab communities were uprooted and exiled. For instance, about three thousand Palestinians remaining in Faluja and Iraq-el-Manshie were, in violation of the Israeli–Egyptian armistice agreement, pressurized into leaving Israel. General Avner (the head of the regional military regime) wished to honor Israel's commitments but Allon managed to put the fear of God into the villagers. After spreading rumors to the effect that survivors of the Alexandroni Brigade, who had lost many comrades-in-arms in their neighborhood, were hell-bent on exacting revenge, he let it be known that the villagers' security could not be assured. Allon's scaremongering, which for good measure included incidents of physical assault, paid off. The intimidated residents of Faluja and Iraq-el-Manshie ultimately requested assistance in moving to Gaza. Although Allon acted on his own and against the explicit orders of the chief of staff, he was never reprimanded.[71]

The unanticipated mass flight of the Palestinians was soon regarded as a blessing for it enabled Israel to become a state in which its citizens were overwhelmingly Jewish and where problems associated with a large degree of multi-ethnicity were moderated. Jews took over and cultivated abandoned Arab land. About 3 million dunams[72] were involved which were either sequestrated by neighboring collective farms or were utilized for the establishment of new agricultural settlements.[73] The village of Deir Yassin was occupied by orthodox Jews associated with Poalei Agudat Yisrael. It was renamed Givat Shaul Bet at a ceremony attended by the two chief rabbis and the mayor of Jerusalem.[74] In urban areas Jewish migrants were billeted in deserted Arab houses.[75]

Notwithstanding any gains that Israel might have enjoyed from the Arab outflow, it attributed responsibility for the plight of the overwhelming majority of the refugees to the Arab League and expected them to deal with the problem. In pressing its case for the refugee problem to be solved by the recipient countries, Israel cited a number of precedents. These included the exodus of 13 million Germans from Poland and Czechoslovakia, six and a half million Muslims from India to Pakistan, a similar number from North to South Korea and 440,000 Finns separated from their homeland by border adjustments. One might also add that the Turkish–Greek War (1919–1922) ended with one and a half million Greeks displaced from Turkey and half a million Turks displaced from Greece. In all cases, the population movements were accepted as final post-conflict adjustments. None of the refugees demanded or expected to return to their original homes. India's constitution even included a clause (paragraph seven) which deprived refugees leaving India after March 1947 for what is now Pakistan, of their Indian citizenship. The India–Pakistan experience was particularly pertinent. There millions of people relocated within the confines of what was originally a single political entity (the British Raj) to settle among their coreligionists.

In Palestine the situation was not that different, for most of the refugees fled to the West Bank, Gaza and Transjordan, all of which (before 1922) were part of the same country. Of the 726,000 Palestinian refugees, 560,000 or 75 percent sought shelter in those areas. That is, three quarters of the refugees, although having been uprooted from their normal places of residence, continued to remain in what was in essence their original homeland. In 1949, the Jordanian premier announced that the Palestinians living in camps and other parts of his country were all citizens of Jordan.[76] From 1950 onward, after having annexed the West

Bank, the Hashemite regime drew its cabinet ministers evenly from both sides of the River Jordan.[77] The Jordanian parliament was also constituted on the same basis. Nonetheless, Jordanians of Palestinian origin still retained documents identifying themselves as refugees so as to obtain UN and other aid.[78] Normally, as far as the UN is concerned, once refugees acquire citizenship in another country, they cease to be refugees. However, the *sole* UN exception applies to the Palestinians, who in the event of assuming a foreign nationality not only retain their refugee status but are also able to confer it on their offspring.

As for the Palestinians living in other Arab countries, they find themselves in an environment in which the general social milieu is comparable to the one in which they were reared. Their host populations speak the same language and adhere to the same religion as they do. More significantly, both the refugees and their hosts believe that they are all part of the same Greater Arab nation. This has prompted Abba Eban to remark that "the integration of Arab refugees into the life of the Arab world is an objective feasible process which has been resisted for political reasons."[79] Dr Elfan Rees, a former adviser on refugees to the World Council of Churches, shared Eban's belief that a practical solution to the Arab refugee problem was readily at hand. In support of that claim he maintained that within the Arab world there was ample room and land for them and that, "more unusually still," there was sufficient money to make their integration feasible.[80] As it happens, US President Eisenhower, through his emissary Robert Anderson, had in 1955 offered to bear the full cost of resettling the refugees.[81]

Although the Arab refugee phenomenon derived from warfare launched first by the Palestinians and then by neighboring Arab states, the Palestinians and their Arab allies have consistently insisted that the refugees possessed a "right of return." On December 11, 1948, the UN General Assembly passed Resolution 194 which, among other things, was meant to facilitate the return of Palestinian refugees. The resolution, which implied acceptance of Israel and which for that reason was *voted against by all Arab states*, read in part: "the refugees wishing to return to their homes and live at peace with their neighbors should be permitted to do so."[82] Abba Eban interpreted the resolution as meaning "that there is no such thing in the General Assembly Resolution of December 11, 1948 as a 'right' of Arab refugees to return irrespective of Israel's permission."[83] Israel maintained that a "right of return" was neither in accordance with general historical experience nor was it consonant with a willingness to accept the creation of Israel as a fait accompli.

Above all, the Arabs have consistently opposed piecemeal returns of refugees, insisting on the return of the *Palestine nation* as the rightful owners of the country. This "solution" was first formulated in February 1949 by an assembly of Palestinians which called not only for the return of the refugees to their original homes but for the preservation of Palestine (that is all of the original mandate territory) as an Arab country.[84] Since then the demand for the return of the refugees has perennially been submitted not as an alternative for the destruction of Israel but as the means to effect it.[85] For example, in October 1949, Muhammad Saleh ed-Din, Egypt's foreign minister, stated that "in demanding the restoration of the refugees to Palestine, the Arabs intend that they shall return as the masters of the homeland, and not as slaves. More explicitly: they intend to annihilate the state of Israel."[86] Some years later at a refugee conference in Syria, it was decided that "any discussion aimed at a solution of the Palestine problem which will not be based on ensuring the refugees' right to annihilate Israel will be regarded as a desecration of the Arab people and an act of treason."[87] On April 6, 1950, the Lebanese newspaper *Alsayyad* declared that the return of the refugees "would serve as the most effective means of reviving the Arab character of Palestine, while forming a powerful fifth column for the day of revenge and reckoning."[88] Alternatively, Abdel Nasser explained that "if Arabs return to Israel, Israel will cease to exist."[89] Eventually the right of return became enshrined in religious dogma. In 2000, a fatwa, specifically requested by Yasser Arafat, ruled that "any arrangement calling for the refugees to be compensated for their right to return or their settlement outside their homeland [that is, all of Israel] is, from the point of view of the Sharia, null and void."[90]

Despite the fact that the Palestinian refugee issue has constantly been raised by Arab regimes as a means of denigrating Israel and of paying lip service to pan-Arab solidarity, such posturing did not necessarily reflect a heartfelt concern for the lot of the Palestinians.

After the commencement of the Lausanne "conference," representatives of three Palestinian refugee groups arrived uninvited and unsuccessfully requested a hearing. Unlike the official state delegates, they were elected by their constituencies and were willing to live peacefully alongside Israel. Not only were they excluded from all the proceedings but, when they tried to secure an interview with the Egyptian delegation, they were forcefully ejected. In an informal conversation with Walter Eytan, a representative of Israel, an Egyptian counterpart explained that "last year thousands of people died of cholera in my country, and none of us cared. Why should we care about the refugees?"[91]

As mentioned above, after some desultory efforts to assist the Palestinian refugees, responsibility for their care fell on the United Nations Relief and Work Agency for Palestine (UNRWA). Such a procedure was highly irregular. All other refugees throughout the world fall under the jurisdiction of the UN High Commissioner for Refugees (UNHCR) yet the Palestinian refugees were provided with a body *of their own*. Kowtowing to the Arab bloc, the UN accorded UNRWA an unusual degree of autonomy allowing it to determine its own agenda.[92] UNRWA's largesse, financed mainly by the US, has seemingly become *open ended* for, as already mentioned, children born to refugees have also attained refugee accreditation.[93] *The inter-generational extension of refugee status, which has been unique to the Palestinians, helped to ensure the perpetuation of the problem*, as did UNRWA itself. By assuming the sole function of supporting Palestinian refugees,[94] UNRWA has neither seriously promoted resettlement nor has it sought realistic alternatives for resolving the issue.

3

THE INGATHERING OF THE EXILES

The main *raison d'être* of Israel, as made clear in its declaration of independence, is that it would be "open to Jewish immigration and the ingathering of the exiles." With that in mind, Israel unreservedly welcomed Jews from the world at large. From May 1948, the first to appear were mostly young pioneers and army volunteers but from October onward, the era of undifferentiated mass immigration commenced with migrants arriving at the rate of over 20,000 per month. Within Israel's first four years when the pace of immigration was the most hectic (see Table 3.1), its Jewish population, which in May 1948 numbered 650,000, had doubled. To grasp the relative magnitude of such a migratory inflow, it is instructive to contrast Israel's experience with that of America. In the years 1949, 1950 and 1951, the ratio of immigrants per thousand Israeli residents was 266, 154 and 132 respectively whereas the highest ratio ever recorded in the USA, the world's most popular migrant destination, was by comparison a mere 16.1 per thousand.[1] Furthermore, Israel's migrants did not stream into a consolidated, tranquil, and ordered country but, as Ben-Gurion stressed, into "a tender and young one that had arisen in the midst of confusion, anarchy and the tribulations of war."[2]

Approximately half of all immigrants came from British detention camps in Cyprus, from displaced people's camps in Western Europe,

Table 3.1   Number of immigrants arriving in Israel

1948	1949	1950	1951	1952	1953	1954
101,819	239,076	169,405	173,901	23,357	10,347	17,471

Source: Lissak 1999, p. 4

and from various parts of East Europe and the Balkans. The rest were made up of Jews from North Africa and the Middle East. The relative importance of specific countries as sources of immigration is highlighted in Table 3.2. Collectively the nine countries listed accounted for 82.4 percent of the immigrant total. Other countries that contributed at least 3,000 immigrants included Yugoslavia, Germany/Austria, Czechoslovakia, Hungary, France, Syria/Lebanon, Egypt and India.

The general character and complexity of the immigrants differed from those of the Yishuv. Immigrant families had more children and, as an overall group, they contained a relatively higher proportion of people above the age of 64. Such factors, combined with the disinclination of women from Arab countries to seek paid employment, caused the active Israeli work force, as a percentage of the total population, to decline from 44 in 1948 to 35 in 1954.[3] As a corollary, the burden of sustaining the economy fell on a relatively smaller number of individuals.

The general level of human capital flowing into the country, as measured by the possession of skills and professional knowledge as well as by basic standards of health, was very low. In 1954 12 percent of all immigrants (22.5 percent from Arab countries) had never been to school, compared with 4.1 percent of the established population.[4] Even among those immigrants that did attend primary school, 40.8 percent dropped out prematurely. With respect to health, as many as 10 percent of all immigrants were either chronically ill or were suffering from diseases, such as polio, tuberculosis, trachoma, and syphilis.[5] So pervasive were migrant medical disorders that one observer warned that the state faced the danger of becoming one big hospital for the Jewish people.[6]

Usually, migrant-receiving countries vet potential applicants on the basis of their employment prospects, age, and standard of health. But Israel could not readily resort to such criteria since the Jews of Yemen, Iraq, and East Europe had only a narrow window of opportunity in which to emigrate before being firmly entrapped within oppressive

Table 3.2   Major country sources of migrants to Israel during
              1948–54

Country	Poland	Romania	Bulgaria	Turkey	Iraq	Yemen	Iran	Morocco	Libya
Number	108,184	121,885	38,248	35,483	125,305	49,182	27,748	67,859	32,616
% of total	14. 7	16. 6	5. 1	4. 8	17. 0	6. 7	3. 8	9. 2	4. 5

Source: Lissak 1999, pp. 8–10. Migrants from Algeria and Tunisia are included with those
from Morocco.

anti-Jewish regimes. Even so, a half-hearted attempt was made to curb
the numbers of those chronically and seriously ill. Overseas emissaries
were instructed to screen potential immigrants for health disorders
and to deny visas to those that failed to make the grade. But in practice
most officials turned a blind eye.[7] So much so that on one occasion, all
passengers on a ship from Bulgaria had formerly been residents of an
old age home.[8]

In order to make sense of the country's new social kaleidoscope,
coming as Israel's new citizens did from such a variety of regions, brief
reviews of the circumstances and travails of Israel's major migrant communities are set out below.

Immigration of the Yemenite Jews:
Operation Magic Carpet

Between January 1949 and September 24, 1950, some 48,818 Yemenite
Jews were shepherded to Israel in a project known as Operation Magic
Carpet that entailed 430 separate flights.[9] The culmination of the
project marked the virtual liquidation of Jewry's oldest diaspora community. While it is not known definitively just how long there had been
a Jewish presence in Yemen, it is generally believed that it would, at the
very least, have spanned a period of 2,600 years. For the most part, the
Yemenite Jews lived in complete isolation from the rest of their brethren, maintaining their Jewish identity by a stubborn adherence to their
faith. They diligently upheld the study of the Torah and Talmud, prayed
three times a day, kept the Sabbath and conscientiously abided by all the
tenets of the Jewish religion.

Present-day Muslims and their apologists like to claim that Jews in

Muslim countries fared far better than in Christian Europe. Granted that no concerted attempt was made to annihilate them and that they were accorded the status of *dhimmi* (a protected people of the Covenant), they were nonetheless treated poorly. In twentieth-century Yemen, Jews were subject to humiliating discrimination and abuse. They were forbidden to ride horses and had to dismount from their donkeys on meeting non-Jews. Walking in a street, they were required to be on the side opposite to that of a Muslim. They could not wear brightly colored clothes and were not permitted to leave their residential areas after nightfall. At a moment's notice, they could be dragooned into performing unpaid labor, including the cleaning of public latrines. In terms of a law passed in 1922, every fatherless Jewish boy under the age of thirteen could (regardless of whether his mother was still alive) be forcibly converted to Islam.

The moment Israel came into being, the Jews of Yemen readily turned their eyes toward Jerusalem in the expectation of being redeemed there. Although not familiar with modern Zionist dogma, their enduring bond with the Jewish religion in which the centrality of Israel is firmly anchored made it seem perfectly natural for them to uproot themselves without further ado and set out for Israel. With their departure being arbitrarily authorized by Yemen's ruler, Iman Ahmed, the Jews liquidated whatever meager assets they possessed to trek to Aden via the Aden Protectorates.

On leaving Yemen they were required to pay a poll tax and then, as they passed through each Aden Protectorate, additional exactions were extracted. Their odyssey was very trying. A few had recourse to buses but most made their way on foot or on donkeys, taking many weeks to span inhospitable desert terrain. Exposed to the blazing sun by day and to sharp drops in temperature by night, many did not survive the journey. Those that did so usually arrived in Aden in tatters, barefooted, exhausted, and emaciated. Many were stricken with eye diseases, with septic ulcers and malaria.

The British, fearing that Aden was being subject to an uncontrollable ingress of Yemenite Jews with serious health disorders, sealed the border. Those on the wrong side of it found themselves in grave peril. Without a roof over their heads they were surrounded by increasingly resentful Arabs.[10] However with an Israeli guarantee that they would be expeditiously processed and escorted to Israel, Britain relented and granted them passage.

In Aden under the auspices of the Jewish Joint Distribution Committee, the Yemenite Jews were concentrated in a desert camp at Hashed where they received rudimentary medical treatment, were inoculated against typhus and smallpox and were fed, clothed, and sheltered. They were also instructed in matters relating to hygiene and in adjusting to life in a modern society. Most had never before slept in a bed, sat on chairs, worn trousers, laced shoes or employed eating utensils.

Transport arrangements were made with an American aviation company called Alaska Airlines (later renamed the Near East Transport Company) which had recently conveyed Jews from civil war-torn China to Israel. Deploying its small fleet of C-54 Skymasters and Curtis Commandos, the company carried Yemenites by the plane-load. Passengers assembled and took off from an RAF base in Aden and, after an eight-hour non-stop flight, landed at Israel's Lydda Airport. The journey, which slightly exceeded 1,700 miles, followed a course that skirted over the Red Sea and the Gulf of Aqaba to enter Israel over its southern port of Eilat. Navigating with exceptional finesse, the pilots did their utmost not to enter Arab airspace.

Operation Magic Carpet constituted the largest air convoy of civilians of its time. On each flight nearly twice as many passengers were taken on board as was the norm. This was facilitated by the removal of standard seating and its replacement by rows of plywood benches, positioned on both sides of a narrow aisle. Three to four people sat to a bench secured by one safety harness spanning their laps. Had not the scrawny Yemenites been grossly underweight, all this would not have been possible. During flights the passengers invariably sat passively, dozed off or dreamily stared through the windows, taking the new chapter in their lives in their stride.[11] On arriving in Israel, they usually prostrated themselves to kiss the ground. With their journey behind them, the severely malnourished and ailing were cared for. The pitiful condition of many Yemenite infants was later described by Ben-Gurion. On a visit to an army hospital he saw "children and babies who were more like skeletons than living human beings, too weak to cry, many of them unable to absorb food."[12] Ben-Gurion considered that encounter "as one of the most horrifying sights" that he had ever witnessed.

Plate 3.1   *Yemenite Jews trudging toward Aden*

Immigration of the Iraqi Jews: Operation Ezra and Nehemiah

Shortly after Iraq attained independence in 1932, its Jewish citizens (whose ancestors had settled in the country nearly 2,500 years earlier) began to integrate themselves into the new state's social milieu. Among other things, this was manifested by Sassoon Heskail and Menahem Daniel, respectively being appointed as minister of finance and as senator. However, on June 1, 1941, the state's early halcyon years came to an abrupt end. A pro-Nazi regime instigated a Baghdad pogrom that led to the death of 180 Jews. From then onward, Iraqi Jews could no longer reasonably expect to live out their lives free from terror and molestation. The groundwork for anti-Jewish sentiment in Iraq was sedulously prepared by Dr Fritz Grobba, the chargé d'affaires of the German consulate. Through the acquisition of a local newspaper, *al-Alam al-Arabi*, Grobba published a serialized version of Hitler's *Mein Kampf*.

Two years after the Second World War (that is in 1947) under the supervision of Shlomo Hillel, a prominent Iraqi Zionist, 50 young Jews flew from Baghdad to Palestine in a C-46 cargo plane piloted by two American mercenaries. On the night of their departure and under cover of darkness, they clambered through a hole in the airport's fence to lie on the edge of the tarmac. The plane that was to fly them taxied in their direction. It then turned with its lights blazing to face the control tower, allowing its youthful passengers to board through a rear door without being seen. Just before dawn the plane furtively touched down on an improvised landing strip at Kibbutz Yavneel. Fraught with unacceptable risks, that adventure was never replicated.

With the advent of Israel's War of Independence, the situation of Iraqi Jews deteriorated drastically. They were summarily dismissed from the public service and those practicing medicine had their licences revoked. Jewish draftees were impressed into hard-labor gangs and Jewish students were barred from attending high school. Hundreds of Jews, arrested under suspicion of being Zionists, were interrogated and in some cases tortured.[13] Then in a show trial, in which the defense was not permitted to present its case, Shafiq Addas, an assimilated Jew *par excellence*, who had even made lavish donations to the Palestinian cause, was sentenced to death for plotting to smuggle arms into Israel. The

Plate 3.2   *Yemenite Jews on a flight to Israel*

presiding judge, Abdullah al-Naasni, was a Nazi sympathizer who had been detained by the British during World War Two.[14] On September 23, 1948, Addas was publicly hanged in Basra.[15] The ghoulish display of his body openly dangling on a rope induced even more non-committed Iraqi Jews to identify themselves with Zionism.

For want of a better alternative, Iraqi Jews slipped across the border to Iran where they were granted exit permits to proceed to Israel via Europe. On occasion with the cooperation of Iranian Airways, they travelled directly from Iran to Israel. The numbers in question were inconsequential but the Iraqi regime, put out by the spectacle of some of its citizens fleeing the country, ruled attempted or actual emigration to Israel a capital offense. Then suddenly on March 4, 1950, thanks to a concerted international campaign, the government changed tack. Jews were granted permission to leave the country at the cost of forfeiting their nationality.

The emigrants were able to transfer only a fraction of their total wealth and, as they began disposing of their immovable property, furniture and house prices plummeted. Eventually, in March 1951, all their assets were frozen. Nevertheless, by February 1952, 104,000 Jews, representing 95 percent of their community, left for Israel. The airlift commenced on May 21, 1950 and, although at first the planes flew via Cyprus, from March 1951 they flew straight to Israel.

That the evacuation of the Jewish community proceeded smoothly was in no small measure due to key members of the government having a personal financial stake in the enterprise. A deal was struck between the American charter company Near East Air and the Iraq Tours Travel Agency. The airline was to fly the Jews while the travel agency (whose board included Tawfiq al-Suwaidi, the Iraqi prime minister) was to collect a hefty commission.

As with other immigrants arriving in Israel, the Iraqi Jews were at first housed in *ma'abarot* (transit camps) where (as outlined below) they endured years of hardship and deprivation. To their dismay, they found themselves forming the largest migrant contingent within such camps.[16] Hillel had in fact been advised by Levi Eshkol, then treasurer of the Jewish Agency, to caution Iraqi Jews to stay away. He reasoned that "right now we lack the ability to absorb them. We don't even have tents. If they come, they'll have to live in the street."[17] Instead, Hillel chose to heed the words of Ben-Gurion which were "tell them to come quickly. What if the Iraqis suddenly change their minds and rescind the law? Go and bring them quickly."[18] In face of serious and generally held reservations that an unplanned mass migration to Israel might overwhelm the state, Ben-Gurion, by the force of his personality and stature, imposed his will to have all would-be immigrants accepted with minimum delay. To some extent both of Hillel's interlocutors were correct. The state could not afford to house them but neither could it afford to abandon them.

Jews from Egypt

For the most part, Jews in Egypt had lived securely as an enclave community immersed in French and European culture. But by November 1945 their situation worsened. A pogrom coinciding with the 28th anniversary of the Balfour Declaration saw the destruction of a Cairo synagogue as well as a number of other Jewish public buildings. This was followed by a series of decrees that impinged on the Jews' capacity to earn a living. For example, certain professions, such as medicine, were reserved exclusively for Egyptian citizens, which meant that only 5,000 of Egypt's 75,000 Jews were eligible. During 1948, various incidences of anti-Jewish mob violence took their toll. Twenty Jews were killed in June, another 150 were either killed or seriously injured in July, in August three rabbis were murdered and in September 19 Jews died as a result of the blowing up of their houses.[19] With the removal of emigration restrictions in August 1949, Egyptian Jews sought haven abroad. Between 1948 and 1954, 19,869 left for Israel, with the total rising to 21,382 by the end of 1956.

Jews from Libya

On November 4, 1945, a pogrom erupted in Tripolitania. 130 Jews were murdered and a number of Jewish women raped.[20] Nearly three years later, that is, in June 1948, there was yet another pogrom in which, according to one correspondent, individuals were "literally cut to pieces."[21] Those outrages, combined with a sharp economic downturn that reduced Libya's Jews to penury, propelled over 32,000 to settle in Israel.

Jews from Morocco

Unlike the Jews of Egypt, who largely identified with Europeans, those of Morocco, who in 1951 totaled 225,000, were socially isolated from both the indigenous Muslim population and from the French. Most were destitute. Malnutrition was rife and over half the community lived in one-roomed quarters. Their material plight was the mainspring in causing them to leave but they had also maintained a long-held spiritual affinity with Israel. The Zionist movement had established a presence in Morocco in the 1930s, and during Israel's War of Liberation hundreds of Moroccan Jews rallied to its defense. By the end of 1954, 37,029 had migrated to Israel.[22] After Morocco attained independence in 1956 and became a member of the Arab League, the Jews were subject to legislative and social discrimination. By 1956, a further 60,000 made their way to Israel, to be followed between 1961 and 1963 by an additional 84,000.[23] Not all Moroccan Jews chose to live in the Jewish state. Nearly one third, particularly among the more educated, went to France and Canada.[24]

Jews from Syria

Virulent anti-Semitism in Syria received a boost in December 1937 with the visit from Germany of Baldur von Schirach, head of the Nazi youth movement. Von Schirach not only bolstered anti-Jewish propaganda within Syria's German schools but he encouraged responsive Arabs to emulate him. By the end of the Second World War, the 13,000-odd Syrian Jews were desperately poor. Apart from six doctors, hardly any had a profession. The community was so impoverished that had aid not been sent from abroad, many would simply have starved.[25] Muslims used the Arab–Israeli conflict as a stick with which to beat their Jewish neighbors. As early as October 1945, a leading cleric, Mustafa Al-Siba'i, preaching from a Damascus mosque, threatened that "if the Palestine problem is not solved in favor of the Arabs, the Arabs will know how to deal with the Jews living in their countries."[26] Nearly two years later, when Jewish property was torched in Aleppo, firemen refused to douse the flames. Freedom of movement of Syrian Jews was severely curtailed. They could neither emigrate nor travel from one city to another. Their children could not enter secondary schools and general job prospects were officially restricted. No Jew was eligible for public service and trading licences were systematically withheld. In 1949, all Jewish bank accounts were frozen. Despite emigration being illegal and troops being ordered to fire upon Jews crossing the border, many fled into Lebanon and then to Israel. By 1954, a third of the community, some 4,375, had succeeded in doing so.

Jews from Iran

As in Yemen and Iraq, Jews had lived in Iran for nearly 2,500 years. By 1948, they numbered between 80,000 and 100,000. They were confronted with a pattern of anti-Semitism and persecution similar to that which prevailed in Arab countries. In 1936, under the sway of intensive Nazi propaganda, the government dismissed Jews from the civil service and restricted their entry into high school. In the free professions, they were up against a brick wall. They were barred from practicing law, almost none qualified as engineers and only 70 or so were allowed to become doctors, dentists, or midwives.[27] During the course of Israel's War of Independence, fanatical mullahs incited their congregants to commit acts of anti-Jewish violence. Fortunately, the Jews were permitted to emigrate and, between 1948 and 1954, 27,748 settled in Israel. By 1958, their presence rose to 39,000.

Jews from Turkey

Turkey's Jewish population, which in 1948 amounted to 82,622, generally enjoyed good relations with the host population. Anti-Semitism did not particularly flourish there but a 1942 law authorizing the imposition of a wealth tax ruined many a Jewish businessman. The upshot of that impost was that by 1944 Turkish Jews had difficulty in sustaining their communal institutions. Although the Turkish Jews were not discriminated against, they, like other minority ethnic communities not fully integrated into Turkish society, experienced a sense of estrangement. One young Jewish professional recounted: "I can't talk to a Turk on equal terms: it's his country, not mine, and he won't let me forget it."[28]

When Israel was established, the Turkish Jews were somewhat

uneasy. Turkey openly supported the Arabs and looked askance at anyone wishing to settle in the Jewish state. After a period of vacillation, in October 1948 the regime issued the Jews carte blanche to emigrate. The response was overwhelming. By December 31 that year a total of 32,985 had proceeded to Israel,[29] with a few more thousand following in later years. The Turkish Jews were not assisted by the intervention of any Israeli or world Jewish organization. Their migration was essentially self-financed. It was motivated by a combination of economic hardship, feelings of alienation, and a desire to lead a full national Jewish life within their own homeland.

Jews from Romania

The 350,000 Jews living in Romania in May 1948 constituted East Europe's largest post-Holocaust Jewish community.[30] Confronted with a strong likelihood of renewed anti-Semitism as well as poor economic prospects, most Romanian Jews were more than willing to leave for Israel. After blocking the exit to all but a handful of the elderly or invalids, in November 1949 the government permitted the emigration of several thousand Jews per month. Then in May 1950, in the midst of internal social unrest, the wholesale departure of the country's Jews was seen as a panacea to the communist regime's difficulties. Among other things, the authorities were counting on raising a large bounty in return for opening its frontiers. This was effected by demanding that the migrants travel on Romanian vessels at grossly exorbitant charges and through the levy of an exit tax. Although Haim-Moshe Shapira, Israel's minister of immigration, complained that "we are dealing with robbers," Israel felt that it had no course other than to pay the "ransom."[31] By so doing, it facilitated the entry, between 1948 and 1954, of some 121,888 Romanian Jews.

Jews from Bulgaria

The Jewish community in Bulgaria was the only European one which uprooted itself in its entirety to settle in Israel. The duration of the migration was short. It began in October 1948 and ended in May 1949. Apart from having to meet a per capita exit tax, Jews leaving the country

encountered no serious obstacles. The cost of the head tax was borne by
Israel. After bargaining with the Bulgarian government, its immigration
agents remitted over three million dollars.[32]

The near complete evacuation of Bulgarian Jewry reflected its almost
universal attachment to Zionism. It has been estimated that in 1947,
over 19,000 of the 50,000 Jews living in Bulgaria were registered members of one Zionist organization or another.[33] This meant that unlike
other communities pouring into Israel, the Bulgarians were already
affiliated with many of the host country's political parties. This made it
easier for them to adapt to their new surroundings.

Jews from Poland

Taking advantage of an unexpected government edict permitting emigration to Israel, Jews began leaving communist Poland in November
1949. The amount of goods and money that they could take was severely
curtailed and at least 2,000 key workers, including physicians, were
denied exit permits.[34] Including those that fled Poland before the communist advent to power, between 1948 and 1954 some 108,000 Polish
Jews made Israel their home. Jewish Agency functionaries involved in
the transfer and absorption of Polish Jews advocated that they be given
housing and other privileges not available to migrants arriving contem-
poraneously from Middle Eastern countries. Realizing that many Polish
Jews had been hesitant in deciding whether or not to migrate, and bearing in mind their potential benefit to Israel (on account of their skills
and professions), it was feared that reports of excessive hardships would
deter others from following suit. Although Ben-Gurion emphatically
declared that special treatment for Polish Jews was "out of the question," some funds were unofficially mobilized on their behalf to alleviate
settling-in problems.[35] In addition, apartments in more desirable parts
of the country were "found" for them.[36]

The reception and absorption of immigrants

Receiving and integrating such an enormity of immigrants over a matter
of a few years imposed tremendous strains on the country. This was
especially so in view of the cascading nature of the migratory influx.

Just as Israel was being inundated by the sudden arrival of thousands upon thousands of immigrants from one source, it would suddenly and unexpectedly be confronted by the arrival of a multitude of others from yet another country. The first large-scale *aliyah* (immigration to Israel) began in October 1948 with the appearance of the Bulgarian Jews accompanied by former inmates of displaced persons camps in Germany, Austria, and Italy. Three months later, the airlift of Jews from Yemen got under way and in February 1949, that is, one month thereafter as the country was buckling under the weight of dealing with them all, Jews from Turkey turned up. In November 1949, well before the immigrants in place were adequately housed, the Jews of Poland began arriving, to be followed, in May 1950 by a massive number of new entrants from both Iraq and Romania. Government officials were beside themselves. Civil servants and social workers required for the task at hand greatly exceeded those available, both in absolute and qualitative terms. Personnel with insufficient training and experience had to improvise within newly formed bureaucratic structures. Lines of demarcation were indistinct and communications between formulators and executers of policy often went awry.

With the rate of immigration being beyond the control and discretion of the government, planning for a manageable and orderly rate of migrant intake was simply not possible. Sometimes on a particular morning, the authorities had next to no inkling as to the number of incoming migrants due later that day. Nor for that matter were they aware of the expected arrival times or of the nature and category of the immigrants in question.[37]

Housing the new immigrants was no mean feat. Prior to their arrival, people were already residing in accommodation that was considerably more crowded than accommodation available in, say, Sweden, Poland, Austria, France, or Czechoslovakia.[38] The first migrants to set foot in Israel, that is those from Europe and Bulgaria, had the fortune of being able to move into domiciles previously belonging to Arab refugees.[39] The more desirable Arab residences located in Haifa, Jerusalem, Jaffa, Acre (now Akko), Ramlah, and Lydda (now Lod) were serviced by reasonably good municipalities. Once the option of utilizing Arab property was exhausted, immigrants were placed in tents and huts while awaiting the completion of low-cost homes. This meant that the sequence of

Plate 3.3   *Immigrant families from East Europe sharing a communal dormitory*

the arrival of the immigrants had a large bearing on their relative living conditions and hence on their general social status.[40]

Israel simply lacked the economic and technical wherewithal to be able (in the short run) to replicate existing housing standards. With meager state finance, resources available for housing construction were threadbare. 18,000 new apartments were indeed completed by the end of 1949 but, given the existing economic circumstances, they were jerry-built. All were minute, bereft of internal doors and plastered walls. The kitchens were tiny and the bathrooms had only a shower and toilet (no bath). In the course of time, areas in which they were sited simply became new urban slums.[41]

For many immigrants, their introduction to Israel occurred at a reception camp where they slept in asbestos huts or in surplus British army tents. Sometimes, thousands of incoming Jews would be transferred to a particular camp within a single day. For example, on April 11, 1949, 5,340 were deposited at the main camp, Sha'ar Ha'aliyah, where the harried staff members were hard pressed to arrange food and bedding for them.

Usually camp residents were medically examined and provided with advice as to what steps they could take to secure employment and some form of permanent housing. Those who were unable to do so languished in the camps at public expense. Stopovers in reception camps, which totalled 40 by December 1949, were meant to last no longer than a few days but for a large proportion of immigrants that was not the case. In time nearly 200,000 were living under canvas.[42] Officials began to fear that prolonged stays in the camps were cultivating a state of mind that eroded personal initiative and the desire or ability to fend for oneself. By a process of natural selection, long-term camp residents were composed of the more socially maladroit, with the camps becoming breeding grounds for criminality. Black market activity was endemic. For example, many immigrants illegally sold their subsidized food rations. To maintain a semblance of law and order, Sha'ar Ha'aliyah was fenced in and camp inmates were not free to come and go as they pleased.[43]

In general, the reception camps left much to be desired. Although they provided free food and board, living conditions were suboptimal. Frequently, groups of fifty or more men, women and children slept in a common hall. Residents had to wait for hours at a stretch to access showers. Electrical power was sporadic and non-existent at night. The camps "swarmed with mosquitoes, flies, mice and rats. The cesspools of the toilets overflowed and the dining hall was thick with grime."[44] Unsatisfactory hygienic conditions gave rise to an increase in infant mortality which was already adversely affected by malnourished mothers arriving in Israel in an undermined state of health. During the summer of 1949, intestinal disorders were widespread. Due to a critical shortage of hospital beds and medical supplies, as many as half of afflicted camp children died.[45]

Eventually, those who could not readily find alternative accommodation were transferred to another type of transition camp called *ma'abarot* (plural of *ma'abarah*) which first saw the light of day in May 1950. Unlike the camps, *ma'abarot* generally did not contain communal dining facilities and residents had to prepare their own food. They also had to earn their own keep. As with the camps (which began to be dismantled), the *ma'abarot* were composed of makeshift quarters, usually one-roomed tin or timber shacks or even tents, without flooring and furnished with narrow iron cots and straw mattresses. On occasion two families shared a large tent.[46] Faucets and latrines were sparsely installed and hot water was usually unavailable. *Ma'abarot* situated in rural areas encountered water stoppages when available supplies were diverted for agricultural purposes, while those adjacent to Tel Aviv found their water polluted.[47] Ablution blocks were located on the *ma'abarots'* perimeters and use of them entailed long lines, regardless of the weather. In one *ma'abarah*, there were only 50 toilets for 4,000 people which caused it to be permeated by the stench of excrement.[48] "Toilets" were often simply dug-out pits. One reason for such a state of affairs was that the country was experiencing a critical scarcity of pipes and lacked sufficient foreign exchange to make good the shortfall.

Apart from the unpleasant physical environment, immigrants, as Hillel observed, had to cope with "countless people from different backgrounds and outlooks speaking a cacophony of languages and the short shrift or condescending treatment they felt they were getting from the camp staff."[49] Overworked absorption staff members were generally perceived as officious and uncaring. Sometimes frustrated immigrants assaulted them or, as Bein discovered, took to "barricading them in their offices."[50] Sammy Michael, an Iraqi Jew, recalled his days in a *ma'abarah* as if "all those in it were thrown into a human garbage heap by anony-mous pale faced people from the big city."[51] Most disheartening of all was the impact those circumstances had on his father. The image he conjured up of him was that of "an old man, saddled with a family, without a dime, wandering about without a shred of hope of securing a chance to provide for his kin . . . he never regained his spirit."[52]

The winter of 1949–50 in particular was most inclement, with snow falling throughout the country. Fierce rainstorms lashed the *ma'abarot*, leveling nine of them. On one occasion, the roof of a shelter, weighed down by snow, caved in, leading to four deaths.[53] Most *ma'abarot* became seas of mud and the cold was all-embracing and penetrating. Neither sufficient heating facilities nor an adequate supply of blankets and warm clothing were on hand. To provide a measure of relief to young children, appeals were directed to members of the established population to take them in on a temporary basis. The response was disappointing. Very few were willing to help out for fear of bringing a sick infant into their homes. Secular Jews that were prepared to do so aroused the opposi-tion of the religious parties that seemed less concerned about a person's immediate physical needs and more about a possible temporary suspen-sion of his or her spiritual nurturing.

In principle the *ma'abarot* as their name (transition camps) implied, were meant to serve as temporary way stations until immigrants could be permanently settled. But faced with intractable budgetary problems, as well as a deluge of oncoming migrants, they expanded to number 127 scattered throughout the land. The *ma'abarot* took on the charac-ter of villages by having their own schools, kindergartens, synagogues, stores and elected management committees. The schools were gener-ally staffed by new immigrants with inadequate training and even less knowledge of Hebrew. Attempts were made to locate *ma'abarot* within the orbit of existing municipalities in the hope of providing better medi-cal and educational services as well as greater employment prospects. However, stringent opposition from, for example, the mayors of Tel Aviv and Ramat Gan, who felt that the proximity of *ma'abarot* would unfavorably affect their lifestyles, compelled the government to place them in less salubrious localities. As a result, many *ma'abarot* were situated alongside small towns or far from existing settlements, with-out ready access to public transport. Often they had no telephones or electricity. The *ma'abarot* endured for a lengthy period, with 56 percent of their denizens remaining in them for between four and eight years.[54] By the end of 1952, thanks to a radical decline in the immigration rate, *ma'abarot* began to be wound down but it took more than six years for the process to be completed. Some, such as Kiryat Shmona, were destined to become kernels of development towns.

The overwhelming majority of immigrants preferred to live in urban areas and between 1948 and 1954 the population of Israel's three major cities (Tel Aviv, Haifa, and Jerusalem) increased by 55 percent.[55] According to Eisenstadt, a leading Israeli sociologist, immigrants usually settled "in new neighborhoods where they were more or less concentrated and, from the ecological point of view, relatively segregated."[56] In time, the establishment of development towns was seen as an attractive alternative (see chapter 4).

To counter immigrant preferences in favor of cities, the government, in as much as it was able, directed immigrants to the agricultural sector where by the close of 1952 some 85,000 found a niche for themselves. 50,000 were absorbed in 167 immigrant farming settlements formed between May 1948 and December 1952, while the rest joined existing kibbutzim and moshavim[57] (see glossary). This contrasts with pre-state farming immigrants who were usually attached to established rural communities. (It also heralded the termination of the kibbutz as the leading cynosure of would-be agronomists.)

Jews from Yemen accounted for nearly a quarter of all immigrant land settlers. Their attitudes to farming contrasted sharply with those from Morocco, who unfavorably associated such activities with the Arab peasants in their country of origin and who considered it shameful to be similarly employed.

Not all would-be farmers were aware of the choices available to them. One young Jew from Morocco explained that, shortly after he and his family entered the country, they were asked if they would like to live in a moshav. Thinking that a moshav meant a city, they agreed to it with alacrity. Before they knew it, they were bundled onto a truck that drove southward into the night to enter their new settlement while it was still dark. After resting in tents, they awoke the next morning to view the local landscape. "There was only sand piled up to the sky, not even a green branch, no birds, no greenery, no cars, no road, no houses, nothing . . . I did not know what to do, I sat alongside a shack and cried and cried and cried."[58]

The anguish endured by that unfortunate person partly arose from the fact that the government, largely driven by military considerations, pursued its population decentralization policy with extreme haste. It was anxious to place people alongside the state's new borders to guard against the return of Arab refugees and the infiltration of Arab marauders. With time seeming to be of the essence, many new immigrants were dumped on remote sites without the prior installation of adequate economic infrastructures. On account of the Holocaust, the ranks of Zionist pioneers willing to place national interests above their own needs were severely depleted. Consequently, the policy of consolidating border areas and other thinly populated Jewish ones was perforce borne by the new immigrants. Furthermore, the channeling of newcomers into farm settlements arose from the near bankruptcy of the Jewish Agency. With a sense of impending financial disaster, the Agency wished to wash its hands of the responsibility of housing them.

At one stage, the government settled people from different countries and cultures in the same villages. It was thought that the common challenges facing the novice farmers would unite them but invariably that hope turned out to be an illusory one. Contrary to expectations, immigrants were unwilling to forsake their distinct identities to be submerged in a cultural and social melting pot. Frictions based on ethnic and other differences soon surfaced and were the cause of the disintegration of many settlements. Taking note, the government eventually took care to ensure that villages were more uniformly composed.

To enable immigrants to earn a living, employment was offered in the context of miscellaneous projects, of which many served no practical purpose other than providing pretexts for doling out welfare payments. The government hesitated to support immigrants directly on an ongoing basis lest they be discouraged from entering the work force and, with that in mind, it insisted that all able-bodied men below the age of 45 seek paid employment. Those failing to do so were subject to the withdrawal of free access to food and shelter. Obtaining work frequently entailed adapting one's calling in accordance with local labor market conditions. This applied to 60 percent of all immigrants.[60] For breadwinners who had previously been shopkeepers and petty traders and who then had to

become farmers or general workers, the transformation was both physically and psychologically challenging. Not only, as already mentioned,
did many balk at farm work but they also resented being employed as
unskilled laborers. As one young man complained, "I do not want to do
here all the things that only the Arab riffraff did in Morocco. I did not
come to Israel to become like one of them. We are better than they, [sic]
we are stronger – why should I perform all this manual labour?"[61]

Obtaining work usually necessitated lining up at an employment
office from 4.00 a.m. When the office doors would finally open, pan-
demonium would break out. Applicants would shout and jostle in what
had previously been a "queue," for the jobs on offer were few and far
between. In particular, Mizrahi immigrants (those from Arab countries)
resented the preferential treatment received by western Jews. David
Haham from Iraq plaintively remembered that on entering Israel:

> they [the Jewish Agency] transported us in open lorries to the
> Ma'abarot. They did not have tents, food and work chits ready for us.
> Yet the Romanians were transported in buses, given a warm meal in a
> cooperative restaurant, issued with food and work chits and in fact on
> the day following their arrival in the country, they set off to work in
> good jobs. . . Whereas what was our lot? To labour on road construction
> where you would not find a single Ashkenazi [western Jew]."[62]

Although mass immigration was of course welcomed, for without it the
state would not have flourished, long-term residents were not enamored
with the likes of many of their new cohabitants. Apart from the low
educational levels obtained by most immigrants from North Africa and
the Middle East, their general traits and customs differed substantially
from those of the pre-state Yishuv. These were manifested in their own
Hebrew idiom, their distinct religious liturgies, their relations between
the sexes, their family life, and their leisure activities. Standard Zionist
concepts such as pioneering, collectivism, socialism, and modernism
meant nothing to them. The prejudices of the established community
were manifested by describing Mizrahi immigrants pejoratively, calling
them, among other things, primitives, ignoramuses, and boors. Such
views were openly expressed in the media. One writer referred to beliefs
that "the ongoing immigration was suffused with a low moral tone and

a miserable cultural standard, all of which was likely to drag the fledging state down into the depths of Levantinism, making it akin to other states of the region."[63] Another compared the immigrants, especially those from Morocco, unfavorably with the Arabs, complaining that they were "given to the play of primitive and wild instincts."[64] The liberal newspaper, *Haaretz*, reported that "you will find among them [the immigrants] dirt, card games for money, drunkenness and fornication. Many of them suffer from serious eye, skin and venereal diseases; not to mention immorality and stealing."[65] The charge of unlawfulness was frequently leveled against immigrants, for they were over-represented in criminal activity. Some maintained that not only were the immigrants unsuited to local requirements in terms of their productivity and will to work but in many instances they were more miserable in Israel than they had been abroad.[66] Even their potential as reliable soldiers was questioned. Ben-Gurion was no less scathing than others. He thought of the immigrants as "riffraff and human dust, without any language, education or roots and without imbibing the tradition and vision of the nation."[67] He certainly had no intention of respecting their traditions and culture for he was adamant that all newcomers had to fit into a melting pot so that a homogeneous Israeli nation would emerge.[68] As far as he was concerned, immigration to Israel involved a one-way process of absorption, integration, and elevation of newcomers, without regard to any possible interaction between them and the veterans.[69]

The verbal and written barbs directed toward the immigrants hit their mark. The mortification of the newcomers was poignantly expressed by Bar-Moshe who wrote: "We left Iraq as Jews and arrived in Israel as Iraqis. It was both sad and ridiculous. After the Iraqi rulers and their press made us appreciate our Jewish identity, here in Israel our brothers and coreligionists stress our Iraqiness."[70] Some Mizrahis, instead of exhibiting legitimate pride in their own traditions and achievements, internalized the prejudices of the veteran community. A teacher from Iraq disclosed how she and others "began to adopt the notion that we were not proper Jews."[71]

The integration of Israel's disparate Jewish population was not easily achieved. Even to this day, the country is riven by differences in ethnic origins. Few Mizrahis are represented in the top echelon of Israeli society, such as among cabinet ministers, army officers, high court judges, university presidents and so on. However, among operative unifying forces the feeling that all Jews are kinsmen sharing the same religion and destiny has been a powerful one. The very realities of life in Israel have been instrumental in melding people from vastly different backgrounds into a homogeneous national body. With Israel constantly at war with its neighbors, external threats tend to draw its Jewish citizens closer together. In that respect, the army has played a key role. By requiring most able-bodied men and women from different backgrounds and walks of life to serve within its ranks, it has subjected them to a common experience and mission.

4

EARLY SOCIAL, ECONOMIC, AND POLITICAL DEVELOPMENTS

As the Israelis emerged from their War of Independence, they looked upon their new state with immense pride. Songs extolling comradeship and personal sacrifice were standard radio fare. A significant proportion of high school students belonged to pioneering youth movements and kibbutz members were still esteemed for their idealism.

While there was a small well-heeled stratum, the average citizen enjoyed fairly Spartan living conditions. Few owned private motor vehicles, clothing was austerely simple (locally produced shoes with wafer-thin soles were manufactured from used leather)[1] and many cabinet members wore open-necked shirts. Buses that served as the main means of transport were exceedingly crowded. Passengers jammed into them compressed one against the other in the midst of thick acrid tobacco smoke. On occasion, they also found themselves brushing against live poultry.

The heterogeneity of the country's newly arrived migrants was reflected by the variety of foreign languages spoken in the streets and differences in dress codes. Holocaust survivors with numbers tattooed on their forearms were omnipresent. Considering that the population was relatively small, residents were readily able to rub shoulders with the country's leaders as they officiated at local and national gatherings. An air of solidarity pervaded and on the whole most Israelis were moderately upbeat about their future.

Israel's first general election took place on January 25, 1949. All adult residents of 18 years of age and over, whether Jews or Arabs, were enfranchised. Moved by the historic occasion, many voters presented themselves at election booths with tears streaming from their eyes.[2] The election was meant to establish the membership of a Constituent Assembly yet no attempt was made to draft a constitution since that would have necessitated a highly contentious determination of the public role of religion. As far as the extreme orthodox Jews were concerned "only the laws of the Torah shall be decisive in all realms of life in the State."[3] Under such circumstances, the Constituent Assembly simply became Israel's unicameral parliament, or Knesset, and in practice many of the modalities of a British unwritten constitution were adopted.

Twenty-one parties or lists contested the 120 seats available on the basis of proportional representation in which the entire country constituted a single constituency. Parties or factions submitted lists containing their candidates and were awarded seats on the basis of the share of the total vote accruing to each list. Candidates on each list were ranked in order of preference so that if a list obtained, say, four seats, the first four names appearing on it would be elevated to the Knesset. Such an electoral procedure had been the norm within the Jewish community of Palestine in the pre-state era. Even had a change been deemed desirable, because a large section of the population was still under arms, an election based on local constituencies would not have been feasible. In practice, what was meant to serve as a temporary expedient turned out to be perdurable. This occurred because the system of proportional representation generated a proliferation of small parties with an interest in maintaining the status quo.

Supporters of proportional representation have argued that it embodies the essence of democracy in that the composition of the Knesset provides a true reflection of voter preferences. Since in Israel no party has ever commanded a majority in its own right, the system has led to chronic government instability and to political blackmail by junior coalition partners. Policy measures forced on a hapless prime minister may actually negate the wishes and interests of members of his or her party and of the public at large. That is, the electorate is never assured that a newly installed administration would enjoy the confidence of most voters.[4] Not only may incumbent governments be out of public favor but the opposition, which in Israel is invariably a loose coalition of disaffected parties from both sides of the political spectrum, has never been able to present itself as a potential alternative. Ben-Gurion believed that Israel's fragmented opposition was "good only for negation, for opposition without responsibility."[5] Proportional representation has been far less democratic than its advocates would have us believe. Until fairly recently, lists of candidates were drawn up by party machines without any consultation with rank-and-file members, reducing the Knesset to a club of party elites.[6] For the most part, Israeli citizens have been deprived of local parliamentarians who could represent their regional interests and to whom aggrieved individuals could turn.

With 15 percent of the voters being newly arrived migrants, and with the Herut (rightwing nationalists) and Mapam (Marxist Zionists) parties having recently been formed, the 1949 election's prospective outcome was uncertain. No reliable survey of voting intentions had been conducted. While Mapai (social democrats) under Ben-Gurion's stewardship was the country's dominant party, both Herut and Mapam were considered credible contenders. In the main, the election campaign dwelt on the question of who could best take credit for Israel's existence and recent victories.[7] Herut under Menahem Begin, the former commander of the Irgun, claimed to have been instrumental in causing Britain to leave Palestine. Begin was an alluring and fiery orator. His public appearances attracted large crowds, especially among the disadvantaged Mizrahi community. At the other end of the political barricade, Mapam vaunted its crucial role in the War of Independence through its involvement in the Palmah. Having many youthful leaders, it strove to present itself as a refreshing alternative to Mapai, which it accused of being defeatist and out of touch with its working-class base. Mapai in turn portrayed Mapam as a pro-communist party beholden to Moscow, while both Mapai and Mapam likened Herut to a fascist party threatening Israel's democracy. The acerbic nature of each party's propaganda whereby opponents were venomously slandered set an unfavorable precedent for future generations of Israeli politicians. Ben-Gurion himself was party to that tradition. He particularly loathed Begin and refused to refer to him in the Knesset by name, describing him instead as the member sitting next to Dr Bader.[8] He later mellowed somewhat writing that "with us disputes are not those of people who are more or less normal but of fanatics. There is simply no measure to our disagreements."[9] Ben-Gurion partly attributed that phenomenon to a prolonged dispersion in exile that deprived Jews of the art of statecraft.

The results of the 1949 election, as for all subsequent ones, are contained in the Appendix (p. 334). Despite a significant demographic shift, the recent formation of Israel, the war for its survival, and changes in national priorities (the absorption of immigrants and the stimulation of economic growth), the election outcome reflected the political constellation that had existed in the pre-state period.[10] In part this was because most established parties had a direct hand in administering immigration reception camps in accordance with their relative strength. This enabled them to create a feeling of migrant dependence on them for securing employment, housing, and other favors. As to the immigrants themselves, coming as they did from a multitude of different countries, they neither constituted a homogeneous group nor were they endowed with their own authentic leadership. Rather than voicing issues that directly concerned them, they tended to accept and abide by the political norms and views of the veterans.[11]

A post-election coalition government under Ben-Gurion's leadership was formed. It consisted of Mapai, the United Religious Front (an alliance of religious parties), the Progressives (liberals), and a Mizrahi faction. On February 16, 1949, the Knesset elected Dr Chaim Weizmann as Israel's first official president. (He had been appointed provisional president by the provisional national council that had ruled in the interim between the Declaration of Independence and the establishment of the first elected government.) Weizmann had nourished the hope that as president he would play an active role in Israel's political life. He would have liked on the odd occasion to preside at cabinet meetings, to have had some influence on foreign policy, and to have had access to cabinet minutes.[12] All these were denied to him. He had to rest content with merely fulfilling ceremonial duties. In Richard Crossman's view (a Labour member of the UK parliament), "the constitutional decision to make the President powerless was not taken on its merits but as a precaution against an otherwise inevitable clash between two great and completely incompatible personalities, the first President and the

First Prime Minister [Ben-Gurion] of Israel."[13] Weizmann resented his exclusion from the seats of power. In his political isolation, he referred to himself as the "prisoner from Rehovot" (his home residence) and complained that the only thing that Ben-Gurion would let him get his nose into was his handkerchief.

Since its formation, Israel has been governed by a series of coalition cabinets subject to recurring crises. Often the crises revolved around fairly minor disputes. In Ben-Gurion's day, when such spats led to deadlock, he simply resigned, thereby forcing a change of heart on the part of coalition obstructionists wishing to be re-included in the successive government. Such was the case in October 1950 when Ben-Gurion wished to increase the number of cabinet ministers from 12 to 13. When the religious front opposed the change, Ben-Gurion forced the issue by bringing down the government. In the ensuing negotiations for a new government, a compromise was reached. The religious front agreed to a 13-member cabinet, provided the additional minister (who was to oversee the ministry of industry) was not affiliated with any party. The bone of contention was simply one of the relative cabinet representation of each party.

The next government crisis was rather more serious. In September 1949, Israel had introduced free compulsory school education for all children between the ages of five and fourteen. Parents had the choice of sending their offspring to one of four school streams. On offer was a Labour stream, with an emphasis on pioneering and socialist values, a general non-political stream, and the two streams of Mizrahi and Agudat Yisrael respectively that were religiously orientated. (Mizrahi was Zionist and mainstream orthodox while Agudat Yisrael was decidedly more obscurantist and essentially anti-Zionist.)

A bitter rift emerged between the religious and secular parties in relation to the education of immigrant children. Within immigrant camps, the government had suspended the application of the four-stream system. In its place, it installed a unified one, with optional classes in religion. That expedient was supposed to have been warranted on account of the ephemeral nature of the camps and the consequent large turnover of students. But the religious parties complained that students from traditional Jewish backgrounds, such as those from Arab countries, were being subjected to anti-religious tuition.

In January 1950, a parliamentary commission chaired by Gad Frumkin, a retired high court judge, was established to examine charges that the religious tuition of immigrant children was inadequate. Although three of the five commission members were secularists, the commission concluded that there was some substance to the religious parties' complaints. The minister of education had inappropriately attributed to migrant camps an extraterritorial status not subject to general law. Thus parents were unfairly denied the ability to choose the nature of education that their children were to receive.

The commission also examined education within newly formed moshavim (see glossary) associated with the Histadrut (trade union movement) and concluded that, as in the migrant camps, this left much to be desired. The labor stream did in fact contain a religious subset (the labor religious stream) that was supposed to cater for the needs of religious members. However, it was found that the religious component in that subset was far too superficial. As a remedy, the commission recommended that moshav children be provided with access to a standard religious school.

With Ben-Gurion refusing to accept the commission's findings, the religious parties rebelled, causing his government to be defeated in a no-confidence vote. Ben-Gurion resigned and a new general election was held in July 1951. By October 1951, after exhaustive bargaining, Ben-Gurion cobbled together a coalition consisting of Mapai and the four separate religious parties. The schooling crisis was resolved by deciding that in immigrant camps composed exclusively of Yemenite Jews, education would be imparted only within a religious school. In other camps immigrants would be afforded the choice between a religious and non-religious one. As it happened, local officials often breached the spirit of the agreement. One parent described how a public employee, on hearing that he had registered his child in a religious school, turned against him "brutally like an enemy and roared at me like a lion: 'I don't want it, I don't want it.'"[14]

On December 7, 1953, Ben-Gurion, after months of prevaricating, resigned. Having been active in public life for over forty years, he felt that he needed some time out. It was not his intention to retire permanently but rather to distance himself from the hurly-burly of political life to indulge in reflection and writing. Early in 1953, on an excursion

from Eilat he stumbled across Sde Boker, then an obscure Negev settlement consisting of a few shacks populated by a small group of young
adults. Striking up a conversation with the settlers, he learnt that they
had fought in that area during the War of Independence and that they
had decided to farm there. As he later wistfully recalled, that encounter
filled him with envy. "Why," he asked "was I not able to participate in
such a venture?"[15] The appeal of Sde Boker remained with him and
upon retiring he and his wife, Paula, joined its ranks. Working part-time
as an "ordinary" member, Ben-Gurion wished to symbolize the importance of pioneering and to call upon Israeli youth to populate the Negev,
an undertaking dear to his heart. Abiding by the wisdom of Confucius,
Ben-Gurion subscribed to the view that a spiritually elevated person is
one that initially does only what he would demand of others and then
to demand from others only what he himself does.

At first he labored at shoveling manure and, when it became obvious by his panting that that was too taxing for him (being 67 years of
age and subject to frequent bouts of ill health), he tended to the sheep.
Abba Eban believed that Ben-Gurion "was totally immune to the
seductions of personal comfort,"[16] initially rejecting air-conditioning
so that he would be on an equal footing with his fellow kibbutz members. However, the kibbutz did provide him with a small four-roomed
wooden house with a study that was infinitely more spacious than the
shared rooms of the others and Paula ensured that he was not lacking
in food to his liking. From his new desert abode, Ben-Gurion conferred
with visiting colleagues, who either sought his advice or enabled him to
keep track of important political and other developments.

While Ben-Gurion set a sterling personal example of devotion to pioneering, he was unable to persuade Israeli youth to emulate him. This
was certainly not for want of trying. He addressed numerous gatherings
of young people hoping to imbue them with a new national pioneering
vision. But only a relatively small number from the moshav as opposed
to the kibbutz movement uprooted themselves (for a limited duration)
to assist immigrants in border areas to adjust to their new lives as farmers. Most of his young listeners reacted to his long-winded speeches
with disdain, interjecting with whistles and shrieks. They contemptu-
ously labeled his entreaties as "Zionism" to which they did not seem able
or willing to relate.[17] The heroic period of the formation of the state and

Plate 4.1   Ben Gurion (left) and Paula (second from right) at Sde Boker

the massive ingathering of the exiles was at an end. Zionism had become thoroughly institutionalized and, by contrast with an earlier epoch where the spirit of voluntaryism prevailed, Israel's citizens, by and large, became preoccupied with their own personal pursuits. Ben-Gurion, like Don Quixote, tilted at windmills hoping to smash what he termed "careerism" and replace it with bygone values. It was a hopeless task.

With Ben-Gurion's departure, Moshe Sharett, who retained his portfolio as foreign minister, was elevated to the premiership. Sharett, like most leading politicians, did not suffer from false modesty. When news of Ben-Gurion's imminent retirement was announced, Sharett told his wife Tzipora that he vastly overshadowed all other prospective candidates in terms of his ability to be a unifying factor in the Knesset, the government, the state, and the nation.[18] Much to his chagrin, Ben-Gurion proposed that Levi Eshkol be awarded the post. Only when Eshkol declined did Sharett's colleagues by default turn to him. In his new government, Pincas Lavon (on Ben-Gurion's strong recommendation)[19] was appointed as minister of defense and, immediately before Ben-Gurion stepped down, Moshe Dayan replaced Mordechai Makleff as chief of staff with Shimon Peres being made director general of the Defense Ministry. Makleff would have liked Yitzhak Rabin to succeed him but, because of Rabin's prominent involvement in the Palmah which Ben-Gurion regarded as having been under the sway of leftists, Ben-Gurion preferred Dayan. He did harbor some misgivings as to Dayan's integrity and personality but Peres was able to reassure him.[20]

From the onset of the British mandate in the early 1920s, both Ben-Gurion and Sharett were prominent Zionist figures. They worked closely together and appreciated each other's qualities but they differed considerably. Ben-Gurion was a past master in realpolitik and controlled the political machinery of Mapai and the Histadrut with an iron hand. He did not shrink from making bold decisions. By virtue of the strength of his convictions he, more than anyone else, paved the way for Israel to declare its independence. Sharett by contrast made his mark on the diplomatic front where his erudition and linguistic skills were put to good use. By inclination he preferred to resolve disputes, whether internal or external ones, by force of reason and give and take. To some extent that was the cause of his ultimate undoing. Not being sufficiently resolute, he tentatively steered the helm of government at a time when his country was being buffeted by a gathering storm of violence and conflict with its neighbors. Commanding scant respect from some of his more contumacious ministers, he failed to rein in their waywardness. This was particularly the case with Lavon who, on becoming the minister of defense, instantly metamorphosed from a confirmed dove to an out-of-control hawk. Behind Sharett's back, Lavon contrived a series of outlandish military actions of which fortunately few saw the light of day. One activity (reviewed in chapter 7) with which Lavon was closely associated involved Jewish agents in Egypt who were arrested and tried. Following that contretemps, Lavon resigned in February 1955. Because the defense ministry was in such disarray, Ben-Gurion was prevailed upon to return from his self-imposed exile in Sde Boker to replace Lavon under Sharett's leadership.

Israel's third general election was held on July 20, 1955, by which time the population had grown to 1,789,000. The election took place following the General Zionists (a conservative party which had subsequently joined the government) refusal to abide by the rule of collective responsibility. The General Zionists abstained in Knesset motions that censured the government's supposed role in the Kastner trial (outlined further below).

Before the 1955 election, a section of Mapam broke away to form a new party, Ahdut Ha'avodah. Unlike Mapam, Ahdut Ha'avodah was more leery of the Soviet Union and more inclined to support stronger military responses to Arab provocations. The elections resulted in losses to Mapai and gains to Herut (see Appendix). Since Mapai lost votes to Ahdut Ha'avodah and Herut gained at the expense of the General Zionists, the changes did not reflect a seismic shift in support between left- and rightwing parties. What effectively happened is that, on account of a deteriorating border security problem (discussed in the following chapter), both the leftwing and rightwing electorate swung to more activist defense parties within their own camps. After the elections, Sharett continued to head a Mapai-dominated government until in November 1955 he was superseded by Ben-Gurion. Ben-Gurion's new coalition government included Mapai, Mapam, Ahdut Ha'avodah, the Progressives and the two Hamizrahi (moderate religious) parties which fused in 1956 to form Mafdal (the National Religious Party).

The Kastner Trial

As already mentioned, the proceedings of the Kastner Trial[21] provided the catalyst for Sharett's government's downfall and for his eventual replacement by Ben-Gurion.

The trial itself had its origins in war-torn Europe. Shortly after the Nazis occupied Hungary in March 1944, Dr Israel Kastner, as head of the Budapest-based Jewish Committee for Rescue and Assistance, established and maintained ongoing contacts with the Gestapo, particularly with Adolf Eichmann. During those sessions, he explored avenues to staunch the transfer of Hungarian Jews to Auschwitz. The sessions between Kastner and Eichmann had frequently been described as negotiations. But as the writer Weitz reminds us, they were in practice conversations between a hangman and his potential victim during which the SS officer reposed in an armchair while his Jewish interlocutor stood before him with much discomfort.[22]

One scheme floated by Eichmann and his subordinate Kurt Becher entailed the release of a million Jews in exchange for 10,000 trucks loaded with merchandise to be supplied by the western allies. The Germans promised that the equipment would be deployed exclusively against the Soviet Union. In May 1944, Joel Brand, Kastner's colleague, was flown in a Luftwaffe plane to Istanbul to promote the plan. In attempting to establish direct contact with high-ranking Jewish Agency officials, including Moshe Sharett, Brand was arrested by the British at the Turkish–Syrian border. For that reason, he was unable to complete his mission, which at any rate had little if any realistic prospect of success. Neither Britain nor America had any intention of assisting Germany to prolong the war or of allowing any wedge to be driven between them and their Russian ally. In the interim, Kastner was able to obtain Eichmann's agreement, supposedly given as a gesture of his goodwill to the western allies, to permit the dispatch of a special train to transport 1,685 Hungarian Jews to Switzerland.[23]

Selecting the train's passengers was an unenviable assignment with the list of designated passengers constantly being revised right up to the final moment. This reflected the prodigious amount of pressure put upon Kastner and his fellow committee members by desperate claimants well aware that their lives depended on being accepted. Allowing for a significant number of wealthy individuals who were required to help finance the venture plus miscellaneous communal officials who were difficult to overlook, there was nonetheless a large contingent of Zionists of all persuasions as well as extremely religious anti-Zionist Hasidim. Despite 19 members of Kastner's family having been included, the majority of his and his wife's relatives were not.

After the war, Kastner, in December 1947, migrated to Palestine where rumors circulated about him and his exploits, some complimentary and some otherwise. In August 1952, subscribing to the view that Kastner was essentially a Nazi collaborator, Malchiel Gruenwald, a Hungarian-born member of the Mizrahi party, wrote as much in an obscure publication, "Letters to Friends in the Mizrahi," that he himself edited and distributed. The article was downright defamatory, accusing Kastner of saving his family and political associates (through the medium of the special train to Switzerland) at the cost of sacrificing Hungarian Jewry. Without mincing his words Gruenwald described Kastner as the indirect murderer of his dear brothers.[24] When the attorney general's attention was drawn to Gruenwald's screed, he decided (against the advice of the minister of justice) to press a criminal libel suit against him. That the action was taken by the attorney general and not by Kastner was a direct outcome of Kastner being both a public official (the spokesman for the ministry of commerce and industry) and of his having a relatively high profile in the ruling Mapai party. As far as is known, Kastner personally evinced little interest in pursuing the case.

The trial took place in the Jerusalem District Court, presided by Judge Benjamin Halevy, with Amnon Tal as the state prosecutor. A number of issues were at stake. These included whether or not Kastner had collaborated with the Nazis and facilitated the slaughter of Hungarian Jews (by concealing from them knowledge of what awaited them at the extermination camps). Gruenwald also intimated that Kastner had cooperated with Kurt Becher in stealing Jewish property collected as "donations" for organizing the train to Switzerland and that he had testified at Nuremberg on Becher's behalf. The proceedings opened on January 1, 1954 and lasted a year and a half. As they unravelled, the press gave them widespread coverage with readers becoming steadily traumatized by the sad and tragic accounts that emerged. The trial marked a milestone in the growing appreciation among Israelis of the full dimensions of the Holocaust, an appreciation that was to deepen during the Eichmann trial almost a decade later.

Nearly 60 witnesses testified, including Kastner, who at first impressed Halevy as having saved the lives of thousands of Jews. Immediately after Kastner's opening remarks, the judge suggested to the defendant that he withdraw his accusations but Gruenwald declined to do so.[25] Then as the trial progressed, Kastner's reliability as a witness was seriously put in doubt by the legal acumen of Gruenwald's attorney, Shmuel Tamir, a founding member of the Herut party. When Tamir was approached by poverty-stricken Gruenwald to take on his case, he enthusiastically agreed, setting aside his usual fees. Tamir sensed that the trial offered him a chance to settle political scores with the Mapai establishment, which he wholeheartedly loathed. He banked on attracting the public limelight in the process and of earning the reputation of being a notable public figure.

Since Kastner had been associated with Mapai well before World War Two, had served a Mapai minister (Dov Joseph) on arrival in Israel, and had been placed on the party's 1949 and 1951 electoral candidate lists, Tamir was able to present his client's defense in political terms. He depicted Mapai's leaders as having betrayed the Jewish nation by abandoning European Jewry. Moshe Sharett was singled out as being responsible for Brand's arrest, while Kastner was alleged to have followed his and other Mapai leaders' directives.[26] Ludicrously described as British lackeys, Sharett and his associates were alleged to have sabotaged Brand's mission in order to reduce pressures for Jewish immigration to Palestine in compliance with the UK White Paper. All the while, the Jewish Agency, in Tamir's learned opinion, "remained silent about the Holocaust, prevented resistance to it and directly aided the Germans, even if it had no desire in furthering genocide."[27]

Incensed by the tone of Tamir's arguments both as they related to him and to his party, Sharett resolved to clear the air. He planned to do so by means of a keynote speech to be delivered at Kibbutz Ma'agan on July 29, 1954, where there was to have been an official unveiling of a statue commemorating Jewish paratroopers dropped over Nazi-held territory. Among those present were surviving paratroopers and the families of the seven that had perished. Immediately prior to the opening of the ceremony, a letter sent by the State president was to be delivered by an overflying Piper Cub. The parcel containing the message became entangled in the plane's wheel carriage and as the pilot tried to retrieve it, his aircraft nosedived into the awaiting assembly, leading to one of Israel's worst civil disasters. Seventeen lost their lives and another 24 were injured. Among those killed were four of the original paratroopers and a wife and only son of a paratrooper that had met his death in Europe. Sharett's address was perforce postponed until much later.

Meanwhile a turning point was reached in the trial whereby Kastner's credibility was grossly undermined. This occurred when Tamir presented him with a copy of an affidavit that he had submitted at the war's end in favor of Becher. Previously Kastner had asserted that he had merely summarized, in a neutral tone, his past dealings with him. But it now became evident that Kastner had actually written that Becher had done all in his power to save Jews and that he deserved "the fullest possible consideration."[28] Putting himself deeper into a rut, Kastner falsely claimed to have acted on behalf of the Jewish Agency, a peccadillo that some ascribed to Kastner's long-standing obsession to be seen as a leading communal functionary. Whatever his motive, the revelation that Kastner had aided a high-ranking SS officer played directly into Tamir's hands. Instead of Gruenwald appearing to have a charge to answer, Kastner began to be seen as the defendant, with the case rapidly becoming identified by the press and the public at large as the "Kastner trial."

Kastner's standing fell even further when Katrina Senesh, the mother of the late Hana Senesh (the country's most idolized and legendary woman paratrooper who was executed in Budapest) was cross-examined. In response to Tamir's questioning, she disclosed that she had desperately sought an interview with Kastner in the hope that he would intercede on her incarcerated daughter's behalf. Day after day and to no avail she presented herself at Kastner's office. Yet Kastner had refused to see her because by acting overtly on behalf of a partisan he would have compromised his dealings with Eichmann.

On June 22, 1955, after a nine-month recess, Halevy found that all of the defendant's assertions, save that Kastner had been implicated in stealing Jewish property, were warranted. This was tantamount to confirming that Kastner did indeed serve the Nazis as Gruenwald had alleged. Halevy was particularly brutal in his summation, claiming that Kastner "had sold his soul to the devil."[29] According to Halevy, Kastner facilitated the slaughter of the Jews of Cluz (a Romanian town temporarily annexed to Hungary), as well as other Hungarian Jews, by withholding from them knowledge of the Nazis' true intentions. By so doing he deprived them of the opportunity of organizing resistance or attempting to flee. So obsessed was Kastner (in Halevy's judgment) with the fate of the special rescue train that he willingly tolerated the sacrifice of hundreds of thousands of excluded passengers.

The Israeli historian, Tom Segev, described Halevy's judgment as "one of the most heartless in the history of Israel, perhaps the most heartless ever."[30] There is the suspicion that Halevy had borne a grudge against the Mapai establishment for not supporting him, before the trial opened, in his bid for promotion to the High Court.[31] In a scathing article in an American journal (*Commentary*), Walter Laqueur mused over whether Halevy deliberately postponed issuing his findings until the approach of the general elections scheduled for July 1955 so that news of the verdict would lessen Mapai's electoral prospects.[32] Bowing to pressure, Laqueur withdrew that innuendo.

Amidst the uproar that followed Halevy's ruling, the attorney general, with the backing of highly placed government members, immediately appealed to the High Court. Since the original case was initiated by the government, Kastner had no legal basis for lodging his own appeal and, in order to provide him with an avenue to clear his name, the government felt that it had no alternative other than to act on his behalf.

Both Herut and the communists censured the government for allowing the attorney general to pursue the libel suit in the first instance and for compounding the impropriety of that decision by challenging the lower court's ruling. Herut claimed that had Kastner not been linked to Mapai, Sharett would readily have disowned him. The outcome of the trial placed Mapai's reputation among the electorate under a cloud. As already intimated, its General Zionist coalition partner served notice that it would not support the government in a Knesset vote of no confidence. It claimed that by not fully considering the true facts and circumstances pertaining to the whole issue, the government had acted rashly in appealing against Halevy's verdict.[33] Given little choice, Sharett resigned to form a temporary government (without the General Zionists) as a prelude to the July 1955 general elections.

In addition to the trial's political ramifications, there was some negative resonance abroad, thanks in part to the pro-Soviet Israeli communists. Their newspaper *Kol Ha-am* proclaimed that Kastner's contacts with Eichmann reflected the Nazi collaboration of the entire Zionist movement.[34] Such a contemptible anti-Semitic calumny became stock-in-trade not only of the world communist movement but also of leftwing anti-Zionists.

Needless to say, Kastner, who was not present when Halevy delivered his judgment, was devastated. For years his activities in Budapest were a source of pride and at a sudden stroke his halo of glory became a mark of shame.[35] With a superhuman effort, he continued with his normal daily routine. He shunned overtures from friendly kibbutzim and entertained no thoughts of leaving the country. Perhaps more painful to him than anything else was the odium directed toward his family. His nine-year old daughter Susie was taunted by her classmates. Mrs Kastner was refused service in a local grocery store and among the many other indignities to which the family was subjected was the pouring of effluent onto their balcony by a neighbor above them.[36]

In January 1958, after having reviewed the "Kastner case" in response to the government's appeal, the High Court of Israel, with five judges sitting at the bench, issued its findings. Four of the five judges ruled that Kastner be absolved of accusations of having been a Nazi collaborator and of having betrayed both the Hungarian Jewish community and the paratroopers from Palestine. He was, however, censored for testifying in favor of Becher whom the judges viewed as a war criminal. Justice Halevy was severely reprimanded for accepting hearsay evidence, for unduly tolerating trivial lines of inquiry, for improperly questioning witnesses and in general for not maintaining appropriate judicial procedures. In a nutshell, Kastner's name and reputation were officially reinstated and his role in saving numerous Hungarian Jews was reaffirmed. By virtue of the ultimate safe arrival of all the train's passengers in Switzerland, Kastner's biographer claimed that Kastner had the distinction of rescuing a far greater number of his kinsmen than any other Jew.[37] It was certainly not in Kastner's power to save Hungarian Jewry at large.

Kastner did not live to witness his vindication. On March 3, 1957, he was shot on returning home from work and died a few days later. In the face of countless threats to Kastner's life, two bodyguards had been assigned to protect him but because of budgetary constraints they were withdrawn shortly before he was murdered. News of Kastner's assassination shocked the general public whose feelings were summarized by the newspaper *Ma'ariv* which wrote "the man who aimed his revolver at Dr Kastner aimed it at the heart of the entire nation."[38] The Israelis typically expressed themselves caustically when referring to their opponents but it did not dawn on most of them that their outbursts would inspire irresponsible elements to take the law into their own hands. (Nor did they learn from that experience, for years later Rabin met his death at the hands of a religious fanatic egged on by rabid and hateful incitement.) Three young men were charged with Kastner's murder on the basis of confessions extracted from two of them (Ze'ev Eckstein and Dan Shemer) who claimed to have exacted revenge on behalf of the Holocaust victims. The third person (Josef Menckes) pleaded innocence but all three were convicted and sentenced to life imprisonment. Their subsequent appeal to the High Court was unsuccessful.

There were two disturbing aspects relating to the murder and its sequel. It soon transpired that an armed underground extreme right-wing group was in existence. A cache of arms inherited from Lehi and containing submachine guns, hand grenades, ammunition and – of all things – flame-throwers was discovered at Kfar Sabah.[39] In the opinion of the police, Israel was confronting an internal threat that was not only responsible for Kastner's death but which also sought to undermine the very foundations of the country's democratic regime.[40] Luckily, the number of people involved was minuscule and the threat was nipped in the bud. This was not the first time in the state's short history that underground Jewish terrorist cells were detected. In 1951 two separate groups came to light. One, the "Brit Kanayim" (Covenant of Zealots), consisted of religious extremists that specialized in burning cars driven on the Sabbath and in damaging non-kosher butcher shops. Protesting against the drafting of religious women into the army, it had planted a bomb in a café and intended to do likewise in the Knesset. The other group, "Malhut Israel" (The Kingdom of Israel), was equally bizarre. It sought to establish a Hebrew empire incorporating all areas in the early historic Jewish kingdoms. More menacingly, it engaged in military exercises and began to amass an underground arms depot.[41]

The second matter relates to the extraordinary early release in 1963 of all three of Kastner's murderers on the basis of a presidential pardon less than seven years after their initial detention. On the face of it there were no grounds for such leniency. None of the accused expressed the slightest remorse. On the contrary, years later, in 1993, Eckstein declared that instead of shooting Kastner he ought to have drowned him in a sewer.[42]

Finally, in contrast to Tamir's extravagant claims that Kastner had shared in the loot collected by passengers for the train to Switzerland and thereby enriched himself, his widow lived out her remaining years in abject poverty, eking out a paltry income by selling lottery tickets from a street stall.

Early economic problems

Israel's early years were plagued by a multitude of intractable economic problems. When the War of Independence was in train, nearly one sixth of its population was in uniform. That imposed an intolerable strain on the civilian labor force entrusted with meeting the country's basic requirements. Furthermore, the onset of an unprecedented inflow of immigrants coming just after the cessation of hostilities considerably exacerbated matters. This was especially the case since the state had perforce to prepare for a potential "second round." Even had Israel not been at war and immigrants not arriving at such an extraordinary rate, the very recent establishment of the state entailed formidable teething problems in their own right.

There was an immediate need to obtain capital for investment purposes and for the acquisition of essential products from abroad. The exclusion of the Israeli pound from the sterling bloc adversely affected the country's foreign exchange balance. Foreign reserves fell to such a low point that the ability of the state to finance the importation of products such as wheat, flour and oil was put in doubt.[43] The raising of funds internally was also problematic on account of the limited size of the country's national income, the inchoate nature of the civil service and because the population was not accustomed to paying taxes.[44] In 1950, taxes as a proportion of Gross National Income amounted to only 13.0 percent. (By 1959 they had risen to 26.8 percent.)[45]

Fortunately, the Jewish Agency, funded by World Jewry, assumed responsibility for immigrant housing and for fostering agricultural settlements. This still left the government with the need to attend to a host of other pressing needs, ranging from defense, education, the provision of public infrastructure, internal security, the establishment of development towns, and so on. In Israel's first financial year, the budget deficit amounted to 40 percent of revenue. Then during the following two years, it exceeded revenue by a factor of two.[46] Essentially, the budget was financed by the expansion of the money supply. Subsequent inflationary pressures were partly moderated by a combination of price controls and product rationing.

Rationing of elementary necessities (including clothes) came into effect in March 1949. It arose following a serious shortfall in agricultural output as a consequence of the abrupt exodus of Arab farmers, the mobilization of Jewish ones, and war damage.[47] Particularly scarce were vegetables, fruit, milk, eggs, and meat. The system of rationing was meant to guarantee that the average per capita daily calorie intake would be in the 2,700–800 range.[48] Two food items seemed to have predominated. One was frozen fish (especially cod fillets) imported from Northern Europe and the other was locally grown eggplant (aubergine). Of the latter, Dr Zvi Dinstein recollected that there "were about 20 different ways of cooking it; it could, for instance, be used to make a sweet or a sour cream salad, a bitter 'apple sauce,' an ersatz 'chopped liver,' a soup, or a pudding. It could be fried, baked, boiled, sautéed, or scrambled. People became sick at the sight of it."[49] In addition, average diets mainly but not exclusively included bread, some potatoes and other vegetables, olives, and skimmed milk cheese. Three eggs were allocated per person per month and virtually no meat was available. Children had access to milk, fruit, and eggs. Chicory was used as a substitute for coffee. The public obtained its food rations by registering with specific retailers who in turn were supplied on the basis of their customer numbers. Hotels maintained two different sets of menus, one for Israelis and another for overseas visitors.

Rationing, as the Israeli economist Nadav Halevi noted, "ensured a fairly equitable distribution of basic necessities among the entire population."[50] By limiting general consumption, it also facilitated a reasonably high level of investment. On the down side, it engendered a thriving and widespread black market stimulated in part by the frustration of excessive queuing, since not all rationed goods were simultaneously available. Individuals from a wide range of social backgrounds participated, with members of the kibbutz movement being no exception.

In 1951, management of the economy began to change course. A restrictive monetary policy combined with a curb on deficit government spending was introduced. A year later a new currency was issued with new notes being exchanged for old ones at only 90 percent of their face value. At the same time, the old notes ceased to be legal tender.[51] The currency was then substantially devalued (from 0.57 to 1.8 Israeli pounds to the US dollar) and price controls were lifted. Rationing began to be phased out and from February 1952 it no longer applied to major food and clothing items.

Controls continued to be enforced in relation to foreign exchange whereby a multiple exchange rate system determined specific foreign exchange rates for various economic sectors or enterprises in keeping with national priorities. Faced with persistent foreign trade deficits, rather than drastically reducing imports, the government sought additional foreign resources to finance them.[52] To some degree, it succeeded. After the 1949 elections, the US recognized Israel de jure and approved a $100 million loan from the Export–Import Bank. The loan provided a temporary boost to Israel's overburdened and flagging economy but it fell short of establishing a sufficient basis for sustained development. In 1952 the US began to provide Israel with general economic assistance. This was supplemented by the floating of loans through the Israel Bonds Organization and by private donations to the US-based United Jewish Appeal. Still, an insufficiency of foreign exchange continued to act as a break on the rate of growth of national income.

German reparations

Desperate to keep Israel's economy afloat, in January 1951 Ben-Gurion decided to seek reparations from Germany. Hoping to avoid direct dealings with any German authority, in March 1951 Israel submitted a claim amounting to $1.5 billion to the occupying powers, that is, the United States, the Soviet Union, Britain, and France, for Jewish property pillaged by the Nazis.[53] The sum in question was estimated to be the amount of capital that Israel required for settling and rehabilitating Holocaust survivors. In turn, the United States, Britain, and France indicated that Israel's claim ought to be considered by the Germans themselves. (The Russians simply did not respond.) As it happened, Konrad Adenauer, West Germany's chancellor, soon expressed a willingness to provide compensation, paving the way for discussions between Israel and West Germany, first secretly and then openly. The Israelis insisted that the Germans unequivocally accept collective responsibility for war crimes inflicted upon the Jewish people. But in a speech delivered in September 1951 to the Bundestag, Adenauer simply stated that "the overwhelming majority of the German people abominated the crimes committed against the Jews." Since "the unspeakable crimes" were committed in the name of the German people, they necessitated "moral and material indemnity."[54] Faced with the realization that such equivocations would neither satisfy Israel nor World Jewry, Adenauer modified his stance. On December 6, 1951 in a meeting with Nahum Goldmann, head of the World Jewish Congress, he finally accepted government responsibility for Germany's Nazi past and an obligation in principle to provide one billion dollars as West Germany's share of the amount sought by Israel.[55] (When Israel subsequently requested the other third, that is, five hundred million dollars, from East Germany it was met with stony silence.) On December 30, given Adenauer's manifest desire for reconciliation, the Israeli government decided to enter into open negotiations with its German counterparts.

Adenauer's personal anti-Nazi record notwithstanding, most Israelis abhorred the prospect of obtaining what they considered as Danegeld from their former tormentors. Misgivings were voiced by the Israeli press and by many members of the Knesset. Spearheading the opposition against German reparations was Begin (on behalf of Herut) and the leftwing Mapam Party that likened West Germany to a neo-Nazi state.[56]

Begin made opposition to any deal with Adenauer his personal crusade. It rescued him from the political wilderness arising from his party's dismal performance in the 1951 general election where its representation fell from fourteen to eight seats. So depressed was he by that turn of events that he contemplated withdrawing from politics to pursue a legal career.[57] When the second Knesset convened in August 1951, he was absent from the swearing-in ceremony. While abroad to buff up his spirits, he received news of the impending reparations negotiations, which he seized upon as a vehicle for making a political comeback. Recouping his former self-confidence, he returned home to mount a challenge to Israel conducting talks with Germany. The main thrust of his argument was that there was no such thing as a German without Jewish blood on his or her hands and that the acceptance of German money would cast a slur on Jewish honor leading to "eternal shame."[58] As far as Begin was concerned, negotiating with Germany was "the ultimate abomination, the like of which we have not known since we became a nation."[59] That political opportunism might possibly have motivated Begin is indicated by his having earlier suggested to Sharett that Israel "demand compensation for Jewish property plundered by the Germans."[60] Nevertheless, his defenders maintained that it was not German money he objected to but the process of negotiating for it.[61]

On January 7, 1952, the Knesset began debating the government's decision to negotiate with Germany. Threatened with potential public disorder by reparation opponents, the government took the precaution of diverting traffic from sensitive areas, erecting barbed-wire roadblocks and mobilizing a large number of police donning riot gear. A few hundred meters from the Knesset, Begin harangued a large crowd (estimated at 15,000) from a balcony of the Aviv Hotel in Zion Square. He declared that every single German, Adenauer included, was a Nazi murderer. Adding a dramatic tone to his bombast, Begin forecast that reparation opponents would be rounded up and herded into concentration camps where they would not be cowed. "Either freedom or death," he shouted, "no surrender." For extra effect, he went on to announce that Israeli police were equipped with German-made gas canisters, "the same gases that asphyxiated our parents."[62] A highly emotionally charged mob then followed him to the Knesset, breaking through police barricades, overturning parked cars and hurling rocks. Windows were shattered and some stones burst into the parliamentary chamber. With residual tear gas fumes wafting in, one parliamentarian fainted. As the debate continued, loud interjections interrupted speeches and mutual recriminations between Begin and Ben-Gurion were exchanged with each calling the other a hooligan. (Begin was suspended from the Knesset for three months for unbecoming behavior.) After trying in vain to subdue the rioters, the police summoned the army and only after six hours of continued mayhem was calm restored. In the process, 92 policemen and 36 rioters were injured.[63] Two days later, Ben-Gurion carried the Knesset with a vote of 61 to 50. Recognizing that any compensation, no matter how large, would not constitute restitution for the loss of human life or expiation for Jewish suffering, Ben-Gurion held that the reparations were necessary to deprive the Jewish murderers of the material benefits of their plunder.[64]

The historic Knesset vote did not put an immediate end to Begin's rabble rousing. In March, addressing a rally in Tel Aviv, he invited his audience to withhold taxes and went on to suggest that the government (as if it were a non-elected one without public support) existed by force of bayonets. Begin then obliquely called for open rebellion by declaring "we [presumably the ex-Irgun members within his party] have experience in breaking the force of bayonets."[65] Word spread that after the meeting the audience was to be incited to march toward key Histadrut buildings and set them ablaze. As a precaution, workers from labor settlements, armed with short clubs secreted in their clothes, attended the assembly. Begin was informed of their presence and as the meeting concluded he advised his supporters to disperse peacefully, which they did.[66]

Begin's general inflammatory remarks made a deep impression on Dov Shilanski, a Herut stalwart, who in October 1952 was detained outside the Israeli Foreign Ministry carrying a bomb set to detonate within minutes of his arrest. Shilanski was sentenced to imprisonment for a period of 21 months.[67] Concerned with such unsavory developments, Shmuel Merlin, the Herut party's secretary, expressed his misgivings to Begin. Failing to obtain adequate reassurances, Merlin resigned. Never again did he converse with his former leader.[68]

On March 18, 1953, Israel and Germany concluded a reparations agreement by which West Germany was to provide Israel with $750 million worth of goods and services over a 12–14 year period. In addition, $107 million were earmarked for a committee representing world Jewish bodies. Most of such funds remained in Israel. Many feared that West Germany would not honor its undertaking but their skepticism was unfounded.[69] The reparations agreement provided Israel

Plate 4.2   *Begin protesting against German reparations. The Hebrew reads: "Our honor will not be traded for money. Our blood will not be atoned with merchandise. We will erase the shame"*

with much needed capital equipment, including 41 merchant ships, 4 tankers, a floating dock, a steelworks, and a copper smelting plant.[70] Israel also obtained raw materials such as iron and steel, copper, lead, rubber, wheat, and sugar. What is more, West Germany began to make restitution payments to individual Nazi victims and by the end of 1965 those living in Israel had received $9 billion.[71] The resources that Israel obtained contributed significantly to the improvement of its economy. In the opinion of a leading Israeli bank, "the receipt of German reparation goods was one of the factors which led to the steep rise in the living standards of the Israeli man-in-the-street."[72]

Ben-Gurion hailed the reparations agreement as a remarkable achievement, for it was not extracted by the threat of force but by the strength of moral imperatives.[73] Apart from its economic value, it represented the first time in Jewish history that Jewish victims or the state representing them had been compensated by a nation that had oppressed them.

General economic growth and development

By 1954, when the Bank of Israel (the country's central bank) was established with David Horowitz as its first governor, the economy recovered and continued to grow at an impressive rate. This occurred as a result of expansionary fiscal and monetary policies, the elimination of almost all direct non-monetary controls and the provision of protection to local industries by means of import quotas.[74] Besides reparations transfers, other growth-promoting factors included the rise in the work force, the adaptability of migrants to local labor conditions, the ready availability of entrepreneurs and experts in important fields of economic enterprise, a large increase in investment, and a buoyant consumer demand.[75]

Between 1950 and 1960, gross national product rose annually by an average of 10 percent, enabling annual per capita income to increase by 6.5 percent. Such rates were among the world's highest,[76] exceeding even those of Japan.[77] Concomitant with a rise in incomes was a rise in living standards. This is suggested by a relatively small increase in the demand for foodstuffs as opposed to general consumer items such as clothes, shoes, furniture, and entertainment.[78] More concretely, there was a sharp drop in infant mortality rates, a rise in life expectancies, a decline in housing density (number of people per room) and an almost universal access (of the Jewish population) to running water and electricity. In the latter half of the 1950s, the unemployment rate consistently declined, falling from 9.2 percent in 1953 to 5.8 percent by 1958.[79]

Those who remained unemployed were assisted by public works programs. They were means tested and allocated a minimum number of employment days per month. Wages paid were lower than those on the open market but at least the jobless were assured of a basic income. As a by-product of the public work schemes, the excess supply of labor was somewhat curtailed, which also helped sustain real wages.[80]

Within the industrial sector a degree of structural change was afoot. There was a relative decline in the production of clothing and foot-wear, an expansion of diamond polishing (which, with citrus products, commanded a lion's share of total exports) and the establishment of an automobile tire plant. However, progress fell short of the country's long-term potential. The development of manufacturing was hindered by various inauspicious circumstances. In the absence of peace, Israel had to divert much of its scarce resources to defense. Between 1950 and 1960, the yearly expenditure for the maintenance and improvement of the IDF amounted to an average of 9 percent of GNP.[81] Not fac-tored into that outlay was the economic cost of the draft that withdrew thousands of potential employees from the work force. Israel's ongoing conflict with its neighbors gave rise in the spring of 1950 to an Arab campaign to impose a trade and investment embargo on the Jewish state. Enlisting the support of non-Arab Muslim countries, the Arab League threatened to boycott any company, including shipping and general transport ones, which had commercial ties with Israel.

On the agricultural front, Israel's capacity to produce its own food needs improved considerably. Whereas in 1952 70 percent of food requirements emanated from abroad, by 1958 (with a vastly enhanced population) only 29 percent did.[82] The surge in agricultural output arose from increased land use, the establishment of new farms, and the adoption of productivity enhancing measures. State-owned land that had previously been held by the British Mandatory Government and which had been denied to Jews was widely distributed. Added to that, Jewish farmers came into possession of large quantities of abandoned Arab property (discussed at greater length in chapter 7). Kibbutzim in particular were substantial beneficiaries, with their control of land rising from 468,000 dunams[83] in 1947 to 1,602,000 in 1952.[84] Furthermore, between 1948 and the end of 1952, 229 new farm settlements were added to the 277 that had existed in 1947.[85] Output per dunam was enhanced by an increase in irrigation and farm mechanization, the widespread use of fertilizers and pesticides, agricultural research, and the dissemination of agronomic techniques and know-how.

Of all the economic sectors, growth in the building industry was the most dynamic. Between 1948 and 1955, nearly 150,000 apartments were constructed, mainly by government and Jewish Agency-owned companies.[86] To appreciate the effort Israel expended, it should be noted that in the period in question an average of 19 new apartments were made available to every 1000 inhabitants, compared with four for the Soviet Union, six for Poland and ten for West Germany.[87] (The three latter countries were also faced with acute housing shortages.)

A large number of homes were built in development towns which were often situated in relatively remote areas in keeping with the government's decentralization policy. While most development towns began from scratch, some, such as Kiryat Malahi (originally Kastina), were grafted onto existing hamlets or townships, usually abandoned Arab ones. Among the development towns were: Ashkelon, Beit Shemesh, Kiryat Shmona, Shlomi, Eilat, Yeruham, Beit Shean, Sederot, Hatzor Hagalit, Mizpe Ramon, Kiryat Gat, Ofakim, Ashdod, Dimona, Netivot, Maalot, Natzeret Ilit, Beersheba, Ramlah, Lod, Safad, Tiberias, Afula, and Acco. Within Israel's first decade some thirty development towns and villages came into being,[88] to be followed in the early 1960s by Arad and Karmiel. In some instances towns officially designated as development ones were already well established urban centers like Tiberias, Afula, and Safed.

Employment in development towns primarily revolved around a single labor intensive enterprise, such as a textile factory or a food processing plant. With most residents being poorly educated immigrants and with the small pool of skilled and professional workers seeking their fortune elsewhere, incentives for capital intensive companies to invest in development towns were all but non-existent.

Under Ben-Gurion's inspiration, a grandiose settlement program was inaugurated in the Lahish area, which included the area where, during the War of Independence, the Egyptians were stationed in and near Faluja. In February 1954, Ben-Gurion commissioned Alhanan Yeshai, a co-resident of Kibbutz Sde Boker, to sound out government and Jewish Agency regional planners as to whether they would look kindly on fostering a bloc of settlements in the Negev. After being stonewalled, Yeshai perchance met with Ra'anan Weitz who was in the process of preparing a similar proposal. Weitz then visited Ben-Gurion and the two thrashed out a program involving the development of a large land area containing numerous farming communities supported by service centers. Since, in Weitz's view, the realization of their plans depended on Levi Eshkol, who was minister of finance, Yeshai approached him to enlist his support. As was his wont, Eshkol was at first equivocal but on being pressed for a definite response, he replied, "Look, the old man is mostly right and what would happen if he is right this time and I am not? You know what, Alhanan, go and tell him that I am in favour of it."[89] Thus the Lahish settlement scheme got under way. Within the next two and a half years, 22 farm settlements of various types and sizes sprang up, supported by two rural centers and the new city of Kiryat Gat. Within the latter a number of agricultural processing plants, a textile factory, and various educational institutes were established. It was cautiously anticipated that Kiryat Gat's population would reach 8,000–9,000, yet by 1980 it had surpassed 20,000 and continued to expand vigorously thereafter.[90]

Government control, income inequality and allied issues

The Israeli economy was characterized by a high degree of state dirigisme. That is, the government and quasi-government bodies assumed control of the direction of most of the country's resources. This was so despite the economy being a mixed one with a vibrant private sector. Israel's inordinate defense outlays plus the magnitude of the burden of absorbing so many immigrants over so brief a time span fostered state intervention, as did the fact that foreign government and private aid was vested with the regime and its associated organs. Included in the public sector were the Jewish Agency, the Jewish National Fund, the Foundation Fund (Keren Hayesod) and the Zionist Organization.

Those organizations in conjunction with the Histadrut pursued national objectives as interpreted by Mapai.

The government's all-embracing economic management gave rise to a system of patronage between politicians and public officials on the one hand and the general public on the other. Political parties scrambled for access to the levers of power in order to channel funds to their own vested interests. To that end, the distribution of cabinet portfolios and the appointment of senior bureaucrats were of paramount importance. With many ministries being largely staffed by political party cronies, an ethos of administering to the public without fear or favor was alien to the civil service. Through their connections with the powers that be (described in Hebrew as *proteksia*), a new category of upstarts (known as "jobniks") ensconced themselves in cushy lucrative posts, some of which were pure boondoggles. The new elite were able to skim off privileges not only in the sphere of employment but also in relation to housing, education, health, automobiles, luxury items, and foreign travel. Since those distant from officialdom were liable to become relatively under-privileged, the practice of *proteksia* was widely resented and led to the undermining of civilian morale.[91]

Increases in income inequality turned out to be not a passing phe-nomenon but a permanent feature of the country's social landscape.[92] Beside the question of *proteksia*, two other factors in particular were significant. First, the more educated veterans were generally better placed than recent arrivals in securing higher paid employment. This meant that during the course of the 1950s, the differential in average wage earnings between new immigrants and old timers widened. At first immigrants received close to 80 percent of the salary of the established population but toward the end of the decade their average relative income fell to around 70 percent.[93] Second, recipients of monthly German pensions enjoyed annual incomes in excess of 30 percent of the national average.[94] Nevertheless, there were some social and eco-nomic considerations that ameliorated income inequality. Thanks to the Histadrut, wage differentials, though growing, were still relatively modest. A progressive taxation system was gradually being put in place, elementary education was free, almost everyone had medical insurance and home ownership became near universal on account of the general availability of low interest rate mortgages.[95]

Trends in the Kibbutz movement

Israeli kibbutzim represented a unique social experiment in the search for a just and egalitarian society. Organized along lines of complete equality, the kibbutzim epitomized a truly democratic and voluntary communist commune where people contributed according to their abilities and received according to their needs. Kibbutzim, which were entirely self-contained, provided members with employment, housing, basic consumer goods, education, childcare, welfare services, cultural facilities, comradeship and support in old age. Made up of enthusiastic idealists, kibbutzniks (members of kibbutzim) contributed disproportionately in the struggle for Israel's independence and ongoing defense.

In 1948, kibbutz members accounted for 8.12 percent of the Jewish population. By 1960, though their numbers had risen from 58,204 to 77,955 (that is, by 34 percent), their overall representation receded to 3.63 percent.[96] Numerous forces accounted for their relative decline. New immigrants overwhelmingly wished to live in urban areas. Of those that could be persuaded to venture into farming, most preferred to settle in moshavim where private ownership and initiative existed. In the past, kibbutzim drew upon graduates of pioneering Zionist youth movements in Eastern and Central Europe. But in the aftermath of the Second World War once surviving youth movement activists were absorbed, additional recruits could only be found within Israel and western countries. Such sources by no means measured up to the traditional ones. As if that were not enough, living standards in most kibbutzim lagged behind those of the rest of the population. Tempted by new openings in the public service and other sectors of the economy, many members, including prominent ones, forsook the kibbutz movement.[97] A general diminution of the need for stoic self-sacrifice in the framework of the transition from pre-state strife to post-war relative normalcy vitiated the ties that bound members to a social community that required of them the suppression of personal ambitions for the sake of the common weal.

Kibbutzim were criticized for providing little, if any, help to new immigrants, especially those from Arab countries. They were faulted for not including them in their schools and work force. Such strictures were only partially warranted. For instance, one Iraqi immigrant recalled that in 1953, when his family was staying in a *ma'abarah*, he and his four siblings attended a kibbutz boarding school free of charge.[98] Nevertheless, that was a rare exception. Apart from the costs that would have been entailed in teaching immigrants, kibbutz education aimed at instilling collective and pioneering values that were at variance with those of immigrant parents. A large and indiscriminate intake of non-kibbutz students would therefore have made the attainment of kibbutz pedagogical objectives somewhat more elusive.

As for employing outsiders, for good or for bad, such an option conflicted with a basic kibbutz tenet of being totally self-reliant and not deriving benefits from the "exploitation" of hired hands. While in later years kibbutzim looked upon the use of external personnel as both desirable and natural, throughout the 1950s it was only with extreme reluctance that they took on a limited number of outsiders. In 1952, in response to government incentives and political pressures, they employed more than 6,000 workers.[99] Ironically, kibbutzim were never in the slightest bit averse to "hosting" volunteers who toiled for board and lodgings only. Nor, as Ben-Rafael remarked, did they ever consider returning surplus land to the state which on account of insufficient farm hands they could not utilize.[100]

The kibbutz movement was organized into a number of kibbutz federations that provided their constituents with financial and other assistance. At Israel's formation there were the three socialist federations of Kibbutz Meuhad, Hever Hakvutzot and Kibbutz Artzi, a small number of kibbutzim associated with the Progressive Party and a small religious kibbutz federation. The federations were distinguished by differences in the nature of the kibbutzim they supported, ranging from small and intimate ones to all embracing large collectives with some memberships exceeding a thousand. Furthermore, they were based on differing world outlooks and party affiliations.

By the beginning of the 1950s, a crisis evolved within the Kibbutz Meuhad Federation. It climaxed in 1951–2 with members being divided between those that uncritically abided by the ideological and practical dictates of the Soviet Union and those that pursued a more moderate pro-western orientation. Essentially, this reflected the fact that, while most members supported the Marxist Mapam party, a large minority favored Mapai. Each faction was troubled by the possibility of a change in political influence as newcomers were taken in.[101] One outstanding bone of contention revolved around the issue of whether or not to glorify the Soviet Union within kibbutz schools and public assemblies. The reference to Russia by some as their "second homeland" affronted those with less starry-eyed visions of the "workers' paradise" and who found reports of growing Soviet anti-Semitism deeply disturbing. In allocating key kibbutz administrative posts, candidates' attitudes to communism and to Ben-Gurion's policies were taken into account.[102]

In those days, ideological convictions were passionately upheld and were the defining characteristics of their adherents. Within the narrow confines of a kibbutz society, many found it difficult, if not impossible, to continue living closely with those whose views they found abhorrent. Nerves became so frayed that in some kibbutzim partitions were erected in common dining rooms so that members could enjoy their meals without having to face their antagonists. Incidents of physical assault were not unknown and, on at least one occasion, police intervention was sought.[103] With the cleavage between members being so profound, kibbutzim either bifurcated or appreciable numbers left for more compatible surroundings. In 1951, as some Kibbutz Meuhad settlements and members realigned themselves with the Hever Hakvutzot Federation, it was renamed Ihud Hakibbutzim v'Hakvutzot.

Religion and the state

Within Israel there has never been a clear separation of state and religion. Marriage, divorce and burial proceedings have always been under the exclusive control of religious authorities. On the Sabbath and other Jewish Holy Days, operations of business enterprises, entertainment outlets and public transport are all severely, if not totally, proscribed. Such a state of affairs arose, among other things, through the clout and intermediation of religious political parties which, throughout Israel's brief history, have been present in virtually all its governments. With the combined religious parties usually not securing more than 15 percent of the popular vote, it would seem that Mapai (the leading party) had the option of excluding them from the corridors of power. But its two major prospective secular partners, Mapam to its left and the General

Zionists to its right, frequently submitted coalition entry pre-conditions that were incompatible with Mapai's social democratic ideals.

During the 1950s, the religious parties, by virtue of their willingness to abide by just about all aspects of Mapai's general program provided it met their basic theocratic demands, presented themselves as malleable coalition partners. Apart from being preoccupied with ritualistic dogma and norms, they rarely focused on ethical issues and have never expressed an interest in seeing them raised in the Knesset.[104] Their prime objective has been the promotion of "conspicuous" religion embodying form rather than content. From Mapai's point of view, granting them a measure of leeway seemed a small price to pay in promoting policies that it regarded as being of critical importance to Israel's security, economy, and social wellbeing. When, in December 1959, Mapai could have comfortably formed a coalition without any religious representation, Ben-Gurion still invited Mafdal (the National Religious Party) to participate. He hoped to rely on it as a counterweight to the Mapam and Ahdut Ha'avodah parties.[105]

Of the religious parties, the two of the Mizrahi (later combined into Mafdal) were ardent Zionists. Although Agudat Yisrael had an anti-Zionist past, it took part in the general political process and was included in the first elected government. In that sense, it differed from the Neturei Karta (Guardians of the City) that in 1937 seceded from it. During the first election, the Neturei Karta posted a proclamation advising Jews that by voting they would be party to "the establishment of an heretical regime that rebels against the kingdom of heaven."[106] As Amram Blau, one of their sages affirmed, the Zionists "have dispossessed Israel [the Jewish people] and call themselves by her name. Having seized dominion over her, they claim to be her representatives and her rulers, while the real Israel, the people of the Lord, the people of the Torah, the Holy people, cries out against this obvious falsification."[107] To this day, Neturei Karta adherents have not recognized Israel and, while still living there (in Mea Shearim, Jerusalem), they pay no taxes nor do they cooperate with any of the state's officials. Effectively, they are a law unto themselves.

The participation in the central government of the religious parties with secular ones was replicated within municipal authorities. By such means, a religious minority was able to impose a degree of orthodox

Jewish laws and practices on a largely secular population. In pursuit of those objectives, the official orthodox establishment secured government disbursements. Legislation enacted in August 1949 stipulates that one third of the cost of providing Jewish religious services shall be borne by the central government and the remaining two thirds by local authorities.[108] Through control of the Ministry of Religious Affairs, the religious parties have funneled vast amounts of money to their followers. But the matter did not rest there. In 1961, Dr Joseph Burg, as minister of social welfare, proudly informed the National Religious Party (Mafdal) that he was depositing "great sums" into the party's coffers. His director, Dr Kurtz, explained that under Burg's leadership, the Ministry was increasingly assuming a party character and, in support of that contention, he cited the fact that of 60,000 Israeli pounds targeted for development, 54,000 were submitted to religious bodies.[109]

Such dealings were criticized by Professor Yeshayahu Leibowitz, a devoutly orthodox Jew, who complained that "only in the state of Israel, which transformed religion into a function of the secular government, has the Jewish religious community been corrupted and become accustomed to financial dependence upon a secular authority."[110] Liebowitz's views were similar to those of President Weizmann who wrote: "We must have a clear line of demarcation between legitimate religious aspirations, on the one hand, and on the other hand the lust for power which is sometimes exhibited by pseudo-religious groups . . . Israel cannot put the clock back by making religion the cardinal principle in the conduct of the state."[111] Far from questioning the propriety of state subsidies, the religious bloc has incessantly complained that they were insufficient.[112] As if to make matters worse, no provision was ever made for the participation of reform or conservative Jewish denominations, which are not permitted to undertake wedding ceremonies, issue divorces or convert people to Judaism. This has meant that Jews in Israel have had far less freedom to choose their mode of religious observance than Jews in the diaspora.[113]

While the non-religious camp was prepared to tolerate what came to be known as the status quo in public religious affairs, it took exception to the unrelenting efforts of the religious parties to extend the status quo's boundaries. A number of religious spokesmen, such as Yeshayahu Bernstein, openly admitted that there was "no doubt as to the duty to coerce in order to enforce compliance with the Mitzvot (religious commands) of the Torah, *provided you have the power*."[114] What has emerged in Israel is that while orthodox Jews are in no way compelled to adjust their behaviour to meet with majority standards, non-observant ones are increasingly required to comply with certain religious restrictions, especially in relation to marriage and divorce.[115] Without question, *compelling all* Israeli Jews to marry in keeping with Jewish orthodox dogma constitutes religious coercion.[116] The religious sector has indeed recognized this. Hazzani, a Mizrahi stalwart, openly wrote that his party was responsible for the continuation of religious legislation and thereby for the imposition of religious coercion.[117]

One issue that on the face of it ought not to have involved religious considerations was the question of male military conscription. Conscription was meant to be universal, but the law allowed for the minister concerned to exempt certain individuals. Mounting a shrill campaign in the late forties and early fifties against conscription, the Haredim (God fearing extreme orthodox Jews) argued that Yeshiva students (students of a religious academy) ought not to serve in the army. It was claimed that the time spent there would have a deleterious effect on their religious education. In all likelihood what the Haredim really feared was that their cloistered youth would be exposed to a wider and alien social milieu. What influenced the government in their favor was that, in the wake of the Holocaust, there was a dearth of young Talmud students.[118] Such an outcome evoked Ben-Gurion and others to sympathize with the desire of the Haredim to refurbish their reservoir of learned rabbis. That of course meant that the Yeshiva students won the day. In later years, contrary to Ben-Gurion's expectations, their ranks ultimately swelled to many thousands of fit and able young draft shirkers.

The controversy over conscription also centered on women called upon to perform non-combat service roles. In the face of overwhelming opposition from a wide range of religious bodies, it was decided that, unlike secular women, religious ones would not be drafted into the IDF. (Women who were married, pregnant or had children were also exempt.) However, in 1953, despite impassioned opposition from Chief Rabbi Herzog and the Haredim, a law was passed, with the backing of members of the religious kibbutzim and elements of Hapoel Hamizrahi, requiring eighteen-year-old religious women to undertake civil public service.[119] Article 8 of the law in question (the National Services Law) clearly specified that opportunities to maintain a religious way of life were to be granted. Ben-Gurion personally promised that the women would be lodged in religious settlements and where possible in proximity to their homes.[120] Ben-Gurion's gesture failed to satisfy the Haredim who likened the law to one that violated the *halaha* (religious laws and practice) and which ought to be defied, if need be at the risk of death. Such a response was a direct continuation of their earlier opposition in 1951 when the legislation was first mooted and when a religious fanatic attempted to bomb the Knesset. Instead of enforcing the law, the authorities decided to turn a blind eye to the women that flouted it. While that may have reduced social tensions, it both derogated respect for the rule of law and violated the general dictates of fairness.

Perhaps of all the rifts across the religious–secular divide, the question of determining just who is a Jew has been the most vexing. The issue has its origins in the 1950 Law of Return that grants all Jews (except those posing a threat to public health or to the state) an automatic right to migrate to Israel. Not by accident did the Law refrain from specifying how a Jew is defined. In 1958 Israel Bar-Yehuda, the minister of the interior, instructed his officials to record a person as being of Jewish nationality if he or she in good faith declared that to be the case. Similarly, if both parents, irrespective of their own Jewish status, indicated that they wished their child to be accepted as a Jew then the child had to be so registered. That directive, which embodied the established but *unwritten* practice of four of Bar-Yehuda's predecessors, was at odds with the orthodox definition of a Jew whereby only the offspring of a Jewish mother or recognized converts to Judaism are deemed to be Jewish.

So incensed was Mafdal by Bar-Yehuda's injunction that it withdrew from the government. It argued that if children that the Rabbinate did not recognize as being Jewish were registered as Jewish nationals, then on reaching maturity, the Rabbinate would be unable to marry them. As a corollary, unwelcome pressures for the introduction of civil marriages would arise. At stake was whether the designating of someone as being a Jewish national rested with the elected Israeli government or with the non-elected orthodox clergy. After the 1959 general election with

Mafdal's return to the front bench and with its securing the ministry of internal affairs, the imbroglio was temporarily defused by the abrogation of Bar-Yehuda's ruling.

Foreign affairs

Toward the end of 1948, Israel applied for membership of the United Nations. For the application to be successful, the Security Council had to recommend it to the General Assembly for its approval. However, Israel failed to gain Security Council backing for want of support from Britain and France. The French delegate felt that "one should not forget that the Arabs are opposed to the State of Israel," whereas the British spokesman requested that the issue of Israel's UN membership be deferred for an unlimited period.[121] A positive outcome was secured when Israel reapplied in March 1949. The Security Council then endorsed Israel's application by a vote of seven in favor, one against (Egypt) and one abstention (Britain) and by May the General Assembly had given its blessing. Thirty-seven member states assented, twelve (including six Arab and three Muslim states as well as India, Burma and Ethiopia) were opposed and nine abstained. Among the latter were Britain, Belgium, Denmark, Greece, and Sweden. Upon the announcement of the General Assembly's vote, Moshe Sharett, the head of the Israeli delegation, approached the dais to deliver his maiden speech. As he did so, the Arab representatives stormed out in a fit of pique.

At first Israel wished to remain detached from either the communist or capitalist blocs. It was motivated by a desire to preserve the backing of the Soviet Union, which voted for the partition of Palestine and which supported Israel in 1948–9, at a time when Britain sought to undermine the Jewish state and the US refused to arm it. Above all, Israel hoped that ultimately the Jews in Eastern Europe and Russia would be permitted to emigrate.[122] In September 1950, Israel, much to the displeasure of the US, supported China's application for UN membership. Later that year, as China entered the Korean War, Israel abandoned its neutral posture to place itself firmly within the western camp. Such a move would have been taken sooner or later given Israel's need for US economic assistance, the Soviet Union's wooing of the Arabs, and the growing animosity of the Third World.

Thanks to the Arab and Muslim states, the communist countries and their Third World allies, Israel had consistently been treated as a UN member with less than full standing. It has constantly been excluded from the Security Council and at one stage was not assured the elementary right of participating in all UN-sponsored forums. In 1950, on encountering obstacles in attending a UN Food and Agriculture Organization Conference, Israel proposed that the UN guarantee all members ready access to such gatherings. Much to Israel's astonishment, its resolution was overwhelmingly rejected. Only four of the forty states that participated voted in its favor.[123]

During Israel's first 19 years, on only one fleeting occasion did it secure UN support. In 1950, Egypt denied vessels sailing to and from Israel access to the Suez Canal. By the terms of a charter drawn up in 1881 in Istanbul by maritime powers (a charter which Egypt endorsed), in both times of war and of peace, free and open passage within the Canal was to be made available to all ships (including battleships) irrespective of their flags of origin.[124] The exclusion of Israeli and other vessels plying goods to and from Israel also violated the spirit of the Israel–Egypt armistice agreement that officially terminated the state of war between the two countries and which was meant to serve as a prelude to a formal peace treaty. On September 1, 1951, following the lodgment of a complaint by Israel, the Security Council reaffirmed Israel's right to traverse the Canal. Egypt in turn treated the Security Council's resolution with contempt.

On September 28, 1954, an Israeli merchant ship, the *Bat Galim*, embarked from Ethiopia in an attempt to sail through the Suez Canal. As expected the ship was seized and its crew of ten arrested. Much to Israel's horror, the crew was also beaten and tortured.[125] Above all, the western powers showed total indifference to Egypt's non-compliance with the 1951 UN Security Council resolution. In the opinion of Walter Eytan, an Israeli diplomat, "they appeared to be less vexed with Egypt for this violation of Israel's rights than with Israel for provoking it."[126] The British Embassy in Tel Aviv reported that the approach of the *Bat Galim* to the Suez Canal was none other than an Israeli ruse for "extorting from the Security Council an effective ruling against Egypt."[127]

During the same year (1954), the Soviet Union vetoed a UN Security Council resolution sanctioning an Israeli development project at Bnot

Yaakov along the Syrian–Israeli boundary. Abba Eban, Israel's UN representative, then realized that henceforth "the UN Security Council would be closed to Israel as a court of appeal or redress."[128] In May 1956, when a report on the Israeli–Arab conflict drafted by the UN secretary general Dag Hammarskjöld was submitted to the Security Council, Ahmad Shukeiri, Syria's representative and later chairman of the PLO, objected to the use of the term "peaceful settlement on a mutually acceptable basis." Deferring to Arab, Iranian, and Soviet opposition, the offending text was duly deleted![129]

Western states were also party to the UN's unwarranted vilification of Israel. During the 1950s, both Britain and the USA routinely condemned Israel. As the British officer Meinertzhagen observed:

> It is an odd fact that the Arabs can utter on platforms, in their Press and on the radio, the wildest, most savage threats of annihilating every Jew on the soil of what they continue to call Palestine; but if an Israeli says that his people intend to defend themselves, screams of shocked protest come from our Foreign Office and the world in general."[130]

In 1953 Dulles informed the US Senate that it was in America's vital interest to improve its relations with the Arabs, especially as its standing (in Arab eyes) had consistently deteriorated since the Israeli War of Independence.[131] By sponsoring a UN Security Council resolution censoring Israel for preparing to divert water from the Jordan River (see chapter 7), Dulles felt that the US had "a heaven-sent opportunity to prove to the Arabs that America was their friend."[132]

The inexorable UN hostility, or at best indifference, to Israel was more or less inevitable. Arab member states, whose numbers rose from four in 1948 to eleven in the mid-1950s, represented over fifty million people as opposed to less than two million Israelis. Newly liberated Third World countries viewed the Arabs as their natural allies and, like the Soviet Union, they courted Arab favor. With their backing, Arab and Muslim states succeeded in excluding Israel from Third World forums which in turn became platforms for anti-Israel propaganda. Clear evidence of this was manifested in the opening conference of "non-aligned states," which convened in April 1955 at Bandung, Indonesia. Among the countries present were Turkey, Pakistan, and Iraq, which had all concluded a military pact with the UK but Israel, which then had no military alliance with any Great Power, was pointedly excluded. Setting a pattern for future "non-aligned" gatherings, the Bandung conference unanimously adopted a pro-Arab resolution proposed by Egypt's president, Abdel Nasser.

In emphasizing its empathy with the Arabs, the Soviet Union lost little time in demonizing Israel. By November 1955, Nikita Khrushchev, the communist party's first secretary, proclaimed that "ever since the first days of Israel's existence, Israel began to threaten its neighbors and to adopt unfriendly policies toward them."[133] Khrushchev's statement was sharply at odds with Russia's previous stance. For example, in March 1949, Yakov Malik, the Soviet UN representative, made it clear that the Soviet Union supported Israel's application for UN membership since Israel was "a peace loving state."[134] A sinister aspect of Soviet hostility toward Israel was that the country as such was held accountable for its "sins" and not simply the government in power. When, in October 1956, Israel, France and the UK were in conflict with Egypt, Russia recalled its ambassador from Israel but not from the other two belligerents. By 1957, Russia fabricated the libel that every time the United States wished to suppress any Arab liberation movement, it used Israel as a tool for such purposes.[135]

To offset its growing isolation, Israel tried to align itself with a major western power. It first turned to Britain with an expression of interest in joining the British Commonwealth but its overtures were brusquely spurned. No more success was met by putting out feelers to the USA.[136] In the early 1950s, the USA was prepared to provide military assistance to Egypt, Syria, and Iraq but when Israel requested similar treatment, it was, as Sharett discovered, "pushed to the back of the queue and offered not weapons but only military infrastructure."[137]

In exasperation, Ben-Gurion, in April 1955, informed his fellow citizens that at stake was not what the Gentiles say but rather what the Jews do.[138] That comment was generally and mistakenly interpreted to imply that Ben-Gurion hubristically assumed that the Jews could do as they please without taking foreign opinion into account. But Ben-Gurion merely wished to caution Israelis that, irrespective of whatever goodwill they might occasionally garner, they simply could not rely on outsiders to extricate them. Lacking hard and fast friends, Israel's fate rested in its own hands.

Although Israel had acquired widespread formal recognition, its frontiers were not regarded as inviolable. For varying reasons, both the UK and the USA wished to reduce Israel's territory. In April 1955, Israel informally learnt from a British member of parliament, Herbert Morrison, that Britain and the USA had reached a joint understanding embodied in a document named Project Alpha. They agreed that in the event of a conclusion of a peace treaty between Israel and the Arabs, Israel was to cede parts of the Negev. In exchange Israel was to receive the Gaza Strip along with all its Palestinians.[139] In September 1955, in a speech delivered at Guildhall, London, Anthony Eden, Britain's foreign minister, gave some indication of the contours of the Alpha plan. He declared that the solution to the Arab–Israeli conflict required a compromise that would ultimately require Israel's borders to fall somewhere between the present armistice lines and the positions suggested in the UN 1947 partition resolution.[140] Such a generous British offer of Israel's territory would still have left the Arabs dissatisfied. An internal report of the secretary general of the Arab League maintained that the Arabs not only expected Israel to withdraw to the *proposed UN 1947 boundaries* and to permit the return of all refugees but that they also required of Israel that it relinquish part of its attenuated land for refugees who might opt not to live there.[141]

By November 1955, US secretary of state Dulles provided Israel with full details of Project Alpha. In Dulles's version, there was to be a transfer of a large area of the Negev to Jordan and Egypt to enable them to maintain a territorial link with one another. Israel, if it so wished, could obtain the Gaza Strip *in exchange for transferring to Jordan compensating territory*.[142] The essence of the US–UK understanding is summed up in a joint unpublished memorandum that stated that "Israel must make concessions. The Arabs will not reconcile themselves to reaching a settlement with Israel with the present boundaries."[143] Such a conclusion was rather extraordinary, considering that both Egypt and Jordan, because of their war of aggression against Israel, were already holding large amounts of Palestinian land to which they had neither legal nor moral claims. Furthermore, contrary to what Morrison reported, Project Alpha never stipulated the word "peace," rather it alluded to an Arab "acceptance of Israel's existence."[144]

Both the USA and UK applied relentless pressure on Israel to solve the Arab refugee problem. On a visit to Israel in May 1952, Henry Byroade, the US assistant secretary of state for Near Eastern affairs, suggested to Ben-Gurion that he limit Jewish immigration to permit the wholesale return of Arab refugees.[145] This call was repeated by Byroade two years later in an address to a Jewish audience in Chicago where he added the proviso that Israel should abandon its Zionist mission by ceasing to consider itself the center of World Jewry.[146] Byroade's demand was couched in language that would have delighted the Arab League, for he described the Jews as sharing only a commonality of religion and not of nationhood.

As for Jerusalem, in November, 1949, Herbert Evatt, the Australian foreign minister, proposed in the UN General Assembly that the city be granted international status in keeping with the November 1947 UN partition resolution. (It came to light that Evatt had done so in order to obtain Catholic support for the Australian Labor party in a forthcoming general election.)[147] Evatt's resolution, approved by a large majority on December 10, had the backing of a host of Catholic states, communist countries and the Arab and Muslim bloc. As had subsequently become par for the course with many UN General Assembly resolutions, this one was based on rank prejudice and pure hypocrisy. When Jewish-held Jerusalem was systematically and repetitively bombed by the Arab Legion in 1948, the UN stood by with its hands folded doing nothing to assist the beleaguered Jews who were supposed to have received the protection of an international governor and police force. For four hundred years (1517–1917) the Christian world was reconciled to Turkish Muslim control of the city and when in 1948 the UN intermediator Count Folke Bernadotte favored handing it over to Transjordan, it raised no outcry. Only when the Jews, who had constituted a majority in Jerusalem since 1874, claimed sovereignty to the western part, in which there was not one of the seven major holy sites,[148] did members of the UN once more press for its internationalization. As Dulles put it, the "world religious community has claims on Jerusalem that supersede the political ones of any particular state."[149]

Sensing the danger that the November 1949 resolution posed, Ben-Gurion persuaded his cabinet to transfer all government offices, including the Knesset, to Jerusalem as a means of asserting that the city was indeed Israel's capital.[150] Sharett was against flouting the UN, as was Eliezer Kaplan, the minister of the treasury, who believed that "the transferring of the capital to Jerusalem was a fatal error and an unnecessary provocation."[151] Though expected protests from the Vatican, France and other Catholic countries eventuated, the risk of openly defying the UN paid off. Because Jordan had also opposed the city's internationalization, it was virtually certain that Britain would veto any attempt to impose it. Although no foreign state ultimately acknowledged West Jerusalem as Israel's capital, foreign diplomats and heads of state soon began to meet with the Israeli prime minister there. In December 1952, they proceeded to Jerusalem to attend the swearing-in ceremony of Israel's second president.

While Israel respected the holy sites of non-Jews in West Jerusalem, Jordan desecrated Jewish holy sites in its part of the city. In the words of Monsignor Oesterreicher (a catholic priest and scholar):

during Jordanian rule, 34 out of the Old City's 35 synagogues were dynamited. Some were turned into stables, others into chicken coops. There appeared to be no limit to the sacrilege. Many thousands of tombstones were taken from the ancient cemetery on the Mount of Olives to serve as building material and paving stones. A few were also used to surface a footpath leading to a latrine in a Jordanian army camp."[152]

Not once did the UN General Assembly issue Jordan with merely the mildest of rebukes. Evidently, the UN's declared zeal for the protection of the holy sites in Jerusalem did not apply to Jewish ones.

5

THE SCOURGE OF ARAB INFILTRATION

As mentioned at the conclusion of chapter 1, although Israel's War of Independence formally ended in July 1949, the struggle for Israel's survival has continued ever since. It is understandable that the Arabs, who regarded all of Palestine as their patrimony, would have objected to the UN partition resolution. From their perspective, there was no justification for hiving off territory they considered theirs for the purposes of allowing people, whom they perceived as foreigners, to establish a state in which some of their kinsmen would have had a minority status. But if the Arab position had been upheld, the Jews, who had deep historic and religious ties to Palestine, would, unlike the Arabs, have remained totally stateless. As the Jews saw things, there would have been no serious miscarriage of justice had the Arabs accepted the 1947 UN resolution. It would only have meant that half a million out of an estimated total of forty million of their compatriots would have lived in a Jewish state where they would have been granted full citizenship and enjoyed civil rights not available in any other Arab country. Even in terms of the partition of Palestine, the Jews believed that the Arabs would not have been hard done by. Of what was originally all of mandated Palestine, the British in 1922 set aside 77 percent for the exclusive use of Arabs in an area that became known as Transjordan. The UN partition scheme applied to the remaining 23 percent of Palestine. After Israel emerged from its War of Independence, it possessed merely 18 percent of the original mandated area. In other words, it laid claim to *far less* than 1 percent of all land within the Arab World.[1]

Within days of the war ending, the Arab media began to vent its anti-Israel spleen. As a case in point, one Syrian journalist wrote that the armistice agreements were a mark of shame that "would endure as long as that abominable state, known as Israel, remains within the heart of the Arab world."[2] In Egypt, a reporter claimed that "the Egyptian blood that saturates Palestine serves as a landmark which guides us to achieve the victory sought by our martyrs."[3] On the official level, despite Article 2 of the UN Charter prohibiting threats of force against any member state, Arab rulers blithely and regularly did so. In April 1953, General Naguib, who momentarily assumed the Egyptian leadership, exclaimed that "the existence of Israel is a cancer in the body of the Arab Nation, which ought to be exterminated."[4] (When Naguib seized power in July 1952, Ben-Gurion indicated that "Israel wishes to see Egypt free, independent, and progressive . . . We have no enmity against Egypt.")[5] In November 1954, mirroring Naguib's approach, the Syrian prime minister informed his parliament that "peace with Israel is not conceivable . . . Even if the refugees would be allowed to return, the Arabs will not conclude peace as long as Jews reside in the midst of Arab states."[6] A popular analogy that gained currency and which still circulates to the present day was the suggestion that just as the Christian crusaders were finally evicted, so too would the Jews of Israel experience a similar fate. That the Jews were returning to their ancestral homeland and that they were redeeming its soil by dint of the sweat of their own brows was a social and historic phenomenon with which the Arabs could never come to terms.

It did not take long for hostilities, albeit on a small scale, to resume. This occurred in the context of cross-border incursions. With Israel's borders being lengthy, tortuous, largely unmarked, situated for the most part in desolate areas and generally not associated with natural barriers, they were relatively easily traversed. At first, very few infiltrators entered Israel with hostile intent. Most wished to return to their former homes, to retrieve some of their abandoned property or to harvest their fields and orchards. Others engaged in theft. In due course, the proportion of infiltrators deliberately setting out to inflict actual bodily harm and material damage rose.

From the outset, the Jordanian and Egyptian governments, wishing to avoid a premature resumption of war, took a dim view of individuals undertaking unauthorized guerrilla-type actions. The capture of documents by the Israeli army confirms that perfunctory efforts by Egypt were indeed made to curb private acts of infiltration. In 1954, roughly 300 Palestinians were mobilized into a "national guard" to serve as an auxiliary force for the Egyptian army to restrain illegal crossings into Israel. However, Jordan and Egypt's ability to restrict infiltrators was limited. For one, their troops were thinly deployed along the frontiers in question. For another, the regimes were irresolute, especially at the local level where officials were wont to overlook border infringements and on occasion provided returning infiltrators with covering fire.

On first being confronted with the occurrence of Arabs stealing across Israel's frontiers, Ben-Gurion and others believed that it called for standard police intervention. Ben-Gurion was not taken aback by its appearance and at a closed cabinet meeting he showed some understanding of the perpetrators' motives.[7] A special border unit (Hael Hatsfar) was formed and by 1950 it contained 600 men, including 100 Circassians. Three years later, it expanded into a force numbering 1,500 and was renamed Mishmar Hagvul (border patrol or border Police). While Mishmar Hagvul sought to detect and prevent border infringements, the army undertook reprisal actions to punish and deter trespassers engaged in violence.

Over the period 1951–6, Israel lost hundreds of its citizens as a result of acts of terror perpetrated by Arab intruders and the need to combat them. The precise death toll is not known. Ben-Gurion put it at 884, while the historian Morris suggests a total of 529.[8] Furthermore, millions of dollars of property damage was incurred, not to mention the cost of diverting scarce resources toward securing and protecting border settlements. Transport to and from frontier farming communities, which in 1954 numbered around 300, became hazardous on account of periodic ambushes, mines, and mortar attacks.[9] The sheer brazenness of the saboteurs caused Israelis to fear for their safety and to question whether their state was capable of providing them with a reasonable measure of protection and security.[10] Settlements populated by newly arrived immigrants lacking military experience were most at risk, particularly those without fences, lighting, shelters, telephones, and internal means of communication.[11] In some instances, entire villages were abandoned. It was not just the dread of violence that distressed the farmers but the fatigue associated with night guard duty, for when so rostered, they still had to work the following day.

Unrestrained infiltration presented Israel with an existential threat. In Dayan's judgment, had the IDF not resolutely combated the problem, Israel's borders would have become so porous that it might just as well have had no borders at all.[12] Military sources estimated that between the second half of 1948 and early 1949, some 50,000 Arabs had illegally resettled in Israel.[13] Among IDF concerns was the possibility of deserted Arab villages reconstituting behind Israel's front lines. After having designated certain strips along the Lebanese and Jordanian borders as "security zones" in which only IDF personnel had freedom of movement, interlopers were, in accordance with an order issued in the summer of 1949 by Yitzhak Rabin, shot on sight.[14] The order was rescinded within a week but it took quite a while before border patrols began firing on male infiltrators in self-defense only. Yitzhak Reis of Kibbutz Yad Mordehai mentioned that in the early 1950s Arabs encountered along the northern Gaza border, including wounded ones, were routinely killed.[15]

Captured infiltrators were on occasion treated brutally. In May 1950, more than one hundred Arabs were driven to the Wadi Arava, a depression below sea level in the south of Israel where temperatures soar to unbearably high degrees. At the point where they were to cross into Jordan, an army captain arranged for two buckets of water to be put at their disposal. As he turned his back, refractory soldiers emptied the buckets into the sand. Without having quenched their thirst, the Arabs prompted by shots fired around and above them, ran off in the direction of Jordan. Wandering aimlessly for between two and four days, about thirty died of dehydration and exhaustion.[16] Dayan attributed that outrage to the lack of moral fiber among newly recruited Mizrahi migrants.[17] The callousness associated with the Wadi Arava affair was not unique. Between 1949 and 1953, there were three known pack rapes of Arab women, with two culminating in murder.[18] In one separate instance, three Arab children, whose ages ranged between eight and twelve, were shot and on two other occasions the victims' bodies were mutilated.[19] However, having carefully sifted through Israeli government and IDF archives, Morris found nothing to suggest "higher-echelon inspiration or instruction for the atrocities."[20] After 1953, when dissolute elements within the IDF were reined in, no more came to light.

Reprisal operations in response to the killing of Israelis were slow in getting off the mark and only from 1953 onward did Israel routinely resort to harsh punitive measures. Initially retaliations were undertaken by standard IDF infantry units. But their lackluster performance left much to be desired. In truth, the combat readiness of the Israeli army had deteriorated markedly since the termination of the War of Independence.[21] With most of the IDF's battle-hardened veterans having returned to civilian life, few remained to impart the benefit of their expertise. Edward Luttwak and Dan Horowitz revealed that the IDF was in such disarray "that combat units and command staffs became little more than empty boxes on organizational charts."[22] Due to general economic constraints, the army's budget was cut to the bone. Serviceable weapons were in short supply, soldiers were scantily clothed and fed and their state of morale was abysmal.[23] Lack of discipline and absenteeism without leave was rife and, what is more, drug addicts and criminals were present among the new recruits.[24] The condition of the Golani Brigade which "guarded" the north of Israel typified the chaotic state of the IDF in those days. Most of its commanders had never been under fire, only 10 percent of its soldiers were native-born Israelis or immigrants from western countries, 17 percent knew no Hebrew, 50 percent knew it partially and 30 percent had no formal education. In Uri Milstein's opinion, the "Golani was not a combat brigade but rather a kind of immigrant absorption center."[25]

Insufficiently trained and poorly motivated conscripts sent on missions either failed to reach their targets or disengaged on meeting token resistance.[26] On January 23, 1953, in an action within the Jordanian village of Falama involving 120 IDF troops, the Israelis beat a hasty retreat the moment they were locked in battle with no more than a dozen enemy soldiers.[27] Israeli losses amounted to one dead and five wounded. Incensed by such a half-hearted endeavor, Moshe Dayan threatened to demote any officer under his command who withdrew from combat before at least half of his soldiers were disabled.[28]

By the summer of 1953, Glubb observed that Israel's border security had deteriorated. He identified what he described as a 'new feature' "infiltrators who went only to kill . . . two or three Arabs would appear in Israel and shoot one or two people at night, or throw a hand grenade into a window."[29] To meet that challenge, fighters with better than average education were assigned to border areas and on July 30, 1953, a special retaliatory unit, under Ariel Sharon's command, known as Unit 101 was formed. Unit 101 had its genesis in an early July reprisal raid that the army subcontracted to Sharon, then a student of History and Middle East Studies at the Hebrew University. As commander of the Jerusalem Brigade, Mishael Shaham put it to Sharon that, with the help of trusted friends, he ought to locate and kill Mustafa Samwili and his underlings, thought to be answerable for a series of murderous incursions. (Shaham's felt need to elicit the help of ex-servicemen reflected his lack of confidence in existing IDF units,[30] two of which, the Givati Brigade and the Paratroopers, had already turned him down.)[31] Responding positively to Shaham's request, Sharon selected seven trusted comrades. One of these, Shlomo Baum, was ploughing in his moshav, Kfar Yehezkel, when a jeep drew up alongside him with a letter from Sharon. On reading it, Baum, without any further thought, put aside his plough, packed a bag and, with his personal tommy gun, answered Sharon's call.

Sharon and his friends succeeded in entering Samwili's village where they partially demolished one house and threw hand grenades into another. Although there were no injuries on either side, the boldness of Sharon's group persuaded both Ben-Gurion and Mordechai Makleff, the chief of General Staff, to establish a special body (Unit 101) under Sharon's leadership. When Shaham informed Sharon of their decision, Sharon expressed misgivings relating to his forthcoming university examinations. Shaham replied "Listen son, you have two options, to learn about the deeds of others or have others learn about your deeds. Choose."[32] Sharon reluctantly chose to jettison his studies.

The contingent of the original Unit 101, numbering 45 by October, included both war veterans and young enthusiasts from kibbutzim and moshavim in the Jezreel valley. Prominent among them were Meir Har-Zion (described by Dayan as "the best soldier that ever arose in the IDF"),[33] Mordechai Gur, Rafael Eitan, and Moshe Levi. All of the latter three ultimately rose to the rank of chief of staff.

The unit underwent an intensive commander training program that included the conveying of skills in hand-to-hand combat, weapons use, sabotage, and field craft. By temperament and appearance, the men in the unit formed a motley group. Some were rough and ready while others bore an air of quiet introspection.[34] They became renowned for their bravery and daring and set an exacting standard to be emulated by the rest of the IDF. In his diary, Har-Zion contrasted the difference between serving in Unit 101 and in the regular army. As a conscripted recruit, he was becoming increasingly irritated with the overbearing manner of his company commander, a real martinet who constantly threw his weight around and impressed upon his subordinates that he was a cut above them. At a moment's notice, Har-Zion was transferred to Sharon's unit. Knowing nothing about it, he fronted up to Sharon who was seated with Baum on the flat roof of a house in Abu Gosh. As he approached, Har-Zion stood to attention, saluted and formally reported for duty. Sharon responded by suggesting that he sit down and join them in partaking of some corned beef.[35]

Unlike previous elitist Jewish units, such as Hashomer and the Palmah, Unit 101 did not possess any ideological baggage associated with a political party or movement. Instead it adhered to the conviction that, as a professionally trained military body, its exclusive mission was to serve the general security interests of the state. In the course of various tours of duty, almost all 101 fighters were at one time or another wounded, some on more than one occasion. A large number were killed.[36]

The first serious Unit 101 reprisal action took place in late August 1953 following an attack on a family in Ashkelon that resulted in the murder of the father and the serious wounding of his daughter. Three small squads totaling fifteen men, and led respectively by Sharon, Baum and Shmuel Merhav, crossed into the Gaza Strip on the night of August 28. They headed toward the Bureiji refugee camp with the intention of destroying a house thought to have been used as a terrorist base. Before reaching their objective, Sharon's squad was spotted and set upon by a mob of refugees, some of whom were armed. That in turn necessitated Baum's men shooting their way through the frenzied throng in order to link up with and extricate their comrades. In the process, a number of refugees were killed with estimates ranging from thirteen[37] to twenty.[38] Enraged camp residents, who demanded to be armed, vandalized a nearby police station. To help restore order, the Egyptian authorities temporarily increased border patrols to hinder Palestinians from infiltrating into Israel.[39]

The next significant Unit 101 operation took place on October 14, 1953, when, in a raid combined with the 890th Paratroops Battalion, the Jordanian village of Qibya was assailed. Commanded by Sharon and with the two main forces headed by Baum and Aharon Davidi, 130 IDF soldiers took part. The raid resulted from the murder, the previous dawn, of a young Jewish mother and two of her toddlers. Entering the village of Yehud, Arab marauders threw a grenade into the victims' bedroom. By the light of an internal oil lamp, they were clearly able to discern that, besides the mother, the room contained four children all soundly asleep. That murderous act represented the culmination of the slaughter of 29 civilians and two soldiers since the previous April.[40] In that period, grenades were tossed into Jewish homes in Beit Nabala, Deir Tarif, Beit Arif, and Tirat Yehuda, while in Mishmar Ayalon a house was demolished.[41]

Qibya, with a population of around 1,500 and with 250 houses, was chosen as the target because it was near the border and it was not far from the area where the Arab perpetrators had entered Israel. Although the village was known to have previously served as a sanctuary and staging-off base for Arab bandits, there was no reason to believe that the killers of the Yehud mother and children had indeed set out from there.

The IDF's Operations Branch foreshadowed that the raid on Qibya was to culminate in the destruction of tens of houses. It forwarded its operational plans to the Regional Command supervising the mission, which in turn modified them before passing them on to Sharon. The modifications explicitly made allowance for civilian casualties.[42]

The raid commenced at 9.30 p.m. on October 14. One hundred Israeli troops bearing 600 kilograms of explosives approached Qibya from various directions. At the same time, small diversionary attacks were initiated in surrounding villages and a roadblock was installed to forestall the arrival of Jordanian reinforcements. As the Israelis neared Qibya, Arab Legion guards detected them and opened fire indiscriminately. To their surprise, the Israelis, who were hidden in darkness, did not reply. This unnerved the defenders, causing many to flee. The

Israelis then burst through an external fence and with a concerted volley rapidly took possession of the village. Terrified inhabitants sought refuge in nearby villages. Acting with extreme haste, a large number of houses were dynamited. The Israelis then withdrew to report that somewhere between ten and twelve Jordanians had been killed.[43]

A contrary appraisal was arrived at by the Armistice Committee. It claimed that the incursion entailed the destruction of 41 houses and the killing of 42 civilians, including women, children, and the elderly.[44] Allowing for fatalities among National Guardsmen and Jordanian troops, the total death toll amounted to 69.[45] According to Sharon, his men were unaware that any civilians had remained in the demolished buildings. The streets were deserted and they assumed that the inhabitants had accompanied the retreating Jordanian soldiers.[46] But, as Morris insists, "the [Israeli] troops had moved from house to house, firing through windows and doorways, and Jordanian pathologists reported that most of the dead had been killed by bullets and shrapnel rather than by falling masonry or explosions."[47]

Arabs in Jordan and other countries, as well as the world at large, were appalled. Within Israel, feelings also ran high. Many were disgusted by the IDF's behavior. In trying to deflect criticism, Ben-Gurion announced on radio that the raid was the unauthorized work of vigilante Jewish farmers, angered by the attack on Yehud. To crown it all, Ben-Gurion concluded that a precise audit had been conducted within the army and that, on the night in question, not a single unit, no matter how small, was absent from its base.[48] Affecting extreme displeasure, Sharett (in his diary) referred to that explanation as "a senseless one," for it was "perfectly clear to one and all that the IDF had a hand in the matter."[49] Sharett's moral indignation would have carried more weight had he not finessed the text of Ben-Gurion's broadcast.

In a personal debriefing with Sharon, Ben-Gurion expressed misgivings that Unit 101 might well evolve into a coterie of professional killers. Sharon tried to allay his fears by assuring him that most of his comrades were regular moshav or kibbutz members sensitive to the human rights of others.[50] Many years later, in the course of a private conversation, Ben-Gurion confessed that he was ashamed of the Qibya raid.[51]

In accordance with accepted IDF practice, Jordanian civilians had deliberately been targeted. The severity of Israeli retaliations had not been calibrated on the basis of the principle that the punishment ought to fit the crime but rather according to their potential impact on the behavior of Israel's adversaries.[52] It was hoped that afflicted Arab villagers would pressurize their government to clamp down on further breaches of the peace. Although Dayan appreciated that such a strategy was immoral, he defended it on the basis of its supposed effectiveness. Dayan was not alone in that regard, for Sharett, who usually wished to minimize Israeli reprisals, also subscribed to what he called the military logic of hitting a particular village so that others would be deterred.[53] However, when faced with widespread international censure in the wake of the Qibya raid, Dayan grudgingly conceded that the gains from such a strategy fell short of the losses and that henceforth the army would engage only conventional military objectives.[54]

Not every Israeli reprisal was expected to yield a measure of tranquillity. Some served to raise the fragile morale of the home population, while others were meant to hone the army's fighting spirit and combat ability. In terms of morale, Ben-Gurion maintained that reprisals were a means for demonstrating to new immigrants that in Israel they could depend on their government to protect them from the depredation of their enemies. It was considered important that the immigrants be reassured that, in contrast with their previous experience, Jewish blood would no longer be shed with impunity.[55]

The military establishment held that had Israel not resorted to the use of any counterforce, the Arabs would have interpreted that as a sign of weakness and as a spur for escalating the conflict. Israel believed that peace, or at least the postponement of another war, was predicated on the Arabs realizing that they were militarily incapable of overrunning their country. Hence, as Dayan asserted, effective IDF retaliations provided "a demonstration of the Israel–Arab balance of power as viewed by the Arab governments."[56]

The effectiveness of reprisals is contentious. Where they were followed by more Arab aggression, there is no way of knowing whether the ensuing violence would have occurred regardless and whether it would have involved more or less force.[57] Critics of Israeli reprisals have argued that it was beyond the power of the Jordanian or Egyptian authorities to prevent individuals entering Israel for, at the ground level, local officials and police were known to have sympathized with them. However, the inability of Arab authorities to put a lid on infiltration was not as incon-sequential as Israel's detractors would have us believe. After the Qibya raid, additional units of the Arab Legion were stationed in border areas. This resulted in a sharp decline in infiltration in the vicinity of Qibya and a marked, if only temporary, reduction along the entire Jordanian–Israeli frontier.[58] This led to a significant drop in Israeli fatalities *arising from Arabs coming from Jordan*. Whereas there were 57 in 1953, a year later they receded to 34 and by 1955 they fell to 11.[59] Sharett suspected that neighboring Arab governments did indeed possess the means to check infiltration. They were well placed to source information relating to potential incursions and, lacking all moral scruples, they could readily have employed all the necessary force to root out the practice.[60] That IDF missions may, on occasion, have been efficacious is suggested by an article appearing in mid-1954 in the *Jordanian Daily*. The writer, Yussuf Hana, called for stringent measures to curb infiltration precisely to avoid violent responses.[61] After the Sinai Campaign, which could in fact be regarded as a super-retaliatory action, border friction between Israel and Egypt and Israel and Jordan decreased substantially, in fact to virtually nothing.

A disturbing side effect of Israel's policy of retaliation is that it engen-dered or exacerbated international hostility toward the Jewish state. Successive episodes of the murdering of either small groups of Israelis or individuals failed to make world media headlines. After all, since such actions appeared to be the product of private non-government initia-tives, UN observers concluded that Arab regimes were not involved. But when Israel's patience snapped and it struck back, the casualties it inflicted were widely reported with barely any explanation of the context in which they occurred. Israel was frequently accused of overreacting to a single and relatively minor transgression, as if there were none preceding it. The UN, in Israel's opinion, routinely failed to distinguish between Arab acts of aggression and Israeli acts of defense. As one Israeli scholar summed up the situation, "while world public opinion was not really shocked by the sight of wholesale acts of murder perpetrated since the armistice against hundreds of unarmed Israelis, it generally seethed with anger whenever Israel retaliated."[62] Abba Eban believed that the Arabs felt free to murder Israeli citizens and generally flout the terms of armistice agreements "in the certainty that the Security Council would not adopt even the mildest resolution of criticism."[63]

Ben-Gurion understood that it was extremely difficult for many of Israel's well-wishers "to understand our [i.e. Israel's] unique situation and the methods imposed upon us to defend ourselves . . . What is clear is that no Soviet, British or American regime would tolerate a continuous state of the deliberate slaughtering of its citizens by organized gangs encouraged by a neighbouring government."[64] Inevitably a chain of events would arise whereby reprisals would follow provocations in a seemingly endless cycle of violence obscuring the true origin of the problem, namely armed Arab infiltration. This phenomenon was to repeat itself at the beginning of the twenty-first century. Throughout the early 1950s, Israel constantly expressed its readiness to abide in full by all armistice provisions. What it was not prepared to tolerate was a state of affairs in which the Arabs could readily violate the peace and then mobilize world opinion against Israel for defending itself. Ben-Gurion held that "an agreement which is infringed by the other party can no longer be honoured by us."[65] For the restoration of calm borders, the armistice agreements had to be *mutually* enforced.

By January 1954, Unit 101 was integrated into the parachutist brigade (by merging with the 890th Battalion) to form a new body known as Unit 202, again under Sharon's leadership. The paratroopers, ever loyal to their former commander, Yehuda Harari, did not take kindly to Sharon's appointment. As Sharon later wrote: "at the formal ceremony on the parade ground to mark the transfer of command I was greeted by hoots and whistles of derision."[66] After transferring most disgruntled officers to other units, Sharon was left with a reliable core which included Aharon Davidi who was to become his deputy. With careful nurturing, the two components of Unit 202 became so well fused that it was difficult to distinguish between those that originated from the 890th Battalion and those from Unit 101.[67] Until December 1955, Unit 202 undertook all of the IDF's retributive actions against Egyptian-sponsored acts of murder and sabotage. Whenever Unit 202 was about to embark on a mission, it would recall men on leave over the radio with coded messages such as "all citizens in Ramat Gan who were bitten by dogs on Tuesday are urged to report to their local infirmaries."[68]

Throughout 1954, despite the decline in the number of infiltrators arising from Jordan, there was nevertheless no let up in Arab violence. The worst case occurred in March when an Israeli bus was waylaid while ascending Maale Akravim (Scorpions' Pass), a desolate Negev elevation on the road to Eilat. With the driver meeting death instantly, the bus veered backward until it struck an embankment. The attackers then boarded the bus and fired at all passengers, including women and children. Eleven were killed, while three who were wounded were thought to be dead. Since there was no accompanying robbery, it was obvious that the attack was purely a terrorist one.[69] Under Sharett's insistence, instead of launching a reprisal raid, Israel lodged a complaint with the Israeli–Jordanian Mixed Armistice Commission, which refused to condemn Jordan for want of concrete evidence. In protest, Israel withdrew from the Commission. (It later transpired that the gang hailed from Egyptian-held territory.)[70]

At the end of 1954, that is, on December 8, five Israeli soldiers on an intelligence-gathering mission were captured inside Syrian territory. One of them, Uri Ilan, after having been subject to a grueling interrogation, committed suicide. His captors hastily returned his body. A note scratched out with a pin was found in his clothes declaring that he died as a loyal patriot. The IDF then forced a civilian airliner to land in Israel on the false pretext that it had entered Israeli airspace. The plane's passengers and crew were to be used as bargaining pawns to secure the return of the remaining detainees. Forty-eight hours later, faced with a resounding international condemnation of Israel's gross infringement of international law, Israel released the plane along with its passengers and crew. In denouncing those responsible, Sharett argued that Israel had to choose between being "a state of law and a state of piracy."[71]

The year 1955 heralded a significant increase in border tension and bloodshed. On February 28, 1955, in an operation named Black Arrow, the IDF killed 36 Egyptian troops (plus two civilians) and wounded 30 others during a raid on an Egyptian military barracks in Gaza in direct response to the murder of an Israeli cyclist, not far from Rehovot. Identity papers accidentally dropped by the Arab intruders indicated that they were in the service of Egyptian intelligence.[72]

The Gaza raid, undertaken by 149 paratroopers under Ariel Sharon's overall command, involved not only the Egyptian barracks but also an attack on a nearby railway station and the ambushing of a reinforcements column. As with the raid on Qibya, the Israelis, surprised by the reprisal's unexpected deadly outcome, presented a misleading report of the dynamics of that engagement. They claimed that an IDF unit under fire in Israeli territory gave chase to the enemy and that in the course of the pursuit a battle raged in Gaza. But most of the Egyptian dead had been traveling in a relief truck that was brought to a halt by an improvised roadblock where the Israelis attacked them with machine guns and hand grenades. In that clash alone, 22 Egyptians were killed.

Once again, Prime Minister Sharett was disturbed by the country's bungled public relations effort. Who could believe he wrote "that such a complicated operation could 'develop' from a casual and sudden attack on an Israeli army unit?"[73] Sharett tried to dissociate himself from the raid by informing an American journalist that had Ben-Gurion not returned to the defense ministry, it would never have occurred. Such an assertion is at odds with Sharett's diary entries that indicate that, regardless of whether or not Ben-Gurion was a cabinet member, the operation would have been given the green light. Following the recent hangings in Cairo of two Israeli agents, Sharett noted (again in his diary) that to square accounts Israel was obliged to respond disproportionately to the next Egyptian armistice violation and that the killing of the Israeli cyclist fitted the bill.[74]

The United Nations reproached Israel, claiming that the raid on Gaza was entirely unjustified. This troubled Sharett but Ben-Gurion remained unruffled. He noted that when in May 1951 his country lost 38 soldiers on its own soil in a five-day battle with Syria at Tel-Mutilla, the UN did not intervene. Israel, in Ben-Gurion's view, ought not to trouble itself with an international moral code that manifested double standards. The stigmatization of Israel was not the consequence of any of its actions for "it occurred beforehand at a time when we were as innocent as doves."[75]

Regardless of the criticism to which Israel was subject, there is no gainsaying the fact that it was the murder of a Jewish cyclist near Rehovot by Egyptian intelligence agents illicitly reconnoitring in Israeli territory that finally sparked the Gaza confrontation. As the historian David Tal remarked, "it is probably safe to say that without the murderous attack that preceded it, the Gaza raid would not have eventuated."[76] The killing of the cyclist was not an isolated occurrence. Since May 1954, the Egyptian army had been sending its men into Israel with malicious intent. Just over a month before the Gaza raid, i.e., on January

21, an IDF soldier was killed by a 12-man Egyptian army unit and a few days later two Israeli tractor drivers were fired upon, leading to the death of one of them and the wounding of the other.[77] Benny Morris, a scholar well known for exposing negative aspects of the IDF, viewed the Egyptian raids as demonstrating "a growing belligerency and adventurousness among Egyptian officials."[78] Morris's version is in keeping with Glubb's summation that from 1954 onward, "incidents in the Gaza Strip became far more numerous than those on the Jordan front." This was because "the Egyptian revolutionary government were desirous of incidents, for they were posing as the great military power which was about to defeat Israel."[79]

Kennet Love, a confidant of Nasser, insisted that the Gaza raid "transformed a stable level of minor incidents between the two countries [Israel and Egypt] into a dialogue of mounting fear and violence."[80] What he did not explain was why Israel ought to have tolerated the continuation of "a stable level of minor incidents," when the Egyptian–Israeli armistice agreement committed both sides to a *total* cessation of hostilities. In any case, it would seem that the Egyptians had every intention of ultimately escalating the border conflict into a full-scale war. Confirmation for this was forthcoming from Major Saleah Saleh, a member of the Egyptian government. On January 9, 1955, nearly two months before the Gaza raid, he declared that "Egypt will strive to erase the shame of the Palestine War even if Israel should fulfil all UN resolutions. It will not sign a peace with her. Even if Israel should consist only of Tel Aviv, we should never put up with that."[81]

As a means of deterring Egypt from pursuing further acts of aggression, the Gaza raid failed. A month later, infiltrators from the Gaza Strip struck at Patish, a new immigrant village in the northern Negev some 17 kilometers from the border. Having bypassed a number of other Jewish settlements, the terrorists were drawn to Patish by the sound of singing and gaiety. A wedding was being celebrated with the entire new migrant village participating. Creeping up in deadly silence, the intruders neared the reception area to discharge their submachine guns and hurl hand grenades at the innocent victims. A young woman, Varda Friedman, a volunteer instructor, was killed and 22 people, including a number of children, were injured. Had it not been for one of the settlement watchmen who readily returned the attackers' fire, the casualty rate would have been considerably higher.[82] With much indignation Ben-Gurion advocated that Israel forcibly dislodge Egypt from the entire Gaza Strip. But after a stormy debate, the cabinet, siding with Sharett, rejected his proposal by a vote of nine to five.[83]

By April 1955, the Egyptians had formed their own official detachment of armed infiltrators, known as Fedayeen (literally "those who sacrifice themselves). The move was formally proclaimed in a government communiqué that made it clear that "there will be no peace on Israel's border because we demand vengeance, and vengeance is Israel's death."[84] Elaborating, Hassan el Bakuri, an Egyptian minister, declared that "there is no reason why the Fedayeen filled with hatred of their enemies should not penetrate deeply into Israel and turn the lives of its people into hell."[85] By establishing a paramilitary organization to create havoc in Israel, Egypt deliberately flouted a key clause of the Israeli–Egyptian armistice agreement. The clause in question read:

> No element of the land, sea or air, military or paramilitary forces of either Party, including non-regular forces, shall commit any warlike or hostile act against the military or paramilitary forces of the other Party, or against civilians in territory under the control of that Party."[86]

The Fedayeen, who numbered over 700, were drawn from the ranks of the Palestinian-manned Gaza-based national guard, as well as from inmates released from gaol in return for pledges to participate in raids against Israel.[87] Supervised by Egyptian army officers, they received special training and were issued with a basic living allowance. Bonuses were awarded for the successful completion of missions. So esteemed were the Fedayeen's dastardly acts that their officer in charge, Mustafa Hafez, saw fit to highlight the performance of one recruit as a means of helping him evade prosecution for murder. Writing on his behalf to the governor of Gaza, Hafez cited the fact that on August 29, 1955 his protégé killed four Israeli civilians (three in an orange grove and one at a power plant) and that on the following day he ambushed a private vehicle, killing its three occupants. Hafez's appeal ended as follows: "taking into account his wonderful deeds, we request that merciful consideration and appreciation be given to his past record of sacrificial actions . . . and that you close the file against him."[88]

In July 1956, Mustafa Hafez was assassinated. The Israelis had provided an identified Egyptian double agent with a package with instructions to hand it over to a supposed Israeli operative in Gaza. As expected, the double agent informed Mustafa, who unhesitatingly opened the parcel and by so doing detonated a deadly explosion. Six months later, his counterpart in Jordan, Salah ad-Din Mustafa, met with a similar fate.[89]

An ominous aspect of the training of Arab terrorists and the general dissemination of anti-Israel sentiment within the Arab world and within Egypt in particular was the widespread recruitment of ex-Nazi war criminals and collaborators. Although the Arabs were infatuated with Hitler and were more than willing to draw on support from his surviving henchmen, they did not for a moment flinch at depicting both Israel and Zionism as being Nazi-inspired. In the early 1950s, many ex-Nazis settled in Egypt where they adopted Arab nom de plumes. The director of the Cairo-based Institute for the Study of Zionism, Alfred Zingler, styled himself Mahmoud Saleh.[90] His assistant, Dr Johannes von Leers, who had served on the staff of Goebbel's ministry, became known as Omar Amin. In 1957, according to the German newspaper *Frankfurter Ilustrierte*, Egypt had welcomed over 2,000 ex-Nazis. Two in particular, Arich Altern (Ali Bella) who was a high ranking member of the Gestapo, and Walter Baumann (Ali Ben Khader) who had participated in the extermination of Jews in the Warsaw Ghetto, became military instructors in Palestinian refugee camps. The significant ex-Nazi presence in Egypt did not in the slightest degree detract from its popularly perceived image as a "progressive anti-imperialist state." Syria likewise became a beneficiary of German military advice.[91]

It has widely been asserted that Operation Black Arrow (the Gaza raid) was instrumental in persuading Egypt to conclude an arms agreement with Czechoslovakia (or to be more exact with Russia) on September 27, 1955 that tilted the strategic Israel–Egypt balance decisively in Egypt's favor. According to such an argument, a needless and precipitate action by Israel pushed Egypt's back to the wall. The large loss of life experienced by the Egyptian army which exposed its general weakness was said to have tarnished Nasser's prestige and standing, both within his own country and within the Arab world as a whole. To redress that situation, Nasser supposedly felt the need to match Israel's strength.

Conventional wisdom suggests that, after unsuccessfully appealing to the West for military assistance, Nasser turned to the Soviet bloc which responded favorably. Such an outcome was allegedly facilitated by Chou En-Lai, the Chinese premier who at the Bandung Congress in Indonesia in April 1955 promised Nasser that he would use his good offices to help Egypt secure Soviet arms. A few weeks later, Chou notified Nasser that Russia was highly receptive to an application for military assistance and was now awaiting a direct approach to Daniel Solod, its ambassador in Cairo. However, in departing from that narrative, Motti Golani in his book maintains that "the Soviets had offered to sell arms to Egypt as early as 1953, and [that] the Czech deal had been in the making since at least late 1954."[92] Whatever the case, once Nasser broached the subject with Solod, he was informed that Russia "would be delighted to oblige with the supply of *any quantity* of arms."[93]

The Russians proved to be completely accommodating. Perhaps their only reservation was that officially the transaction was to appear as an Egyptian–Czech one to serve as a cover, though not a convincing one, for their own direct involvement. In light of the fact that during Israel's War of Independence, Czechoslovakia was Israel's main arms supplier, the irony of that stipulation was not lost on the Egyptians. The Soviets provided Egypt with a prodigious amount of modern weapons, of a type and caliber that had hitherto not been available to any Middle Eastern combatant, including tanks, artillery, planes, and submarines. Payment, to be deferred, was to be made in Egyptian cotton.

As an ardent pan-Arab nationalist with global leadership ambitions, Nasser had perforce sooner or later to adopt an extreme anti-Israel position. A year before the Czech–Egyptian arms deal was announced (and well before operation Black Arrow) Nasser emphasized to his biographer, Anthony Nutting, the importance of equipping his army with modern weapons as an indispensable precondition for consolidating his political power.[94] In the absence of the Gaza raid, the appetite of the Egyptian armed forces for increased armaments would still have had to be satiated.[95]

In Moshe Sharett's opinion, which seems to have been shared by the Soviet foreign minister, Vyacheslav Molotov, it was not so much the Gaza raid but the formation of the Baghdad Pact that led to the Czech–Egyptian arms deal.[96] Nasser in deliberating with Richard

Crossman, a UK Labour member of parliament, *identified the Baghdad Pact* along with operation Black Arrow as *both* being responsible for the worsening of the security situation in the region.[97] Mohamed Heikal, Nasser's confidant, also claimed that his leader felt seriously threatened by the Baghdad Pact.[98] What perturbed Nasser was that Iraq, Egypt's rival for pan-Arab hegemony, had adopted a key role in the alliance. On top of that, Nasser loathed the idea of Arab nations entering into formal defense agreements with the West. It stood at odds with his commitment to the Third World. Glubb, who closely monitored trends in the Arab world, wrote that when the Baghdad Pact was concluded "the Egyptian government was immediately roused to resentment," and that on acquiring Soviet arms "Nasser had succeed in trumping the Baghdad Pact."[99] One might have expected of Glubb, a staunch Israeli foe, to include Israel's Gaza raid as a factor in Nasser's calculations but, significantly, he failed to do so.

Subsequently, Egypt claimed that it needed to acquire more arms to redress an Israeli advantage resulting from Israel's arms negotiations with France that began in 1954 and continued until March 1955. In reality, all that Israel had then managed to achieve was a commitment from France for the supply of 12 outdated jets (that had then not been delivered) plus some artillery, bazookas, and light tanks. Such a consignment would only have partially offset the weapons that Iraq and Egypt had recently obtained from the West. [100] Hardly grounds for causing Nasser any concern.

A widespread belief shared by gullible European and American commentators that Nasser was forced to embark on a path leading to war is belied by the facts. When in early 1956 Eisenhower dispatched Robert Anderson to the Middle East as his personal envoy, Nasser constantly and consistently rebuffed every suggestion that could have paved the way for a peaceful resolution of Egypt's conflict with Israel. He rejected any notion of meeting with Israelis face to face or of conducting indirect negotiations with them. Rather he demanded conditions that no Israeli government could ever concede, such as the complete repatriation of the Palestinian refugees and a "return" to the 1947 proposed UN partition borders.[101] Why, as the historian Mordechai Bar-Zohar asked, did Nasser permit Anderson to visit him in Cairo in the first place? Providing his own answer, Bar-Zohar concluded that, among other things, Nasser hoped to forestall potential American arms shipments to Israel by issuing vacuous statements purporting to depict himself as a man of peace.[102] Whatever soothing words Nasser may have used in impressing naive westerners, Glubb held that he was none other than an inveterate liar who exuded charm and sincerity.[103]

As for the Fedayeen, at the end of August 1955 they attacked targets deep inside Israel's territory, reaching to within 18 kilometers of Tel Aviv. The raids were combined with the shelling of Israeli border positions and continued for a full week. More than a dozen Israelis were killed.[104] From the Egyptians' point of view, their actions constituted reprisals for Israel's occupation of demilitarized zones and the slaying, in a gun battle, of an Egyptian officer and two volunteers.[105] Then on August 31, the IDF attacked an army base at Khan Yunis in which 37 Egyptians were killed and 45 wounded.[106] So miffed was Nasser that on September 12 he threw down the gauntlet by prohibiting Israeli civilian aircraft from overflying the Gulf of Aqaba.

With Egypt beginning to take possession of arms from Czechoslovakia, Dayan took the view that retaliatory raids against it ought to become more devastating so as to precipitate a full-scale war in which Israel would overrun the Gaza Strip. He feared that on integrating and mastering its newly acquired weapons, Egypt would challenge Israel in a "second round" at a time of its own choosing. That being the case, Israel had to act while it still had the facility to do so. (A further indication of Arab intentions appeared on October 19 when Egypt and Syria concluded a mutual defense pact providing for a joint military command under Egyptian leadership.) Dayan's prognosis was shared by Ben-Gurion who on October 23 instructed him to prepare contingency plans for the capture of the Straits of Tiran, the Gaza Strip and the Sinai Peninsula.[107] In practice this meant that a year later when the Sinai Campaign was launched, "the Israeli army was ready for war, its units equipped and trained, its plans laid down to every minute detail and its borders fortified."[108]

In the meanwhile, the IDF began to perform more vigorously. On October 27–8, Sharon and Meir Har-Zion commanded a section of Unit 202 against an Egyptian stronghold in the Sinai town of Kuntilla. At nightfall, paratroopers set out in the cold desert darkness for an exhausting three-hour trek. Arriving at Kuntilla just as a change of guard was taking place, the Israelis so startled the Egyptians that they offered little resistance. All told, ten Egyptians were killed and 29 were captured, as opposed to the loss of two Israelis.

The Kuntilla raid caused Egypt to station troops in Israeli territory where they dug in near Nitzana, a kilometer from the border. The IDF was called upon to eject them and, on November 2, the first army-to-army battle on Israeli soil took place since the War of Independence. At a cost of five Israeli lives, the Egyptians suffered grievously. They lost 81 men and another 55 to captivity, plus a fair amount of equipment.[109] Perhaps realizing that they were at fault, the Egyptians appealed neither to the Armistice Commission nor to the UN Security Council.

On December 11–12, 1955, following Syrian shelling of Israeli fishing boats on Lake Kinneret (which occasioned no bloodshed), the IDF retaliated. Conducting a three-pronged attack with land forces coming from the north and south and water-borne fighters from the west, the IDF destroyed a number of Syrian positions adjacent to the lake. Forty-nine Syrians were killed and 30 taken as prisoners while Israel lost six men and twelve were wounded. Taken aback by its scale and the losses inflicted, Ben-Gurion remarked that the "operation was much too good."[110] Nevertheless, he strongly defended the action. Although Lake Kinneret in its entirety plus a ten-meter wide strip along its eastern coastline were part of Israel's sovereign territory, Syria positioned its army right along the lake's edge. Despite appeals by General Banica, the head of the UN team of observers, that the Syrians refrain from undertaking hostile activities in the area, in 1955 alone Syria violated the armistice agreement on 108 separate occasions. After Israel's retaliatory raid, General Burns, who served on the Syrian–Israeli Armistice Commission, submitted a report to the UN. In it he wrote that a staff member had interviewed a captured Syrian officer who had informed him that he was under orders (in contravention of the armistice agreement) to fire upon Israeli vessels that approached to within 200 meters of the edge of the lake.[111] Be that as it may, in a communication to Ben-Gurion, Dayan frankly admitted that the problems of Israeli fishermen in Lake Kinneret were the least of his worries. What really motivated him was the possibility that Egypt, in the face of an attack on its new-found ally, would feel duty bound to rally to its support, thus provoking an all-out war.[112] In this respect, he was disappointed. The Kinneret raid was denounced by the UN Security Council as well as by some members of the government coalition.

As the year 1955 drew to a close, the Egyptian army commander in Gaza called upon the Fedayeen to widen their "actions within enemy territory, including bombings and acts of sabotage, the severance of transport and the creation of panic in Israel."[113] Then in February 1956, the commander of the Egyptian 3rd Infantry Division ordered his officers to ready themselves "for the inevitable campaign against Israel, with the intention of fulfilling our exalted aim, namely the destruction and annihilation of Israel in the shortest possible time and in the most brutal and cruel battles."[114] Preparations to implement the commander's instructions included a mock-up of an Israeli settlement constructed near Abu Ageila and Egyptian maneuvers involving exercises in overrunning the Nitzana area and the seizing of Beersheba.[115] Perhaps the strongest indication of Nasser's hostile intentions was the dramatic change in the overall deployment of Egyptian forces in Sinai. Up until 1953, the Egyptian army, by maintaining only one brigade in the entire peninsula, was clearly not poised for an attack on Israel. But soon after Nasser and his fellow officers attained power, they shifted their army's center of gravity toward Sinai where, by the beginning of 1956, the major bulk of the army was concentrated. Ten out of Egypt's 16 brigades were positioned in the northeast corner of the peninsula, all of which were better equipped than those of Israel.[116] New roads and airstrips were laid specifically for military purposes and a large supporting infrastructure of fortifications, workshops, ordnance depots, and general storage facilities were constructed, most of which were situated in close proximity to Israel's borders.[117] In short, the Egyptian military build-up in Sinai far exceeded reasonable defense needs.

By April 1956, a spate of clashes, initiated by the regular Egyptian army, erupted along the Israel–Egyptian border. On April 5, after the Egyptians rained 120-mm mortars on the kibbutzim of Kfar Aza, Nahal Oz, Kissufim, and Ein Hashlosha, the IDF shelled Gaza city with mortar of like caliber, killing four soldiers and 58 civilians.[118] This was followed during April 7–11 by a bout of Fedayeen activity that led to the death of 14 Jews, including a teacher and five children who were at prayer in a synagogue at Kfar Habad, just ten kilometers east of Tel Aviv.[119] Press photographs of the synagogue's torah scroll smothered in blood horrified the nation.[120] From Cairo, Ahmed Sa'id, a prominent radio broadcaster, exultantly challenged Israel to "Cry for your future, night and day! Wait for your death at any moment because the Fedayeen are everywhere."[121]

Roi Rutenberg, a founder of Kibbutz Nahal Oz, was among those Israelis who died during the April engagements. He was shot while on horse patrol in his settlement's fields. The attack occurred a week after both Egypt and Israel reaffirmed their willingness to abide by the 1949 armistice agreement. Rutenberg, whose face was clubbed beyond recognition, had his eyes gouged out. At his funeral he was eulogized by Dayan who exhorted the mourners as follows:

> Do not be deterred from seeing the enmity that consumes the lives of hundreds of thousands of Arabs that surround us and who long to destroy us. Let us not avert our gaze lest our hand be weakened. This is the fate of our generation. We need to be vigilant and armed, strong and resolute, for otherwise the sword will fall from our hands and we will be annihilated.[122]

Inspired by Fedayeen attacks staged from the Gaza Strip, the Jordanian army, having in March 1956 divested itself of Glubb Pasha and most other senior British officers, began to throw its weight more overtly behind locally based Fedayeen. Writing in April 1956 in the Arab journal *Al Mitahak*, Shafik Atsheidat, a one-time Jordanian minister, outlined his country's change of policy. He acknowledged that it had previously been one of restraint but, with the departure of Glubb, it was incumbent upon Jordan to prepare an army from among Palestinian refugees that would be sent "into every area of the region called Israel to burn, murder and destroy."[123] Taking their cue, the infiltrators killed whoever they encountered. They shot at automobiles, blew up houses and water installations, mined roads and derailed trains. The wanton mayhem continued for months on end. In early September, in the vicinity of the Hebron hills, Jordanian soldiers fired on a group of 30 IDF reservists engaged in a map-reading exercise within Israeli territory. The Jordanians dragged six Israelis across the border where they finished them off and mutilated their corpses by removing their genitalia.[124] A couple of days later, that is on the night of September

11–12, two IDF paratrooper companies headed by Sharon blew up a Jordanian police station in the same vicinity and ambushed a column of Jordanian reinforcements. Some 20–29 Jordanians were killed. Israel casualties numbered one dead and three wounded, among whom was Meir Har-Zion, whose life was saved by a doctor performing, under fire, a tracheotomy with a penknife.[125] On September 22, a Jordanian soldier machine-gunned four to death and wounded 16 participants at an archaeology conference at Kibbutz Ramat Rahel. The next day just out of Moshav Aminadav, a few kilometers southwest of Jerusalem, a mother and her ten-year-old daughter were attacked while harvesting olives. The daughter was killed and her hand was severed to be taken away as a souvenir.[126] Elsewhere, a young tractor driver was murdered near Kibbutz Ma'oz Haim in the Beit Shean Valley.[127] During the night of September 25, Israel in turn struck at the Husan police fort and adjacent Arab Legion positions, causing the deaths of 37 soldiers and National Guardsmen, as well as two civilians. The reprisal was from Israeli's point of view a costly one for in the heat of battle, as well as in an ensuing traffic accident, it had lost ten men.[128]

The Israeli assault on the Husan police fort did not put an end to trans-border violence. On October 9, two Jewish workers near Even-Yehuda, 14 kilometers within Israel, were murdered and disfigured. (Their ears were cut off.) Outraged by such ongoing atrocities, which included the recent slaughter of five workers near Sodom, and convinced that the Jordanian authorities had orchestrated the latest violation, the Israeli cabinet authorized a significant reprisal. The Israeli government was particularly affronted by King Hussein who, on being notified of the identity of infiltrators responsible for the killing of eight Israeli citizens, promptly released them from custody.[129]

At 9 p.m. on October 10, under the command of Mordechai Gur, a paratrooper brigade with armor and artillery support attacked a Jordanian fortress adjacent to Kalkilya. With illuminated floodlights trained on the fortress, the Israelis bombarded it with 25-pound shells. Two hours later, it was stormed and overpowered. Then after ensuring that it was devoid of soldiers and horses, it was demolished.

Meanwhile an Israeli blocking force to the east of Kalkilya on the road to Azun, which was meant to ambush Arab Legion reinforcements, was itself surreptitiously encircled and outgunned. Some of its officers were shot dead, while one was in a state of shock. A 21-year-old lieutenant assumed command. He and the remaining able-bodied men scurried up a steep hill that contained disused trenches. There, after securing their wounded and mobilizing those among the injured still capable of handling a weapon, they awaited the final Jordanian onslaught. Approaching Legionnaires screaming out minatory war cries were undaunted by Israeli submachine gunfire and the launching of anti-tank grenades. In utter desperation, an IDF signalman radioed for the hill to be bombarded. By a stroke of luck, he had previously been in the artillery and was able to direct Israel's 155-millimeter cannon stationed 13.5 kilometers away. The response was almost immediate. Artillery shells saturated the hillside and scattered the Jordanians, while the Israelis sheltering in trenches, escaped unharmed.[130] Even so, they were running low on ammunition. This induced Dayan to improvise a rescue operation and, as an added measure, the air force was alerted to bomb enemy positions. Dayan intended to dispatch an infantry battalion to the imperiled paratroopers but Sharon, realizing that it would not arrive in time, sent an armored column instead.[131] Traveling furiously with its lights on high beam, the column reached its destination at 2.30 a.m. The wounded were placed inside the troop carriers while others perched themselves along the vehicles' outer perimeters. That arrangement was less than satisfactory. Fire from Legionnaires, who had meanwhile regrouped on Zuffin Hill, exacted an additional toll of five deaths and 20 wounded.[132] During the planning stages of the operation, Sharon had suggested that Zuffin Hill be seized "to insure against any emergencies."[133] But his suggestion was rejected. Both Ben-Gurion and Dayan were mindful of the possibility of the raid becoming too ramified, causing Jordan to call upon Britain for military support in terms of a Jordanian–British defense treaty. In a post-operation debriefing, Sharon bitterly inveighed against the decision not to adopt his Zuffin Hill proposal. For his troubles, he incurred Dayan's wrath.[134]

When the overall dust of the Kalkilya operation had finally settled, the IDF had suffered 18 fatalities and 68 wounded.[135] Enemy losses amounted to approximately one hundred. Total Israeli casualties would have been higher still had the paratroopers not fought with complete abandon. Their heroism is exemplified by Yirmeyahu Burdanov, a demobilized lieutenant. Like many other veteran parachutists, Burdanov spontaneously turned up "to give the youngsters a hand." He joined the units besetting the fortress at Kalkilya and then boarded the leading half-track heading to the rescue of those near the roadblock. On returning to base, it was discovered that a damaged vehicle was missing. Burdanov peremptorily ordered the driver of the half-track, nominally commanded by Major Moshe Breuer, to turn back. Dressed in civilian clothes, Burdanov attached a tow-cable to the incapacitated vehicle. Unfortunately, his white shirt attracted Jordanian fire and he was killed, as was Breuer just a minute earlier.[136]

So embarrassed was the High Command by the extent of Israeli losses that it initially withheld full information from the general public. Considering all aspects of that dismal outcome, Dayan concluded that Israeli retaliations had run their course.[137] The Arabs had begun to anticipate IDF responses and allow for appropriate counter moves. Now more than ever, Dayan was convinced that Israel's sole remaining option was the launching of a pre-emptive war.

As a prelude to Israel pursuing decisive action against Egypt, in June 1965 Ben-Gurion demanded Sharett's resignation. From the moment in February 1955 that Ben-Gurion had returned from Sde Boker, he was more than ever conscious of his differences with Sharett. Sharing his thoughts with Zeev Shraff, the cabinet secretary, he said he felt that Sharett was nurturing a generation of cowards and that he was determined to thwart him.[138] In the interest of creating a more harmonious relationship between the defense and foreign ministers and of ensuring the support of the foreign minister in the event of war, Sharett was replaced by Golda Meir. For Ben-Gurion it was a heart-wrenching decision. He described his mixed feelings to the Knesset thus: "as a long-standing comrade and friend I am personally very distressed that things have come to this but, bearing in mind the needs of the country, I see much to recommend it."[139]

6

OPERATION KADESH: THE SINAI
CAMPAIGN

Nasser's arms deal with the Soviet Union provided the Egyptians with a tremendous military boost. It included 230 of the latest tanks, 200 MIG-15 jet fighters, 50 Ilyushin bombers, 200 armored personnel carriers, two destroyers and six submarines.[1] Even beforehand, the Arabs had enjoyed a significant numerical advantage in terms of arms and men. Now as Dayan observed, "it was not only the disparity in quantity but also the superiority in quality [of weapons being shipped to Egypt] which decisively upset the arms scales."[2] The MIG-15 jet outperformed the modest number of Meteors and Ouragans that Israel possessed, while the firing range of the Soviet-made tanks was at least twice as far as that of Israel's M-3 Shermans. This, according to Bar-On, Dayan's adjutant, nullified the superb manpower quality of the IDF for "even the most courageous of pilots could not outfly faster planes, and even the most daring of gunners could not hit tanks outside their range."[3]

The transfer of such an immense and unprecedented quantity of armaments to Egypt was deeply troubling. In Sharett's judgment, the change in the balance of arms between Israel and the Arabs was not one of varying degrees of grey, rather it was "the difference between black and white."[4] Ben-Gurion feared that unless Israel could somehow or other fully, or at least partially, match the new Egyptian arsenal, a full-scale war was inevitable. While he was confident that Israel would pull through, he envisaged the cost of victory as being horrendous, "more terrible than what we paid in 1948."[5]

In vain hope, Israel knocked on the doors of the US and the UK. In late 1955, it submitted a modest request to the US for, among other things, 48 F-Saber Jets and 60 M-49 Patton tanks.[6] In March 1956, after months of prevarication, the US formally rejected Israel's application. As the US secretary of state, John Dulles, briefed President Dwight Eisenhower, the US needed to turn down Israel's appeal for arms "not on its own merits" but so as not to appear to be too pro-Israel.[7] In October 1955, that is a month after the Czech–Egyptian arms deal was announced, Dulles and Harold Macmillan, the then UK foreign secretary, agreed that "we must avoid being pushed by the Russians into a position of opposition to Arab interests . . . Our guiding principle is that we should not be moving in to supply Israel with arms on a large scale to offset those supplied by the Iron Curtain."[8] This approach chimed with a warning by Henry Byroade that "furnishing Israel with weapons will push the entire Arab world into the communist camp."[9] Dulles invented a disingenuous rationale for denying Israel the means to defend itself. He held that since the Arabs were considerably more numerous than the Israelis, Israel in the long run could never attain the ability to absorb armaments to the extent that they could. Therefore it was pointless, if not self-defeating, for the US to supply Israel with military hardware.[10] Nor was the US administration prepared to offer Israel any protection other than the potential application of the 1951 Tripartite Declaration of the US, UK, and France which purported to preserve the 1949 armistice frontiers. Yet even in that respect, the US was found wanting. When in the autumn of 1955, Abba Eban wished to ascertain whether the US regarded Israel's borders as inviolable, Dulles replied: "The United States could not guarantee temporary armistice lines."[11] Unlike the image the US currently enjoys of being a warm and reliable friend of Israel, throughout most of the 1950s it was somewhat aloof. In a letter sent on April 30, 1956, Eisenhower disclosed to a mortified Ben-Gurion that the US arming of Israel was at odds with peace and world stability.[12] With both the UK and the US refusing to redress the Middle East arms imbalance, Israel, in utter desperation, turned to France.

Arms negotiations with France began in 1954 when contracts were completed for the dispatch of a modest amount of equipment. The items in question had no appreciable bearing on Israel's strategic position. On returning to the Defense Ministry in February 1955, Ben-Gurion authorized Shimon Peres, his department's director-general, to fly to Paris to meet with the new French minister of defense, Pierre Koenig.[13] Koenig, who was well disposed toward Israel, expressed a desire to cooperate fully. Within a matter of months a deal was struck. Israel was to receive a small quantity of light tanks, some artillery, and 24 Mystere-II fighter planes. However, by September, it was learnt that the planes in question were subject to serious defects. Among other things they had a tail wobble. As a stopgap, France proposed selling Israel outdated Ouragan planes with a promise of a shipment of 24 of the more modern Mystere-IV jet fighters once they became available. It soon transpired that Israeli access to them was somewhat problematic. France was manufacturing the Mystere-IV planes in conformity with an offshore agreement with the US and, for Israel to acquire any, America had first to sanction the deal. Worst of all, in November 1955, the French government, having lost the confidence of the national assembly, resigned. A general election was called and not until a new government was installed could the arms agreement be ratified.

During the election campaign, Peres lobbied various French prime ministerial candidates, including Guy Mollet, leader of the Socialist Party. Mollet, an ex-member of the French resistance, was an ardent admirer of Israel who waxed lyrically about Mapai's social achievements. Conferring with him, Peres pointedly asked whether on attaining power the French Socialist Party would, like the UK Labour Party, renege on its backing for Israel. Mollet emphatically stated that that would not be the case. On emerging victoriously from the January 1956 general election, he was able to prove himself. Shortly after Mollet assumed office as prime minister, Peres, bearing a letter from Ben-Gurion, paid him a call. Mollet greeted him with a broad smile and exclaimed, "Now you will see that I will not be a Bevin" (the post-war British Labour Party foreign secretary).[14] Like Mollet, many key French ministers were pro-Israel. For one, Christian Pineau, the new foreign minister who had been imprisoned by the Nazis in Buchenwald concentration camp during World War Two, was an avowed friend of the Jewish state.

While waiting impatiently for America's approval to supply Israel with the Mystere-IV jet fighters, Pineau stressed that he was determined to place them in Israeli hands irrespective of Washington's response.[15] By March 1956, the US reluctantly assented. That month the first consignment of 12 Mystere-IV fighter planes was issued, as was the first batch of French tanks in June. These were followed in the months of July, August and September by a steady flow of additional supplies that enabled Israel to offset its potential vulnerability vis-à-vis Egypt.

The consolidation of French military assistance to Israel was facilitated by ongoing contacts between the two countries' senior defense personnel. One key meeting was held on June 23, 1956 at Veimars, just north of Paris. The Israelis present were Dayan, Peres, Yeshufat Harkabi, Emanuel Nishry, and Joseph Nachmias, while members of the French delegation included Louis Mangin, the political adviser to the minister of defense, General Maurice Challe, France's deputy chief of staff, Abel Thomas, the director-general of the Defense Ministry and several other members of the General Staff as well as intelligence officers. After affirming that Israel was prepared to collaborate with France on any terms, Dayan submitted what he imagined was an unobtainable wish list. It included 200 AMX tanks, 72 Mystere-IVs, 40,000 75-mm artillery shells and 10,000 anti-tank rockets. The French did not bat an eyelid. They agreed to supply all the items requested and went as far as expressing a readiness to draw upon current army stocks if need be. Arrangements for the furtive transfer of the military hardware were made there and then. Ships were to arrive in Israel during the night where they were rapidly to be unloaded so that they could slip out before dawn.[16] So secretive was the entire procedure that Ben-Gurion confided only in his foreign minister, Golda Meir, and his treasurer, Levi Eshkol, who was responsible for securing the 80 million dollars needed to finance it all. Not until August, when deliveries were running smoothly and on schedule, did Ben-Gurion take the full cabinet into his confidence.

French arms sales to Israel were largely derived from a perception that Israel could well serve France as an ally in confronting Nasser. France was beset by an uprising in Algeria, regarded as an integral part of its mainland, and where one and a half million people of French extraction lived. The revolt, which broke out on November 1, 1954, obtained Egyptian backing in the form of finance, weapons, military training, the provision of asylum to mutinous leaders, and the use of a

Cairo-based radio station (*The Voice of the Arabs*) as a rebel mouthpiece. With Nasser identified as a major stumbling block in suppressing the insurrection, the French were keen on toppling him. Anti-Arab sentiment was on the ascendancy within the Fourth Republic as a whole and particularly within military circles. In addition, commercial considerations may also have been at stake. The arms contracts were financially rewarding and offered prospects of scale economies in French weapons production. Since France then maintained limited commercial relations with other Middle Eastern states, it had little to fear by way of Arab reprisals for trading with Israel.[17]

Out of the blue as it were, on July 26, 1956, the anniversary of King Farouk's abdication, Nasser proclaimed that Egypt had nationalized the Suez Canal Company owned and managed by Britain and France. A US refusal to fund the Aswan Dam served as the catalyst in generating that fateful decision. At first, the US was indeed willing to ply Egypt with generous economic assistance. But Nasser's flirtation with the Soviet Union, his recognition on May 16, 1956 of communist China, his antagonism to the Baghdad Pact and his efforts to undermine the Jordanian and Iraqi regimes all told against him. Furthermore, southern US cotton growers, fearful of potential Egyptian competition, had vigorously lobbied Congress not to ratify the Aswan Dam grant. This led Dulles to mention to Ahmed Hussein, the Egyptian ambassador, that the American public rated the Aswan Dam as being by far the most unpopular project on the political agenda.[18] Affecting nonchalance, Hussein claimed that alternative finance was on hand from the Soviet Union. The futility of his gambit was soon brought home to him when Dulles parried, "Well, as you have the money already, you don't need any from us! My offer is withdrawn!"[19] With the UK following in America's footsteps, the World Bank also withheld its support. Left in the lurch, Nasser counted on gaining revenue from the nationalized Suez Canal Company as a means of financing the construction of the dam.

Egypt's nationalization of the Suez Canal Company had an electrifying effect. The governments of Britain and France, which had already harbored long-standing grievances against Nasser (France because of Algeria and Britain because of Egypt's opposition to the Bagdad Pact and its meddling in Jordan), reacted hysterically. They likened Nasser's pronouncement to an act of international piracy threatening their lifeline to Middle Eastern oil fields. Doubts were expressed as to whether the Egyptians were capable of managing the canal and whether all maritime countries would enjoy free access to it. Nasser's stipulation that foreign pilots were not at liberty to sever their employment added to their indignation. Both Britain and France felt that they were presented with a fait accompli that required nothing less than a military riposte. They were prepared to go through the motions of seeking a peaceful resolution which would entail the canal being managed by an international consortium, during which time they would prepare for war. Consultations with interested third parties were to be structured so as to ensure that they would not yield a non-violent alternative. In the interim, British and French armed forces were instructed to be fully operational by the following September. America, by contrast, was anxious to contain the crisis. Eisenhower's special emissary, Robert Murphy, was sent to London to explain that although the US disparaged Nasser's machinations, it believed that a western onslaught would have dire consequences. The West's general standing in both the Middle East and the Third World would be grossly, if not irretrievably, undermined.

Neither Britain nor France had just cause to wage war against Egypt. With the Suez Canal Company registered as an Egyptian enterprise and operating within its own territory, Egypt was legally entitled to nationalize it, especially since it had offered to pay full compensation to all shareholders on the basis of the share prices listed on the day preceding the announcement. In retrospect, that offer was exceedingly generous for Egypt had contributed to the construction of the Canal by supplying free forced labor, lavish land grants, and customs exemptions.[20] What further marred France and Britain's case was the fact that Egypt was formally due to assume full possession of the Canal by 1968.

For Britain in particular, the planned military thrust against Egypt reflected both a resurgence of jingoism and a last-ditch attempt to restore its faded imperial glory. The government was largely composed of members of the aristocracy and established wealth. Nine of the 18 cabinet ministers were old Etonians and all but two had studied at the exclusive Oxford or Cambridge universities.[21] Prime Minister Anthony Eden, Britain's driving force in the campaign against Nasser, was haunted by his country's weak-kneed attitude to the German Nazis and other European fascists during the 1930s. In fact, in 1938, he resigned as foreign secretary in protest against Prime Minister Neville Chamberlain's failure to confront the Italian supremo Benito Mussolini for invading Ethiopia. With Nasser now seen as a new and dangerous dictator, Eden was determined to reaffirm that he was no appeaser or, as one of his junior colleagues put it, that "he had a real moustache."[22]

On July 27, Pineau flew to London to consult with Eden. The two agreed to pursue a joint military campaign dubbed "Musketeer" and appointed General Sir Charles Keightley as its supreme commander with Admiral Pierre Barjot as his deputy. The British were adamant that Israel was neither to be party to their venture nor to be informed of imminent hostilities. With no mean chutzpah, Britain, in a closed Baghdad Pact meeting, warned that it would not permit Israel to exploit the Suez imbroglio for its own ends.[23]

Britain's pretense at seeking a diplomatic outcome was packaged in the form of a conference of selected countries claiming to have grounds for concern for the administration by Egypt of the Canal. Twenty-four states, including Russia and Egypt, were invited. Israel, which had been denied use of the Canal and which of all countries was the most aggrieved party, was pointedly excluded. Egypt and Greece declined to attend the conference that commenced on August 16 and which was held in London. It climaxed on August 22 with a resolution, proposed by Dulles and approved by 18 delegates, to establish an international body for the management of the Canal. The Australian prime minister, Sir Robert Menzies, accompanied by representatives of Ethiopia, Iran, Sweden, and the US, then flew to Cairo to brief Nasser, who on September 9 formally rejected the conference's terms. In an effort to maintain the diplomatic momentum, Dulles brought all his influence to bear in inaugurating yet another conference which convened on September 19, again in London. This gave rise to the formation of a Canal Users' Association to oversee the management of the Canal and collect its tolls. Since Dulles categorically ruled out the use of force, Nasser brazenly ignored it.

The very day that Pineau met with Eden (July 27), Peres and Nachmias were conversing in Paris with Maurice Bourges-Maunoury, France's minister of defense. In the course of their discussion, Bourges-Maunoury casually asked how long it would take, if Israel so chose, to cross the Sinai Peninsula to reach the Suez Canal. Peres answered that it would probably take two weeks.[24] Peres's estimation seemed to amuse both Bourges-Maunoury and some French generals also present. Cautiously, Bourges-Maunoury put it to Peres that perhaps he was being over-optimistic, for the French were sure that no less than three weeks would be required. Peres was then asked whether Israel intended to embark on such an enterprise and, if so, when? (Most military observers had assumed that Nasser would attack Israel once he had weathered the Suez storm.)[25] In turn, Peres explained that Israel's Suez was Eilat, since Israel held that Egypt's unlawful blockade of the Straits of Tiran was insufferable.[26] Coming straight to the point, one of the French generals then demanded to know whether, if France went to war against Egypt, Israel would align itself with it. Peres immediately replied affirmatively. This amazed his staff member Nachmias, who afterward reproached him for making such an unauthorized commitment. Peres reasoned that had he said "no," that would have ended the Israeli–French liaison and that in any case it was obvious that the final word in such matters always rests with the cabinet.[27]

About a month later, that is, toward the end of August, Ben-Gurion acceded to a French request for the use of Israeli airports should the need arise. This encouraged the French to give more serious thought to the idea of incorporating Israel into their budding military endeavor. In September, Admiral Barjot put out feelers to the Israelis, who responded by expressing a readiness in principle to throw in their lot with the French. A series of further explanatory talks followed and in one of them Bourges-Maunoury, again in conversation with Peres, let it be known that France, in cooperation with Britain, was considering launching an attack on Egypt. The problem was that Britain seemed to be frittering away valuable time by exploring a peaceful solution through the Canal Users' Association. With Britain appearing to be less resolute or certainly not on immediate stand-by, Bourges-Maunoury thought it prudent to explore the possibility of forging an exclusive Franco–Israeli pact. What Bourges-Maunoury wanted to know was the date Israel had set for its own campaign, taken as a foregone conclusion. France was anxious to commence immediately but Britain appeared to be willing to wait a few more months. Three factors impelled the French to avoid further delays. They dreaded the prospect of storms brewing over the Mediterranean by late autumn/early winter, they wished to strike while

President Eisenhower was preoccupied with his re-election campaign, and there was a limit to the extent that their forces could remain in a state of alert. Peres relayed the contents of his talk with Bourges-Maunoury to Ben-Gurion, who instructed him to notify the French that their timetable and that of Israel overlapped.

Bourges-Maunoury then made a direct overture to Ben-Gurion who confirmed Israel's willingness to side with France. On September 27, in pursuit of that objective, Ben-Gurion dispatched a team to Paris, headed by Golda Meir, which included Moshe Carmel, Peres, and Dayan. Mordehai Bar-On, head of Dayan's office, served as the delegation's secretary. Among other things, Ben-Gurion insisted that his representatives stipulate the following pre-conditions. Israel could not be expected to open hostilities on its own. The US was to be advised that a joint military action was pending and was to give assurances that it would not penalize Israel. Britain was to sanction the alliance and to guarantee that, should Israel have to defend itself against Jordan and Iraq, Britain would not intervene. Meir and her associates were also instructed to inform the French that it was Israel's intention to wrest control of the western shore of the Gulf of Aqaba to ensure unhindered shipping to and from Eilat.[28] During the discussions, which were held in secret in Louis Mangin's private residence and which became known as the Saint Germain Conference,[29] the French showed a readiness to consider plans for an Israeli–French assault on the basis of it being initiated by Israel with France following in its wake. At that stage, Israel was still unwilling to be the only state to take up arms, albeit for a brief period only. Nonetheless, the talks ended on an upbeat note, with General Paul Ely, France's chief of staff, indicating a predisposition to supply Israel with a considerable stock of weapons from French army stores that, added to the ones already supplied, would vastly improve Israel's fighting ability. Among the items soon to be approved were 100 Sherman tanks, 300 front-wheel-drive trucks, 200 half-tracks, 20 tank carriers, 1,000 bazookas, and miscellaneous ammunition. Provided on a lend-lease basis for the duration of the hostilities, the final shipment arrived just as the Sinai Campaign commenced.[30]

Less than a week later, on October 2, Dulles conceded that the Canal Users' Association's teeth had not been drawn because it never had any teeth in the first instance. This strengthened Eden's conviction that

Britain had no alternative other than to defend its perceived rights by means of force.[31] His resolve in that regard was buttressed on October 13 when the Soviet Union vetoed a Security Council resolution calling on Egypt to cooperate with the Canal Users' Association.[32]

It was now fairly certain that Britain would after all fall into line with France. On October 14, General Challe, as well as Albert Gazier who was deputizing for Pineau, met with Eden at Chequers, the premier's official country residence. Also present was Anthony Nutting, the Foreign Secretary's assistant. Challe outlined a plan whereby the war would open by Israel attacking Egypt. Once Israel secured a significant area of the Sinai Peninsula, Britain and France would enter the arena, ostensibly to protect the Suez Canal. From Britain and France's perspective, such a scenario seemed to provide them with a perfect pretext. They would appear, or so they thought, as if they were restoring a state of peace, disrupted by Israel. Eden received Challe's proposal so enthusiastically that within two days he and his foreign secretary, Selwyn Lloyd, arrived in France to consult with Mollet and Pineau. After lengthy deliberations, the four agreed to adopt the "Israeli Pretext." Eden undertook to sign a memorandum (to be shown to the Israelis) stating that Britain and France would only attack the side that refused to withdraw from the Canal Zone and that Britain would not confront Israel if it in turn was compelled to ward off a Jordanian offensive. Eden personally gave his seal of approval to the French to negotiate with Israel and, after some hesitation, agreed that Britain too would be a direct party to the talks.

On being briefed by the French, Ben-Gurion balked at the idea of Israel providing Britain and France with an excuse to attack Egypt. Although he appreciated that Israel might well be compelled to launch a pre-emptive strike, he did not relish the prospect of his country being singled out by the world at large as an aggressor. He would have been more inclined to endorse Challe's scheme (which he mistakenly attributed to Britain, a mistake encouraged by the French) had he any faith and trust in Eden. It was not inconceivable, Ben-Gurion thought, that Eden was setting up Israel for a fall.[33] Expressing his reservations to Mollet, Ben-Gurion indicated that if despite them Mollet still felt that he ought to attend talks in Paris, he would do so. With Mollet emphasizing that such a meeting was certainly opportune, Ben-Gurion reluctantly foreshadowed his appearance.

On October 21, 1956 Ben-Gurion, with Dayan, Peres, Nehamia Argov (Ben-Gurion's military secretary) and Bar-On, flew in General de Gaulle's personal plane to Sèvres (a suburb of Paris). There (linked up with Nachmias and Artor Ben-Natan) their talks opened with Mollet, Pineau, and Bourges-Maunoury. A little later, Selwyn Lloyd, accompanied by his private secretary Donald Logan, joined in. Lloyd, who tended to relate to Ben-Gurion as a subordinate, exhibited a marked reluctance to converse with the Israelis.[34] Ben-Gurion was later to describe him as a "scoundrel."[35] Dayan wryly recalled that Lloyd "may have been a friendly man, pleasant, charming, amiable. If so, he showed near-genius in concealing these virtues. His manner could not have been more antagonistic. His whole demeanor expressed distaste – for the place, the company, and the topic."[36] He returned with Logan to London before the negotiations were finalized. Patrick Dean, assistant under-secretary of the British Foreign Office and chairman of the Joint Intelligence Committee, replaced him. He arrived with Logan who came back to ensure some continuity.

From the start, Ben-Gurion, by pouring cold water over the proposed role allotted to his country, threatened to jeopardize the proceedings. But thanks to Dayan's tactful intervention, a general agreement was reached. Taking Ben-Gurion aside (before Lloyd made his appearance), Dayan argued that Britain and France had absolutely no need of Israeli military participation since they were more than capable of overwhelming Egypt. What Israel had to offer was the provision of a suitable pretext. That alone constituted its admission ticket to the Suez Club. Ben-Gurion was advised to tread warily and not to squander a golden opportunity to be aligned with western powers in a campaign that served Israel's interests. Failing that, Israel would be left on its own, without a reliable source of arms. Heeding Dayan's words, Ben-Gurion became more pliant. As a result, on October 25, Ben-Gurion, Pineau and Dean signed what became known as the Sèvres Accords. Ben-Gurion, with an impish smile, then conspicuously tucked his neatly folded copy of the agreement into his waistcoat pocket. He was patently delighted with the outcome.

In the immediate aftermath of the accords, Eden treated Ben-Gurion shabbily. Instead of notifying him directly of his confirmation, as he had undertaken, he wrote only to Mollet, who on his own initiative

forwarded Ben-Gurion a copy. Ben-Gurion felt insulted and complained that "Eden didn't behave well."[37] Furthermore, when Dean and
Logan returned from Paris with the signed Sèvres agreement, Eden
was mortified. He had not expected that the protocols would have been
recorded and after having destroyed his own document, he made a vain
attempt to retrieve those of France and Israel. When the Suez War
ultimately got under way, there was never any direct contact between
the IDF and the British army.[38] Because the Sèvres Accords remained a
closely guarded secret, most high-ranking British officers had no idea
that their country was colluding with Israel.

The Sèvres agreement stipulated that the campaign against Egypt
would open with an Israeli "raid" involving a parachute drop at the far
end of the Mitla Pass, some fifty kilometers east of the Suez Canal and
out of the immediate reach of major Egyptian forces. Simultaneously,
an Israeli armored column would enter the southern portion of Sinai,
destroy two Egyptian positions and then proceed to link up with the
paratroopers at the Pass. This would suggest that Israel was merely
undertaking a protracted retaliatory incursion. If by contrast Israel
had opened the campaign by, say, attacking El Arish, the Egyptians
would have assumed that Israel intended to conquer the entire Sinai
Peninsula.[39] Similarly, by delaying aerial attacks on Egyptian airbases,
it was hoped that the Egyptians would be fortified in their belief that
a full-scale war was not imminent. However, by initially leaving the
Egyptian air force intact and thereby capable of bombing Israeli cities,
Israel took a calculated risk. At any rate, the parachute drop was meant
to provide Britain and France with sufficient cause to secure the Canal
from the warring parties. On the morning after the outbreak of fighting,
Britain and France were to issue an ultimatum (termed "appeal" in the
Sèvres agreement) to the two protagonists to stay clear of the Canal. It
was expected that Egypt would not comply especially since it was also
to be asked to accept a "temporary" French and British presence in the
Canal Zone. In that case, both Britain and France would then intercede
(36 hours after the Israeli parachute drop) as protectors of a vital international waterway. Israel undertook not to attack Jordan and Britain in
turn promised not to assist Jordan if it attacked Israel. Should Britain
renege on the agreement, which Israel regarded as a distinct possibility,
the raiding Israeli paratroopers would withdraw. Finally, it was hoped

that Britain and France would recognize Israel's right to retain a section of Sinai in the interest of free navigation to and from Eilat.[40] In a separate agreement, not disclosed to Britain, France was to provide Israel with air cover (by stationing air squadrons in the country) and was to bombard Egyptian bases along the Sinai coast.

Israel's mistrust of Britain was well grounded for it viewed Israel with extreme animosity. In a confidential dispatch to the Foreign Office, John Nicolls, the UK ambassador to Israel, described Israel as "the centre of infection in the region."[41] Not surprisingly, Ben-Gurion perceived Britain as maintaining the world's most hostile anti-Israel government. His suspicion that "Eden wants to be rid of us"[42] was not a fanciful one. During the 1940s, Eden consistently opposed the establishment of a Jewish state in any part of Palestine and, once Israel came into existence, he could never bring himself to refer to it by its proper name, talking instead about "the Jews" doing this or that.[43] Anti-Israel sentiments certainly pervaded the UK foreign office. In late 1955, Evelyn Shuckburgh, as private secretary to the then foreign minister, Harold Macmillan, wrote "we must somehow keep Egypt on our side even to the extent of paying a very high price which may well include having to abandon Israel. It has long been my firm belief that the continued support of Israel is incompatible with British interests."[44] In January 1956, Lloyd in a memorandum to Eden stated that "our credit in the Middle East will be irretrievably lost if there is an Israeli attack on an Arab country and HM Government takes no early visible action to help the Arabs."[45] (That a few months later the UK colluded with Israel to attack an Arab country testifies to the fickleness of Lloyd's foreign policy.) Shortly after Nasser nationalized the Suez Canal Company, MI6 (the British foreign intelligence agency) made contact with would-be Egyptian anti-Nasser conspirators and agreed to provide them with secret information relating to Israel. In his book, *The Arab Secret Service*, Yaakov Caroz, deputy chief of the Mossad (the Israeli Secret Service), sardonically noted that such an arrangement "did not apparently trouble the conscience of the British."[46] Perhaps most sinisterly, during 1954–6 the British High Command devoted an inordinate amount of effort in compiling contingency plans for a war against Israel. Dubbed Operation Cordage, the prospective campaign allowed for the destruction of the Israeli air force, a naval blockade, attacks on Israeli ground forces, and the bombing of Jerusalem, Tel Aviv, and Haifa.[47] Influenced by the tenor of Operation Cordage, British propaganda broadcasts to the Middle East throughout the duration of the Sinai War remained as blatantly anti-Israel as ever. In operational orders both Israel and Egypt were designated as "enemies."[48]

Israel's main objectives in the Sinai Campaign included the impairment of the ability of Egypt to confront it and the opening of the Straits of Tiran to ships of all flags. During the early 1950s when Israel was mired in a series of border skirmishes with Egypt, Jordan and Syria, it was Egypt alone that seemed to have both the will and the might (with its Soviet arms) to undermine it gravely. At a cabinet meeting held in October 1953, two years before the Egyptian–Czech arms deal, Ben-Gurion identified three factors that indicated Arab intentions of attacking Israel, namely improvements in training, the upgrading of military equipment, and a trend toward a unified Arab command.[49] He had already taken a dim view of the future from the moment that it became clear that the Arabs had no intention of proceeding from the armistice accords to peace treaties. Ben-Gurion realized that the continued state of neither peace nor open warfare, afforded by the armistice agreements, was essentially unstable and that sooner or later hostilities would resume. Expounding the elements of what Samuel Huntington later termed "the clash of civilizations,"[50] Ben-Gurion warned against concluding that the Israel–Arab conflict even partly emanated from difficulties of communication or incidental misunderstandings. Rather it reflected an unbridgeable gap between national, social and moral values. As if anticipating later suicide bombers, Ben-Gurion stressed the difference placed on the value of human life by Arabs and Jews and the futility of assessing Arab attitudes to war and peace on the basis of Israeli or western values.[51] In Ben-Gurion's opinion, the source of Arab blood lust was to be found in their Islamic religion "which arose on the basis of the sword and which inculcates living by the sword."[52] Ben-Gurion was under no illusion as to Arab intentions and the nature of the conflict with them. It did not stem from disagreements over borders, the extent of Israel's territory, mutual relations, or spheres of influence but revolved around Israel's very right to exist. The defeat of the Arabs at the hands of Jews deeply wounded their pride and, with their exaggerated sense of honor, they felt an obligation to exact revenge.

Dayan, by contrast, had at first been more sanguine. In May 1955, he opined that "we face no danger at all of an Arab advantage of force for the next eight to ten years."[53] But once he was apprised of the Egyptian–Czech pact, he considered it absolutely crucial for Israel to wage war against Egypt at the earliest opportunity. His sense of urgency was heightened when on October 23, 1956, Egypt, Syria and Jordan entered into a joint military alliance under the nominal direction of Egypt. According to Ali Abu Nawar, the commander of Jordan's Arab Legion, the Arabs would "choose a suitable moment to initiate hostilities that would eliminate Israel."[54] One of Dayan's greatest fears was that, unless Israel prepared for an immediate war, it might well face the possibility of Egyptian tanks suddenly emerging from the Gaza Strip to "engage not an army unit prepared for battle but Jews in an orchard picking oranges."[55]

On October 25, the IDF mobilized 100,000 reservists, ostensibly on account of a looming Iraqi threat. The supposed defensive nature of Israel's mobilization seemed credible in light of Iraq's expressed intention of sending military reinforcements to Jordan. As a precautionary measure, some IDF units were indeed positioned along the Jordanian border. The mobilization was conducted unobtrusively. Wherever possible, instead of broadcasting coded call-up notices, messengers were dispatched to individual reservists. Israel did not want to convey the impression that it was on the verge of waging an all-out war. Ultimately of course the full extent of the mobilization became apparent. Economic activity tapered off due to a sudden loss of manpower. Taxis, buses, and other vehicles requisitioned by the IDF became few and far between, while city streets began to throng with backpackers wending their way to assembly points. Reservists willingly responded to the call-up. What amazed the writer Shabtei Teveth was the almost instant transformation of the Israeli man in the street. From being a consummate individualist, an argumentative cynic, an embittered doubting Tom, riven between parties, ethnic communities, and varying degrees of religious observances, he suddenly became a disciplined soldier imbued with a deep sense of national obligation.[56] As the Israeli mobilization gathered apace, the French rushed additional military supplies to Israel and, as promised, began deploying protective air units within Israeli airfields as well as stationing three warships along its coast.

At the eleventh hour Ben-Gurion canvassed approval for the Sinai Campaign from the leaders of all political parties (except of course the communists). He had already obtained government backing and although the Mapam party indicated that in principle it was opposed to a pre-emptive strike, it agreed to abide by the cabinet's decision. All the Zionist opposition parties lent their support. Begin as head of Herut was particularly appreciative of Ben-Gurion's resolve. He was invited to Ben-Gurion's home where he lay sick in bed with a high fever. On being acquainted with Ben-Gurion's intentions, Begin applauded them and grasped the hand of his old and implacable political foe holding it "as if they were lovers."[57]

As matters were coming to a head, Ben-Gurion affected an air of calm. He anticipated a strong negative reaction from Russia, the US, and the UN. A portent to that effect arrived in the form of a letter from President Eisenhower dated October 27. In it Eisenhower expressed what he termed his "anxiety" on learning about the general mobilization of Israel's forces and advised Israel not to resort to any form of warfare.[58] That letter was followed by yet another delivered on the morning of the opening day of the Sinai Campaign. Again Eisenhower emphasized his anxiety and the need for the preservation of the peace. He also mentioned that he was eliciting the cooperation of both France and Britain. Rather than issuing false promises, Ben-Gurion replied by justifying the readying of Israel's army, citing, among other things, the gathering of Iraqi troops on Jordan's border, the Egyptian–Syrian–Jordanian alliance and the declared intentions of the Arabs to annihilate Israel. Ben-Gurion did not commit himself to restraining his forces and as Bar-Zohar, his biographer observed, any competent political observer would readily have comprehended that Israel was on the verge of war.[59] Eisenhower then tried to invoke the 1950 Tripartite Declaration. But a few days later, on grasping the extent to which the UK and France dissembled their true intentions, he realized that that was not feasible. His allies' intrigues left him seething with anger.

The night before the outbreak of the war, that is, on October 28, 1956, an Israeli plane intercepted and downed an Egyptian air transporter as it flew over the Mediterranean from Syria to Egypt. With 18 Egyptian General Staff officers perishing, the Egyptian army was dealt a serious blow.[60] Further boosting its self-confidence, the IDF had just learnt that only a small proportion of the weapons that Egypt had received from Czechoslovakia were in service. Most of Egypt's pilots and tank crews were still in training.[61] To cap it all, the proposed timing of Israel's onslaught was propitious. The Egyptians had just transferred a large number of troops from Sinai to the Canal Zone in anticipation of an Anglo-French threat. This yielded Israel a numerical superiority in Sinai of 45,000 against 30,000.[62] Finally, in preparation for the general assault, four Israeli Mustangs flew over Sinai severing telephone wires with their propellers and wings.[63] All was then ready for Israel to do battle.

The Sinai Campaign, or Operation Kadesh[64] as the Israelis called it, commenced at close to 5.00 p.m. on October 29, 1956 with a parachute jump (of 395 men) from 16 Dakota transport planes near the Mitla Pass. Originally, the intention was to deposit the paratroopers at the western end of the pass, enabling them to block the entrance of Egyptian forces but preliminary aerial photographs suggested that that location was already occupied. There were signs of tank tracks, fortifications, and the presence of tents. The landing site was therefore switched to a far less satisfactory spot adjacent to the Parker Memorial east of the pass. On D-Day a further aerial reconnaissance disclosed that, contrary to earlier indications, no Egyptian soldiers were in the area. The new findings were relayed to Raphael Eitan, commander of the parachute drop. He and his men were already at their departure base but Eitan, in consultation with Meir Amit from army intelligence, decided to adhere to the amended plan.[65] To avoid detection by enemy radar, the planes conveying the paratroopers and their ten Meteor jet fighter escorts kept to a very low altitude. Only within minutes of their destination did they ascend to 1,500 feet in preparation for the jump in which 13 sustained moderate injuries. By error, the men were dropped three miles to the east of their designated landing, which meant that they had to undergo a two-hour hike to reach the Parker Memorial.

Settling in for the night, the paratroopers received eight jeeps, mortars, four 106-mm recoilless guns, ammunition, cigarettes, food rations, jerrycans of water and gasoline, all of which were parachuted and supplied by the French, flying Nordatlas air planes directly from Cyprus.[66] The paratroopers' ability to fend for themselves was enhanced by the existence of remnants of Turkish bunkers and trenches[67] and after some

Map 6.1 *The Sinai Campaign*

brief harassment from the Egyptian Air Force, a light fog securely blanketed them. The next morning, a battalion of the 2nd Egyptian Infantry Brigade that had driven overnight from the Suez Canal reached the Mitla Pass. The Egyptians were strafed by the Israeli air force, which, with assistance from the paratroopers, held them at bay. Deterred from emerging from the eastern end of the pass, the Egyptians remained well within it, digging in along its slopes and ridges.

The moment the paratrooper contingent became airborne, a column of the 202 Paratrooper Brigade, commanded by Sharon, crossed into Egypt via Kuntilla (taken with only minimal effort) to proceed overland to the Mitla Pass. On their way they encountered two Egyptian strongholds. They overcame the first (Thamad) within 40 minutes and the second (Nahkl) within 20 minutes. The attack on Thamad, which was enclosed by minefields and barbed-wire fences, began at six the next morning with the Israelis approaching it with their backs to the rising sun. That plus the thick clouds of smoke and dust thrown up by the rapid movement of their tanks and half-tracks made it difficult for the Egyptians to discern them. Finally around midnight on October 30, Sharon and his men joined up with their fellow paratroopers at the Mitla Pass. The going was more arduous than anticipated. Six of Sharon's 13 tanks broke down well before reaching the border staging area.[68] Of 153 trucks promised, only 46 were supplied. None were equipped with wheel spanners so that those that had punctured tyres were abandoned.[69]

As the Sinai Campaign opened, Israeli radio announced that the IDF was engaged in combating fedayeen. To convey the misleading impression that nothing other than an unusually large reprisal operation was in play, the announcer went on to declare that the IDF's actions followed on the heels of Egypt sabotaging Israel's transport facilities. The outbreak of fighting took the world by surprise. It was particularly embarrassing for Eban who found himself reassuring US officials that Israel's intentions were peaceful. Similarly, Sharett first got wind of it from a New Delhi newspaper on his way to a meeting with President Nehru. Nasser too was caught off guard and had suddenly to return substantial forces to Sinai.

On the morning of October 30, Dayan, much to his consternation, discovered that Colonel Assaf Simhoni, who was in charge of the

Plate 6.1 *Israeli paratroopers settling in near the Mitla Pass*

Southern Command, flagrantly disregarded GHQ orders by sending the 7th Armored Brigade into battle 24 hours ahead of schedule.
Simhoni defied authority after the 4th Infantry Reserve Brigade that
was to capture Kusseima was delayed on encountering difficulties in
driving through the desert sand. This set back the infantry's attack by
five hours. Unable to restrain himself, Simhoni forwarded his armored
brigade under Ben Ari to hasten the process. Not being privy to the
political dimensions of the campaign, Simhoni felt that orders for the
7th Armored Brigade to remain inactive for yet another day defied
military logic.

Ben Ari's men arrived at Kusseima just as it was being overrun by the
infantry and then continued westward. By then the Egyptians were able
to gauge Israel's true intentions, placing in jeopardy the momentarily
isolated paratroopers near the Mitla Pass and possibly subjecting Israel's
major cities to bombing raids.[70] With the 7th Brigade being 40 kilometers within Sinai instead of 40 kilometers within Israel, Dayan made
a virtue out of necessity by endorsing Simhoni's movements. Some of
Simhoni's men approached Abu Ageila from the rear and soon captured
it. A large part of the 7th Brigade then continued into the heartland of
Sinai, taking Gafgafa on November 2 in a clash with Egyptian armor
and then drawing to a halt within 15 kilometers of the Suez Canal.

It was not before the evening of October 31 that the rest of the 7th
Brigade could claim the entire Abu Ageila region. A fierce battle raged
for the control of the Ruwafa Dam. At the disposal of the Egyptians
were numerous field guns, anti-tank weapons, and ten 57-mm cannons.
As the fighting intensified, Israeli tanks ran out of ammunition compelling the tank crews to rely on hand grenades and submachine guns.
Had the Egyptians then mounted a counterattack, the Israelis would
have been unable to withstand it. Fortunately for them, the Egyptians
decided to regroup. This enabled the Israelis to replenish their stocks
and, once that was done, they were able to trounce their foes at the cost
of 10 dead and 30 wounded.

In the morning of October 31, the 10th Brigade undertook a perfunctory attack on Umm Katef. On meeting with artillery fire the unit
commander concluded that a daylight assault was inopportune and
withdrew. Dayan then demanded of the brigade that it renew its attack
on Umm Katef by nightfall. In accordance with his philosophy of

bypassing fixed enemy encampments to be dealt with after the securing of primary objectives, Dayan ought to have given Umm Katef a wide berth. But to maintain the campaign's momentum, he wished to secure the surfaced road overlooked by that stronghold. After hasty preparations, two 10th Brigade battalions set out. Once again, they met with failure. One battalion lost its way and the other floundered about until ultimately making contact with the enemy at 4.30 a.m. the next morning. After a brief encounter it disengaged. The 37th Armored Brigade, which was still in the process of being formed and that was to assist the 10th Brigade, impetuously rushed ahead without the protective backing of its tanks. Its advancing half-tracks entered an uncleared minefield to become snagged in the face of heavy fire. With the brigade commander being killed and the officers accompanying him being severely wounded, the attack petered out. Dayan was beside himself. In his Sinai Campaign diary he wrote, "Our attacks on Umm Katef last night and this morning by 10th Infantry Brigade and a unit from 37th Armored Brigade failed. That they failed is certain. Less certain is whether the actions can be called attacks."[71] However, after stiffer Israeli resolve, the enemy gave way. Some would say melted away for the Egyptians at Umm Katef, after displaying exemplary fortitude, were pulling out. (Confronted with an imminent British–French invasion, Nasser had ordered all his forces to abandon Sinai.)

Just before daybreak on October 31, an Egyptian destroyer, the *Ibrahim El-Awal* (of British origin), neared Haifa and began shelling the port, inflicting little damage and no casualties. Having been challenged by the French destroyer, *Cressant*, that shelled it, the *Ibrahim El-Awal* made off at full speed in the direction of Port Said. Within an hour and a half it was tracked by the two Israeli destroyers *Jaffa* and *Eilat*. A frenzied exchange of fire ensued, causing the Egyptian vessel to attempt an escape to Beirut. The Israeli air force was summoned leading to two Oragans firing armor-piercing rockets onto the *Ibrahim El-Awal*. The rockets smashed into the ship's stem incapacitating the steering mechanism and electrical system. As a consequence, the ammunition elevators were put out of order and, with his vessel having been rendered defenseless, the captain ran up the white flag. After radioing his superiors in Egypt of his intention to sink his ship, he received reassurances that the crew's families would be cared for. But the *Ibrahim El-Awal* remained afloat. Water that seeped into it was pumped out and the vessel was towed to Haifa where all but two of the 153 men on board survived.[72] After the *Ibrahim El-Awal* was repaired and renovated, it was renamed *Haifa* and incorporated into the Israeli navy.

Although Dayan had strictly ruled out any attempt to capture the Mitla Pass, Sharon went ahead regardless. At noon on October 31, while supposedly sending a small reconnaissance unit into the pass (for which authorization was forthcoming), Sharon deployed a battalion-sized force, commanded by Mordehai Gur, of half-tracks, light tanks, gun carriers, and jeeps. Sharon was to some extent pressurized by Gur who had been imploring him to send the paratroopers into action. Like Sharon, Gur resented having to cope with enforced idleness while other IDF units were engaged in battle. All hyped up and gung-ho, he wished to lead his men through the pass "no matter what."[73]

The Egyptians awaiting them had ensconced themselves along the pass's ridges and escarpments, taking cover in natural depressions and in caves concealed by rocks. So effective was their camouflage that Israeli planes flying overhead failed to detect them. Instead, the pilots noticed a row of vehicles. Mistakenly thinking that they were occupied, they blasted them and then reported that the entire Egyptian expeditionary force had been eliminated. More specifically, the pilots announced that "there is not a living soul to be seen."[74] Their report gave rise to a false sense of confidence that little untoward awaited Gur's men. Not only were there no Egyptian casualties arising from the Israeli air strike, the enemy was well armed. In addition to personal weapons, it had at its disposal a number of intermediate machine guns, artillery, and heavy mortar launchers.[75] As the paratrooper column incautiously meandered its way through the narrow defile, heavy Egyptian fire rained down upon it. Nevertheless, Gur ordered his men to continue westward on the erroneous assessment that the forces opposing them were inconsequential and that they were on the verge of disintegrating.[76] (This was contrary to the spirit of Sharon's brief that suggested that the patrol turn back on encountering serious resistance.) The more the column advanced, the more the pass narrowed. Soon the driver of the lead troop carrier was shot dead. A machine gunner took over the steering wheel but it broke and the carrier then got bogged down. The rest of Gur's column continued to approach it and in so doing ensured that its vehicles batched into a bottleneck where an insufficiency of space, aggravated by strewn burnt-out Egyptian trucks, did not allow for U-turns. The Israelis were pinned down. The Egyptians dealt out everything at hand, discharging rifles, submachine guns, intermediate machine guns, bazookas, anti-tank missiles, and rifle-propelled grenades. So close were they that from an elevated rock not more than thirty meters away, one of their soldiers lobbed a succession of grenades onto exposed Israeli half-tracks below.[77] Soldiers in the forward half-track were successively picked off. A number of vehicles, including a fuel truck, burst into flames.

Somehow one of the half-tracks succeeded in dislodging an Egyptian hulk, allowing a section of the column to nudge forward and leave the line of fire. The Israelis then made futile attempts to mount the steep ridges, some of which had an 80-degree gradient, but the Egyptians with air assistance frustrated them. At that stage, the column was segmented into three components, one still trapped among the burnt-out vehicles, one that managed to escape and one on the eastern side which had yet to enter the main body of the pass. The latter's commander, Aharon Davidi, was determined to seize the ridges. Not knowing where the enemy lay, he called for a volunteer to drive a jeep through the pass to attract enemy fire so that the location of the Egyptians would be disclosed. Twenty-year-old Yehuda Ken-Dror took up the task. As he drove off, all hell broke loose. Guns roared at him from all sides and from all dugouts. He was hit in his stomach, hands, and feet and grazed on his head and neck. He continued for a while but soon his jeep came to rest. Later after darkness had set in, Ken-Dror, who was mortally wounded, drew on all his remaining strength to crawl back on his belly.[78] (The received history suggests that Ken-Dror volunteered for that fatal assignment. However, that may or may not be so. Davidi remained adamant that Ken-Dror set off on his own volition but three soldiers who were within earshot of Davidi are equally insistent that once no one stepped forward Davidi simply turned to Ken-Dror, who was his personal driver, and ordered him to go.[79] Whatever the case, Ken-Dror carried out his mission with noble valor. His bereaved parents had already lost a son in the War of Independence.)

At dusk, thanks to the intelligence that Ken-Dror's actions had yielded, an Israeli unit succeeded in scaling one of the slopes and then swept it from top to bottom. So steep was the slope's gradient that some of the paratroopers fell, hurtling downward to their death.[80] The unit had to move quickly since, apart from contending with opposition on the slope in question, it also attracted fire from the opposite one. In its haste, it overlooked enemy pockets secreted in small pits so to ensure that the slope was secure, two more hazardous sweeps had to be undertaken. By then, paratroopers from the rest of the brigade who had mounted the eastern ridges were coming to their rescue. Only after nearly ten hours of bitter fighting, including hand-to-hand combat, did the Israelis prevail. It was a costly engagement, entailing 38 deaths (close to a quarter of Israelis killed in the entire campaign) and 120 wounded. Enemy deaths were estimated at 200.[81]

Sharon was neither reprimanded nor disciplined, which was most irregular considering that his brigade's ultimate mission was certainly not to attempt to approach the canal but rather, if need be, to zero in on Sharm el Sheikh in the south, by *circumventing* the pass.[82] As if to make a mockery of the soldiers sacrificed, once the battle was resolved, the paratroopers returned to their original positions, that is, the Mitla Pass was "attacked, captured and abandoned."[83] Some of Sharon's men accused him of "reputation-building at their expense."[84]

In keeping with the Sèvres Accords, Britain and France duly issued their ultimatum to Egypt and Israel calling upon them to stop fighting and to withdraw ten miles from the Suez Canal. As expected, Israel responded positively while Egypt rejected their demands out of hand. On the evening of October 31, after issuing an additional warning, British and French air forces began pounding Egypt's airfields, 48 hours after the opening of hostilities rather than 36 hours as Israel was promised. For operational and political reasons, Britain had postponed its air attacks by 12 hours. Since there was no communication between the UK and Israel, the Israelis reacted with outrage, particularly in light of intelligence reports that the Egyptians were planning a massive air assault against Israel's cities.[85] Dayan fumed: "Those bastards. They make a political agreement in which one of the main clauses, one we insisted on, was an air strike on Wednesday morning, and here they casually postpone the operation by 12 [hours] with no warning, not even an apology, the bastards."[86] Ben-Gurion fearing that the paratroopers at the Mitla Pass would be dangerously exposed to Egyptian planes, toyed with the idea of withdrawing them, an action that would have put paid to the entire Sinai Campaign. However, Dayan dissuaded him from doing so and, once news of the commencement of the British–French air strikes reached Ben-Gurion, he was noticeably relieved. The French and British began to bomb Egypt's air force, much of which was grounded. Within days, around 260 Egyptian planes were destroyed and air harassment of the Israelis ceased.

By the night of October 31, the main focus of the campaign shifted to the northern sector of Sinai centering on Rafah and El Arish. Soon after midnight, the French navy bombarded Egyptian positions around Rafah so as to facilitate an Israeli drive but the French effort was in Dayan's view "a complete flop." Instead of pulverizing the enemy, as Dayan had counted on, "the leviathan gave forth a sprat."[87] Rafah was protected by 13 self-contained fortified strongholds, nestling on slight elevations. Surrounding each one were minefields and multiple barbed-wire fences. Within their inner cores were machine gun emplacements and launching pads for artillery, anti-tank guns, and other heavy weapons. Each fortification had to be invested separately. The tasks were allotted to soldiers of both the 1st Infantry and 27th Armored Brigades. Sappers went ahead to clear paths through the enemy's minefield and then destroy or dismantle sections of the barbed-wire enclosures. In dismantling the mines, the sappers labored under the covering fire of Israeli artillery. Since the Egyptian mines were cast in bakelite rather than metal, standard mine detectors could not be utilized. Instead, the sappers had delicately to probe for them with their daggers. They toiled in the darkness of night covering themselves with blankets under which they lit their flashlights to guide them. At one point, sappers were subject to artillery fire that placed them in a most unenviable situation, for in a minefield, one cannot rapidly scatter about in the interest of minimizing casualties. On that occasion, the Egyptian bombardment was promptly silenced by accurate Israeli counter-fire.

Generally, after the sappers had accomplished their mission, the vanguards of each unit, again under covering fire, were to pounce upon the enemy. In most cases, this more or less went as planned. The Egyptians seemed willing to stand firm as long as the Israelis were repelled but, once their outer defenses crumbled, they readily gave way and often fled. But it was not all plain sailing. In a pre-dawn action against an Egyptian position commanding a vital crossroad south of Rafah, the lead vehicle of a motorized column struck a mine, as did the follow up half-track which was set ablaze. The flames of the burning vehicle illuminated the area around the Israelis, making it necessary for them to advance with a minimum of delay. Sappers worked feverishly to clear an alternative path to find more mines. Only on the third "clearance" and by now in broad daylight, did the attack force manage to storm its objective.[88] In another incident, a company rushing toward the center of a stronghold unexpectedly discovered that the ultimate fence had yet to be breached. Being so close to their adversaries and with no time to spare, private Tuvia Anshal spontaneously leaned on the barbed wire which partially gave way and offered himself as a human bridge for the rest of his unit to pass over.[89]

On the morning of November 1, with Rafah's surrounding strongholds all having been overcome, the 27th Armored Brigade made for El Arish. Early the next day it entered the town to find no opposition. During the previous night, the Egyptian forces had left. The evacuation was rapid and panic-stricken. Posts were instantly deserted as people scrambled to join departing convoys. In the midst of a medical operation, a soldier whose leg was being amputated was forsaken. Not being bandaged, he died from a severe hemorrhage. Eighteen others left without a single carer met with a similar fate.[90] The Egyptian flight from El Arish was so chaotic that a veritable hoard of weapons and supplies was left intact. No effort was made to demolish them. Empty army camps just west of the town were in such good repair that one might have thought that they were vacated for the express purpose of allowing the Israelis to enjoy them.[91] From El Arish, the 27th Brigade pressed on to within easy reach of the Suez Canal some fifteen kilometers off the Egyptian town of Kantara. The day after Rafah was taken, that is on November 2, the 11th Infantry Brigade wrested Gaza City and its northern environs. Then early during the following afternoon Khan Yunis fell and with it the entire Gaza Strip.

The battle for Sharm el Sheikh constituted the closing chapter of Operation Kadesh. It was borne by 1,800 men of the 9th Infantry Brigade (commanded by Avraham Yoffe) with the promise of assistance from paratroopers dropped over Al-Tur on the western coast of the Sinai Peninsula and by paratroopers arriving by way of Al-Tur from the Mitla Pass. On November 2 the 9th Brigade, equipped with topological knowledge gained from a prior scouting mission, proceeded from Ras al Naqb (which had been captured on the evening of October 29) in the direction of Sharm el Sheikh. The brigade's 200 vehicles (none of which were tanks) had to cover some 320 kilometers of rough and trackless enemy territory. In certain stretches, vehicles ensnared in deep sand had to be towed by the half-tracks. Elsewhere, a narrow "goats' pass" had to be widened with dynamite. Should it have wished to do so, the column could not have backtracked, for some sandy inclines were only negotiable in a southward direction.[92]

On November 4, after a grueling trek, the Israelis appeared within sight of Sharm el Sheikh. The Egyptians could not believe their eyes. They took it for granted that no significant ground force could have taken such a route. Nonetheless, anticipating sea and air attacks, including a large parachute drop, the defenses at Sharm el Sheikh were prepared for an assault from any direction. The only advantage that the brigade enjoyed was the possession of armored vehicles. By late afternoon, its reconnaissance unit made tentative contact with the enemy but it was forced to withdraw on encountering heavy fire. Fighting resumed after midnight when a force equivalent to battalion strength once more tried to overwhelm the Egyptians. But that attack too was short-lived. The Israelis failed to clear a path through the minefield and, because of the rocky nature of the ground, digging-in was not feasible. Faced with concentrated machine-gun fire and without the protective cover of foxholes, the offensive was canceled. Early in the morning of November 5, utilizing heavy mortars and relying on the air force to support them with rockets and napalm, the Israelis took on the Egyptians for the third time. On this occasion, after a harsh and intensive struggle lasting 50 minutes, the 9th Brigade's jeeps, under covering fire from the half-tracks, burst through. By 9.30 a.m., Sharm el Sheikh had fallen.[93] The paratroopers converging on the scene arrived just as the battle ended. Israel, which now held the entire Sinai Peninsula (bar a 15-kilometer-wide strip straddling the Canal), assumed control over the Straits of Tiran.

Apart from the failed attacks on Umm Katef, Israel enjoyed sweeping success, which may be attributed to a number of factors, among which was the dash and élan of the IDF, fortunate to engage an enemy whose ranks had been depleted by the transfer of units from Sinai to the Canal

Zone. Supporting the ground forces, the Israeli air force played a useful role. In the Sinai theater of war, air supremacy is critically important. The nature of the terrain is such that for the most part army columns have no choice other than to travel over a limited number of navigable roads. Without adequate air cover, they could readily be mangled in devastating air attacks, as was the fate of the armored Egyptian corps.

In the opening phase of Operation Kadesh, that is before the British and French air forces had joined in, Israel's pilots got the better of their Egyptian counterparts and to a very large extent were able to shield their troops. This occurred despite Israel's relative disadvantages. At Israel's disposal were 143 planes, more or less equally divided between jet fighters and piston-driven aircraft. By contrast, of the estimated 150 to 250 Egyptians planes in operation, all were jets.[94] In no single air encounter did Israel employ more fighters than did Egypt. Often an Israeli air formation audaciously challenged one that was larger still. Egyptian fighter planes never attempted to enter Israel's airspace and only on two occasions did individual bombers discharge their loads in desolate Israeli regions before heading home. No Israeli fighter plane was downed by enemy craft. By flying at rather low altitudes to improve their targeting, the Israelis inadvertently exposed themselves to greater risks. This explains why, except for one Piper Cub, all of Israel's limited losses resulted from anti-aircraft ground fire.

A puzzling aspect relating to the Sinai Campaign is that neither Jordan nor Syria entered the fray. One school of thought argues that Egypt did indeed appeal to its allies but they paid no heed to such adjurations.[95] But that does not seem to be quite the case. Shortly after the Israeli paratroopers landed near the Mitla Pass, Jordan and Syria, in accordance with their pact with Egypt, instructed their forces to prepare for Operation Beisan, a pre-arranged plan to dissect Israel by seizing the coastal town of Netanya. King Hussein of Jordan was all for immediate action but Ali Abu Nawar, his chief of staff, insisted on awaiting Syrian reinforcements that arrived three days late in a state of utter disarray. That delay, coupled with a British warning that if Jordan attacked Israel the Anglo-Jordanian Treaty would not apply, gave Hussein grounds for not interfering. In a personal telephone call, Nasser reassured him that he had acted wisely.[96] In Syria with the president abroad on a visit to Moscow the government was not inclined to undertake any precipitous military move.[97] Syria did however destroy, within its own territory, an oil pipeline running from Iraq to the Mediterranean.

As Operation Kadesh climaxed, the IDF's conquests went to Ben-Gurion's head. In a written communiqué to be read at a victory parade at Sharm el Sheikh, he referred to a new Israeli dominion from Dan in the north to the island of Tiran in the south.[98] Well before the opening of the campaign, that is, at the Sèvres Conference, Ben-Gurion had revealed a plan that was so extraordinary that he himself felt the need to describe it as "fantastic." It involved a radical restructuring of the Middle East. Once Nasser was deposed, Israel would take over the West Bank of Jordan (with the rest of the kingdom to be transferred to an Iraq at peace with Israel), annex southern Lebanon up to the Litani River, and assume permanent possession of the entire Sinai Peninsula, or at least a large part of it.[99] Needless to say, Ben-Gurion's co-conspirators were unimpressed. Such a proposal was neither discussed in the Israeli cabinet nor did it represent official or unofficial government policy. Ben-Gurion's ideas were propounded at a time when the Jordanian regime seemed to be on the verge of collapse. That caused Ben-Gurion to suspect that Britain was hatching schemes of its own without taking Israel's interests into account. He therefore wished to pre-empt big power plans with an Israeli one.[100] Ben-Gurion's intuition was not far off the mark. During 1956, the UK fleetingly contemplated engineering the downfall of both the Syrian and Saudi Arabian regimes as well as the total elimination of Jordan.[101]

Opposition to the Sinai Campaign was near universal but most telling from Israel's point of view was the unremittingly critical stand of the US. Not that Israel was spared any bile from other sources such as the Soviet Union, which was at the time riding roughshod over Hungary. In a deprecatory letter sent on November 5 (which Ben-Gurion thought could have been drafted by Hitler), Russian Prime Minister Nikolai Bulganin suggested that Israel's attack on Egypt had put "in jeopardy the very existence of Israel as a state." The Russians then recalled their ambassador to Moscow. Adding fuel to the fire, Nikita Khrushchev, the Russian Communist Party general secretary, wrote that if Israel persists in its "armed aggression" against Egypt, it might well face Soviet "volunteers."[102] In replying to the Russians, Ben-Gurion reaffirmed Israel's legitimate right to defend itself in the face of explicit Arab threats to destroy it. He made no apologies for the activation of the IDF and gave no hint of being in the slightest bit cowed. In truth, he and his colleagues took the Russian threats very seriously and the possibility of Soviet military involvement weighed heavily upon them. The US was likewise concerned. As a precaution, the Sixth Fleet sailed onto the high seas to avoid a surprise attack.[103]

Immediately after Israel invaded Sinai, the UN Security Council, at the bidding of the US, met to denounce its engagements against Egypt. An American-sponsored resolution proposing that member states withhold all military, economic, or financial aid from Israel if it failed to withdraw to the armistice lines was vetoed by Britain and France.[104] Thereupon, on November 1, an emergency session of the UN General Assembly was convened. In terms of a 1951 UN constitutional amendment, the General Assembly could act whenever the Security Council was deadlocked by the imposition of vetoes. The Assembly called for a cease-fire and for all foreign forces to vacate Egyptian territory. For its part, Egypt was to restore passage of the Suez Canal disrupted by the sinking of vessels at both its northern and southern entrances. A few days later (on November 5), the Assembly also endorsed a resolution forwarded by Lester Pearson, the Canadian UN representative, setting up a UN peacekeeping force. As for the demand for a cease-fire, on November 3 both Israel and Egypt announced that they would comply.

Britain and France had bungled their planned landing of troops, largely because of Britain's insistence on adhering to a tardy timetable. (In keeping with its obsession not to be seen as working in tandem with Israel, Britain refused to put its battleships out to sea until Israel actually went to war.) Britain and France soon found themselves in an awkward situation in which they were officially about to intervene militarily to suppress fighting that had already ended.[105] To extricate them from their self-imposed plight, Israel was asked by France to rescind its undertaking to rest its arms. Affronted by such a request but not wishing to offend France, Israel obliged by declaring that in fact only a de facto as opposed to a de jure cease-fire was in force. In order for a de jure cease-fire to apply, Egypt had to concede that it was no longer in a state of war with Israel, that it would immediately enter into negotiations for a final peace settlement, annul the economic embargo, and grant Israel free and unhindered passage in both the Suez Canal and the Straits of Tiran.[106]

The absence of an official de jure cease-fire was taken by the two European powers as a legitimate justification for their campaign and without any further ado they issued a joint note to the UN reaffirming the need to separate the Egyptian and Israeli armies. The note contained a clause, insisted upon by Britain and contrary to the spirit of the Sèvres Conference, indicating that Britain and France sought the prompt withdrawal of Israeli forces. Having reluctantly bent over backward to accommodate their war plans, Israel felt slighted. Responding to Ben-Gurion's grievance, the French fudged by claiming that the clause in question was meant to refer to (non-existent) Israeli troops within the Canal Zone. Expressing his displeasure during a conversation with leading UK Labour politician Richard Crossman, Ben-Gurion, having recalled that Israel had once offered to join the British Commonwealth, sarcastically snapped: "The offer is withdrawn."[107]

On November 5, notwithstanding the fact that Israel had finally agreed to an unconditional cease-fire, the Anglo-French force belatedly landed in Egypt. The two western powers parachuted into Port Said, took command of bridges linking up with the mainland, and assumed control of the local airport. They then headed southward along the length of the Canal. At that point, the Russians, after having mercilessly crushed the Hungarian uprising, threatened to intercede on Egypt's behalf. Bulganin crudely hinted at the possibility of Soviet rockets armed with nuclear warheads crashing down on England and France. This led to a widespread fear that a third world war was imminent. To preclude such a possibility, America was prepared to compel Britain to scuttle its Suez project by deploying its economic might to topple the pound sterling and by withholding financial aid for British oil imports from non-Middle Eastern sources. Such moves would have drastically damaged the fragile British economy.

By November 6, bowing to international opposition but also in part to a rising ground swell of internal criticism, Eden, in a state of nervous exhaustion, announced that Britain was abandoning the Suez Campaign. Later that day France felt that it had no option but to follow suit.[108] By December 22, both countries had repatriated their forces. Their Suez endeavor turned out to be a calamity and their relations with the US were deeply flawed. The British, who cherished the illusion of enjoying an intimate partnership with America, were especially aggrieved. Few doubted that had the Panama Canal been nationalized, the US, impervious to international condemnation and without consulting the UK, would instantly have despatched its marines.[109]

Israel tried to stall for time for as long as possible, insisting on retaining Sharm el Sheikh, the Gaza Strip and a strip of land linking the two. On November 7, the UN General Assembly reiterated its demand for the immediate withdrawal of *all* foreign troops. It was a striking rebuke to Ben-Gurion's tactless and provocative victory speech presented to the Knesset that same day. With unsparing exaggeration, not to mention absurdity, he declared that not only was the Sinai Campaign the greatest and most glorious in the annals of the Jewish people but also one of the most remarkable in world history.[110] As far as he was concerned, the armistice agreement was dead and buried.[111] Yet President Eisenhower, among countless others, did not concur. He wrote Ben-Gurion a letter that, though politely worded, unambiguously stated that he was expecting the full implementation of all UN directives. In addition, Herbert Hoover Jr (the US acting secretary of state) informed Israel that if it failed to abide by the UN resolution, the US would deprive it of all forms of aid, enforce UN sanctions against it, and have it expelled from the UN.[112] The harshness of Hoover's communication reflected the United States' need to counteract the spread of Soviet influence in the Middle East which capitalized on the Anglo-French debacle and on growing anti-western sentiments within Arab and Third World countries.

Replying to President Eisenhower, Ben-Gurion submitted a photocopy of an order issued on October 15, 1956 (that is before the Sinai Campaign) by the head of Egypt's Third Division, Major-General Ahmad Salam. In it Salam insisted that "every commander had to prepare himself and his subordinates for the inevitable struggle with Israel, to attain our elevated goal: the destruction and elimination of Israel in the shortest possible time by means of the most savage and cruel encounters."[113]

All that was to no avail. Faced with rumors that Russia had begun transporting Soviet personnel and arms by both sea and air to the Middle East – rumors that subsequently proved to be false – Israel reluctantly accepted the UN's directive in principle on November 8.

The decision was broadcast by Ben-Gurion at 12.30 a.m. on local radio. Listeners were alerted to it after the late night news. With undisguised sorrow, Ben-Gurion recounted that the cabinet had convened twice during the previous day and, after comprehensively reviewing the pressures mounting against Israel, it felt duty-bound to take steps to diffuse the situation. The letters by Bulganin and Eisenhower were then read out, followed by Israel's official replies. In the letter to Eisenhower, Ben-Gurion assured the president that neither he "nor any other authorized spokesperson of the government of Israel had indicated that we had intended to annex Sinai."[114]

Israel, however, insisted that since conditions relating to its security were still to be met, its withdrawal would perforce be phased. From December 3, the IDF began to pull back in stages. In so doing it indulged in a scorched earth policy. Roads and railway tracks were uprooted and military buildings and installations were razed to the ground.[115] By January 15, 1957, Israel had departed from all Egyptian territory save Sharm el Sheikh and the Gaza Strip, both of which it was still hoping to retain. But the US as well as the UN remained adamant that they too had to be relinquished. Dag Hammarskjöld, the UN secretary general, was particularly abrasive. He related to Israel in an imperious manner, the likes of which he at no time demonstrated to any recusant Arab state.[116] Accusing Israel of endangering world peace, he questioned its future existence.[117] (Ben-Gurion regarded Hammarskjöld as a veritable anti-Semite.)[119] Eisenhower, although less offensive, restated his previous demands for a complete and unconditional withdrawal.

Impassionedly, Ben-Gurion denounced the double standards of the world community and asserted that Israel would never countenance such unfair treatment.[120] Judging from its own history, Israel thought that the US ought to have been more understanding. In March 1916, after having being harassed by armed Mexican bandits, the US invaded a small portion of Mexico and remained there until early in 1917. The US secretary of state, Robert Lansing, informed the Mexican government (which unlike that of Egypt did not suggest that it was in a state of war with its neighbor) that it was impossible for the US to station its troops across the entire length of its border. The only recourse open to it was "to visit punishment or destruction on the raiders . . . especially when the neighboring state makes no effort to prevent these attacks."[120]

Slowly but surely, with the US media and Congress coming round to the view that Israel harbored legitimate grievances, Eisenhower mellowed somewhat and began to show a more sympathetic appreciation of Israel's predicament. On February 20, 1957, in a nationwide radio and television broadcast, he publicly conceded that Israeli military action against Egypt resulted from grave and repeated provocations. Although he went on to state that "military force to solve international disputes cannot be reconciled with the principles and purposes of the United Nations," he also mentioned that no nation has the right to hinder free and innocent passage in the Gulf.[121] Taking up Eisenhower on the latter point, Israel requested that the US use its good offices to persuade other nations to deliver similar pronouncements.

A few days later, in a meeting with Dulles, Eban was told that the US was predisposed to a French suggestion for resolving the deadlock. It entailed the issuing of a manifesto by the US, France, Britain, Canada, Australia, Norway, and other countries recognizing Israel's claim to free navigation in the Bay of Eilat. Should such a right be denied, Israel would be entitled to assert it by force. In return Israel was to complete its withdrawal. Eban, after consulting with Ben-Gurion, signaled Israel's readiness to endorse the French initiative. The promised declaration was soon in hand as was a reassurance that the UN would place an Emergency Force in Egyptian territory along the Israel–Egypt border. On March 1, 1957, after definitively agreeing to withdraw from Gaza and Sharm el Sheikh, Golda Meir addressed the UN General Assembly. (She had previously liaised with her US and French counterparts who were in practice co-sponsors of her newly formed position.) She announced that Israel's complete withdrawal was contingent on the realization of two critical demands. That is, the UN would administer the Gaza Strip until the conclusion of a final peace treaty between Israel and Egypt and that the proposed UN Emergency Force would be charged with preserving the cease-fire as well as Israeli access to the Straits of Tiran. Should Israel ever again be denied that access, it would feel free, in terms of Article 51 of the UN charter, to respond militarily. Following Meir to the podium, the US delegate, Cabot Lodge, delivered a speech that was not only insufficiently supportive but in part at variance with what Israel had been led by Dulles to expect. Lodge backed Israel's stand on the Straits of Tiran but not on Gaza. However, a soothing letter from Eisenhower seemed to clear the air. With that letter in hand, Israel on March 6 vacated the Gaza Strip. To Israel's dismay, instead of Gaza being administered by the UN, Egyptian-inspired riots caused the UN to flinch, allowing Egypt to assume full civil control. Fortunately, the UNEF remained in Gaza to position itself along the frontier with Israel. As for Sharm el Sheikh, it was handed over to the UNEF on March 8.

Israel's decision to withdraw in full from Egyptian territory was unavoidable. Nonetheless it was bitterly opposed by Herut. Haim Landau, its spokesperson, maintained that although Nasser had not defeated the IDF, Ben-Gurion had.[122] An editorial in the party's journal melodramatically reflected the angst of those who unrealistically would have preferred Israel to dig in its heels. It proclaimed that "one's heart is shattered by terrible pain and anger and the human mind is stunned in the face of the realization of the fearful nightmares that have descended on us in the wake of Meidenak and Auschwitz. The surrender [of Egyptian territory], the shameful surrender, whole, complete, cruel, ridden with absolute disgrace."[123] In a more subdued tone, Dayan expressed the conviction that the one and only way to ensure freedom of passage in the Straits of Tiran involved Israel retaining a physical foothold at Sharm el Sheikh. He foresaw that "no guarantee in the world [including commitments made by Nasser] would prevent the infringement of international contracts that would arise, if not immediately or the next day, within one year or at most ten."[124]

Shortly after the Sinai Campaign, the Australian prime minister Sir Robert Menzies observed that "the United Nations made Israel a victim of a double standard of belligerent rights." It accepted Egypt's assertion that it could deny Israel access to the Suez Canal because Israel and Egypt were in a state of war with one another but at the same time it compelled Israel to withdraw from Egyptian territory including the Gaza Strip which Egypt illegally conquered. Menzies avowed: "I cannot believe this kind of thing is a triumph of international justice."[125] Paul-Henri Spaak, one time foreign minister of Belgium and acting president of the UN General Assembly, arrived at a similar conclusion. He wrote (in *Foreign Affairs*) that, confronted with regular Egyptian violations of the armistice agreement, the UN could not bring itself to intervene but as soon as Israel sent its troops into Sinai there was uproar. "All who stood by with folded arms in the face of the terrible suppression of the Hungarian uprising were beside themselves in reprimanding Israel. Justice of this sort is nothing but a travesty."[126]

Operation Kadesh, which cost Israel the lives of 172 soldiers and caused 817 to be wounded, did not attain all the results for which Ben-Gurion and others had hoped. Nasser was not deposed, Egypt's ties with the Soviet Union were strengthened, no territory ensuring Israeli access to the Straits of Tiran was permanently gained, and peace with the Arabs remained elusive. Critics of Israel's Sinai Campaign have likened it to a "war of choice," implying that it was not strategically imperative and that it was motivated by a desire to acquire more land. Foremost among such detractors was Avi Shlaim who, in a preface to a book by Motti Golani, reasserted the standard anti-Israel canard of an Israel greedy for territorial expansion.[127] Yet within the very same book that Shlaim so praised, Golani stated that for Israel, the "war was a means to an end: a sustainable peace with the Arab world."[128] As far as the Israeli defense establishment was concerned, Israel's "choices" were limited to it biding its time until the Arabs attacked it at their leisure, or foreclosing such an option by means of a pre-emptive strike. The Israeli writer Uri Milstein holds that had Israel not initiated the Sinai Campaign in 1956, an Arab offensive, comparable to the Yom Kippur War, would probably have eventuated. Should such a war (involving a surprise Arab attack) have occurred, Israel, in Milstein's view, might well have succumbed.[129] Israel was not alone in assuming that Nasser was intent on destroying it. In April 1956, George Kennedy Young, the deputy director of MI6, confided to the CIA that according to their sources, Nasser aimed at nothing other than the total destruction of Israel.[130] Given Nasser's chronic hostility, Israel was reluctant to return land that it had taken. However, there is no doubt that the strategy it formulated during 1955–6 was essentially a response to its deteriorating security situation. Mordehai Bar-On, a stalwart of the Israeli Peace Now movement, attests that it certainly did not "reflect a renewed arousal of an appetite and will for territorial expansion for its own sake."[131] Skeptics need only to be reminded that, years after the Six-Day War, Israel once again returned the Sinai Peninsula to Egypt, this time on its own volition in exchange for peace and without any big power threatening it with sanctions.

The actual achievements of the Sinai Campaign were not negligible. Spoils of war included the capture of 100 tanks, a large hoard of weapons, and sufficient fuel to meet civilian needs for a year.[132] Although the Soviet Union rapidly replenished Egyptian losses, between March 1957 and May 1967 there was not a single Egyptian violation of the armistice agreement. Ships freely sailed to and from Eilat, the anomaly of the Nitzana region (within Israel) being demilitarized was remedied, a UN peacekeeping force was stationed in the Gaza Strip and Sinai and the general state of military tension between Israel and Egypt abated. Since the Egyptian army did not reoccupy its Sinai bases, the peninsular effectively became demilitarized.[133]

On the other hand, little progress was achieved with regard to the Suez Canal. Israeli ships continued to be denied entry but at least other vessels carrying non-strategic cargo to and from Israel were accorded rights of passage. By early 1959, this "privilege" was canceled on the spurious grounds that Israel was developing trade ties with African and Asian states at a rate that displeased Egypt.[134] While Israel objected to not having access to the Suez Canal, it made the distinction between being deprived of its rights in the Canal as a potential user and its rights of access to the Gulf of Aqaba as a full partner stemming from its geographic presence in Eilat.[135]

The speed, daring, and success of Israel's military campaign strengthened the IDF's professional pride and the self-confidence of the entire nation.[136] In the years preceding the campaign, the Israelis constantly lived under the shadow of war. With the Sinai Campaign projecting Israeli power and with Nasser realizing that the IDF was far too formidable, the Israelis enjoyed a decade of relative tranquillity in which they felt secure and non-threatened. Also, within the international political arena there was a relaxation of tension, for proposals by western powers to revise Israel's frontiers so as to curry Arab favor (such as project Alpha) were ultimately put to rest.

The campaign also yielded valuable strategic lessons. One of Dayan's shortcomings was his misjudgment of the effectiveness of the IDF's tank corps. He failed to appreciate that heavily armored tanks, which could advance in the face of enemy fire, were in reality more mobile than lighter vehicles used by the mechanized infantry. His prejudice stemmed from the indifferent performance of Israel's tank "battalion" in the War of Independence. Not taken into account was the paltry amount of tanks then on hand. Israel had only thirteen, ten of which were of pre-war vintage. They were subject to frequent mechanical breakdowns arising from shortages of skilled mechanics and spare parts.[137] By October 1956, Israel possessed 250 Sherman tanks plus another 200 light ones, complete with an adequate stock of spare parts, repair kits, and tank transporters.[138] The armored corps boasted a high standard of technical and strategic competence and was eager to show its mettle.

As a result of the Sinai Campaign, Dayan absorbed the lessons of the 7th Brigade's startling success in capturing Abu Ageila and in sweeping effortlessly across Sinai. Tank brigades were given the recognition that was their due. Their strength was very much consolidated. Extensive efforts were also made to iron out flaws in the IDF's technological, logistic, and operational capabilities. Naturally, the air force and navy also received due consideration. Improvements and innovations in the IDF served Israel well when in May 1967 Nasser once again inflamed the region by unwittingly setting in motion a chain of events that led to the June 1967 Six-Day War. By then Israel was significantly more capable of fending for itself.[139]

Postscript

A tragedy occurred within Israel just as the Sinai Campaign was about to begin. Arab villages near the border with Jordan, in an area known as the "small triangle," had regularly been subject to a daily curfew starting at 9 p.m. and ending early the following morning. On the opening day of the Sinai Campaign, it was decided that the curfew was to commence at 5 p.m. The imposition of the curfew and its extension was a prudent security measure. Most of Israel's Arabs were not reconciled to living in a Jewish state and their passivity could not be taken for granted. As early as April 1956, Dayan had noticed that the Arabs were adorning their homes with pictures of Nasser.[140]

Alas, many inhabitants of Kfar Kassem were away from their village when changes to the curfew schedule were announced. Major Shmuel Melinki, the commander of a battalion responsible for Kfar Kassem, inquired of his senior officer, Brigadier Yashka Shadmi, what was to become of such villagers. It seems that Shadmi replied in Arabic with the expression "may God have mercy on them." From this Melinki inferred that they were to be shot.[141] As a result, some 49 Arabs, including 17 women and children, were killed on returning from work. From the court record, we learn that the first to die were four quarrymen peddling bicycles. "When they had gone some fifteen meters along the road toward the school, they were shot from behind at close range."[142] A short while later, a shepherd and his son herding their sheep met with a similar fate. One group recognized as bona fide residents was lined up and shot as were passengers alighting from a bus.[143]

Both the military censor and the government tried to suppress news of the massacre. But the story unfolded by word of mouth and the authorities were forced to relent. With the Kfar Kassem slaughter officially being acknowledged, the Knesset rose for a minute of silence. Ben-Gurion described the outrage as a dreadful atrocity and a sum of 5,000 Israeli pounds was issued as compensation to the victims' families.[144] In a cabinet meeting held on November 11, Ben-Gurion admitted: "I am sorry that the death penalty was cancelled. In this case we should have used it, so the lesson would be heard and seen."[145] Much of the media likened the carnage in Kfar Kassem to atrocities perpetrated by the Nazis. On December 7, in the Labor daily *Davar*, Natan Alterman, Israel's poet laureate, wrote "no human society can exist in which such depravity occurs without its quivering with anger."[146] "Rabbi Benyamin" (an alias of Joshua Radler-Feldman) pleaded with the Jewish clergy "to publicly confess this great crime, go to Kfar Kassem to beg forgiveness, exoneration and atonement."[147] But as the writer Boaz Evron lamented, "the religious leadership have been silent in utter indifference. Not one single religious personality has stood up to save the honour of the Jewish religion."[148]

A committee of inquiry headed by Judge Binyamin Zohar and assisted by attorney Hoter-Yishai and Abba Hushi was commissioned with investigating the circumstances leading to the massacre. The committee suspected that the order to shoot curfew violators originated from Shadmi. But in the face of Shadmi's categorical denial and given that his instructions to Melinki were issued in private, the committee reluctantly gave Shadmi the benefit of the doubt. Melinki, his deputy, Lieutenant Gavriel Dahan (who passed on Melinki's orders to his unit at Kfar Kassem) and six others, including conscripts from the Druze community, were court marshalled. Melinki was sentenced to 17 years in prison, Dahan and Shalom Ofer to 15 years and five others to seven years. Just three years later they were all released. Shadmi, who was acquitted of murder, was fined less than one US cent for exceeding his authority.[149]

Each year on the anniversary of the massacre, Kfar Kassem holds a memorial service. Despite repeated appeals to the government to send an official representative, it took 41 years for it to do so. In 1997, Moshe Katsav, the minister of tourism, visited the village to convey his government's apology. After thanking Katsav for his gesture, Ibrahim Sarsour, the village head, entreated him to return 1,500 dunams of land confiscated in 1959 and handed over to a Jewish settlement.[150] There is no indication of that request ever having been granted.

7

INTERLUDE BETWEEN WARS

On the political front

In July 1959, Ben-Gurion resigned as a result of a no-confidence motion supported by two of his coalition partners, Mapam and Ahdut Ha'avodah, in clear breach of the practice of collective ministerial responsibility. The motion in question, which gave rise to a general election in the following November, concerned the sale of arms to West Germany. Hoping to benefit from anti-German sentiments at Mapai's expense, the two dissident parties asserted that the transaction had not received government approval. However, Ben-Gurion in the Knesset, by quoting from cabinet minutes, showed that the deal had indeed secured cabinet assent.

The resulting election, the first since the victorious Sinai Campaign, enabled Mapai to trade on the glory in which Ben-Gurion still basked by flaunting the slogan: "Say yes to the Old Man." Both the Communist Party and Herut, the main instigators of the no-confidence motion, had misjudged the mood of the electorate since voters were by and large not excessively perturbed by Israel's relations with West Germany. With the country enjoying economic growth and a measure of calm, there was general satisfaction with the status quo. In the end, Mapai secured its highest number of Knesset seats (47) since the State's formation (see

Appendix). By December 1959, having patched up his quarrel with his former coalition partners, Ben-Gurion formed a new government composed of Mapai, Mafdal (the National Religious Party), Mapam, Ahdut Ha'avodah, and the Progressives.

Although the 1959 elections raised Ben-Gurion's personal political stature to new heights, his senior Mapai colleagues did not necessarily see eye to eye with him on all matters. Their loyalty was conditioned on Ben-Gurion not threatening their positions and on his continued ability to ensure Mapai's parliamentary dominance. Beneath the surface a ground swell of discontent was brewing that in 1963, coupled with other factors, paved the way for Ben-Gurion to relinquish both the premiership and defense portfolio.

The Mapai old guard noted with growing dissatisfaction that Ben-Gurion was grooming junior members for high office. Among other things, they took umbrage at his assertion that the fulfilment of Mapai's mission depended on it projecting a more youthful image than its rivals.[1] Statements of that kind induced them to coalesce into an unofficial cabal which, while not necessarily sharing general common ground, was united in believing that some counterweight to Ben-Gurion's power and influence was required. Prominent among the faction were Lavon, Sharett, Meir, Zalman Aran, and Pinhas Sapir. Among Ben-Gurion's young acolytes were Peres and Dayan. Peres, in his capacity as director of the Ministry of Defense and after 1959 as deputy minister of defense, was frequently assigned secret missions to European capitals that Meir, as foreign minister, believed ought to have resided within her domain. Primarily left to the day-to-day supervision of Israel's overseas embassies, she became increasingly frustrated at not being able to play a strategic role in formulating and articulating foreign policy. Added to that, Meir resented the self-assertiveness of the likes of Peres and his peers whom she regarded as being excessively ambitious and cynical.[2] Dayan as the newly appointed minister of agriculture antagonized the veterans by advocating national values over traditional working-class ones. This brought him into direct collision with Histadrut functionaries whom he accused of being purveyors of lip service to socialism. Enjoying all the perks of office, they in turn derided Dayan for his apparent lack of social ideals. What really roused their ire was an invidious comparison that he publicly made between the youth that in the previous 15 years had "crawled between rocks and thorns with rifle in hand," fighting in the War of Independence and the Sinai Campaign and "those that have been sitting for twenty-five years in the fifth storey of the building of the [Histadrut] executive committee."[3] Eventually, in the context of the Lavon Affair, the underlying tensions between Ben-Gurion and the Mapai old guard surfaced. To make sense of it all, an account of the Lavon Affair follows.

Although the Lavon Affair burst into the political arena in the early 1960s, it arose from events that occurred nearly a decade earlier. As already noted (in chapter 4) on December 7, 1953, Ben-Gurion resigned to take leave of absence in Kibbutz Sde Boker. Sharett, who retained his foreign ministry portfolio, succeeded him as prime minister, while Lavon took over as minister of defense. The day before Ben-Gurion's departure, Moshe Dayan replaced Mordechai Maklef as chief of staff.

Both Makleff and Dayan were wary of Lavon who had a penchant for hatching reckless military ventures. Their distaste of him was shared by Sharett in whose opinion Lavon "incessantly advocated acts of lunacy, inculcating the army command with the diabolical notion of igniting the Middle East, fomenting dissension, bloody assassinations, attacks on objectives and assets of the Powers, acts of desperation and suicide."[4] Berl Katznelson, the labor movement's guru, summed up the general feeling about Lavon by describing him as "a brilliant mind within an ugly soul."[5] Lavon in turn had a particularly low regard for Dayan, Sharett, and Peres. But above all his behavior toward Sharett was most improper. He seldom briefed him on military matters and on the odd occasions when Lavon did present Sharett with reports they (according to Dayan) "did not contain the whole truth."[6] In May 1954, in order to curb Lavon's excesses, Sharett formed a quasi-legal committee made up exclusively of five Mapai cabinet ministers to oversee foreign and defense matters. It consisted of Sharett, Lavon, Meir, Eshkol, and Aran. Non-Mapai ministers were not only excluded but they were also kept in the dark as to the committee's existence. That arrangement was at odds with the maintenance of cabinet solidarity and normal democratic norms.

During 1951 a special military intelligence section, known as Unit 131, responsible for undercover operations in enemy territory was established. After having trained about a dozen Egyptian Jewish recruits, the unit sent them home at the end of 1953 to await further instructions. On assuming office, Lavon was deeply troubled by an impending Egyptian–British rapprochement. Due to American pressure, the British agreed to enter into negotiations with Egypt to withdraw their troops from the Suez Canal zone. The Americans believed (wrongly as it turned out) that Egypt, on no longer hosting foreign troops on its soil, would be more amenable to the idea of entering into an anti-communist alliance with Iraq and other Middle East states. What worried Israel is that not only would Egypt's army have been improved by its acquisition of abandoned airports, bases and ammunition dumps but the absence of British forces in the area might well have emboldened Nasser to undertake more reckless anti-Israel military ventures.

Lavon and Benyamin Givli (who despite his shameful role in Meier Tubiansky's execution[7] had been elevated to the directorship of military intelligence) canvassed various means to frustrate any British undertaking to withdraw from Egypt. One option considered was the activation of the dormant section of Unit 131 to engage in sabotage. They hypothesized that by targeting British objectives, Britain would mistakenly conclude that the attackers were Egyptian government-inspired and as a consequence would immediately terminate negotiations to vacate the Suez Canal Zone.

In July 1954, the Israeli operatives in Egypt made a few desultory attempts to create havoc, none of which involved British property and none of which caused any serious damage. An incendiary device carried in the pocket of Philip Nathanson, one the conspirators, emitted smoke as he entered the Rio Theater in Alexandria. He was promptly arrested and his detention led to the apprehension of the rest of the group who were all tried for treason. Two were hanged, one was tortured to death, six received lengthy sentences, and two were acquitted. The Israeli coordinating them, Avri Elad, was later suspected of serving as an Egyptian double agent. Before assuming the role of the saboteurs' minder, Elad had been cashiered from the IDF for theft. But having an Aryan appearance, he was readmitted provided he went to Egypt to coordinate the underground group. To bolster his cover, he adopted the alias of Paul Frank.

In retrospect the sabotage plans were naive in the extreme, reflecting a total lack of political savvy.[8] They involved the dropping of crude and ineffective fire bombs into public post boxes, the planting of similar devices in American libraries in both Cairo and Alexandria, and finally, in response to a coded message from Israel (given through the medium of a radio cooking program), "attacks" were planned on four cinemas and the baggage storeroom of Cairo railway station. It was that latter operation that brought Nathanson to a cinema in Alexandria. On the international front, Israel was acutely embarrassed. It failed to forestall a British military withdrawal, completed by June 1956, while at the same time, it antagonized the Egyptians.

Internally, the question arose as to who had authorized the ill-fated operation. At first both Givli and Lavon suggested that the unit in Egypt must have seized the initiative of its own accord. But when Mordehai Ben-Zur, the commander of Unit 131, informed Dayan that he had acted on Givli's advice, Givli insisted that he had followed Lavon's injunctions, supposedly issued on July 16 in the course of a private conversation. (In point of fact, initial sabotage attempts commenced nearly two weeks earlier, on July 2.) On consulting his diary Lavon noted that he did not meet with Givli on July 16. He then maintained that Givli sought the go-ahead from him on July 31, by which time the entire group had been rounded up.

On January 2, 1955, to clarify matters, Sharett appointed a two-man commission, consisting of the Supreme Court president, Yitzhak Olshan, and Yaakov Dori, Israel's first chief of staff. Expected to determine just who had authorized the Egyptian operation, the commission, after interviewing both Givli and Lavon, felt that it lacked sufficient grounds for arriving at a definitive conclusion. What remained as a source of puzzlement to it was the fact that Lavon had not reprimanded Givli for supposedly acting out of turn.

Exasperated with Lavon's general conduct and seeing him as a growing liability, Sharett made it clear to him that he no longer enjoyed his confidence. As a result on February 2, 1955, Lavon resigned and later that day Ben-Gurion acceded to Sharett's request to replace him. Months later, with Ben-Gurion's assistance, Lavon assumed the role of general secretary of the Histadrut, while Givli in turn was transferred to another posting. For all intents and purposes, the Lavon Affair was shelved. But a hint of what was later to come lay in Lavon's letter of resignation. After expressing his pent-up anger at what he regarded as disreputable treatment by his former comrades, Lavon reserved the right to lodge his complaints at his leisure with an appropriate public body. The ostensible reason given by Lavon for his resignation, which was forwarded to the government and the Knesset's Committee for Foreign Affairs and Security, was that a proposal of his for a thorough reorganization of the defense ministry had been rejected.[9] No responsibility whatsoever was accepted for the Unit 131 disaster.

Then suddenly in August 1960 the affair resurfaced. In the course of Elad being tried in Israel for illicitly holding secret documents, new information came to light. It appeared that military intelligence documents had been doctored on Givli's instructions (to implicate Lavon as the initiator of the ill-fated action) and that Elad, after having been coerced by Givli, had given false evidence to the Olshan-Dori Commission. To get to the bottom of it all, Ben-Gurion approached Haim Laskov, who was then chief of staff, to set up a military board of inquiry consisting of the Supreme Court judge Haim Cohen as its chair, along with two colonels. (Cohen was temporarily accorded the rank of colonel.) The board was to investigate whether documents were indeed forged and whether former witnesses to the Olshan-Dori Commission had committed perjury. Because the board concentrated on the allegation of forged documents and was neither required nor expected to review the totality of the affair, Lavon concluded that he was denied an opportunity to clear his name. He wished to have it established unequivocally that he did not order Givli to activate the Egyptian section of Unit 131. On being asked by Lavon to be publicly exonerated, Ben-Gurion explained that he had not passed judgment upon anyone and nor would he take it upon himself to pass judgment.[10]

Disappointed at not obtaining natural justice, Lavon decided to pursue the matter with the Knesset Foreign Affairs and Security Committee. His first appearance was made on October 4, 1960. The next day, a headline in *Haaretz* read "Lavon reveals intrigues and forgeries that compromised him as defense minister." Never before had deliberations of the Knesset committee been leaked to the press. The presumption was that it was Lavon's doing. His alleged misuse of the committee as a forum meant, according to Sharett, that it had been turned into a "scandal factory."[11] Within the ensuing three weeks, Lavon presented his case on four separate occasions.

Fueled by a constant output of "confidential off-the-record comments," the Israeli press ran stories hinting that Lavon was a victim of a conspiracy to protect Ben-Gurion's protégés. Dayan and Shimon Peres were among those uppermost in mind. Based on "information" that Lavon and his associates provided them, the press not only created the misleading impression that they were somehow implicated but that the scandal tarnished the entire defense establishment.[12] At one point in his submission to the Knesset committee, Lavon alluded to "acts of corruption perpetrated by officers and clerks in the Defense Ministry." He refused to name those involved and, while conceding that he was not sure how many there were, he added, "I am told that there are tens of them."[13] To counter Lavon's allegations, which incidentally were never pursued while Lavon served as minister of defense, Peres submitted substantial documentary evidence but his efforts were overwhelmed by the deluge of charges that Lavon kept submitting.[14] Some reports even suggested that Ben-Gurion had originally pulled strings behind the scene as a means of displacing Lavon from the government and preparing the way for his own return.[15] Egged on by the opposition parties and their journals, the public began to perceive that at issue was a legitimate demand for justice being denied by an obdurate premier pursuing his own hidden agenda. Because of military censorship, most citizens had absolutely no idea as to what the fuss was really about. They were unaware of the ins and outs of the bungled Egyptian operation and its sequel nor were they any the wiser regarding the precise role of the key players. What they did know was that there was some serious rupture within the regime's upper ranks, being used as grist to the mill by Mapai's opponents.

On October 15, 1960, Haim Cohen announced the findings of his committee. In essence there was insufficient evidence to confirm suspicions that documents were forged. Given the investigative committee's conclusions and outraged by the malicious rumors that Lavon and his supporters were spreading, Ben-Gurion demanded a judicial inquiry to establish definitively just who had issued the order for the Egyptian operation. So too did Givli who, having just returned from abroad and been heartened by Cohen's ruling, reasserted that he had acted on Lavon's explicit direction. Because Sharett and others feared that a judicial inquiry might unearth the prior existence of the unauthorized cabinet defense review committee from which non-Mapai ministers had been excluded, they did not take kindly to Ben-Gurion and Givli's demands. Instead, through Eshkol's maneuvering, they commissioned a seven-member government committee and persuaded the Knesset Foreign Affairs and Security Committee to suspend its hearings.

Although not being legally empowered to summon witnesses, the government committee consulted with, among others, Givli's secretary who confirmed that at her boss's insistence she had altered a copy of a letter previously sent to Dayan. Givli himself was neither questioned nor invited to appear. From the start, members of the government committee were determined to bury the affair even if it meant exonerating Lavon. On December 20, 1960, they ruled that Lavon had not issued the critical operational order to Givli. Thereupon, Givli, acting on legal advice, withdrew his own demand for a judicial inquiry and as a result of his implicit admission of guilt, was discharged from the army.

Ben-Gurion who had a misplaced faith in Givli's integrity, refused to accept the committee's verdict. He found it beyond belief that a high-ranking IDF officer would take it into his head to initiate a delicate military operation without being ordered to do so. While his colleagues were simply more than anxious to call it a day, Ben-Gurion would not settle for anything less than a full judicial inquiry. As far as he was concerned, not only had the government committee favorably judged a fellow politician but it ought not to have been convened in the first place. In Ben-Gurion's view, the widely held principle of the separation of the powers of the judiciary, legislature and executive body had been flouted, creating a precedent that was liable to impair Israel's rule of law and democracy.[16] What is more, the government committee violated its own mandate which was merely to recommend the appropriate legal procedure for resolving the controversy. Although it was not supposed to draw its own conclusions, it did so for the sake of party peace and unity. What Ben-Gurion found particularly galling was that by clearing Lavon of responsibility for the affair, innuendos against Dayan, Peres and himself were lent an air of credibility. He was not far wrong. In cinemas showing current newsreels, Lavon's appearance elicited general applause whereas Ben-Gurion's aroused derision.[17]

In January 1961, Ben-Gurion resigned as prime minister in protest against the government committee's findings. As he put it "my current resignation from the government emanates from what my conscience dictates and from my fear for the rule of law and justice in the state."[18] Despite maintaining that his departure had nothing to do with Lavon's own behavior, Ben-Gurion mounted a personal vendetta against him. When Lavon first approached him about the suspected forgeries, he was not unsympathetic. But after Lavon invented one anti-IDF smear after another, he saw him in a totally different light and likened him to a wolf in sheep's clothing. Not being able to subject him to the legal forum of his choice, Ben-Gurion, through faithful proxies, endeavored to destroy his political career. Troubled by the course of such events, 150 distinguished academics and writers signed a manifesto that inveighed against Ben-Gurion. They expressed disquiet at his constant attempts to impose his will and at the readiness of some of his loyal underlings to do his bidding. As one writer observed, Ben-Gurion began to be "seen as a querulous and vindictive grudge bearer."[19]

Nonetheless, many party colleagues were appalled by the way Lavon, without justification, dragged the IDF through the mire, tarnishing its image with unsubstantiated allegations of corruption. Their feelings were summarized by Giora Yoseftal who asserted that "a public representative who fights for his rehabilitation by casting suspicion on the basic values of our social and political life can no longer represent us."[20] On February 4, 1961, in a secret ballot, Mapai's central committee voted to have Lavon removed from his post as general secretary of the Histadrut.

A few days later, Ben-Gurion was prevailed upon to form a new government. But on account of the odium insidiously attached to him by Lavon and his cohorts, the Mapam and Ahdut Ha'avodah parties would have dealings with him. This meant that a general election had to be held. It was scheduled for August. The constant and forceful stream of anti-Ben-Gurion invective had hit its mark, causing Mapai to lose five of its seats. Although Mapai still remained the single largest Knesset party, Ben-Gurion was unable to stitch a government together. That task was undertaken by Eshkol. Through patient and tactful bargaining, he eventually managed to assemble a coalition on Ben-Gurion's behalf consisting of Mapai, Ahdut Ha'avoda, Mafdal and Poalei Agudat Yisrael. In November 1961 it secured Knesset endorsement.

To everyone's dismay, on resuming office Ben-Gurion once again tried unsuccessfully to have the findings of the previous government committee relating to Lavon annulled. This caused his relations with the old time Mapai guard to become strained. He had already irrevocably slighted Sharett by publicly declaring that he had been incapable of securing adequate weaponry during the 1950s. Later, in May 1963, on the eve of the completion of the Dimona nuclear reactor (see below), Meir wanted to comply with the inexorable pressures that the US was applying for Israel to abandon its nuclear program.[21] She feared that the continuation of the project was likely to jeopardize Israel's relations with the US. Ben-Gurion thought otherwise, taking a dim view of what he regarded as her superficial grasp of the country's strategic imperatives. Then with an apparently cavalier attitude to German scientists working in Egypt (see below), he crossed swords with Iser Harel, the head of the Mossad (Israel's secret service organization), precipitating Harel's resignation. This caused Meir, who had close personal ties with Harel, to chide Ben-Gurion for not appreciating Harel's worth.

In the general political arena, Ben-Gurion's friendly policy toward West Germany evoked strong opposition from both rightwing and leftwing parties. For some unexplained reason, Ben-Gurion convinced himself that Herut was taking advantage of the anti-German alignment to prepare the groundwork for a fascist dictatorship. He became so detached from reality that on May 13, 1963, he informed the Knesset that Herut "glorified and praised Hitler, holding him up as an exemplar."[22] That outburst acutely embarrassed his comrades. On June 15, Meir paid Ben-Gurion another call to complain bitterly that IDF soldiers were inappropriately being trained in a West German army base. In a rancorous exchange Meir added that she was so mortified by the Defense Ministry executing foreign policy that she was thinking of resigning. But the following morning it was Ben-Gurion who resigned with the intention of leaving both the government and the Knesset. (At the last moment he was persuaded to retain his parliamentary seat.)

Ben-Gurion never provided any explanation for stepping down. While the accumulation of all of the above described incidents certainly unsettled him, it would be safe to say that in essence the Lavon Affair which Ben-Gurion refused to put behind him and which continued to gnaw at his soul was the key factor in lessening his grip on his party and government. His never ending obsession with the affair had colored his judgment, thus distancing him from almost all of his long-term allies.[23] Disappointed with his colleagues for placing political expediency above what he regarded as an important legal principle, he became somewhat wary of the hurly-burly of political life.

He was succeeded by Eshkol who, like his predecessor, also assumed the role of minister of defense. Meir remained foreign minister, while Sapir replaced Eshkol as minister of finance. By the year's end and of no inconsequential significance, Yitzhak Rabin replaced Zvi Tzur as chief of staff. With Eshkol beginning to adjust to his new responsibilities, Ben-Gurion now domiciled at Sde Boker viewed events from a distance. He certainly did not like what he saw. His hackles were raised when Eshkol and other Mapai party stalwarts made efforts to bring Lavon in from the cold and to reconcile themselves with him and his not insignificant number of supporters. Then, in what further galled him, it was decided that a plank in the party's platform favoring reform of the electoral system (which Ben-Gurion had so ardently pursued) was to be temporarily suspended. Both such measures were taken to placate Ahdut Ha'avodah in negotiations for a joint electoral ticket to be known as Hama'arah (the Alignment). In Ben-Gurion's eyes, Eshkol had also committed the cardinal sin of permitting the remains of Ze'ev Jabotinsky to be brought to Israel for an official reburial. Jabotinsky, be it noted, was the founder of the Zionist Revisionist Movement which ultimately gave rise to the Herut Party. All this resulted in Ben-Gurion excoriating Eshkol. He asserted that Eshkol was grossly unfit to be prime minister and that he himself was prepared to lead Mapai in the next election. But his party did not rally to his cause. Instead, its central committee overwhelmingly re-endorsed Eshkol.

Toward the end of June, 1965, Ben-Gurion gathered his closest supporters to a meeting at his home to announce that he was forming his own electoral list to be called Rafi (an acronym of Rishimat Poalai Yisrael, the Workers of Israel List). The new group had eight Knesset members, all of whom were drawn from Mapai. At first some Rafi adherents, including Dayan and Peres, wanted to have it both ways. Although associated with an alternative electoral list, they still wished to retain their Mapai membership. They justified their position by claiming that they represented the genuine essence of the party, a claim that was given short shrift when in August 1965 they were formally expelled.

With Rafi forced to appear as a party in its own right, it began to formulate a political platform that differentiated it from its mother party. Apart from favoring electoral reform entailing the replacement of the existing proportional representative system by one based on regional constituencies, it advocated economic liberalization, curtailments of the right to strike within public service sectors, the nationalization of health care delivery, improvements in the quality of life, and environmental protection. Rafi attracted a number of public luminaries such as Yoseph Almogi, Mapai's former Haifa party boss, Haim Herzog (a future state president), Teddy Kollek (a future mayor of Jerusalem) and Yitzhak Navon (another future state president).

Among the rightwing opposition parties former General Zionists within the Liberal party voted to enter an alliance with Herut, known as Gahal (a Hebrew acronym of Gush (block) Herut-Liberals). Ex-Progressives, who were opposed to such a move, seceded from the Liberals to establish the Independent Liberal Party. At the other end of the political spectrum, the Communist Party bifurcated into the New Communist List (Rakah) and the Israel Communist Party (Maki) which consisted mainly of Jews, led by Moshe Sneh who no longer wished to deprecate basic Zionist principles. Of the two, Maki had a smaller following.

The November 1965 general elections yielded an unexpected outcome (see Appendix). Pollsters and media commentators were confident that Rafi under Ben-Gurion's stewardship and with the illustrious Dayan at his side would significantly challenge Hama'arah, the new Mapai–Ahdut Ha'avodah alignment. Yet it only gained ten mandates, causing Ben-Gurion to attend few subsequent Knesset sessions. Mapai retained its dominance and Eshkol formed a new cabinet consisting of Hama'arah, Mapam, Mafdal, and the Independent Liberals. With Meir no longer a cabinet member, Abba Eban became foreign minister.

In June 1, 1967, on the eve of the Six-Day War and in response to immense public pressure, the coalition was widened to include both Rafi and Gahal. Eshkol transferred his defense portfolio to Dayan while Begin became a minister without portfolio in a government of national unity. In December, Rafi, without Ben-Gurion, merged with Ham'arah to form the Labor Party. Although Dayan signaled his intention to displace Eshkol as prime minister, in reality it was Eshkol whose status was enhanced for he now headed a party that superseded Mapai and from which Ben-Gurion was excluded.

The economy

In the latter half of the 1950s, Israelis experienced significant advances in living standards which continued steadily until the mid-1960s, by which time the population numbered two and a half million. In 1965 real per capita income was 77.6 percent higher than it was ten years earlier.[24]

Although the benefits of economic growth were widely spread, the upper social echelons reaped disproportionate gains. From 1954 to 1958 the share of GDP of those in the two highest income deciles rose from 38 to 41.5 percent. On the other hand, the shares of those in the two lowest income deciles fell from 7 to 5.3 percent.[25] To some extent, the increase in income inequality resulted from the payment by West Germany of reparations to individual Jews in addition to state transfers. The enhanced affluence of Israel's privileged was reflected in a rise of private car ownership, the widespread establishment of up-market restaurants, the increased patronage of tourist hotels by locals, more foreign travel, and the consolidation of exclusive suburbs such as Savion, Herzlia Pituah, and Har Hacarmel.[26]

After several years of feverish economic growth, the balance of trade continued to worsen as imports rose excessively. Consequently, in 1962, the Israeli lira was drastically devalued from 1.8 to 3 liras to the US dollar. Because Israel was highly dependent on the importation of raw materials, the devaluation generated an inflation rate of 20 percent compared with a previous bout of price stability. Widespread industrial unrest compelled the government to index wage increases to inflation. Although this mollified adversely affected workers, the wage indexation nullified the trade gains that the economy ought to have derived from the devaluation. Not only that, but the payments gap steadily widened. While the trade deficit averaged 330 million dollars per annum during the period 1957–1960, it registered 570 million by 1965.[27] The rise could be partly accounted for by large increases in military spending and by a wages blow-out that far exceeded increases in productivity. With more money on hand, consumer spending rose with some of the additional

Table 7.1   Number of immigrants (in thousands)

1955	1956	1957	1958	1959	1960	1961	1962	1963	1964	1965	1966
37.5	56.2	71.2	27.1	23.9	24.5	47.6	62.3	64.4	54.7	30.0	15.0

Source: Tzur 1997, pp. 80–1; Shaham 1998, p. 231.

expenditure being directed abroad. Had Israel been able to depend on a consistently large net inflow of foreign capital, its overall balance of payments might well have been positive. But its external financial sources were shrinking. German reparations payments were coming to an end while the US was reducing its aid allocation to Israel on the grounds that its economic growth had paved the way for self-reliance.

To rectify the worsening balance of payments crisis, the government reduced its budgetary outlays and slightly prised open the highly protected Israeli economy to foreign competition. This was done to restrict local demand and to induce manufacturers to adopt efficiency-enhancing production techniques to enable them to make greater inroads within the world market. As it happened, measures meant to gently moderate the growth of living standards were applied at an inauspicious moment of time. Several large construction projects had just been completed. These included the national water carrier, the port at Ashdod, an oil pipeline between Eilat and Haifa and extensions of the Dead Sea potash plants. This meant that workers serving in those areas were now seeking alternative employment. So too were many in the building industry which was encountering a downturn in the demand for housing as immigration in 1966 tapered off (see Table 7.1). In addition, industries newly exposed to cheap imports began trimming their staff, as did those feeling the pinch in the face of a general fall in consumption following the government's budgetary constraints. Although the unemployment rate for the country as a whole, which stood at 3.5 percent in mid-1966, was by no means excessive, a number of development towns suffered badly. In some, 20 percent of the available work force was without work.[28] Since Israel did not maintain an open-ended comprehensive unemployment insurance scheme, the unemployed were hard pressed to find the means to sustain themselves. Despairing of their future prospects, many sought salvation by migrating to countries such as the US and Canada. The result was that emigration in 1966, which largely included young adults, exceeded immigration. With Israel meant to be a beacon for Jewish immigration rather than a source of augmentation for diaspora communities, the loss of manpower that emigration entailed put in question the state's long-term viability. Not surprisingly, emigrants were characterized as being traitors and deserters. They were alleged to have lacked the moral fiber to live as proud and free Jews in their own country, choosing instead the fleshpots of exile.

The Eichmann Trial

In the very early days of the state's existence, general public awareness of the Holocaust was comparatively low key. Holocaust survivors, who settled in Israel and who numbered close to half a million, strove to reconstruct their lives without dwelling on past traumas. They seldom recounted their gruesome experiences and, even had they done so more frequently, it is doubtful whether veteran Israelis would have lent them a sympathetic ear. Having just emerged from a life-and-death struggle of their own, the Israelis could only identify with the ghetto fighters whom they regarded as bestowing honor on the Jewish nation and with whom they could readily empathize.

Eventually, the significance of the Holocaust began to be officially appreciated. In 1953, Yad Vashem, an institution memorializing the Holocaust, was established by law and situated alongside Har Herzl in Jerusalem where the fallen in the War of Independence were buried. As the bill's sponsor, Ben-Zion Dinur remarked, it is notable that Yad Vashem is located "here in Jerusalem, in the heart of the nation, here in the heart of Israel, here where everything needs be concentrated."[29] In other words, Israel was assuming the role of representing Jewry at large and of being responsible for commemorating its salient historic events. In 1959 this became even more so with the passing of a law determining an annual Holocaust memorial day.

Nonetheless throughout the decade of the 1960s, the capture and subsequent trial of Adolf Eichmann was for the Israelis the most important factor in stimulating Holocaust awareness. Eichmann, as is commonly known, was a key figure in the organization and logistics of the Holocaust. Shortly after the war, although being high on the list of wanted Nazi fugitives, he eluded the Allies and vanished. In the autumn

Plate 7.1   *Eichmann at his trial in Jerusalem*

of 1957, after years of futile searches, Harel received a tip-off from Dr Fritz Bauer, a German (Jewish) public prosecutor, that Eichmann was believed to be living in Argentina,[30] having arrived there in 1950 by means of Red Cross documents issued by the Welfare Department of the Vatican.[31] The information originated from a Jew in Buenos Aires whose daughter was seeing a young man named Nicolas Eichmann. (Adolf Eichmann had a son Nicolas who was born in Germany). Nicolas's address was provided and in early 1958 a Mossad agent was sent to conduct a surveillance of the house in question. He reported that he could not track down Eichmann and in any case it was most improbable that he would have been living in such an undesirable locality.[32] Eventually, in December 1959, Bauer provided the Mossad with an address he had just obtained from an anonymous source. It too was dated but a neighbor referred Mossad agents to Garibaldi Street, in a suburb of Buenos Aires.[33] There they discovered that the person believed to be Eichmann went by the name of Ricardo Klement. All doubts that Klement and Eichmann were one and the same were dispelled when on March 21, 1960, the day of the Eichmanns' silver wedding anniversary, Adolf returned home bearing a bouquet of flowers. Moments later sounds of celebratory merriment issued from the house.

Harel, with a hand-picked team, flew to Buenos Aires to oversee the planning and arrangements for Eichmann's capture set for May 11. On the day in question, as Eichmann alighted from a bus on returning from work, two men tackled him as he was momentarily blinded by high-beam automobile headlights. On being shoved into a car, he was bound, forced down onto the floor, and covered with a blanket. Within an hour, he was placed in a safe house where after some initial hesitation he admitted to his true identity and disclosed his SS serial numbers. Eichmann remained a prisoner in Buenos Aires for a week. Harel wanted to make sure that his family did not report the kidnapping to the police. As he anticipated, they failed to do so lest his kidnappers kill him. Having searched for him throughout the night, contacting friends and acquaintances and inquiring at local hospitals, they themselves went into hiding.[34] On May 20, dressed in an El Al attendant's uniform, Eichmann was injected with a substance that dulled his senses yet enabled him to remain ambulatory with the support of two El Al "colleagues." Bemused customs officials who assumed that Eichmann was suffering a bad hangover did not intervene and as a result he was edged into an awaiting El Al plane. Twenty-four hours later, Eichmann landed in the Jewish state. With unrestrained emotion Ben-Gurion informed the Knesset that he was under arrest in Israel and awaiting trial.

Within days, the Argentineans protested that their sovereignty had been violated. They insisted that Eichmann be returned to Argentina and that the Mossad agents in question be punished. Not obtaining a satisfactory response, they appealed to the UN Security Council. An Israeli apology failed to placate them and only in August after a mutual recall of ambassadors was the issue resolved. A joint communiqué announced that both countries regarded the incident as closed.

Against the advice of Nahum Goldmann, president of the World Jewish Congress, and others that Eichmann should be arraigned before an international court, Ben-Gurion was adamant that only Israel, the center of world Jewry, was entitled to try him. Ben-Gurion determined that Eichmann's trial would encompass not only the individual transgressions of the accused but also the entire range of the Holocaust.[35] He wanted to impress upon young Israelis the precarious nature of Jewish life in the diaspora and the need to ward off Hitler manqués threatening their country. Likewise, Gideon Hausner, the newly appointed attorney general who headed the prosecution team, intended to "design a national saga that would echo through the generations."[36]

A special police division, "Bureau 06," that at one stage employed more than 50 people, was established to interview Eichmann. Throughout the eight-month period of his interrogation, Eichmann cooperated freely. He replied to all questions and initialed each of the 3,564 pages of the recorded transcript to signify that they were authentic. Innumerable documents from the Nuremberg trials and the archives of various European countries formed the main legal basis for obtaining a conviction. They were carefully scrutinized and sifted, with only the most incriminating being submitted as evidence. In addition, survivors were expected to corroborate the written records and to recount their personal experiences with vivid effect.

The appointment of the three judges of the Jerusalem District Court under whose jurisdiction the proceedings were to take place presented some difficulties. Normally the president of the Jerusalem District Court decided who was to serve. But the incumbent was Justice Benjamin Halevy, the very judge who in the Kastner trial (see chapter 4) likened Eichmann to the devil. Under such circumstances both Yitzhak Olshan, president of the Supreme Court, and Pinhas Rosen, the minister of justice, thought that it would be most improper for Halevy to adjudicate. When with unseemly stubbornness Halevy insisted on exercising his right to nominate himself as presiding judge, a change in the law was contemplated. This in turn caused a political furore when Herut cried foul by complaining that Halevy (admired by the Revisionists for his support in besmirching Mapai's record in rescuing Jews from the Holocaust) was being discriminated against. The issue was resolved by means of a compromise. Supreme Court Justice Moshe Landau assumed the role of presiding judge, accompanied by Yitzhak Raveh and Halevy. All three were German-born.

The trial opened in April 1961 in the auditorium of the Bet Ha'am theater where Eichmann was enclosed in a bullet-proof glass cubicle. He was charged under the Nazi and Nazi Collaborators Punishment Law for having played a leading role in organizing and executing the Holocaust. During his interrogation, Eichmann had stated, "I am prepared to be punished for the black events and I know that the death sentence awaits me. I do not request mercy for I do not deserve it."[37] However, from the court dock he pleaded not guilty. Dr Robert Servatius, a lawyer from Germany, defended him and was financed by the state. More than 600 foreign correspondents covered the case. The carefully chosen 110 Holocaust survivors provided chilling testimonies of the dreadful experiences that they had endured. No grisly details were spared. The court was packed with onlookers, an overflow crowd being provided with a televized view in a nearby convent. Almost the entire Jewish population keenly followed the proceedings broadcast on radio.

Among the details emerging from the trial was the warm and close association between Eichmann and the Mufti of Jerusalem, Haj Amin al-Husseini, who headed the Palestinian national movement. It emerged that on being asked by al-Husseini for a special adviser to solve the Jewish problem in Palestine as "efficiently" as was being done in Europe, Eichmann nominated his assistant, Dieter Wislicency.[38] Years later the PLO, the Soviet Union, and anti-Zionists in western countries distorted the historic record by inverting victims and perpetrators. Instead of the Palestinians being seen as having had intimate ties with the Nazi regime, Israel began to be portrayed as having inherited the Nazi mantel.

By December 1961, Eichmann was found guilty of crimes against the Jewish people and of crimes against humanity. In May 1962, after an unsuccessful appeal to the High Court, he was hanged. As he mounted the scaffold he blessed Germany, Austria, and Argentina. His body was cremated and his ashes were scattered four kilometers out at sea.

The Eichmann trial represented an important milestone in Israeli society. Beforehand, most Israelis shared little affinity with their fellow Jews abroad. But thereafter with the frailty of Jewish existence and the importance of maintaining a national haven in Israel indelibly printed on their minds, they acquired a better appreciation of their Jewish roots. Israeli nationalist sentiments became somewhat less exclusive vis-à-vis their overseas brethren and as the historian Tom Segev put it, Holocaust commemorations provided "a way for secular Israelis to express their connection to [their] Jewish heritage."[39] Apart from acquiring a more sympathetic attitude to survivors living within their midst, young Israelis, who followed the trial's proceedings no less avidly than their older counterparts, internalized the lessons of the Holocaust, chief among which was the need for a strong sovereign Jewish state. When in May 1967 Arab states converged on Israel's borders and openly declared their genocidal intentions, Israeli soldiers were resolved that they would not allow a second Holocaust to be visited upon them. Such determination was in no small way derived from their awareness of the twentieth-century Jewish European tragedy that befell their people, an awareness that was derived first and foremost from the Eichmann trial.

Inter-ethnic Jewish tension

Israeli social scientists assumed that with the passage of time differences in economic and social conditions experienced by Mizrahi and Ashkenazi Jews would narrow but a study conducted by Amir indicated that by the end of the 1960s they had not done so and may even have increased somewhat.[40] The Mizrahim were particularly disadvantaged by the 1966 economic recession in which they bore the major brunt of unemployment. On the other hand, there is an alternative view that holds that, in the wake of the Six-Day War, those on low incomes secured a significant earnings boost. Such is the assessment of the Bank of Israel which concluded that "the standard of living of families of Asian and African origin improved relative to the standard of living of all families."[41] An investment bonanza that commenced in 1967 not only gave rise to a relative labor shortage but, as low-paid Palestinian hands entered the Israeli work force, the Mizrahim found that they in turn were able to rise up a few rungs in the socio-economic ladder. Such a phenomenon is common within countries absorbing or hosting migrant workers. Nevertheless, on average the Mizrahim remained worse off than the Ashkenazim. Whether or not they were in fact positively discriminated against, 80 percent believed that to have been the case.[42] Their relative deprivation was readily discernible within Israel's large cities where Mizrahi Jews constituted the majority in lower-class neighborhoods.[43] In some districts, they were even disproportionately represented in crime and juvenile delinquency, which added fuel to their woes by generating an empathy gap along with the income one.

In July 1959, Mizrahi Jews (mostly of Moroccan origin) violently voiced their pent-up frustration in the Haifa quarter of Wadi Salib, an overcrowded and poverty-stricken quarter at the foot of Mount Carmel, previously inhabited by Arabs.[44] The commotion began on July 8 as an immediate result of a drunken brawl at a local café triggered by a patron named Ya'acov Elkrif. On arrival at the scene, one of two police officers attempting to arrest Elkrif, who was throwing bottles at them, impetuously drew his pistol and fired at him. Noise of the shots drew a large crowd that began stoning the offending constable and his colleague. Among various deprecatory expletives, the refrain "the police have murdered one of us" was widely and loudly broadcast.[45] As Elkrif was rushed to hospital, the law enforcement agents took refuge in their patrol car. Among oncoming reinforcements was a senior police officer who patiently and sympathetically listened to the crowd's grievances and by so doing extricated all of his men.

The following morning, activists of a little heard-of organization styled "United North African Immigrants" incited the local population to join them in a protest march. The response was both instant and significant, with around 200 volatile residents following in the footsteps of the group's spokesman David Ben Harush, who led them to a police station in the nearby Hadar district. There they demanded that a delegation be permitted to visit Elkrif in hospital to establish that he was still in the land of the living. With their request having been acceded to, the crowd, at the suggestion of the police, began to disperse. Not all were so easily assuaged and as those most disaffected passed through the Hadar district, they wantonly damaged or set fire to shop windows, parked cars, and public buildings associated with the ruling Mapai party. The mayhem lasted from eleven in the morning until the evening when a combined force of regular and border police quelled the disturbances but not without both inflicting and incurring numerous injuries.

Manifestations of unrest quickly spread to other parts of the country, first in Acco and Tel-Hanan, then a week later in Kiryat Shmona where Mizrahi laborers demonstrated against the detention of those seeking improved working conditions. They clashed with police that blocked their way, injuring 11 of them. Then on July 24 in Wadi Salib a boisterous crowd massed in front of the Hadar cinema to voice its disapproval of Mapai functionaries that were inside. The next day, to everyone's surprise, Ben-Gurion and Dayan visited the troubled district. Ben-Gurion, who was clearly worried about Mizrahi agitation becoming nationwide, called for the imposition of forceful measures to restore calm. Then a week later, public violence once again came to pass in Wadi Salib in response to the convening of yet another local Mapai meeting. Sixty demonstrators were taken into custody, including Ben Harush who in his attempt to resist arrest discharged his pistol into the air. All this was followed by anti-establishment rallies in Migdal Ha'emek, where a Histadrut building was set ablaze, and in Beersheba.

Leading Mizrahi activists, including Ben Harush, were tried and sentenced to terms of imprisonment for violating public order. Ben Harush was also charged with unlawfully possessing a firearm. At the opening of his trial, the presiding judge made her feelings abundantly clear by declaring that "anyone appearing before me stating that he is a Moroccan shall be doubly punished."[46] After an unsuccessful attempt to recuse the prejudiced judge, Ben Harush sought to use the court as a platform to articulate Mizrahi grievances. But with the media and almost all politicians taking a dim view of the rioters' behavior, they were widely perceived as hooligans by a public disinclined to consider the underlying causes of their discontent.

Nonetheless, the events of Wadi Salib compelled the establishment to reappraise its melting-pot policy. What became known as the ethnic problem was ranked by Ben-Gurion as second after defense in terms of the country's most challenging issues.[47] Shaken by the disturbances, the government tried to redress some of the rioters' complaints. Expenditure on immigrant housing was increased as were grants to families with large numbers of children.[48] Parties of all shades included more delegates with a Mizrahi background on their electoral lists. But such gestures were merely token ones. In the newly formed December 1965 Knesset, only 12 percent of the parliamentarians were Mizrahi Jews.[49]

Mizrahi dissatisfaction, voiced mainly by immigrants from Morocco, did not at the time translate into a resounding Mizrahi political challenge. Wadi Salib activists stood for the Knesset under a list of their own but they failed to secure any seats. Unlike immigrants from other Arab countries, barely any of the leading Moroccan Jews settled in Israel. For the relatively poorly educated ones that went to Israel, this meant that in addition to having to cope with the tribulations of adjusting to a new life in an unfamiliar environment, the absence of most of their traditional leaders left them rudderless and with an enhanced sense of alienation.

Israel's Arab minority

At the beginning of 1949, there were 156,000 Arabs within the new Jewish state.[50] By around 1959, the Arabs of Israel numbered close to 220,000 and represented approximately 11 percent of the total population. 70 percent were Sunni Muslims, 21 percent Christians, and 9 percent Druze. The Arab natural population growth rate since 1948 at 4.0 percent per annum was among the highest in the world and far in excess of the Jewish one of 1.7 percent.[51] That factor, combined with a marked decrease in Arab infant mortality, a return to Israel of about 40,000 Arabs through a family reunification program, as well as the fact that few Arabs emigrated, meant that despite mass Jewish immigration, the share of Arabs in the total population never receded.[52] (It was 12 percent in 1966.) Israeli Arabs are concentrated in four regions. Sixty percent live in the Galil (Galilee), 20 percent in the "Little Triangle" along the highway between Afula and Hadera, and the rest in Haifa and the Negev.

Before the founding of the state of Israel, the Zionists solemnly promised that its Arab citizens would enjoy complete equality and would have access to all manner of posts, even the most senior ones. When the state was declared, the declaration included clauses that reaffirmed such promises. In practice, they have not been fully upheld, especially in the state's early years when the lot of its Arabs was far from satisfactory. That does not mean to say that the Arabs were deprived of all basic rights or that they experienced no improvements in their general living conditions. Rather the balance sheet contained both pluses and minuses.

On the negative side, the biggest drawback was the subjugation of close to 85 percent of the Arabs to military rule. That entailed the suspension of normal laws, including the right to civil trials, within the areas where it was applied and the subjection of the Arab population to the arbitrary whims of military governors. Internal travel permits were required and were issued for only limited time periods, and destinations and night curfews were enforced.

Arabs were subject to an overarching military control because they were regarded as a potential fifth column likely to aid the enemy. Interestingly, the mirror image of that view was upheld in Arab countries where, as the writer Dvora Hacohen, noted, Jews "were seen as a national minority associated with the Zionist movement – the enemy of the Muslim Arab world."[53] Military rule was also invoked to help seal the country's borders against the return of Arab refugees, for most Arabs lived in proximity to Israel's neighboring countries. Those in the Galil were close to Lebanon, the "Little Triangle" was tangent to Jordan, and Bedouin in the Negev were wont to roam into Egypt and Jordan. Yitzhak Shani, the chief military governor of the Arabs, argued that the abolishment of military rule would be tantamount to opening "the border areas to undisturbed infiltration [of Arabs] and to increasing penetration toward the interior of the country."[54] But those that doubted the wisdom of such a policy claimed that it guaranteed and perpetuated the animosity of the Arabs without significantly improving the country's security.[55] By circumscribing the formation of municipalities in Arab areas, military rule not only deprived many Arabs of a say in matters of direct concern to them but it limited the range of public services that such municipalities normally provide, such as education, health, sewerage and roads. Arab schools, for example, continued to be poorly endowed with books, equipment, adequate toilets, and playing fields. Bureaucratic stumbling blocks tended to minimize subventions from the Ministry of Education which claimed that it was unable to provide supplementary aid to villages lacking recognized local authorities such as municipalities or local councils.

The various local military governors extended their authority to matters which had absolutely no bearing on defense, such as the issuing of business licences, building permits, approvals of state loans, financial allocations for agricultural equipment, and so on. They were able to do so since they were not subject to any administrative civilian authority. This gave the ruling political party (Mapai) considerable political leverage over the Arabs who supported it in the hope of securing some form of patronage. Various Arab election lists compiled by Mapai functionaries certainly did not represent standard political Arab parties with distinct ideologies or programs. Rather they were crude but effective devices for channeling Arab votes their way. In some cases, voting papers marked by different symbols for the same list were distributed to alternative villages so that it would be apparent which villages failed to endorse them. Not surprisingly, in the 1951 and 1955 general elections, Mapai secured 66.9 and 64 percent respectively of the Arab vote, nearly double the proportion that it received from the Jewish community.[56]

Efforts to terminate military rule began to gather momentum in the late 1950s. In July 1959, the majority of a committee of government ministers, chaired by justice minister Pinhas Rosen and which represented all coalition political parties, proposed abolishing it. Rosen emphasized that there was no justification for singling out Israel's Arab community for military rule considering that it did not manifestly engage in subversion or treason.[57] There was no evidence of the formation of any underground guerrilla force or of the perpetration of any anti-state violence. On the contrary, most of the Arabs, albeit reluctantly, came to terms with their new-found situation. Even so, the minority members of the Rosen Committee, who carried the day in the Knesset vote and who were associated with Mapai, favored only minor reforms. By January 1962, the issue was re-ventilated. On the surface, the prospects for annulling military rule seemed to be promising. Opposition parties such as Mapam, as well as the General Zionists and the Progressives (the two of which two had coalesced into the Liberal Party), and surprisingly even hardline Herut concluded that restrictions specifically affecting Israel's Arab community no longer served any purpose. Within Mapai, there were those who expressed similar views but party discipline compelled them to vote against any change. With some coalition members siding with the opposition, the Mapai-led government was at first just short of being able to command a parliamentary majority. That was soon made good by bribing Agudat Yisrael. In return for granting it a banking license, it closed ranks with Mapai and its allies. A 1964 Knesset vote to reaffirm military rule was passed by the slimmest of majorities, that is, by 57 to 56. Only in December 1966 was military rule finally abrogated.

In terms of agriculture, where the Arabs in the late 1950s constituted

20 percent of the country's total farming community, output per capita had been considerably smaller than that attained by the Jews. In 1955–6, it was less than a quarter.[58] Educational standards among Arab peasants had for generations been abysmal but, more significantly, the tendency of Arabs to bequeath land equally to their ever-growing number of offspring resulted in excessive land fragmentation, leaving each heir with suboptimal farm-size holdings. Under such circumstances, mechanization and the use of other inputs and techniques that might have raised production were not economically feasible. Customs relating to land inheritance were by no means the main cause of an insufficiency of land per Arab farmer. The problem largely resulted from absolute reductions in the land area at the disposal of numerous Arab villages, combined with a high population growth rate. For illustrative purposes, the Organization of Arab Farmers in Israel listed land losses encountered by nine Arab villages as a result of the turmoil during the War of Independence and of measures taken thereafter. It appears that from 1948 to 1959, the area that those villages encompassed shrank from 298,000 to 46,800 dunams.[59] In overall terms, something of the order of 2.3 to 2.8 million dunams of land previously owned by Arabs fell into Jewish hands.[60] The land transfers were facilitated by the terms of the Fallow Lands Act, the Law of Abandoned Property, and a law relating to the acquisition of real estate. There were some Arabs in Israel who for one reason or another had temporarily been separated from their original villages. Designated as "present absentees," they were usually not permitted to return to their former homes or to restore villages that the IDF had razed. In this respect, the experiences of the Arab villagers of Yikrit and Biram were particularly shameful. Immediately after the war they were evacuated from their homes near the Lebanese border with a firm guarantee that their removal would be of a strictly limited duration. With that guarantee not being fulfilled, the villagers in desperation appealed to the Israeli High Court but, while the legal proceedings were pending, the army demolished their homes and explicitly reneged on its formal undertaking.[61]

Apart from land issues, Arab farmers found themselves concentrating on crops such as olives and tobacco that were not readily amenable to mechanization and which required intensive care. Unlike many of the products cultivated by Jews, olives and tobacco were not protected from foreign imports and, in instances where Jews did grow tobacco, they (but not Arabs) were granted subsidies.[62] Perhaps worst of all, the Arabs were compelled to market their produce through authorized monopsonistic buyers who paid them no more than a third of their crops' market value.

Incidences of government or official discrimination against the Arab sector were manifold. Here just a few are cited. In 1965 the national water carrier piped water underground or over less desirable land belonging to Jewish settlements. But in respect to land cultivated by the Arab villages of Skhanin and Araba, the carrier was placed above ground on fertile soil. The conduit was only 4 meters wide, yet a strip with a width of 93 meters was expropriated, so that, all in all, the villagers forfeited 3,000 dunams of land.[63] While Arabs were able to lease land from the Israel Lands Administration, the terms of the leases were usually for no more than a year compared with the standard 49-year leases issued to Jewish settlements. The Arabs hired land at market rates whereas the settlements paid peppercorn rents.[64] The Ministry of Social Welfare had a deliberate policy of issuing lower welfare payments to indigent Arabs compared with those provided for poverty-stricken Jews.[65] Furthermore, the Ministry of Housing allocated a paltry amount to ease accommodation shortages in the Arab sector. For example, in 1962–3, only 1.2 percent of its budget was set aside for non-Jewish Israelis.[66]

The proportion of the Arab population employed in the farm sector fell from over 50 percent at the beginning of 1948 to 41.5 percent by 1961.[67] The securing of employment in other fields of the economy was hindered by the Arabs lacking training in skilled work and knowledge of Hebrew, and by the limitations to their spatial mobility imposed by military rule.[68] For tasks requiring identical skills and education, Arab wage and salary earners in the state's first decade were paid less, sometimes as little as half that of their Jewish counterparts. They were grossly under-represented in the public sector and civil service, where in 1959 only 2 percent of such employees were Arabs.[69] Even in spheres where one might have expected them to have a reasonable presence, their numbers were remarkably sparse. There was no Arab in the office of religious affairs and only four (out of a staff of 30) were engaged in the Arab section of the Israeli Broadcasting Cooperation.[70] Of those Arabs completing high school, the teaching profession presented itself as the only one with reasonable job prospects.

The Arabs had not been able to identity fully with the new state. Prior to 1948, that is before the flight of Palestinian refugees, they constituted a majority of the land's population and then suddenly they became a minority living under a non-Muslim regime. Although Arabic was accorded the status of an official language, Israel's national anthem relates to the country's ethnic Jewish majority only, as do other state symbols such as the national flag and the menorah[71] (see glossary). As an added issue, the 1950 citizenship law presented the Arabs with certain limiting factors in acquiring citizenship. The act stipulated that Israeli citizenship could be obtained on the basis of residents being listed in a population census conducted in November 1948, by being born in Israel after the state had been founded, by virtue of subsequent legal immigration, by marrying an Israeli and, finally, by applying for naturalization. The latter procedure required, among other things, a demonstration of the ability to speak Hebrew and the final ruling was subject to the arbitrary discretion of the minister of the interior. Fortunately, over time the general issue of Arab citizenship faded into the background, as more and more Arabs were automatically nationalized through birth.[72]

On the positive side, the Arabs enjoyed a fair measure of political and legal entitlements which enabled them to participate in the political arena and to seek redress against administrative abuse through the High Court. Their general situation improved significantly and tangible gains were recorded in the areas of education and health. Within the state's first decade, the number of Arab school teachers and pupils rose by nearly five- and threefold respectively. A shortage of teachers in the early 1950s (accounted for by most having taken refuge in surrounding countries) was one of the primary causes that retarded Arab education. Lack of buildings and equipment was of course another significant determinant but, by the end of the 1960s, Sabri Jiryis, a self-exiled Israeli-Arab writer highly critical of the policies of the Jewish state, conceded that "all Arab villages, even the remotest ones, now have elementary schools."[73] The standard of Arab education gradually improved. There was even a slow rise in the number of students acquiring tertiary training. On the health front, medical clinics were established within a number of Arab rural communities. Partly as a result, the Arab infant mortality rate declined from 96 per thousand (births) in 1948 to 42 per thousand in 1966[74] (but it was nevertheless still twice as a high as the Jewish rate).

By the early 1960s, with the country enjoying a more acceptable measure of security and with the economy booming, the government began to pay more heed to the needs of its Arab citizens. It drew up a five-year Arab development plan that aimed to complete the provision of basic utility services, the expansion of housing and the provision of improvements in health, education, and welfare, as well as to assist in modernizing Arab agriculture. Efforts had been expended to improve the productivity of Arab farmers by means of seminars, the provision of advice from trained agronomists, and the encouragement of an increased use of mechanized implements, fertilizer, and pesticides.

Over time, real Arab incomes rose and, although living standards continued to fall short of Jewish ones, the average Israeli Arab enjoyed far more amenities and services than in the past and certainly far more than those available to most Arabs in neighboring states. Seen in the context of Israel's ongoing conflict with its Arab neighbors and given that almost its entire Arab minority had backed efforts to prevent Israel's formation, Israel's approach to them did not compare unfavorably with policies adopted by western countries when they too felt threatened. During the Second World War, the US arbitrarily interned its loyal Japanese minority, and in Australia, young Jewish refugees – of all people – were placed in a rural detention camp simply because they originated from Nazi-held territory. While the Israeli government was less than generous to the Arabs in the early fifties, the fact remains that its finances were in a parlous state. Had the World Jewish Community not come to its rescue, it would have been exceedingly hard pressed simply to provide food and some basic shelter to the impoverished Jewish immigrants from Arab lands, many of whom arrived with little more than the shirts on their backs.

Consolidation of Israel's military strength

For a few years after the Sinai Campaign, relations with France remained close. French arms continued to be delivered to Israel on an ongoing basis and it seemed that the Jewish state could in the medium term depend on France to satisfy its strategic needs. Nonetheless, with

Ben-Gurion and others appreciating the risks inherent in being too reliant on a single foreign source, attempts were made to secure military hardware from additional countries. The US was the most preferred supplier but, conscious of its need to forge friendly ties with Arab states, the US was disinclined to buttress overtly Israel's defensive wherewithal. What it was prepared to do was to finance the transfer of arms from Britain and West Germany. Britain obliged by providing Israel with two submarines, while Germany from 1958 onward secretly dispatched tanks, helicopters, and other items. In the process, Israel enjoyed a period of close cooperation with what Ben-Gurion termed a "different Germany."[75] Unfortunately, the German arms flow terminated in 1965 when the Arabs got wind of it and vehemently protested.

To lessen its dependence on foreigners in general, Israel widened the scope of its locally made weapons. Production was coordinated and undertaken by a body known as Rafael (the Hebrew acronym for Reshut L'pituah Emtzaei L'hima, that is, the Authority for the Development of the Means of Warfare). Its military industrial plants began to manufacture an assortment of armaments, including the renowned Uzi submachine gun, mortars, cannon, and a wide range of ammunition and shells.[76] Old tanks were modified and equipped with powerful cannons. In the field of aviation, from a small beginning in 1953 when local aircraft maintenance was first undertaken, the available number of aeronautical technicians and engineers was significantly augmented. So much so that by 1960, on the basis of a licensing agreement with France, Israel began assembling its own training aircraft. Rafael placed emphasis on enriching Israel's electronic capabilities. After creating electronic devices to enhance communication and arms fire control, its scientists had by 1956 constructed their own computer. This enabled Rafael to establish a program for the development of ground-to-ground and sea-to-sea rockets. In July 1961 the launching of a rocket named *Shavit* (Comet) 2 was widely reported as a successful stage in Israel's meteorological research. That is, Israel obliquely made it known that it was well on its way to possessing a home-made long-range ballistic missile.

The IDF had also made impressive strides in strengthening its fighting prowess. With more emphasis placed on its armored units, tank crews received intensive training. In the air force, the selection of aspiring pilots was so exacting that, as opposed to the US where 75 percent of novices were allowed to complete their courses, in Israel only 10 percent were.[77] By the mid-1960s, the IDF was highly capable of either deterring potential adversaries or inflicting a resounding defeat on foes that might recklessly misjudge the full extent of its potency. In addition to increases in armaments and improvements in organization, in November 1966 the number of soldiers at its immediate disposal was enhanced by extending the term of male-conscripted service from 26 to 30 months.

Yet Israel had grounds for questioning whether in the long run it could rely exclusively on conventional forces. The country found itself pitted against an implacable Arab bloc with a population that substantially outnumbered its own and with enormous oil-generated wealth, not to mention potential military and capital reserves residing in the rest of the Muslim world. Confronted with such a nightmarish situation, Israel's leaders would have to have been extraordinarily confident, if not foolhardy, to assume that it could always maintain the upper hand simply by relying on conventional military resources. Unlike the Arabs, Israel had no military alliances or guarantees of protection from any foreign source. Also, the country's minute size did not allow for the easy maneuvering of the IDF in the event of a foreign invasion. Israel attained the rare distinction of being the only UN member state whose neighbors explicitly threatened it with total annihilation. The "august" UN body not only tolerated the continued membership of such countries but allowed them to serve in its Security Council. Clearly the UN would never lift a finger to save Israel from extinction. Not surprisingly, Ben-Gurion arrived at the conclusion that Israel had perforce to develop a nuclear shield.

Ben-Gurion's considered need for a nuclear option dates from at least 1948 when unconfirmed indications of uranium deposits were found within the country. A year later a group of students was sent to Europe to study atomic physics to pave the way for Israel to conduct research in atomic science. By 1952, an Atomic Energy Commission, chaired by Ernst Bergman and under the auspices of the Ministry of Defense, was founded and staffed by scientists from the Hebrew University and the Weizmann Institute. It negotiated a deal with the US to assist it in building a one megawatt nuclear reactor stationed at the Nahal Soreq area south of Tel Aviv, to be used for research purposes only. Then within the confines of the 1956 Sèvres Conference, France covertly agreed to cooperate with Israel in nuclear technology by helping to install a 24-megawatt reactor at Dimona. Included was a facility for separating plutonium. Work on the reactor commenced in 1958 under the guise of the construction of a large textile plant.

Israel's pursuit of atomic power did not go internally unchallenged. By 1958, almost all the original members of the Atomic Energy Commission tendered their resignation. Two of them subsequently joined an Israeli body promoting an atomic-free Middle East. From within the cabinet Meir, Eshkol, and Sapir of Mapai joined ranks with ministers from Mapam and Ahdut Ha'avodah in opposing the production of nuclear weapons. They feared that it would ultimately stimulate a regional nuclear arms race that would offset any advantages that Israel might temporarily derive. They were also worried that the high financial costs involved might entail reductions in the IDF's general budget. Despite such dissension, Ben-Gurion prevailed. Work on the Dimona reactor continued as did Israel's development of long-range rockets. Needless to say, all of this was kept under tight wraps and disclosed neither to the entire cabinet, nor to Knesset members, nor to the public at large. Only a select number of politicians, high-ranking IDF personnel and government officials were consulted. A good deal of the funding of the Dimona project was raised from wealthy private donors in Israel and abroad.

In mid-1960, President de Gaulle informed Israel that France would no longer supply it with uranium unless Israel ceased developing an atomic bomb. Unlike his predecessors, de Gaulle did not regard Israel as a strategic ally. Rather, given his desire to mend fences with the Arab world, he looked upon close military ties with Israel as an unnecessary liability. After a hastily arranged visit to Paris, Ben-Gurion conceded that he would eventually declare that Israel's reactor was to be used for peaceful purposes only. In exchange, de Gaulle withdrew his demand for international inspections and confirmed that, while France would no longer assist in the reactor's construction, it would honor its obligations to supply Israel with all promised equipment. In December 1960, *Time* magazine revealed that Israel was developing an atomic bomb and on December 21, 1960, after photographs from a U-2 US spy plane gave the lie to Israel's explanation that work afoot at Dimona was for a new textile plant, Ben-Gurion addressed the Knesset. He averred that Israel indeed had a budding nuclear reactor but that it was to be used exclusively in furthering scientific research in the fields of agricultural and health and for energy generation.[78] Any suggestion that a nuclear weapon was being developed was a "deliberate or unwitting untruth."[79]

Far from being satisfied, the US sought to stymie Israel's nuclear ambition. On January 3, 1961, the US ambassador peremptorily served Israel with a list of questions relating to Dimona that he insisted had to be addressed by no later than midnight. Ignoring the artificial deadline, Ben-Gurion replied within a few days. He did not deal with every point raised but assured the US that Israel would in good time permit an inspection of its nuclear plant by a group of US scientists. As for an unequivocal commitment that Israel intended to harness atomic energy for peaceful purposes only, Ben-Gurion asserted that the US would have to make do with his previous Knesset announcement. In mid-1963, shortly after Eshkol replaced Ben-Gurion, President Kennedy sent the new premier a strongly worded letter indicating that his patience was wearing thin. He would no longer be fobbed off. A timetable of regular US inspections of the Dimona reactor had to be agreed upon. The Israelis (with Eshkol now accepting the need for an atomic bomb) were partially able to meet his demands by decelerating the pace of the process of their nuclear development program and by agreeing in principle to occasional visits of American inspectors in accordance with vaguely defined terms and rights of access. The visits took place in January 1964, January 1965, April 1966, and April 1967. On no occasion did the US scientists detect anything amiss. American concerns were also partially allayed by Eshkol who, on an official visit to Washington in June 1964, assured President Johnson that "Israel will not be the first to introduce nuclear weapons in the Middle East."[80] Taking all these matters into account, for the first time ever the US administration provided Israel with offensive weapons including Sky Hawk planes and Paton tanks.[81] Some defensive weapons, such as ground-to-air missiles, had already been authorized in August 1962 when Kennedy was in office. The general decision to arm Israel partly arose from the US wishing to ply Jordan with weapons to pre-empt Russian shipments. Having struck a deal with Jordan, the US was more amenable to doing likewise with Israel.

Conflict over water

In January 1951, Israel began a project to divert water from the Jordan River and in the process set about work in its part of the demilitarized zone (DMZ). Taking exception to this and arguing (incorrectly in Israel's view) that the Syrian–Israeli armistice agreement did not provide Israel with sovereign rights in that area, Syria lodged a complaint with General William Riley, chief of staff of the UN Truce Supervision Organization (UNTSO). Riley ruled that the project ought to be suspended pending a mutually satisfactory agreement between Israel and Syria. For the time being, Israel complied but at the end of March it resumed work, insisting that it was operating within its own territory. It did not take long for violent confrontations to occur. The first one erupted in early April, involving an Israeli artillery bombardment of Syrian military positions in response to the killing of seven members of the IDF who, dressed as policemen, had illegally patrolled within the DMZ. Then in May Syrian forces penetrated into the Israeli side of the DMZ to be repulsed by the IDF at the cost of 40 of its own men.[82] Israel protested to the UN but, instead of censuring Syria, the UN condemned Israel for its earlier provocation. Israeli work in the area was then put on hold.

In July 1953, Israel decided to divert water from the upper Jordan River at the Bnot Yaacov Bridge (lying east of Mishmar Hayarden) to the Negev. The Bnot Yaacov Bridge site was chosen because it was somewhat higher than Lake Kinneret which is 200 meters below sea level. In addition, water at that source was salt free, which was not quite the case in the lake. Work on the project commenced on September 2, 1953. Syria lost no time in objecting to the operation, maintaining that it was detrimental to its own water requirements. Its complaint was endorsed by General Vagn Bennike, then chief of staff of UNTSO, who ordered Israel to suspend work on the project. Israel was reluctant to comply but it was left with no choice when the US withheld economic aid as a punitive measure.

In October 1953, Eric Johnston arrived in Israel at President Eisenhower's request to mediate between the Israelis and Arabs and to propose a program for the use of Jordan River waters on a regional basis. A protracted period of bargaining ensued. Eventually a plan was submitted which allocated Israel 34–8 percent of the Jordan Valley water.[83] In October 1955, the Arab League rejected Johnston's proposal under the guise of seeking "further study." However, an unwritten and indirectly negotiated understanding was reached between Israel and Jordan, enabling each to draw on the quotas that Johnston had finally recommended. To avert further international repercussions, Israel decided to divert water (in accordance with its recommended quota) from the northwest corner of Lake Kinneret at Eshed Kinnorot, which was unequivocally within its sovereign territory. It was intended that the national water carrier would replenish water along the coastal plane and then continue southward into the Negev.

To prevent Israel from drawing water from Lake Kinneret, Syria called upon the Arab world in general and Egypt in particular to join it in waging a war against the Jewish state. At the 1961 Arab Summit Conference, Syria formally submitted a proposal for all member states to attack Israel forthwith. But under Egypt's influence, the Summit reached a compromise. The Arabs would not open hostilities immediately; rather they would do so as soon as Israel's national water carrier became fully operational. Then in 1964 when that was the case, the Syrians demanded of their fellow Arabs that they fulfil their obligations. Yet Egypt persuaded the majority that instead of attacking Israel, the Arabs ought to support efforts to deprive it of water. With that in mind, in January 1965, Syria inaugurated a water diversion scheme. On Rabin's advice, Eshkol agreed to the IDF sabotaging the Syrian enterprise by destroying its heavy equipment. Between March and July 1965 in a series of Israeli-induced incidents, most of Syria's excavating and dredging machinery was pulverized by tank-fired shells. The Syrians attempted to neutralize the IDF's onslaughts by deploying planes to attack Israel's ground forces but they were no match for the jet fighters that protected them. By the end of July, realizing that they were unable to proceed, the Syrians suspended their operation. The Lebanese, who had also made some paltry attempts to deprive Israel of water, backtracked after encountering an Israeli raiding party and after seeing what had become of Syria's endeavors.

Thanks to its legendary spy, Eli Cohen, Israel knew with pinpoint accuracy the location of each and every dredger, bulldozer, and all other implements required for the Syrian diversion project. In addition,

Cohen furnished Israel with a wealth of information relating to Syria's military establishment.[84]

Cohen was born in Alexandria, Egypt, in 1924 to a devoutly orthodox Jewish family. In February 1957, after participating in an Israeli spy ring in Egypt, he migrated to Israel, where he first worked in the Defense Department, translating and analyzing the Arab press. Bored with that job, he pursued a diploma course in business studies and entered the realm of commerce by acquiring a responsible position in a company running a food store chain. In 1960, only after fully establishing that he had adapted well to Israeli life, did the Mossad recruit him. During his training he demonstrated that he had a brilliant and inventive mind as well as a host of other attributes that made for an exemplary agent. Mossad selected him to be sent to Syria. In preparation for his mission, he acquainted himself with Islamic ritual, studied the history, politics, economics and geography of Syria, and acquired a plausible Syrian-Arabic accent. In addition, he honed his knowledge of Spanish and was taught to speak like an Argentinian. Then in March 1961, using the non de plume of Kamil Amin Taabes, he flew from Switzerland to Buenos Aires where, with Mossad finance, he posed as a Syrian expatriate trader.

Within next to no time, he had ingratiated himself with the Syrian émigré community and was warmly embraced as a true Syrian patriot. Among those that developed a special fondness for him was Major Amin Al-Hafez, a military attaché at the Syrian embassy, destined to become his country's president. In August 1961, having convinced all his Syrian associates that he could no longer bear to remain abroad, Cohen left Argentina armed with a host of recommendations on his behalf to leading members of the Syrian elite. On arrival in Damascus in January 1962, he set himself up as an import–export indent agent and soon became a leading light in Syrian society. Everyone trusted, liked, and admired him. He entertained lavishly and was exceedingly generous to all his newfound friends. In efforts to win his favors, he was given free access to the Golan Heights where he pretended that he was thinking of buying land. His military contacts proudly conducted him round their outposts and positions and he was even shown drawings and plans of their entire defense system. In July 1963, his admirer Al-Hafez seized power and talked about appointing Eli as defense minister. From then on Eli had full and unrestricted access to all of Syria's secrets. Indeed, he furnished Israel with details relating to the fortification of the Golan Heights town of Kuneitra, news of the arrival of Soviet tanks and planes, copies of Soviet suggestions for the conquest of northern Israel, and blueprints for the water diversion scheme.

In January 1965, suspecting that there were unauthorized radio transmissions from the area in which Eli resided and with the aid of Russian technicians, the Syrians tracked the broadcasts to his apartment. Due to previous electrical outages, Eli was powering his transmitter with batteries and on the fateful day in question, there was, unbeknownst to him, another general blackout. His was then the only set operating in the district. Eli was cruelly tortured and, after stoically denying his captors information, he was sentenced to death by hanging. Prior to the execution, set for May 18, he was permitted to write a farewell letter to his wife Nadia, in which he entreated her to remarry, to look after herself and their children, and to pray for his soul. An elderly rabbi was permitted to be present. He wept so profusely that Eli in turn found himself consoling and comforting him. Finally, shortly after three in the morning, Eli was led to the gallows set in a public square illuminated by floodlights. He refused an offer to mask his eyes and in the full glare of the television cameras he uttered the sacred Hebrew prayer, "Hear O Israel, the Lord our God, the Lord is one," and died a hero's death. Poor distraught Nadia went through the agony of watching it all on her television. She attempted suicide but was rushed to a hospital to be saved.

Renewed Arab threats

Egypt and Syria, which in 1958 forged a new political and sovereign entity, "The United Arab Republic" (which lasted until September 1961), continued to receive large shipments of the latest Soviet armaments. This meant that over time they would present Israel with a renewed and serious military threat. For its part, the IDF sought to retain a credible deterrent strength. Ruling out reprisal raids as a definitive response, Israel made it clear that in the event of certain Arab hostile measures, it would initiate a preventive war. Potential Arab measures that Israel regarded as going beyond the pale included the closure of the Straits of Tiran to Israeli shipping, the entry of foreign armies into Jordan, the concentration of large forces along Israel's borders, the diversion of the Jordan's waters to deprive Israel of their use, and an escalation of "guerrilla" assaults within Israel.[85]

Syria's aggressive posturing and its eagerness to ignite the Middle East cauldron affected Israel's attitude toward it. The Israelis began to assert what they regarded as their right to cultivate land in demilitarized zones within their own borders. Adjacent to Tel Katzir, south of Lake Kinneret, they laid a drainage channel and prohibited Arab farmers from crossing over it. That prohibition was ignored and when Israeli soldiers fired in the direction of the trespassers, they in turn were strafed by the Syrians. The encounter escalated into an artillery duel in which an Israeli soldier was killed. That in turn caused Israel to execute its first reprisal raid directed against Syria since the Sinai Campaign. It occurred in February 1960 when an IDF unit entered an Arab village within the demilitarized zone to destroy houses suspected of being used by Syrian forces. Syria appealed to Egypt to rally to its side. While Nasser was not ready to go quite that far, he surreptitiously positioned a large number of troops within Sinai. In response, the Israelis, in what was known as Operation Rotem, unobtrusively mobilized some of their reserves and stationed them along their border with Egypt. The stand-off was soon resolved by means of quiet diplomacy. Both sides backed down but regrettably Egypt concluded that it could march into Sinai without necessarily triggering a full-scale confrontation.[86] Such a mistaken assessment was partly responsible for events leading to the Six-Day War (reviewed in chapter 8).

The next major incident with Syria occurred in March 1962, again after an exchange of fire in Israel's demilitarized zone. The IDF attacked the Syrian village of Nukeit lying to the north of Ein Gev, leading to the deaths of five of their own men and thirty Syrians.[87] As before, the Syrians tried to embroil the Egyptians. But the Egyptians were not prepared to commit themselves at a time not of their choosing. By September 1962, Egypt became even more hesitant. It was actively involved in a civil war raging in Yemen. Siding with the republican rebels against the monarchy (supported by Saudi Arabia), large dispositions of Egyptian forces lent assistance to their newfound ally in a brutal conflict in which, according to Michael Oren, "prisoners were routinely executed, bodies mutilated, entire villages wiped out."[88] As the fighting dragged on, the war drained Egypt of large numbers of men and resources. Only in 1967 did Egypt finally disengage but not before becoming the first Arab country to deploy poison gas against its foes.

On another matter, in July 1962, the Egyptians announced that they had completed a successful trial run of a locally produced rocket capable of reaching as far afield as southern Lebanon. As if to substantiate their claim, rockets nestling in their carriers were displayed in the country's traditional Revolution Day Parade.[89] Word soon got out that German scientists were assisting Egypt in the development of non-conventional armaments. Operatives within Mossad took it upon themselves to cleanse Egypt of the Germans involved. One simply vanished. Others received letter bombs. Many Israelis were convinced that Egypt, with the help of the German scientists, was indeed on the verge of acquiring weapons of mass destruction. Anti-German feeling gathered momentum and endangered the close and cordial ties with Adenauer that Ben-Gurion had so carefully cultivated. Israel was in the process of receiving arms shipments from Germany and the last thing Ben-Gurion wanted was to endanger that flow. Suspecting that there was little basis for the growing hysteria, Ben-Gurion asked Meir Amit, head of the General Staff's intelligence branch, for an independent assessment. He reported that Egypt's potential capacity to realize its ominous objectives was minuscule. Their rockets lacked reliable navigational equipment and the Egyptians certainly did not have any access to atomic weapons nor to devastating weapons of mass destruction of any other kind. As already mentioned, in March 1963, Ben-Gurion and Harel exchanged bitter words with Harel arguing that Amit's findings were tailor-made to suit Ben-Gurion's political agenda. In a fit of temper, Harel unexpectedly resigned. He was replaced by Amit. Thereafter the panic relating to German scientists working in Egypt subsided. Those not intimidated by the Mossad's scare tactics were provided with sufficient financial inducements by the West German government to abandon their projects and return home.

In January 1964 at an Arab summit held in Cairo, Nasser suggested that a Palestine Liberation Organization (PLO) be set up under Arab League auspices. His suggestion was readily approved and finance was budgeted for that purpose. Nasser then nominated Ahmad Shukeiry, a former Palestinian who had served successively as the Saudi Arabian and Syrian ambassador to the UN, to be the PLO's first president. Once again the summit concurred. Shukeiry then personally selected the delegates for the PLO's founding conference which opened in May 1964 in East Jerusalem. Off his own bat, Shukeiry drafted a National Charter and a Fundamental Law for the nascent organization. At that time both the Gaza Strip and the West Bank were firmly in Arab hands. If to those regions one adds the eastern part of Jordan, then 82 percent of the original mandated Palestine was Arab held. Within those confines, the Palestinians constituted a distinct majority (even within Jordan alone, where the Bedouin were a rather small minority).[90] Not being content with such a situation, the PLO dedicated itself to the total elimination of the Jewish state. Only then, it declared, would Palestine be liberated. Interestingly, while one of the resolutions adopted at the PLO's founding conference held that the Palestinian body would assume sovereignty over Palestine, it was also agreed that such sovereignty would not abrogate Jordan's annexation of the West Bank![91] The abnegation of Jewish national rights was only one plank in the PLO's platform. It was officially intended that all Jews bar those that lived in Palestine prior to 1918 be expelled. At least that was touted as the desired benign outcome. In reality, many PLO members and adherents expected the Jews to be massacred en masse. As one "militant" confessed, he was among those who thought "that we must slaughter the Jews."[92]

Not to be outdone by Egypt's pretensions to be the leading sponsor of Palestinian rights, the Syrians in the latter half of 1964 sought to form a rival body to the PLO under their direct control.[93] Their army intelligence agents scoured refugee camps in Lebanon in search of volunteers to be trained as Palestinian fedayeen. One of the Syrian agents was approached by Yasser Arafat and seven of his comrades. (Yasser's first name was originally Rahman. He was given the name Yasser by a teacher in memory of a myrmidon of the Nazi collaborator Haj Amin al-Husseini, a cousin of Arafat's mother. The eponymous Yasser was killed by the British while smuggling German arms into Palestine.)[94] Arafat explained that he headed a band dubbed the Movement for the Liberation of Palestine. He and his men had opposed the formation of the PLO for not being sufficiently revolutionary and were hindered by it in that it attracted Algerian funds and facilities that they had previously enjoyed. To the great satisfaction of the recruiting agent, they agreed to cooperate with the Syrians.

Their first task was to draft a communiqué announcing the inaugural military action of their group which they named Fatah, derived by reversing the first Arabic letters of the Movement for the Liberation of Palestine (Harakat-Tahrir Falastin). Fatah means conquest through jihad. The communiqué opens by referring to the group's dependence on God and their belief in the duty of jihad,[95] thus putting paid to Arafat's subsequent protestations that he was striving for a secular democratic state. The heralding of military action in January 1965 turned out to be somewhat premature, for the explosive charges meant to sabotage Israel's national water carrier failed to detonate. No matter, news of the "event" was widely disseminated and instantly Arafat and his associates acquired celebrity status. Orchestrated by Syria, further Fatah raids got off the ground. Many were staged from Jordan in order to complicate matters for Hussein but a large number also originated from Syria. By 1966 a new Syrian regime emerged on the heels of a bloody coup that took the lives of hundreds. Because many of the new rulers were members of the minority Alawi sect that differed theologically from the main stream Sunnis, they felt the need to portray themselves as rabid Syrian nationalists to forestall potential Sunni opposition. One of their first acts was to place Fatah under the command of their own protégé, a Palestinian named Yusef Urabi, who in turn duly dismissed Arafat. Not long thereafter, Urabi's murdered body was found in a refugee camp. Arafat and his cohorts were arrested but were soon released and allowed to proceed to Lebanon. With their departure, the Fatah raids, masterminded by the Syrian Military Intelligence organization (the Deuxième Bureau), continued. They were plainly meant to undermine Israeli society and the Syrians were by no means reticent in expressing such views. Senior government officials explicitly informed Hal Saunders, a member of the US National Security Council, that the Fatah had been given free rein to endanger Israeli lives to such an extent that many, if not most, would leave for the safety of foreign shores.[96]

After facing, for nearly five months, a resurgence of terrorist attacks emanating from Jordan, Israel finally struck back. The deciding factors occurred when on May 25, 1965, six of its citizens were wounded at Kibbutz Ramat Hakovesh, and a day later, when a mother and her two children were seriously injured after their house at Afula was blown up.[97] On the night of May 27, in what marked the end of an implicit understanding with Jordan (dating from the close of the Sinai Campaign) that both countries would refrain from pursuing acts of violence, Israeli soldiers crossed the border to attack Fatah bases near both Jenin and Kalkilya. From then on, as in the 1950s, Israeli reprisal raids within Jordan became a matter of routine. It was an unsatisfactory outcome as the Israelis were well aware that Syria was the controlling force behind all the incursions. Logically, the Syrians should have been hammered instead of the Jordanians but to do so would have been infinitely more problematic. Because the Syrian Golan Heights was so well fortified, a successful Israeli raid would have necessitated a large coordinated assault involving infantry, armor and air power that would have been more akin to the waging of a full-scale war than to a mere reprisal raid.

During the night of October 7, 1966, Fatah detonated explosive charges in West Jerusalem, damaging the supporting pillars of two residential buildings. One woman was seriously injured and three less so. Visiting the scene, Eshkol, by declaring that "the ledger is open and the hand is recording," made it clear that Israel reserved the right to respond should such acts of terror continue.[98] On the following night, as if to taunt Eshkol, four members of an Israeli border patrol met their deaths as their vehicle was mined while driving in proximity to the Syrian frontier. Israel lodged a complaint to the UN Security Council where the Russians vetoed a resolution censuring Syria. Within another two weeks, on October 25 to be precise, there was another incident. A goods train on the Jerusalem–Tel Aviv line was derailed by an exploding mine. Just a short while beforehand, a passenger train had passed over the same tracks. The perpetrators, who adhered to what they styled the Abad Al-Kadar Husseini unit, issued a proclamation that read "Leave our lands, you Zionists!"[99] All that plus an announcement from the PLO's radio station in Gaza promising even more brazen acts to follow tried Israeli forbearance to the limit.

The final straw occurred on November 12, 1966, when an Israeli army truck struck a mine near Arad, killing three seasoned paratroopers and wounding six others. At the scene were footprints leading to Jordan. Convinced that an Israeli reprisal was merely a matter of time, King Hussein of Jordan wrote a letter of condolence to Eshkol in which he indicated that he would do all in his power to prevent such a recurrence. The letter was sent via the US embassy but Walworth Barbour, the American ambassador in Tel Aviv, failed to pass it on expeditiously.[100] The next day, in broad daylight and without having received Hussein's message, Israel, in an operation code-named "Grinder," exacted vengeance on the Jordanian village of Samu, some 17 kilometers south of Hebron. Paratroopers, under the command of Raphael Eitan, backed by tanks and supported by air cover, killed fourteen Legionnaires and six civilians. (Israeli losses amounted to one dead and fourteen wounded.) In the course of the raid, as a Jordanian Hunter aircraft approached, it was shot down by an Israeli Mirage.[101] Damage to property was extensive.[102] Despite prior efforts to ensure that residents vacated their houses, the US military attaché in Jordan who visited the village reported that civilian bodies were found among the ruins.[103] On learning of the overall outcome of the incursion, Eshkol was distressed. It far exceeded what he was led to expect for the IDF had not anticipated any involvement of Jordanian armed forces. Both Ben-Gurion and Dayan were scathing. Ben-Gurion considered it unjust to deploy excessive force against an essentially non-hostile neighbor, while Dayan thought that the raid was needlessly provocative.[104] Of more moment, US President Johnson was outraged. He had previously cautioned Israel against any impetuous venture affecting Jordan and, to make his displeasure plain, he signaled through one of his emissaries, Robert Comer, that if Israel persisted in such behavior, US aid to Israel would be cast in doubt. Eshkol, a man of caution, did not authorize the raid frivolously. He reminded his cabinet colleagues that the Soviet Union vetoed a UN Security Council resolution deploring Syrian complicity in the death of the four Israeli border patrol guards mentioned above. Israel, according to Eshkol, possessed the military might to deter Arab aggression but unless that might was used whenever the need arose, possession of it would be meaningless. On three recent occasions, against the advice of the General Staff, the IDF was restrained. How many more times could that happen he asked. Once? Twice? Three times? At the end of the day Israel had to react.[105]

Meanwhile, in Jordan the Palestinians were up in arms. Complaining that the government left them defenseless, they rioted in all the major West Bank towns. Shukeiry called for a general insurrection but public order was soon restored by means of mass arrests. Hussein not only fulminated against the Israeli raid on Samu but openly ridiculed Nasser. He accused him of hiding behind the apron strings of the UN Emergency Force in failing to come to his aid. Hussein's philippic hit its mark. The next time Hussein rebuked him he would act, as described in the following chapter.

From January 1966 to June 1967, 64 acts of sabotage undertaken by Palestinians were recorded in Israel.[106] They encompassed the blowing up of irrigation pipes, pumps, and electrical installations and the mining of roads and railway tracks. While their overall physical impact was minimal, virtually not a week went by without at least one Israeli becoming a victim of Arab violence. It was not something that the general populace was prepared to put up with ad infinitum.

Foreign affairs

Throughout this chapter, matters having a foreign affairs connotation have been covered in the context of broader issues such as the Lavon Affair, Israel's nuclear reactor, armaments and Germany, the water crisis, friction with the Arabs, and so on. Here only a handful of some other foreign affair issues are adumbrated.

While Israel, by virtue of the Sinai Campaign, was widely condemned, ironically its ability to befriend various Third World countries was not seriously impaired. Within its near geographic region, it cemented warm commercial and even military intelligence ties with Ethiopia and more significantly with the two Muslim states of Turkey and Iran. From Iran Israel sourced most of its oil requirements. The oil was shipped to Eilat, now accessible through the Straits of Tiran, and from there it was pumped by pipeline to refineries in Haifa. Within Africa links were forged with, among others, Senegal, Mali, Guinea, Liberia, Ivory Coast, Togo, Nigeria, the Central African Republic, Chad, Congo, Zaire, Ghana, Uganda, Kenya and Tanzania. All told, just before the outbreak of the 1967 Six-Day War, Israel maintained diplomatic relations with 27 African states.[107]

Israel was viewed as a small newly independent country from which one could obtain assistance without any concern that it might subvert and dominate aid recipients. It generously provided African states with agricultural training, advice on economic planning, guidance in setting

up medical, educational and welfare services, and even support in establishing effective security services. Israel's emissaries and volunteer aid
workers were appreciated for their idealistic enthusiasm and ability to
relate in a non-patronizing way to Third World citizens. It ought to be
stressed that of all donor countries, Israel at the beginning of the 1960s
was among the most principled. In 1961 and again in 1962, it was one
of the few advanced countries that supported a UN General Assembly
resolution calling for sanctions against South Africa. This was done
despite the fact that such an approach was likely to be one that would
cost Israel dearly. And sure enough, in 1963, South Africa blocked the
free flow of funds donated by its 120,000 Jewish community to assist
Israel in absorbing new immigrants.[108] Only after the 1973 Yom Kippur
War, when almost all African states severed relations with Israel in their
frantic rush to curry favor with the oil-rich Arab bloc, did Israel revise
its policy toward South Africa.

At one point, Israel's aid program extended to no less than 65 countries
in Africa, Asia, Latin America, the Caribbean and the Mediterranean.[109]
Were it not for special US assistance, Israel would have been unable to
provide such largesse. Meir had persuaded the American government to
finance many of its overseas aid projects on the basis that by helping to
alleviate poverty, Israel was helping to ward off Soviet encroachments
within the Third World. Ultimately, despite all its best endeavors, most
of Israel's agricultural projects in Africa collapsed. This was partly due
to African countries closing ranks with the Arabs but in the main it followed from the general futility of aiding countries rife with corruption
and ruled by dictatorial regimes that appropriated their states' limited
resources for the near exclusive benefit of their parasitical and non-
productive elite.

In mid-1963, an unanticipated yet welcome rapprochement occurred
between Israel and Jordan which because of its sensitive nature was kept
secret. It began with a clandestine meeting in London between Eshkol's
adviser, Ya'akov Herzog, and King Hussein. By 1965 Meir met with the
Jordanian monarch. The two sides agreed on a procedure for the orderly
sharing of the waters of Lake Kinneret. Also, Israel provided Hussein
with critical intelligence relating to attempts to subvert his regime and
to assassinate him and supported his efforts to obtain arms from the US.
The Jordanians understood that they were not to deploy heavy armor in

the West Bank but on occasions when serious internal disturbances arose, Israel gave Hussein the nod. It was a strange friendship. Hussein would have preferred to live in peace with Israel but the presence of a large Palestinian community within his kingdom as well as the need to comply with Arab League decisions forced his hand. Against his better judgment, he turned a blind eye to Palestinian saboteurs based in his territory. In the context of persistent Egyptian and Syrian efforts to undermine him and portray him as an imperialist agent, he antagonized his Arab adversaries by highlighting their shortcomings in confronting Israel militarily. By so doing, he felt obligated to exhibit an uncompromising anti-Israel stance.

As for Egypt, early in 1963 Sir Denis Hamilton, the editor of the London *Sunday Times*, interviewed Nasser. In the course of their conversation, Nasser informed him off the record that if only he and Ben-Gurion could meet alone face to face, all outstanding issues would be resolved. That declaration was consonant with the Arab practice of beguiling westerners into believing that, contrary to appearances, Arab rulers like Nasser were in reality benevolent peace-seeking statesmen. As soon as the contents of Hamilton's dialogue with Nasser were drawn to Ben-Gurion's attention, Hamilton was invited to visit him in Israel. There he learnt that Ben-Gurion was more than willing to meet Nasser at any venue of his choice, even Cairo. When Hamilton returned to Cairo with Ben-Gurion's tidings, it was evident that Nasser was hoist with his own petard. He lamely maintained that, on account of Ben-Gurion's general untrustworthiness, it was futile meeting with him.[110]

8

THE LEAD UP TO THE SIX-DAY WAR

Following the mid-July 1965 Syrian failure in diverting the waters of the Jordan, artillery exchanges between Syria and Israel abated, helped in part by an Israeli willingness to suspend cultivation in the demilitarized zones. It was hoped that a negotiated agreement could be reached, demarcating just where and how Israel could farm. However, the calm was but the eye of the storm. A series of events took place that rapidly led to a Middle East conflagration with far-reaching and unprecedented repercussions. Despite a let-up in cannon fire, Israel continued to be harassed by small-scale guerrilla warfare. Then, as surveyed in the previous chapter, on February 23, 1966, young members of the ruling Syrian Baathist Party seized power. They were far more extreme than their predecessors in terms of Arab nationalism and in terms of their orientation to communism. Their manifesto declared that: "The revolutionary forces in the Arab homeland, with the Baathists at their head, demand a genuine liberation of Arab Palestine . . . and an end to the Zionist presence."[1] Syria's new leaders imbued with a pseudo-Marxist doctrine of a "popular liberation struggle" held that, by means of a guerrilla insurgency, the Jewish state would be grossly undermined, if not toppled. Putting their theory into practice, they took credit for no less than 75 armed incursions into Israel during the months of February and March 1966.[2]

Twelve months down the track, that is, by March 1967, Eshkol decided to exact a punishing toll from the guerrillas' Syrian sponsors. The plan was to send tractors into the demilitarized regions to draw Syrian fire to which the IDF would immediately respond. True to form, on April 7, the Syrians fired at an Israeli tractor ploughing a field near Kibbutz Ha-On, southeast of Lake Kinneret, and at two other settlements in the same vicinity. Israel replied with an artillery barrage that in turn was met in kind. The IDF then activated its armor but, since it was unable to advance to within range of all relevant enemy positions, the air force, with Eshkol's approval, was summoned. Scores of fighters took off. (Some allege that as many as 130 planes were involved.)[3] As the Israeli planes drew near, they encountered Syrian Migs. A furious dogfight developed which spread deep into Syrian airspace. Six Syrian planes were downed without any Israeli losses. In full view of thousands of Syrian citizens, two of their planes fell on the outskirts of Damascus. With its prestige badly tarnished, Syria looked to Egypt to redeem it in accordance with a mutual defense treaty signed in November 1966. However, Nasser maintained that if he were to muster his forces in response to Syrian–Israeli border skirmishes, all that Israel need do is to "smash a Syrian tractor to draw us in. That is not satisfactory. Only we ourselves will set the deadline."[4] Therefore, unless Syria was invaded by a large ground force, Egypt would retain its own freedom of action.

Some months beforehand – that is, in September 1966 – *Bamahaneh*, a weekly Israeli army magazine, published an interview with Yitzhak Rabin, the chief of staff. Among other things, Rabin casually mentioned that the Syrian regime could not assume immunity should it continue supporting guerrilla operations against Israel. With that in mind, Rabin considered whether the only recourse open to Israel was for it to bring force to bear against "those that direct the sabotage [against Israel] and against the regime that sponsors it."[5] Later, in May 1967, Rabin reiterated that if ever Israel were to undertake acts of reprisals against Syria, they would differ qualitatively from those employed against countries such as Jordan or Lebanon not responsible for terrorists operating from their territories.[6] Not only were Rabin's remarks not followed by any specific action but Eshkol had reprimanded him for speaking out of turn. To dispel any misunderstanding, Eshkol publicly affirmed that the "State of Israel does not involve itself in the internal affairs of other states and their regimes."[7] However, by May 1967, after Israel had in the previous month alone been subject to no less than 14 Syrian-inspired attacks, Eshkol could not resist thinking aloud that "perhaps it might be necessary to adopt means no less drastic than those of April 7."[8] Rabin's and Eshkol's ruminations were interpreted by the Arabs as having a sinister gloss. But by comparison with statements so liberally provided by Syrian officials, Rabin's and Eshkol's pronouncements were the epitome of mildness. Five months before Rabin's interview with *Bamahaneh*, Hafaz Assad, Syria's minister of defense, claimed: "we are facing a war without compromise, a war exclusively for the liberation of Palestine and for the expulsion from it of the invaders."[9] Even earlier, on May 24, 1966, *Radio Damascus*, the Syrian government's mouthpiece announced: "we have decided to drench this land [Israel] with our blood, to oust you, aggressors, and throw you into the sea for good."[10]

Totally ignoring inflammatory Arab pronouncements and feigning consternation at Israel's expression of concern, Russia "discovered" in early May 1967 that Israel was massing 11–13 brigades on its northern frontiers in preparation for a general onslaught against Syria. The invasion forces were reputed to be divided into two fronts, one south and the other north of Lake Kinneret.[11]

The Soviets were in the habit of concocting such fabrications. In May 1966, in a joint statement with Syria, the Soviets declared that Israel was gathering its army within close reach of Syria.[12] On October 3, 1966, the Soviet newspaper *Pravda* wrote that Israel was preparing to conquer Syria and overthrow its regime. In that same month, Dmitri Chuvakhin, the Soviet ambassador, complained to Eshkol that Israel was readying 13 divisions for an attack.[13] Eshkol in turn invited the ambassador to accompany him to the northern region to establish for himself that there was no foundation to such a charge but Chuvakhin declined.[14] According to Aharon Yariv, the IDF's military intelligence chief, during 1966, the Soviets in one way or another raised the issue of a planned Israeli attack on Syria on eight separate occasions.[15]

The culmination of all this was that on May 13, 1967 (or May 12 as some believe)[16] a security officer of the Soviet diplomatic mission in Cairo informed Egypt that Russia had confirmed that Israeli forces were indeed poised to invade Syria and that in Russia's estimate the onslaught would probably occur between May 16 and 22.[17] In addition, on May

13 in Moscow, the Soviet president Nikolai Podgorney personally informed Anwar Sadat, chairman of the Egyptian National Assembly, of the imminence of an Israeli invasion of Syria.[18]

The Egyptians who trusted the Russians implicitly took the latest invasion report very seriously, especially since it was issued on at least two occasions. For its part the Kremlin believed that Egypt was more than capable of standing up to Israel and would act accordingly.[19] Lest for some reason the Egyptians get cold feet, Soviet Marshal Grechko assured them (on May 28) that "our fleet is in the Mediterranean near your shores. We have destroyers and submarines with missiles and arms unknown to you. Do you understand fully what I mean? . . . if something happens to you and you need us just send us a signal."[20]

That year Israel's annual Independence Day celebrations were scheduled to take place in Jerusalem. Out of consideration for the delicate status that Jerusalem held in the international community and because Israel was bound by the terms of its armistice agreement with Jordan not to introduce heavy weaponry or tanks into the city, the traditional military parade planned for May 15 was downgraded. Brushing aside such considerations, Egypt chose to deduce that the units that would otherwise have been on display formed part of Israel's potential invading force. On May 14, to shed light on the situation, Egypt's chief of staff, Muhammad Fawzi, flew to Syria. To his surprise, he observed from the air that there were no signs of any unusual military activity in the area in question. Syria's army was not even placed on a war footing! Fawzi reported to Nasser that: "There is nothing there. No massing of forces. Nothing."[21] Fawzi could simply have saved himself the trip by first checking with the UN Truce Supervision Organization that was well aware of the fact that nothing untoward was occurring.[22] Also revealing was a total absence of any mention by Syria of IDF troop concentrations when on May 15 at the UN Security Council it charged Israel of "aggressive" intentions.[23] On returning home on May 15, Fawzi learnt that Egypt was already moving two infantry divisions into the Sinai Peninsula to augment the one already there.[24] In his inimitable way, Nasser would later brazenly mislead the Egyptian people. Addressing them on the anniversary of the Egyptian Revolution on July 23, 1967, he asserted that with regard to the supposed Israeli troop build-up, "we attempted to verify this information and found that the Israelis were concentrating not less than thirteen brigades on Syria's doorstep."[25]

The massing of Egyptian troops in Sinai took Israel by surprise. Its intelligence service, not yet aware of the Soviet disinformation, first learnt of such developments on the night of May 14 when Israeli leaders were in attendance at a torchlight military tattoo in Jerusalem. Up to then, both Rabin and Dayan had discounted the possibility that in the foreseeable future Egypt would wage war. In April 1967, in addressing Harvard academics, Dayan predicted that there would not be any outbreak of serious hostilities for at least another ten years.[26] A short while before Independence Day, the IDF in its annual security assessment determined that at least for the forthcoming year, Egypt would not become belligerent. With a third of its army bogged down in a civil war in Yemen on the side of the rebels, intelligence officials assumed that Egypt had insufficient scope to place a meaningful attack force in Sinai.[27] Furthermore, Nasser had recently and repetitively asserted that he had no intention of committing his forces to a war against Israel until he was more than satisfied that they were up to such a task. On that basis, Rabin was reassured that the IDF could bring the Syrian regime down a peg or two without having to fear an Egyptian intervention.[28]

Given Nasser's insistence that he would not allow Egypt to be prematurely roped into war, it is rather surprising that he did just that. Perhaps he felt cornered. Considering that Syria was supposedly endangered, any attempt to disavow the Soviet alert would probably have been seen as an Egyptian ruse not to honor its defense treaty obligations. (Alternatively, Nasser may well have interpreted the Russian communiqués as less of a warning and more of an invitation for him to adopt military action against Israel.)[29] Shamed by not aiding Jordan in the previous November during the attack on Samu (see chapter 7), he could ill afford to appear evasive. Whatever the case, it was generally believed, even among high-ranking IDF officers, that by May 14 Nasser was not anticipating an outbreak of hostilities.

In keeping with Nasser's need to be seen to be doing the right thing by Syria, the Egyptian troop redeployment was affected with much aplomb and fanfare. The Israelis, who did not know what to make of it all, first thought that they were witnessing a rerun of the 1960 incident when a sudden influx of Egyptian troops into Sinai was shortly reversed, allowing Nasser the luxury of flexing his military muscles without using them. They failed to appreciate the fact that, in contrast to the previous occasion, Nasser's new opening gambit was being extensively covered by the media at large with the result that the inflamed "Arab Street" was now making it difficult, if not impossible, for him to back off. The IDF did at least take the precaution of placing extra armor along its southern border but no field troop reserves were alerted. As far as the IDF High Command was concerned, as long as the Egyptian Fourth Division, Nasser's main armored corps, remained west of the Suez Canal, it could safely be assumed that war was improbable.[30] What they did not know is that on the morning of May 14, Marshall Abd al Hakim Amer, Egypt's vice president and minister of defense, in conferring with his senior officers, canvassed the possibility of a limited offensive against Israel.[31] (Although Nasser was Egypt's supreme leader, full and unfettered control of the armed forces was delegated to Amer.)

Suddenly King Hussein of Jordan raised the stakes by reminding everyone that Nasser had once left him in the lurch and by accusing the Egyptian army of cowardly hiding behind the United Nations Emergency Force (UNEF). Rising to the bait, on May 16, Egypt instructed the UNEF to withdraw its forces stationed between Rafiah and the Gulf of Eilat and to reposition them in Gaza. The request, submitted in a telegram by Fawzi to Major General Indar Rikhye, the commanding officer of the UNEF, made no bones about the fact that instructions had already been issued to the Egyptian army to be prepared for action against Israel and that the partial displacement of the UNEF was requested in the interest of the full security of its personnel.[32] In other words, the UNEF, that was established to help safeguard the peace, was advised that war was imminent and that it was in its best interest to step aside.

Egypt's request to the UNEF led Israel to call up some of its reserves plus an appreciable number of reserve pilots. Rabin continued to accept Yariv's conviction that the growing Egyptian force in Sinai was essentially a defensive one intended to deter Israel from attacking Syria. However, from his knowledge of the Middle East, Rabin realized that whenever large concentrations of force are massed for a certain objective, one never can tell whether or not they will ultimately be used for some other purpose.[33] Monitoring events from afar and realizing that

Israel might be becoming apprehensive, the US State Department cabled that in its evaluation the growing disposition of Egyptian forces in Sinai was merely a public relations ploy.[34]

On learning of Egypt's request to the UNEF, U Thant, the UN secretary general, informed the Egyptian UN ambassador that there was no provision for a partial evacuation of UNEF. Egypt could either continue to accept the current arrangement or it could instruct the secretary general to withdraw the UNEF in its entirety. Should it choose the latter alternative, then the UN would have no recourse other than to comply. Rather than temporizing so as to defuse the situation, U Thant irresponsibly made public his interpretation as to what options could or could not be taken. This placed Nasser in a dilemma. If he abided by the status quo, he would surely once again be subject to gross vilification by Hussein. Also, considering that Egypt's request for a partial UNEF withdrawal had already been broadcast, along with a televized map indicating the demarcated zone in question, Nasser could hardly have glossed over the fact that an approach to the UNEF had been made. Accordingly, on May 17 he opted for the total removal of the UNEF, thereby seriously undermining the informal post-Sinai Campaign accords.

By May 18, acting on an injunction issued by U Thant, the UNEF began the process of dismantling itself. On May 19 it lowered its flag at the Erez junction in Gaza and the next day Egyptian paratroopers took possession of UNEF positions at Sharm el Sheikh adjacent to the opening of the Straits of Tiran. While the UNEF, with a total compliment of only 3,400 men, could never have served as an effective military buffer between Israeli and Egyptians forces, it did at least provide a psychological and political shield that facilitated a degree of caution on the part of Egypt. With its removal, the Israelis felt the absence of what they regarded as a significant stabilizing factor. Abba Eban, Israel's foreign minister, recalled assurances given in February 1957 by Dag Hammarskjöld, the then UN secretary general, to the effect that there was no danger of a precipitate withdrawal of the UNEF without allowing Israel an adequate opportunity to adjust to changing conditions. With that in mind, he felt that U Thant had acted far too rashly, if not recklessly.[35] Speaking directly with U Thant, Gideon Rafael, Israel's UN ambassador, read him an excerpt from a UN document that stated "relations between the peoples on the opposite sides of the line are such that if the United Nations buffer should be removed, serious fighting would, quite likely, soon be resumed." U Thant asked who wrote the report and when Rafael disclosed that it was submitted on September 7, 1966, to the General Assembly by none other than U Thant himself, the secretary general was acutely embarrassed.[36] With the demise of the UNEF coinciding with additional Egyptian forces pouring into Sinai, Israel decided to draw upon even more reservists and to notch up the number of tanks facing Egypt to 400.[37] (Already the Egyptians were placing 80,000 troops and 800 tanks in Sinai.[38] Later these were to be supplemented by, among others, the arrival of expeditionary units from Kuwait and Algeria.)

Within Israel a pre-emptive strike began to be widely canvassed. The sudden departure of the UNEF as well as the inexorable arms build-up in Sinai were viewed as harbingers of worse to come, causing Eshkol to conclude that the advent of war was a certainty.[39] What really heightened Israel's sense of looming disaster was an incident that occurred on May 17. Two Egyptian Mig-21s were reported as entering Israel's airspace from the Bay of Eilat. The planes flew at a very high altitude to pass over the country's nuclear reactor at Dimona. The Israeli air force (IAF) was unable to intercept them and the planes returned to Sinai unharmed.[40] The flights were seen as heralding an unprovoked aerial attack on the reactor. As of late, grounds have emerged for believing that the planes in question were not Mig-21s piloted by Egyptians but state-of-the-art Mig-25 Foxbats operated by Russians. In an article written by Colonel Aleksander Drobyshesky, chief spokesperson of the Russian air force, and posted in October 2006 on the ministry's web site, reference was made to the commendation of Colonel A. S. Bezhevets, a Soviet pilot, for overflying Israel in a Foxbat.[41] This supports a theory propagated by Isabella Ginor and Gideon Remez that Soviet intrigues in the Middle East were far more menacing than had been formerly realized.[42] However, the evidence, though strongly suggestive, is not conclusive.

On May 18, as the Israeli government grappled with its defense predicament, a letter arrived from US president Lyndon Johnson. The gist of it read: "The United States will not accept responsibility for situations arising from actions undertaken without prior consultation with it."[43] What Johnson was effectively demanding was the right to veto any proposed Israeli military operation. Notwithstanding that, on May 19, Eshkol (on Rabin's advice) decided on a large-scale mobilization of the reservists.

In many cases reservists were contacted in the dead of night. Within a matter of minutes, they had to pack their bags and take leave of their loved ones. The call-up exceeded general expectations. Not only did almost everyone commissioned report for duty but many who for one reason or another were not required begged to be included. As in the days immediately preceding the Sinai Campaign, the streets of Israel's towns and cities thinned out. Few vehicles were seen on the roads as many were requisitioned to ferry troops. On the home front, people volunteered to serve where needed. Neighbors assisted families whose breadwinners were away, drivers scooped up passengers vainly waiting at bus stops, and there was a general uncharacteristic sense of public solidarity.[44] Sensing the gravity of the situation, Rabin stressed that the conscripts should be under no illusions that they had been called upon merely for training or maneuvers. The army was being put on a war footing and the rank and file had to understand what that implied.[45] Rabin was later to record that from May 19 onward, he had not the slightest doubt that the current crisis could only be resolved by force of arms and it was that realization alone that subsequently provided the overriding thrust to his entire course of action.[46]

Observing a general build-up of forces on both sides of the Egyptian–Israeli border, the US sent yet another message to Israel counseling patience and advising it to place its trust in diplomatic moves that the US was overseeing. The US also sought assurances from Russia and Egypt that the potentially explosive situation would be contained and that the Straits of Tiran would remain open to Israeli shipping. On May 22, Eshkol addressed the Knesset. He stated that "Israel is prepared to participate in an effort to strengthen stability and the advancement of peace in our region."[47] But discreetly through the medium of the UN secretary general, U Thant, Eshkol cautioned that, should Egypt close the Straits of Tiran, Israel would view such a move as a casus belli. That very evening, while U Thant was en route to deliver Eshkol's message, Nasser upped the ante. While on a visit to the Abu Suweir airbase at Bir Gafgafa in Sinai, he had become emboldened by the supreme confidence exuded by his pilots. As they spoke of their ability to destroy the entire Israeli air force within a matter of hours, he in turn informed them that henceforth all ships bearing Israeli flags would be barred from entering the Straits of Tiran. Not only were Israeli ships to be disallowed but so too were ships of any nationality conveying "strategic" goods to Eilat. Inspired by his own rising and uninhibited bellicosity, Nasser added: "if the Jews threaten to fight, my reply is 'ahlan wasahlan' [you are welcome] – we are ready for war."[48] For Nasser it was no longer a matter of idle boasting. He had already (on May 13) been briefed by his generals that Egypt could take on Israel and that "we will never be in a better position than now. Our forces are well equipped and trained. We have all the advantages of attacking first. We are sure of victory."[49] Shams Badran, who had been the Egyptian minister for war, on later defending himself at a military court martial told his judges that after Nasser had taken his leave of the pilots at Bir Gafgafa, he and Amer had lingered a little longer. Ever so anxious to make it crystal clear to the airmen that they were not being fed false promises, Amer "told them not to worry, for they would really be going to war."[50] In essence, the decision to close the Straits of Tiran had been taken the day before (May 21) when the Supreme Committee of the Arab Socialist Union (Egypt's sole political party) assembled at Nasser's house.[51] On reminding his colleagues of the serious implication of such a step, Nasser again turned to Amer for reassurance. The marshal obliged by affirming effusively "on my head be it, Boss! Everything is in tip-top shape."[52] Just over six months earlier, well before Israel's supposed military build-up on the Syrian frontier, Amer had already been advocating the closure of the Straits.[53] He had concluded that, unlike the Suez War when Israel was in league with two great powers and Egypt's forces were largely deployed in the Canal Zone, Israel now stood alone without the benefit of French air cover to confront the main brunt of the Egyptian army. All this made Nasser reckon that with his heavily armed and fortified troops massing in Sinai and with fraternal Arab countries backing him to the hilt, he could readily deal Israel a mortal blow.

Elated by the grand challenge he had set himself and beholden to events that he no longer controlled, Nasser delivered one fiery speech after another.[54] The net result was that the general Arab populace was whipped up into a delirious frenzy sending chills down the spines of the Israelis. As Dayan noted, there was an interesting twist to the way things were panning out. Rather than Israel actually threatening to go war against Syria, as the Soviets falsely claimed, Egypt presented Israel with an enormous concentration of troops and threat of force.[55]

On May 23, faced with such a dramatic turn of events, a ministerial defense committee met to consider Israel's next move. At hand was an appeal from the US president for Israel to delay any action for another 48 hours to enable him to use his good offices to reopen the Straits of Tiran. Taking into account the risks associated with starting a war, few showed any overriding interest in launching a military adventure. The ministers were somewhat sobered on learning that in Rabin's and Ezer Weizman's judgment (Weizman was head of the IDF operations branch), the IAF could not simultaneously but only sequentially neutralize both Egyptian and Syrian fighter and bomber planes. Until then, they had taken it as axiomatic that Israel could handle a multitude of fronts with relative ease.[56] On being reassured by Rabin that there was no compelling military reason why Israel could not agree to a delay of 48 hours or even more, Eban was instructed to proceed to America. There he was to establish what the US was doing to resolve the deadlock. (One step that Johnson had already taken, on May 22, was the ordering of the Sixth Fleet to the eastern Mediterranean.)

Shortly after the ministerial meeting, Rabin became somewhat fretful. On the basis of a revised intelligence appraisal, he sought out Eshkol to tell him that he no longer thought that Israel could afford to wait a moment longer but Eshkol was unmoved.[57] Rabin's "new" information was simply a reconfirmation of the continued Egyptian armed forces build-up in Sinai. It was also delivered by Rabin with an element of indecisiveness in that he expressed some reservations as to whether the country was ready for the sacrifices entailed.[58]

Eban's mission was not greeted with enthusiasm by many either within or without the cabinet. Eshkol feared that an agreed delay of 48 hours would stretch into a fortnight and then a fortnight into two years.[59] Others surmised that Eban would return with some flimsy and worthless gestures that would tie Israel's hands. Nor were the Americans pleased. They feared that any course that Israel might subsequently pursue would be seen as involving US collusion.

In the early hours of May 24, Eban left Israel on his flight to the USA via Europe. His first port of call was in Paris where he conferred with President de Gaulle who insisted that, despite all Egyptian violations of the status quo, Israel should never fire the first shot. De Gaulle arrogated to himself the role of *primus inter pares* (first among equals) of the four great powers (US, UK, France, and Russia) which under his sagacious counsel would resolve the Middle East impasse by diplomatic means. An absurd proposition if ever there was one, for it implied that the West and the Soviet Union, which provided the catalyst for the crisis, could reach a consensus. De Gaulle was neither prepared to reaffirm France's commitment to Israel's security nor to censure Egypt for its hostile posturing. Hours before Eban arrived, the French cabinet had accepted de Gaulle's interpretation that the Straits of Tiran were within the territorial waters of Egypt and Saudi Arabia and that Israel had no legal basis for demanding free passage.[60] As if to emphasize the extent to which France was prepared to side with the Arabs, he let it be known that he wanted the four powers to reconsider the Arabs' general demands, including the "right" of the Palestinian refugees to return en masse. When Eban reminded de Gaulle of the statement issued by France in 1957, reaffirming its support of Israel's right of free passage through the Straits of Tiran, de Gaulle with a shrug, dismissed it as no longer having any relevance. "Besides," he added, "I wasn't president then."[61] Israel was beginning to learn the hard way that the shelf life of one state's commitment to another could be short indeed.

As Eban next touched down in London, the reception awaiting him was somewhat more cordial. Harold Wilson, the British prime minister, indicated that he appreciated and supported the need for ensuring complete freedom of shipping in the Straits of Tiran. But he stressed that it was up to the US to assume the lead in securing such an outcome. In any case, as Wilson insisted, a multilateral solution to the crisis needed to be obtained under UN auspices. If Wilson had misplaced faith in the UN, his foreign secretary, George Brown was under no such illusion. Three days earlier he had told the House of Commons that since at the end of the day the UN is merely the sum of its members, "there are clear limitations" as to what one might reasonably expect of it.[62] In any case the irrelevance of the UN was made evident when on May 24 Canada and Denmark failed, thanks to a Soviet veto, to convene a Security Council session to consider the Middle East crisis.

Meanwhile in Israel (on May 24) Weizman, deputizing for Rabin who was out of commission for 24 hours, placed the IDF on full battle alert. Forces were moved to frontline positions in the expectation that war would break out at dawn. However, because of opposition from Eshkol who refused to sanction pre-emptive hostilities, Weizman's orders were rescinded. The following day (May 25), Israel's security situation appeared to have taken a serious turn for the worse. Meeting with Rabin, Yariv, Weizman, and General Haim Bar-Lev, Eshkol was led to understand that Nasser was determined to go on the offensive and that the center of gravity of the threat facing Israel had shifted from the Straits of Tiran to Egypt's massive concentration of force in Sinai. What swayed Yariv's judgment was information just received that the crack Fourth Egyptian Division had finally entered Sinai and was taking up a position between Bir Gafgafa and Tamara. As already stated, the entry of the Fourth Division was viewed by Israeli Intelligence as a litmus test of Nasser's intentions. An additional piece in the intelligence puzzle was the realization that almost the entire Egyptian expeditionary force in Yemen had now been repatriated. Finally, that very afternoon, Egypt had falsely announced that an Israeli attack on the Gaza Strip had been repulsed by Palestinian forces. Yariv feared that that bogus report was meant to provide a ruse for an Egyptian offensive.[63]

The upshot of it all was that Eshkol sent Eban an urgent telegram informing him of the latest developments. Eban was instructed to emphasize Israel's perilous circumstances to President Johnson and to ask him to explain precisely what practical steps his government was taking to diffuse the crisis. Then on the evening of May 25, the generals of the High Command became even more perturbed. They felt that they had reason to believe that Russia had provided Egypt with Israel's strategic plans and that to counter them Egypt was on the verge of destroying Israel's airfields. On establishing from Yariv that an Israel pre-emptive strike could be put off for one more day, Eshkol sent a second telegram to Washington. On this occasion it was addressed to Avraham Harman, Israel's ambassador to the US. It unequivocally demanded that both Harman and Eban notify the American administration in no uncertain terms that within the past 24 hours the situation had become untenable. Emphasizing the extreme gravity of the matter, the telegram went on to stress that unless the US issued an *immediate* statement to the effect that an attack on Israel would be regarded as an attack on the US, there was no telling what Israel might do.

Essentially, recourse to arms had become inescapable. By making an urgent plea to the US, Eshkol was in effect trying to ensure that Israel's impending military operation would be viewed with some understanding, if not sympathy. Be that as it may, despite all indications of a forthcoming Egyptian thrust, Eshkol was loath to launch a preventive war while Eban was consulting with Johnson. Mindful of the fact that the Japanese attack on Pearl Harbor had occurred just when its ambassador was communicating with the US administration, Eshkol wished to avoid such an invidious comparison.

The telegrams imposed on the Israeli foreign minister an unattainable goal for, even had he wanted to, Johnson lacked the constitutional powers to issue such a statement. Before meeting with the US president, Eban had conveyed Israel's concerns to members of the State Department and Pentagon who were far more unruffled than the Israelis. In their opinion, Israel was quite capable of fending for itself. Nevertheless, under Johnson's instructions, Eugene Rostow, the under secretary of state, summoned the Egyptian ambassador and issued him with a blunt warning. The essence of this was that, since the US was committed to preserving the integrity and existence of Israel, a sudden Egyptian attack on it would be tantamount to suicide. Concurrently, Russia was notified of Israel's anxiety.[64] Other than that, Eban's encounter with Johnson (on May 26), for which he had waited nearly a full day, bore little fruit. At the end of a two-hour discussion, Johnson promised that he would do all in his power to open the Straits of Tiran to Israeli shipping but first he intended to exhaust the UN channel. This essentially meant that for the moment, nothing of consequence would be decided. Apart from referring to the UN, Johnson was adamant that "Israel will not be alone unless it decides to go alone" (a phrase actually coined and suggested by Dean Rusk, the secretary of state).[65] After Eban had taken his leave, Johnson, who was despondent about prospects for the immediate future, is reported to have said: "I've failed. They'll go."[66]

That same day in Israel Dimona was subject to another Egyptian overflight. Four Migs cruising in Israeli airspace at an altitude of 52,000 feet proved to be elusive. As with the incident that occurred nine days earlier, this one was taken as an omen of Egyptian intentions to bomb

Israel's nuclear reactor as well as to devastate the country's limited air-fields.[67] An urgent meeting of the ministerial defense committee was held at Eshkol's home. After briefings by Rabin and Yariv, in which the importance of striking the first blow was underscored, dovish skeptics such as Mordechai Bentov of Mapam and Haim Shapira from Mafdal pressed Rabin for more details. Not wishing to divulge any operational plans, Rabin answered that whoever attacks first gains an advantage. More than that, he was not prepared to say. Notwithstanding the strong case presented by Rabin and Yariv, the ministers felt that they really ought to await Eban's return to hear his report.

At around 2.30 a.m. on May 27, both Eshkol and Nasser were awoken to receive a message from Aleksei Kosygin, the Soviet premier. Having done all in their power to bring Israel and the Arabs to the brink of war, the Soviets informed Israel that it was far easier to start a fire than to extinguish it.[68] With that in mind, Israel was warned not to assume the offensive. Even though Kosygin claimed that Egypt was being accorded similar advice, the Israelis at first construed his note as a thinly veiled threat but on second thoughts concluded that by Soviet standards it was not quite so blunt. Walworth Barbour, the US ambassador, who was shown the Russian communiqué, described it as being "moderate in tone and reasonable in content."[69] On the other hand, the contents of Kosygin's message to Egypt had far-reaching repercussions. In it Kosygin revealed that President Johnson had informed him that Egypt was on the verge of attacking Israel and, should it do so, the US would not feel bound to exercise restraint.[70] Those words hit Nasser like a bolt from the blue for Egypt was indeed braced, that very morning, to carry out Operation Dawn, a plan to conquer the southern Negev. A special task force under General Sa'ad Shazli's command was to dissect the Negev by punching through from Egyptian to Jordanian territory to occupy Eilat. The campaign was to be preceded by sweeping Egyptian air strikes that would obliterate Israel's grounded aircraft.[71] Final briefings had already been given to Egyptian air, ground, and naval forces which were in the process of counting down to zero hour. With Nasser now wrongly believing that Israel had full knowledge of his intentions and that the US might intervene on Israel's behalf, Operation Dawn was canceled.[72] Weeks later, Nasser in a note to the Soviets bitterly complained, "you prevented us from inflicting the first blow. You deprived us of the initiative. It was none other than a conspiracy!"[73]

That night (May 27) an Israeli cabinet meeting was convened. Eban, having just returned from the US, reported that the Americans wanted Israel to hold out for yet a few more weeks to allow diplomacy to take effect. The ministers agonized over Israel's dilemma. Some feared that in the event of war the IDF might find itself with a depleted stock of armaments and with no one to turn to for replenishments while the Arabs would be generously supported by Russia. In that light, Shapira ventured that he had more confidence in American promises than in the IDF's ability to succeed.[74] By contrast, others backed by Rabin (who with other high-ranking officers was also in attendance) held that the risk of lying idle far exceeded the risk of Israel taking its fate into its own hands. The longer Israel waited, the more opportunity the Egyptians would have to consolidate and strengthen their forces. With the session dragging on till four in the morning, Eshkol suggested to his weary colleagues that they adjourn for some sleep and reconvene at three the next afternoon (of May 28). Judging by the views expressed by each participant, it was apparent that the cabinet was deadlocked. Nine members, including Eshkol, favored immediate military action while nine were opposed to such a move.[75]

In the interim, the Israelis heard from President Johnson and from Dean Rusk. Johnson divulged that he had been informed by Russia that within Israel it was now widely assumed that there was no alternative to war. According to Johnson, should the Israeli government be guided by such a view, it would be making a terrible mistake. As a friend, the president urged Israel not to act rashly. He offered grounds for believing that the US was achieving steady progress in assembling an international flotilla that would break Egypt's Straits of Tiran blockade. Rusk's warning, relayed by Barbour, was far sterner. It explicitly suggested that there would be a catastrophic outcome if Israel irresponsibly failed to abide by Johnson's request.[76] With those two messages in mind, the cabinet, at its re-adjourned session (on May 28) overwhelmingly agreed to let matters play out for another two to three weeks. Rabin tried to forestall that decision on the grounds that in the end Israel would be faced with far more adverse political and military hurdles. But Eshkol made it clear that the decision rested with the cabinet and not the army.[77] Finally, it was decided that it was imperative that Eshkol address the nation on radio that evening to reassure it that all was under control.

The address turned out to be a complete fiasco. It was written by Eshkol's personal assistants who passed on their draft to Israel Galili, a cabinet minister, who prided himself on his writing skills. In his own hand, Galili superimposed a number of alterations on the typed document. When Eshkol arrived at the broadcasting studio he was rather tired, had a bad cold and, as a result of a recent cataract operation, one eye had an artificial lens that was not stably in place. Moments before the broadcast, he was handed a copy of his speech with its penned amendments. Its contents were somewhat placatory, stressing the need for diplomacy. No ultimatum was issued regarding the closure of the Tiran Straits. At one point Eshkol encountered some difficulty in making out the text. One word appeared to be faintly replaced by another. Not being sure which one to use, Eshkol could be heard murmuring to an aide. Quite possibly he had momentarily forgotten that he was live on air. Not surprisingly, his listeners were dumbfounded. Instead of radiating strength and self-confidence, he came across as a bungling waverer, leaving his audience with an enhanced sense of unease. Rabin wrote that Eshkol's address would be remembered as "the stammering speech."[78] Aside from Eshkol's poor rendition, the content of his speech was found wanting. Although tribute was paid to the IDF's capability of defending the country, undue emphasis was placed on the reliance of outsiders to resolve Israel's quandary. In the process, the confidence of its citizens in their state's means to weather the crisis was severely diminished. Morale among both soldiers and civilians plummeted. It had even been reported that some soldiers, including officers, burst into tears as they listened to Eshkol's faulty delivery.[79]

Immediately after his ill-fated broadcast, Eshkol met with the IDF's General Staff to explain why military action had to be delayed. Even under normal circumstances, a psychological gulf existed between the government and the General Staff, reflecting differences in their makeup. First of all, there was a generational gap. The average age of cabinet ministers was 64 years compared with an average of 43 years for the generals. But, more significantly, only one (Yigal Allon) of the 18 cabinet ministers was born in the country, while 13 of the 18 General Staff members were.[80] Such differences resulted in divergences in temperament and perspective. The timidity of cabinet members who were decidedly more wary of the use of force was seen by the generals as a by-product of their diaspora origins. In meetings with his General Staff, Rabin habitually referred to his political superiors as "the Jews," implying that, unlike them, both he and his colleagues represented a new generation of Israelis untainted by ghetto mentalities and complexes.

By all accounts, the officers had reached the conclusion that the government was totally incapable of rising to the occasion. In their view, since war was unavoidable, it made no sense to wait any longer. Cutting Eshkol to the quick, Sharon declared "your prevarications are going to cost us thousands of lives."[81] Calmly but with suppressed anger, Eshkol reminded the generals that even if Egypt was subdued, it would soon recover but, for Israel to endure, it perforce had to rely on the goodwill of countries like the US and Britain. A responsible government had to ensure that it did not needlessly alienate potential sources of support. It was therefore incumbent upon Israel to demonstrate a willingness to allow a decent interval in which the crisis could potentially be peacefully settled. The generals were unconvinced. Among their concerns was the fact that the IDF's rank and file was becoming increasingly disheartened by repetitive on–off alerts. Rabin suggested that they be advised that though for various political considerations the government had momentarily restrained them, there had been no change in the military situation and that sooner or later they would be called to arms.

Even before the closure of the Tiran Straits, politicians began conspiring to replace Eshkol either as prime minister or certainly as minister of defense. Lacking Ben-Gurion's charisma, Eshkol, a kind and decent man, was widely perceived as being too vacillating. He was in reality no one's fool but preferred, wherever possible, to arrive at crucial decisions consensually. That democratic attribute was wrongly interpreted as a sign of weakness, making him the butt of inappropriate jokes. One of these he himself inadvertently coined. On being asked whether he would prefer tea or coffee, he playfully replied "half and half." Unfortunately, according to his daughter, Eshkol's wisecrack boomeranged to haunt him.[82]

Foremost amongst Eshkol's opponents was Shimon Peres who energetically canvassed to have him replaced by Ben-Gurion who since the Lavon Affair loathed him obsessively. Ironically, at a time when the public was clamoring for a resolute leader to gird the nation for war, Ben-Gurion was averse to it. (So too was Peres whose alarmist views about the IDF's capabilities further sapped the confidence of cabinet doves.)[83] Ben-Gurion feared that fighting would continue for weeks on end and that, without a great power behind it, Israel would be hard pressed to sustain its war effort. He suggested that the country should simply dig in until a more opportune moment arose.

Once it became clear that Mapai was firmly standing by Eshkol as prime minister, efforts were concentrated on having Dayan appointed as minister of defense. After Eshkol's ill-fated broadcast, such efforts gathered momentum. They were no longer confined to Peres and his colleagues but were supported by a large cross-section of the media, politicians, and general public. Mafdal threatened to bolt from the coalition unless Dayan was coopted in the framework of a newly formed government of national unity. It had mistakenly assumed that Dayan would be a restraining influence against IDF pressures to go to war.[84]

As the pro-Dayan lobby was growing from strength to strength, Nasser was becoming ever shriller. On May 28 he told a gathering of journalists that it was not the closure of the Straits of Tiran that was the problem but rather the very existence of Israel. Egypt would not abide coexisting with it.[85] The following day, in an address to the Egyptian National Assembly, Nasser announced that he was ready "to restore the situation to what it was in 1948 [before Israel was proclaimed]."[86]

On May 30, the move to install Dayan was given a sudden boost from an unexpected quarter. Without the Israelis having any foreknowledge, Hussein flew to Cairo to sign a defense pact with Nasser that committed him to take up arms in the event of Israel attacking Egypt. Hussein also accepted a number of other Egyptian dictates that included recognizing Shukeiry and his PLO as the legitimate representatives of the Palestinians, the placing of his army under the command of an Egyptian general, and an agreement to the entry into his kingdom of both Egyptian and Iraqi troops. On contracting with Egypt, Hussein announced that he was looking forward to treading the "road leading to the erasure of our shame and the liberation of Palestine."[87]

Hussein had come to the realization that if he did not align himself with Nasser, his shaky monarchy would be shattered by a combination of Egyptian subversion, local Palestinian discontent, and even a possible Egyptian invasion should Nasser defeat the Israelis. Taking the US ambassador in Amman into his confidence, he admitted that he was flying to Cairo "in order to secure a life insurance policy."[88] Having previously taunted Nasser for his reluctance to combat Israel, Hussein could now hardly remain on the sidelines.

Dayan realized that the entry of Jordan into the anti-Israel axis was a sure sign of war for, had Hussein thought otherwise, he would not have thrown in his lot with his erstwhile adversaries.[89] Meanwhile on June 1, the Egyptian General Abdul Munin Riad assumed authority over the Arab Legion. Among his war plans was the concentration of four Iraqi brigades opposite Netanya and in the Jenin hills as a prelude to severing Israel at its thin waistline.[90] Two Egyptian commando units were assigned to Jordan to be put to use either or both in attacking Jerusalem or seizing Eilat. Among Arab Legion documents later found were plans for operation "Rad," which entailed a night raid on Motsa lying on the outskirts of Jerusalem. The village was "to be razed to its foundations without allowing for a single survivor or anyone fleeing from it."[91] With Israelis finally sensing that they could dally no longer, the clamor for Dayan, the hero of the Sinai Campaign, to assume the reins of the country's defense ministry became deafening.

Eshkol did not take kindly to the notion of incorporating Dayan into his government. By his close association with Ben-Gurion, Dayan was too tainted a political rival. Golda Meir warned Eshkol that if Dayan were to become minister of defense Eshkol would be unfairly deprived of the honor of victory. Weizman, who barged into Eshkol's office unannounced, spoke in similar terms albeit far more theatrically. With tears in his eyes he shouted, "The state is ruined. All is wrecked." Then more to the point he exclaimed, "Eshkol, just issue the IDF the order to go to war and we will win. What do you need Moshe Dayan for? Who needs Yigal Allon? Our army is powerful and is simply awaiting your order."[92] But in the face of a universally perceived need to coopt opposition parties into a government of national unity, Eshkol reluctantly bowed to Rafi and Gahal's entry preconditions (also shared by Mafdal for remaining in the cabinet) that Dayan be appointed as minister of defense. Accordingly, on June 1, Eshkol relinquished his defense portfolio in favor of Dayan, while Begin and Yosef Sapir of Gahal were appointed cabinet members without portfolio. On the face of it, it seemed strange that a dove like Shapira had so eagerly promoted Gahal's entry into a government of national unity. After all, Gahal's leader, Begin, was a hawk par excellence. But Shapira had noted that, like him, Begin had advocated the return of Ben-Gurion to power.[93]

Israel now had a government of national unity whose long-term significance was not fully grasped. Until then, Begin had been treated by the ruling Mapai establishment as a political pariah. Suddenly he was regarded with respect as a responsible politician whose cooperation was sought in Israel's hour of need. By bringing Begin out of the political wilderness, conditions were being met which paved the way for him becoming, in 1977, Israel's first non-labor prime minister.

For Eshkol, the decision to renounce his defense portfolio in favor of Dayan was an acutely painful one that tormented him right up to his dying day some two years later. But he could hardly have done otherwise, for he had already proposed a compromise. He would remain as prime minister, Allon would become defense minister and Dayan would be made deputy prime minister. When this was put to Dayan he rejected it out of hand, countering with a preference to replace Yeshayahu Gavish as the commander of the Southern Front. Rabin out of deference to Gavish was most put out, as was Yisrael Lior, Eshkol's military attaché who thought that Dayan's suggestion was just one other indication that he lacked the common touch and had no regard for the feelings of others.[94] As it happened, the notion of appointing Allon as minister of defense was a non-starter. Not having seen active service since the War of Independence and having little public following, Allon was not widely perceived as being suited for that portfolio. He certainly would not have been accepted by Rafi and Gahal. At noon on June 1, Allon made things easier for Eshkol by renouncing his candidature. The irony is that but for the need to assuage a public driven by hysteria there was no other reason why Eshkol need have relinquished the defense portfolio. He oversaw it in his usual efficient way, had a good rapport with Rabin, and readily supported all measures necessary to ensure that the IDF was able to meet the challenges of the day. It was Eshkol who finally made it possible for Israel to source the American arms market. In Rabin's view, that feat alone "ought to insure that Eshkol's name be inscribed in gold on Israel's pages of history."[95]

In addition to the anguish that Eshkol experienced by deferring to

Dayan, he also had to put up with the churlishness of Rafi. On indicating Rafi's willingness to enter the government of national unity, Peres informed Eshkol that he and his comrades continued to regard his premiership as a national liability of the highest order. Ever since Rafi had failed dismally in the previous general election, Ben-Gurion had poured scorn on Eshkol. In his dotage, Ben-Gurion became increasingly vindictive. He criticized his political opponents without letup and employed innumerable devices to discredit them. Eshkol was the main target of his attacks and among Ben-Gurion's calumnies was an unwarranted accusation that Eshkol had been negligent with regard to Israel's defense. Moreover, Peres, as Ben-Gurion's lieutenant, constantly denigrated Eshkol. As far as Eshkol was concerned, Peres's barbs were far more biting than those of Begin who was at least courteous and eloquent.[96]

To understand more clearly just what fueled the drive to divest Eshkol of his defense portfolio, it is necessary to delve into the three-week interval between the entry of Egyptian forces into Sinai and the outbreak of the Six-Day War, when almost the entire Israeli Jewish population was seized with a powerful sense of foreboding. With hostile Arab forces increasingly massing along their frontiers and with the neighboring states of Egypt, Jordan, and Syria firmly in alliance, the Israelis felt that an iron ring was being clamped around their fragile homeland. In June, Iraq committed itself to the fray and began dispatching an expeditionary force into Jordan. Other Arab countries from near and far foreshadowed their participation either by way of manpower, finance, or by imposing an oil blockade against countries thought to be friends of Israel. Lebanon, Algeria, Tunisia, Libya, Sudan, and Kuwait all announced that they were on a war footing, with some of them being in the process of sending token contingents to Cairo. In Gaza, hordes of armed Palestinians were filmed brandishing rifles and baying for Jewish blood. Cartoons appearing in the Arab press were intimidating. One from the Syrian paper *al-Jundi al-Arabia* depicted a heap of skulls, each marked with the Star of David, lying within the smoking ruins of Tel Aviv.[97] The Arabs were certainly not coy in declaring that the demise of the Jewish state was avidly being sought. The Cairo-based radio station *Voice of the Arabs* made it clear that a total war would be waged against Israel "which will result in the final extermination of Zionist existence."[98] Mullahs called for a jihad and one of Radio Cairo's hit songs exhorted the Arabs to smite, kill, burn, and destroy the Israelis. "Itbah, itbah, itbah" (that is, "massacre, massacre, massacre") ran its refrain.[99] On June 2, General Murtagi, the commander of the Egyptian forces in Sinai, issued an Order of the Day that enjoined his troops to "reconquer anew the robbed land of Palestine."[100] Just prior to the outbreak of the Six-Day War, on being asked in an interview on French television what plans he had for Jews born in Israel, Shukeiry, the head of the PLO, simply drew a finger across his throat.[101] Elsewhere, in answer to the same question, Shukeiry responded "those who survive will remain in Palestine, but I estimate that none of them will survive."[102]

With western countries expressing reluctance to help restore Israel's right of passage through the Straits of Tiran and with Russia and then France throwing in their lot with the Arabs, Israel was becoming increasingly isolated. (On May 22, both Britain and France announced that the 1950 Tripartite Declaration guaranteeing the inviolability of all Middle Eastern states' borders no longer applied.) Throughout Israel, people reflected on the Holocaust and wondered whether a similar fate lay in store for them. Rumors circulated that the Tel Aviv Independence Park was being consecrated to allow for 20,000 burial sites. Estimates of possible war fatalities ranged from 10,000 to 100,000.[103] Thousands of additional hospital beds were made available and large quantities of antidotes for poison gas were stockpiled.[104] Anxious civilians began to hoard items such as sugar, rice, flour, canned goods, candles, and toilet paper, and very soon they were no longer freely available.[105]

Not everyone was overcome with despair. Volunteers gladly stepped into the breach to help out in hospitals, the postal service, kibbutzim, and in other places experiencing serious manpower shortages on account of the draft. Civilian encouragement was also given to frontline troops. The Hebrew daily *Ma'ariv* reported an incident in which a kindergarten teacher walked 30 of her charges to a nearby reservist unit. The soldiers, delighted at the arrival of the toddlers, feted them by doling out candy, sweeping them up in the air, and joining in with them by singing their nursery rhymes. At one point one of the infants spontaneously stepped forward and plaintively pleaded: "Soldiers, look after us and our state and our flag."[106] With most having children of their own, they were deeply moved.

Even those within Israel's military hierarchy who were confident of a victorious outcome harbored some misgivings. It had never dawned upon them that Nasser would so audaciously throw down the gauntlet. They had assumed that he appreciated Israel's relative strength and would therefore not recklessly provoke a non-winnable war. But now they had to contend with a large element of irrationality.[107] Against what normally would have been their better judgment, some senior officers, including Motti Gur, personally dug defense trenches around their homes.[108]

Israel had 250 planes, some 1,300 tanks and 250,000 men under arms[109] but most of its equipment was fairly dated. By and large, new American weapons in the pipeline did not arrive prior to June 1967.[110] On the other hand, Egypt, Jordan and Syria were in possession of 554 planes (420 of which belonging to Egypt), 1,430 tanks and 276,000 men. Of Egypt's forces, 100,000 men were stationed in Sinai by June 5.[111] (According to one authority, the Arab world as a whole could field 900 planes, 5,000 tanks and 500,000 men.)[112] However such figures make no allowance for qualitative differences and in this respect, bearing in mind factors such as general education, training, organization, planning, and above all motivation, Israel's manpower capabilities were distinctly superior.

The IDF's enforced idleness, as the futile search for a political resolution of the crisis continued, seemed to sap Israel's ability to launch a pre-emptive strike. It was thought that the more Israel waited the more would an IDF offensive be problematic. Conversely, if the Arabs were to strike first, Israel would suffer extensive human and material losses. As the waiting period lengthened, members of the General Staff began to question ever more vocally whether the government had the political backbone to seize the bull by the horns. The Israeli economy could not sustain a prolonged state of full mobilization and, in the event of the reservists being discharged, the Arabs whose armies were stationed at unprecedented strength along Israel's borders would have been incapable of resisting the temptation to attack.

At a personal level, Rabin found the strain unbearable. He had not slept for a number of nights, ate little, sipped innumerable cups of black coffee, and smoked incessantly. On May 22, he visited Ben-Gurion who hectored him for even contemplating a war without Israel first securing a great power ally. According to Ben-Gurion, by mobilizing the reservists, Rabin "led the state into a grave situation."[113] Ben-Gurion's disparagement was totally unfounded, for the mobilization of the reservists was undertaken in direct response to a massive and growing accumulation of Egyptian forces within easy reach of Israel and not the other way round. By contrast with Nasser, Rabin tried to augment his army's combat readiness with as little fuss as possible. In his memoirs Rabin wrote that on the night after having seen Ben-Gurion and even for days thereafter, Ben-Gurion's admonitions ("You have led the state into a grave situation. You bear the responsibility") kept ringing in his ears.[114] To add to his woes, on May 23 Rabin was subject to a dressing-down by Shapira. After wondering how Rabin had the temerity to go to war when all signs pointed to the contrary, he asked: "Do you want to bear the responsibility for endangering Israel?"[115]

As mentioned above, on May 23 (when the closure of the Straits of Tiran became known), Rabin, along with his senior colleagues implored Eshkol to authorize an immediate preventive strike. Unwilling to be pressurized until all other options were exhausted, Eshkol refused. Rabin's nerves frayed. Pouring out his heart to Weizman, he revealed that he was deeply depressed because he could not escape the feeling that he (along with the political hierarchy) had brought the country to such a terrible impasse, far worse than anything encountered since the War of Independence.[116] Weizman advised Rabin to compose himself and assured him that he would yet enjoy the kudos of leading Israel to victory.[117] A doctor was called who injected Rabin with a sedative. He was out of commission for more than 24 hours and was officially diagnosed as suffering from nicotine poisoning. Having patiently and meticulously crafted detailed and ingenious war plans, Rabin should have known that the IDF was more than a match for Israel's enemies. But given his sensitive and self-effacing nature, he humanly succumbed to last-minute doubts.[118] On recovering, Rabin offered his resignation to Eshkol who sensibly and compassionately indicated that he had no problem with him. And there is no reason why he should have had. In his capacity as chief of staff, Rabin was strong, authoritative, and professional. In his ground-breaking book, Gluska concluded that if one had to designate just one person responsible for the smooth running of the IDF and its decisive victory in the Six-Day War, "surely without a shadow of doubt it would have to be Yitzhak Rabin."[119] As for Ben-Gurion's asperity, the historian Teveth suggests that it may well have been influenced by what had become a personal vendetta to discredit Eshkol. At issue was Ben-Gurion's erroneous belief that Eshkol was incapable of leading the nation in war and coping with subsequent political pressures.[120]

On June 1, when news of Dayan's elevation to the defense ministry was released, there was a collective sigh of relief. As the historian David Shaham observed, the calm that instantly arose reflected an irrational belief that "since Dayan stood by the helm of defense, all danger had passed."[121] It now seemed obvious to all and sundry that Israel would shortly begin to assert itself.

In his new ministerial capacity, Dayan first turned his mind to the IDF's operational plans. He rejected the notion of the campaign against Egypt opening with an attack on Gaza and instead endorsed an alternative strategy of pushing into the heart of Sinai by means of three main frontal offensives.[122] Only once northern Sinai was in Israeli hands was the IDF to secure the Straits of Tiran and Sharm el Sheikh. Explicit instructions were issued that on no account were Israeli units to near the Suez Canal. Dayan maintained that approaching the Suez Canal would be "political madness."[123] Preoccupied with the need to destroy the backbone of the Egyptian army, the last thing he wanted was to incur any foreign intervention on the pretext that Israel was threatening an international waterway. Dayan also thought that if Israel reached the banks of the Canal, "Nasser would never accept a cease-fire and that the war would drag on for years."[124] As for IDF forces bordering Jordan and Syria, they were to maintain a strictly defensive posture. No existential threat was perceived as emanating from those two countries and, as far as Israel was concerned, its exclusive war aim was the extirpation of the danger that Egypt posed. Dayan was most explicit on that point, ruling out minor territorial grabs in, say, the Latrun salient, as long as Jordan remained passive.[125]

On June 2, France, in a gesture to the Arabs, imposed a "temporary" embargo on the supply of armaments for which Israel had already paid. (The provision of spare parts was exempted.) By contrast, the US began to display a greater implicit understanding of Israel's plight. It seemed that there was reason for believing that America no longer unequivocally insisted on Israeli passivity. The change in the US attitude resulted from the collapse of Johnson's effort to organize an international fleet (referred to as the "Regatta") that was meant to challenge Egypt's blockade of the Tiran Straits. Neither the US defense establishment nor the US Congress was in the least supportive of the project but more telling, only two countries, Australia and Holland, agreed to supply vessels. Canada at first seemed willing to cooperate but soon withdrew fearing an impairment of its relations with the Arabs. Even Britain, the Regatta's so-called co-sponsor, pulled out. The UK cabinet concluded that there had been a permanent change in the disposition of forces in the Middle East "to the disadvantage of Israel which both she and the western powers would have to accept." As a corollary the ministers determined that it was not in "British interests to restore the right of innocent passage in the Straits of the Gulf."[126] The estrangement of most western countries was revealing. Jews throughout the world felt a sense of déjà vu in observing that, as far as the bulk of the international community was concerned, their state was expendable. Only by virtue of Israel's own military resources could it hope to survive.

All the while Dayan projected an air of nonchalance, conveying the impression that he was far from driving his country into armed conflict. He addressed the media by stating that Israel had missed the boat for an instant military response and that it was far too early to determine whether further diplomatic steps would be sufficiently promising.[127] By so doing, he hoped to lull Egypt into believing that it need not necessarily maintain an extraordinary high level of vigilance.[128] To help foster such an impression, many reservists were given weekend furlough and on Saturday, June 3, Israel's beaches swarmed with swimmers and sunbathers who seemed to be casually enjoying their leisure. That same day two Egyptian battalions landed in Jordan, as did the advance guard of the Iraqi army. A brigade of Kuwaiti soldiers was on its way to Sinai and additional forces were expected from both Libya and Sudan.[129]

By nightfall Eshkol summoned, among others, Rabin, Allon, Dayan, Eban, Amit, Yariv and Harman to meet with him. At Eshkol's behest, Amit had flown to the US on May 31 to confer with the US intelligence fraternity and with Robert McNamara, the US secretary of defense. Amit's brief was a re-evaluation of US policy should Israel fire the first shot. In meeting with his professional counterparts, Amit gained the distinct impression that the US was no longer explicitly insisting that Israel not go to war. Rather with the question of the armada becoming nothing more than an acute embarrassment, Amit was led to understand that the Americans now wished Israel to relieve them of their maritime commitment.[130] Also Eban had just received a message from Ephraim Evron, Israel's minister in the US, who had learnt that the president had of late expressed a far greater sympathetic appreciation of Israel's dilemma, which Eban interpreted as constituting a green light for action.[131] With all that information in mind, everyone agreed to recommend to the cabinet that it authorize an immediate strike against Egypt.

Finally, on June 4, the cabinet met to make its fateful decision. Giving serious weight to Amit's findings and to Dayan's insistence that war was the only option on the table, the cabinet at long last voted to give the IDF the go-ahead at a time of its own choosing.[132] (The IDF's D-Day of June 5 was essentially dictated to it by the fact that the main body of the Iraqi forces was expected to enter Jordan on the night of June 6.)[133] The cabinet's decision was neither easily nor automatically arrived at. Even at that late hour, some members toyed with the idea of waiting at least another week. Zorach Warhaftig of Mafdal was reluctant to throw caution to the wind. He recommended sending a boat to the Straits and only after it was shelled by Egypt would Israel be patently entitled to defend itself. Such a notion was scotched by Dayan and others who pointed out that the dispatch of a trial boat to the Straits was as good as sending Nasser a telegram saying "Israel is about to go on the offensive."[134] With the dye finally cast, Israel adopted rather modest war aims. It sought to extricate itself from the threat of extinction, to reassert its right to navigate through the Straits of Tiran and to restore the status quo ante.[135] No Arab land was coveted.[136] Among Israel's political grandees, the lack of practical interest in widening the state's frontiers was best exemplified by Ben-Gurion. Just over three weeks before the Six-Day War, Ben-Gurion was approached by Geulah Cohen, a nationalist firebrand, and enquired as to what she should tell her grandson should he ask what the homeland's borders are. Without any hesitation, Ben-Gurion replied "The borders of your homeland, my grandson, are the borders of the State of Israel as they are today. That's it."[137]

9

THE SIX-DAY WAR AND ITS AFTERMATH

At 7.45 a.m. on June 5, swarms of Israeli jet fighters, including some locally made and adapted training planes, took off and headed over the Mediterranean. Others flew directly to Egyptian airbases in Sinai and via the Red Sea to a base in Luxor. Excluding 12 fighters that were held back for air defense, just about the entire Israeli air force was involved.[1] The decision to launch the air strikes at around 8.30 a.m. Egyptian time was a shrewd one. Because conventional wisdom suggested that surprise air attacks normally occur at sunrise, the Egyptians were usually then on maximum alert. Should nothing untoward occur, an all clear would be given, after which they would relax their guard and their pilots would have breakfast. As the sun further ascended, the morning mist would lift, affording a clear view of the terrain. On the morning of June 5, visibility was exceptionally good and there was no wind.

To evade radar detection, the Israeli planes flew at precariously low altitudes. As they passed over the Mediterranean, they were almost lapped by the waves. Complete radio silence was imposed, even in the event of pilots having to jettison their aircraft. Ultimately, those making for the Egyptian heartland banked south and then a little later from a westerly direction, after momentarily soaring upward, they swooped upon Egyptian airbases. The Israeli raids were composed of two main waves. The second one, which commenced at 9.45 a.m., had no need to fly at low altitude or observe radio silence. It was also assisted in its navigation by thick columns of smoke billowing from previously bombed airfields. In addition to ground covered by the first bombing wave, six Egyptian airbases that had previously been left untouched and in which some enemy craft sought sanctuary were dealt with. In general, in the bases that Israel struck the damage inflicted was so extensive that planes were neither able to take off nor land. Bombs, known as Durendals, which had been secretly developed in partnership with France rendered large craters difficult to repair since time-delayed explosions went off sequentially. After having hit the runways, Egypt's interceptor jets were destroyed by cannon fire and rockets. Finally, the enemy's bombers were dispatched. Egypt's practice of parking its planes by category, with certain types assigned to specific bases or clustered together, facilitated the IAF's selection of targets. Toward noon, 286 of Egypt's 420 warplanes were destroyed.[2] Nearly a third of Egypt's pilots were killed[3] while Israeli losses amounted to nine planes and six pilots.[4]

Israel's air offensive had caught the Egyptians off guard. Yet on June 2, based on a premonition, Nasser had forecast to his senior officers that the Israelis would strike on June 5. Neither Marshall Amer nor Sidqi Mahmoud, the air force commander, took him seriously and no special precautions were taken.[5] On the contrary, most of Egypt's anti-aircraft batteries and missiles were inoperative on the orders of Amer who was flying in Sinai on that fateful day. Not securing a usable Sinai airstrip, Amer's plane finally touched down at Cairo International Airport.[6] Amer, who had consistently sought an opportunity to challenge Israel, was elated. The long-awaited showdown had arrived. Rushing by taxi to Supreme Headquarters and being blissfully ignorant as to what had transpired, he bellowed out a series of orders for Egypt's air force to cover his army in its prospective march on Tel Aviv.

Once it became known that Egypt was at war with Israel, Syrian planes attacked Kibbutz Deganyah A, Tiberias, Megiddo, an airfield in the Jezreel Valley, and Kibbutz Ein Hamifratz near Haifa. The Jordanians harassed Netanya and the Kfar Syrkin airfield, while the Iraqis rocketed Nahalal. By around noon, the IAF was able to divert some of its fighter planes away from the Egyptian theater and as a result the entire Jordanian air force was eliminated (20 Hunters and 8 others), as was half of that of Syria (53 out of 112 planes), while Iraq forfeited 10 of its aircraft.

The moment the IAF embarked on its path-breaking mission against Egypt, so did the IDF's land units. Three separate armored columns, under the overall command of Gavish, pushed into Sinai to engage Egyptian defenses in grueling battles. Meanwhile, Israel radio laconically announced that "in the early hours of this morning fighting has been raging along the Southern front between Egyptian air and armored forces moving toward Israel and our forces that have set out to block them."[7] Dayan's order of the day to the IDF was also publicized. In it Dayan specified that "we have no aims of conquest. Our sole purpose is to put an end to the Arab objective of vanquishing our land."[8] No firm details were disclosed. The announcements served to convey the impression that Egypt caused the outbreak of hostilities and that Israel was striving to ward off an invasion. By so doing, it was hoped that the international community would not demand an immediate cease-fire through the UN and that the US would feel free to support Israel.

Fortuitously Israel's public relations strategy was assisted by an outburst of Egyptian rodomontade. Nasser's regime flagrantly boasted that it had downed 40 Israeli planes, its bombers had set Tel Aviv aflame, and its forces had penetrated into the Negev in the preliminary stage of overwhelming the "Zionist enemy."[9] One Cairo radio station broadcast in Hebrew that Palestinian fighters were roaming the streets of Tel Aviv and, far from being cowed, "they were spreading death."[10] Such vainglorious fantasies were in no small measure the result of a dearth of concrete information. The Egyptian air force was loath to report its undoing and communications from the Sinai front did not provide reliable accounts of the strength of the Israel forces being encountered. With the continuation of a news blackout in Israel, foreign correspondents picked up on the Egyptian pronouncements and soon the western media presaged dire consequences for the Jewish state. This had the fortunate by-product of generating widespread sympathy for Israel's plight, especially among overseas Jewish communities where solidarity with Israel was, inter alia, expressed by youth volunteering to come to its aid. Later that day when the Security Council finally did meet in New York, neither Israel nor Egypt was in the least bit interested in securing a cease-fire. Arab UN ambassadors were convinced that everything was going their way and that they would soon be able to proclaim victory. Delighted communist and other friendly delegations tendered their congratulations.[11] Under such circumstances, the Security Council adjourned. Only at midnight Israeli time did Rabin and Mordechai Hod (the air force chief) announce to the world at large that Israel had virtually wiped out its adversaries' air forces.

Egyptian ground defenses in Sinai were daunting. Built over the years since the Sinai Campaign, they consisted of clusters of bases, "often as deep as twenty miles."[12] At their core were fortified installations, supported by artillery, tanks, anti-tank guns, machine-gun nests and multiple trenches surrounded by minefields. Protecting them were peripheral outposts that were themselves small-scale versions of the central bastions. Throughout most of the first day of the war, the IAF was preoccupied in crippling the air forces of Egypt, then those of Jordan, Syria, and Iraq. This meant that on June 5, Israeli ground forces entering Sinai had to face solidly built Egyptian strongholds without the benefit of any meaningful air support.

Of the three Israeli columns entering Sinai, the most northerly one, consisting of two armored brigades and commanded by Israel Tal, set out to demolish a fortified area lying between Khan Yunis and El Arish, as well as to surround the Gaza Strip. Tal succeeded in disposing of the Egyptian defense alignment along the coast northeast of Sinai to reach the outskirts of El Arish but his advances were not without cost. In trying to break through into Khan Yunis, six lead tanks were knocked out and many soldiers were killed. Then, once Khan Yunis was subdued, Tal's men bypassed Rafah to move in a southwesterly direction where they confronted formidable enemy positions that dealt the Israelis lethal blows. Only by calling upon the IAF and by resorting to heavy artillery were they able to prevail. Nor was the capture of El Arish plain sailing. On nearing it on June 6, the Israelis took it for being deserted but as they entered the city they were fired upon from what seemed to be every conceivable source.[13] Not till midnight was El Arish finally secured. Similarly, it took an entire day of repetitive assaults to vanquish Rafah. Although Dayan forbade the IDF from using Rafah as a staging post to enter the Gaza Strip, when the Israeli settlements of Nirim and Kisufim became subject to heavy enemy fire, Rabin, without authorization, ordered the Strip to be taken. By the evening of June 5, the IDF occupied a ridge overlooking Gaza City and the next day the city fell.

To the south, Sharon's column consisting of three brigades containing armor, artillery, infantry, and paratroopers emerged from the vicinity of Nitzana in the Israeli Negev. As his men challenged the Egyptian position at Umm Qatef (near Abu Ageila) which had an extraordinary array of weaponry plus some 16,000 defenders, they incurred a large number of casualties.[14] Nevertheless, the Egyptians were overwhelmed by Sharon skillfully maneuvering his tanks to approach them from both the northeast and west while surreptitiously advancing a large contingent of infantry and paratroopers, not to mention close to 90 artillery pieces. By unleashing the largest barrage of shells in Israel's short history, the IDF destroyed the Egyptian defenses, paving the way for the following morning's fall of Abu Ageila.[15] It was quite a remarkable victory because the well-armed Egyptians, not taken by surprise, ought to have held their own. What decided matters in the IDF's favor was the determination of its men to press on regardless of all pitfalls, combined with an ability to perform with a high degree of military professionalism. They were well-coordinated, flexible in combat and adapted proficiently to the physical environment.[16]

While Sharon's fighters were thus engaged, Avraham Yoffe's two armored brigades slipped across the border over sandy stretches that were left unguarded because they were deemed to be impassable. Yoffe then rushed to the rear of the Egyptians facing other oncoming Israelis to intercept enemy reinforcements arriving from Western Sinai. By midnight, when two Egyptian armored brigades were spotted heading in his direction, Yoffe was ready. Protagonists from both sides dimmed the lights on their tanks and dueled in the dark, firing blindly at one another. The exchanges continued until daybreak, by which time IAF support enabled Yoffe to claim victory.

During June 6 various armored corps battles took place, leading to the destruction of hundreds of Egyptian tanks. Israeli losses, by contrast, were considerably smaller. By evening Amer, who by then had acquired a more sober perspective of his army's prospects, directed the withdrawal of all Egyptian forces to the entrances of the Mitla and Gidi passes. The order was shortly cancelled but already many officers had abandoned their units and, to add to the chaos, Israel had successfully jammed Egyptian radio communications.[17] Amer felt that in light of Israel's dominance of the skies and the collapse of Egypt's first line of defense, a withdrawal was necessary to ensure the safety of the remainder of his army. It was not a decision that the General Staff endorsed. Half of Egypt's forces were still intact and hundreds of pilots had survived to fly planes that were expected from Algeria. Israel's troops having fought non-stop for over 24 hours were fatigued, whereas on the Egyptian side a large number had yet to see action. In short, the relative standing of the Egyptian forces was not quite as bleak as Amer had concluded. However, the chaotic and panicky retreat that Amer's order fostered was a significant factor in the Egyptian army's rapid undoing. Coming across roads clogged with thousands of stationary vehicles, the IAF was presented with a golden opportunity to wreck havoc upon them.

On June 7, the IDF finally took possession of the entire Gaza Strip and overran enemy bases in central Sinai. Yoffe's men then raced westward to cut off retreating Egyptian forces at the mountain passes. In the early evening, a battalion of Yoffe's brigade reached the entrance to the Mitla Pass ahead of the enemy. There they arranged a collection of wrecked vehicles in such a way that oncoming columns would perforce be funneled directly into their line of fire. At the battalion's disposal were nine tanks. Six were situated at the entrance of the pass and three on an elevation above it. Throughout the night the Israelis stood their ground, staving off frontal attacks by Egyptians anxious to reach the safety of their mainland.

Meanwhile also on June 7, complying with Amer's withdrawal order, almost all of the original 1,600 Egyptian troops stationed at Sharm el Sheikh fled. Two Israeli torpedo boats arrived on the scene at 11.30 a.m. At 1 p.m. they were joined by helicopter-borne paratroopers who set to work mopping up the small remnant of Egyptian forces still in the general area. All this enabled Dayan to declare that Israel's access to the Straits of Tiran had been restored.

On June 8, the fighting in Sinai peaked. Recalling the disaster that befell his country, Mahmoud Riad, Egypt's foreign minister, wrote that on that day alone "all tanks, trucks, guns and equipment east of the passes were demolished."[18] En masse, Egyptian soldiers wandered listlessly on foot toward the Canal. Many died of thirst, hunger, and heat exhaustion.

Thousands were taken prisoner and in accordance with Rabin's strict instructions were – with few exceptions – humanely treated.

By the end of the day, the IDF laid claim to the entire east bank of the Canal, bar Port Faud. In New York at the UN Security Council, in response to a call for an unconditional cease-fire, the Egyptian representative Mohammad El Kony had intended to declare that his country would fight until the last drop of blood. Just before doing so, he was called away. Moments later he re-entered the hall with tears streaming down his face to announce that Egypt would abide by a cease-fire if the same could be said for Israel.[19]

The Egyptian compliance with the UN cease-fire resolution prompted Dayan to annul his prohibition for the IDF to advance right up to the Suez Canal. (During the war, Dayan was prone to inconsistencies.) Glossing over this particular about-face, Dayan contended that since Egypt finally agreed to an unconditional cease-fire, its forces ought to be completely displaced from Sinai to prevent them from menacing the IDF's western flank. Furthermore, should the UN call for a general withdrawal of troops from the canal zone, Israel "ought to have an area from which to withdraw."[20] The Egyptians were indeed intent on preserving a foothold in Sinai and as a result, residual and sporadic fighting continued for a short while, causing 50 additional Egyptian tanks to be destroyed. But when quiet finally reigned on the morning of June 9, the entire Sinai Peninsula was in Israeli hands.

At the outbreak of the war, Israel thrice warned Jordan to hold its fire and assured it that, if it did so, it would come to no harm. This was done through the auspices of the General Odd Bull, chief of the UN Truce Supervision Team, by direct communication between Israel's lieutenant colonel Gat and Jordan's colonel Daud and finally through the US.[21] The message sent via Bull read: "We are engaged in defensive fighting on the Egyptian sector and we shall not engage in any action against Jordan, unless Jordan attacks us."[22] Well before the War, in December 1966, General Elad Peled presented Rabin with an analysis of the consequences of Israel capturing the West Bank. After considering all aspects of the issue, Peled concluded that expected disadvantages far outweighed expected benefits. Peled and the IDF hierarchy in general felt that Israel's interests would be better served by that territory remaining in King Hussein's domain.[23] In keeping with Israel's non-aggressive

Plate 9.1 *Israeli troops in Sinai*

Plate 9.2 *Evacuating Israeli casualties in Sinai*

intentions, the IDF deployed only three brigades equipped with a limited supply of tanks along its Jordanian border. That is, contrary to what has often been alleged, Israel was certainly not itching for a fight with Hussein in order to divest him of his kingdom.

Israel's offer not to harm Jordan was issued even after Jordan had opened fire. It was hoped that after satisfying his new-found allies with a few warlike gestures, Hussein would remain inert. But such hopes were dashed. Toward midday Hussein issued his reply through Sa'd Jum'a, the Jordanian prime minister, who in a radio broadcast decreed: "We are engaged in a war of honor and heroism against our common enemy. For years we have longed to wipe away the shame of the past."[24]

Hussein's tragic error of entering the military arena was partly a result of his hearing Amer's fanciful claims that Egypt had by far the upper hand. Such a version of events seemed to be confirmed by a Jordanian radar station detecting hundreds of aircraft flying over Sinai in an easterly direction. The assumption was that they were Egyptian fighters but in reality they were Israeli jets returning home. In a telephone conversation in the early morning of June 5, Nasser, who was not fully informed until late in the afternoon, assured Hussein that Israel was reeling from defeat. Accordingly, Hussein's Legion shelled the airport at Ramat David as well as Tel Aviv and its surroundings. As already mentioned Jordanian planes (before being destroyed) carried out a bombing raid on the Kfar Sirkin airport and undertook sorties near Netanya and Kfar Saba. Then at 11.15 a.m., West Jerusalem was bombarded. Six thousand shells were fired into it and as a consequence, over a thousand people were injured, 150 seriously with 20 subsequently dying. Damage to property was extensive. More than 900 buildings were struck, including the Hadasah Hospital at Ein Kerem where the famous Marc Chagall stained glass windows were damaged.[25] As the Israeli historian Avi Shlaim observed: "Had King Hussein heeded Eshkol's warning, he would have kept the Old City of Jerusalem and the West Bank. No one in the cabinet or the General Staff proposed the capture of the Old City before the Jordanian bombardment began."[26] Also of note is that while Hussein had shown no compunction in raining down shells on West Jerusalem, Dayan took pride in the fact that Israel neither bombarded East Jerusalem nor any other Arab city in the West Bank.[27]

What sealed Jordan's fate was its capture of the UN building known as Government House situated in no man's land in south Jerusalem. From there it fired mortars at Kibbutz Ramat Rahel and the Jewish quarter of Abu Tor. Moreover, it maintained a favorable launching post for attacking West Jerusalem. Fearing that the investment of Government House was but a prelude to an assault on the Israeli-held enclave of Mount Scopus, the IDF wrested it from the Jordanians. The battle for Government House that commenced shortly after midday was a bitter one entailing hand-to-hand combat and grenade attacks. By early evening when the Jordanians were ultimately defeated, of the two Israeli infantry companies that took part, only ten soldiers were still capable of further fighting.[28]

Throughout much of the day Eshkol was urged to widen military objectives to include the West Bank. Allon and Begin, at a cabinet meeting requested by Begin, impressed upon Eshkol that the country had a golden opportunity to capture East Jerusalem, an opportunity that in their view Israel could ill afford to squander. Shapira, on the other hand, dissented. He feared that the conquest of Jerusalem would lead to pressures to internationalize the city.[29] Nevertheless, Allon and Begin secured majority support. The discussion then moved on to the possible administration of conquered territory. Eshkol thought that they should proceed "in the foreknowledge that we will eventually have to vacate [East] Jerusalem and the West Bank."[30] With that in mind, Eshkol put it to Dayan that the IDF ought to take the Old City.[31] But being somewhat cautious, Dayan recommended that it merely be besieged since a full frontal assault could result in unwanted damage to holy places.

At the northern end of what became known as the West Bank, a limited thrust into the Dotan valley near Jenin was set in motion to forestall an Arab Legion attempt to approach Israel's coast line. Most of the tanks of a Jordanian armored battalion present in the area were destroyed by the IAF. The few left unimpaired relocated to Jenin. Late in the afternoon, two additional Jordanian armored battalions appeared, one of which made straight for the Israeli ground forces.[32] Reeling under pressure, the Israelis fought back in a battle that continued throughout the night. At dawn on June 6 with the IAF's reappearance the Israelis gained the upper hand and by midday, with Rabin's approval, Jenin was taken.

There were also some other forays into the West Bank. At 4 p.m on June 5 the Harel Brigade, under Uri Ben-Ari, left its staging post near Kibbutz Kiryat Anavim and crossed the northern border of the Jerusalem corridor to perform a flanking operation in support of a move to defend Mount Scopus. On entering Jordan it ran into a dense minefield at Radar Hill which immobilized many of its tanks, causing its infantry to advance without armored cover. But by midnight, thanks to stubborn perseverance, the Israelis were able to continue eastward to the northern outskirts of Jerusalem and before noon the next day they reached Mount Scopus. Elsewhere, to Jerusalem's west, Latrun – which during the War of Independence had fended off successive Israeli attacks – fell after offering little resistance. So too did a number of nearby villages.

In Jerusalem, Moti Gur's paratroop brigade (having just been transferred from Sinai) planned to penetrate Jordanian lines to advance via Sheikh Jarrah to Mount Scopus and occupy other key positions. Despite inadequate street maps, almost no updated aerial photographs and insufficient military intelligence, they intended to tackle the Jordanians at around midnight but logistical difficulties stalled them until the early hours of June 6. Facing them were 5,000 Legionnaires and 1,000 Palestinian guardsmen armed with mortars, machine guns, and howitzers. The paratroopers were divided into three battalions. The 66th Battalion under Yossef Yoffe assailed the police academy that was surrounded by as many as six distinct barbed wire fences that had to be cleared by Bangalores (a slender 1.8 meter rocket used to demolish fences and clear minefields). After intense fighting, the Jordanians withdrew to Ammunition Hill. Pursuing them, the Israelis met with counter-charging Legionnaires discharging Bren guns and hurling grenades. Almost all of the Israeli front line was struck down. Those that followed and who bore backpacks too wide to negotiate enemy trenches continued over open ground where they were hit not only by the enemy at Ammunition Hill but also by troops from adjoining sites. By first light the Israelis ultimately burst into the Jordanian commander's bunker to find that he and the remnant of his men had just slipped away. The battle for Ammunition Hill gave rise to the loss of 35 paratroopers and was the most costly one in Israel's conflict with Jordan.[33]

Meanwhile, the men of Yossif Fradkin's 28th Battalion made it to the American Colony after being subject to heavy mortar fire. En route to the Rockefeller Museum (their ultimate objective), they mistakenly entered Nablus Road (today known as Dereh Shehem) just as the Jordanians had expected. Awaiting them at point-blank range were batteries of bazookas and anti-tank guns. A furious exchange of fire ensued that culminated in the retreat of the Jordanians and the retirement of the surviving Israelis to the YMCA of the American Colony. On learning that Uzi Eilam's 71st Battalion had overrun the suburb of Wadi el Joz, Fradkin's men were sufficiently re-energized to seize the Rockefeller Museum where Gur then located his forward headquarters.

Additional conquests of Jerusalem were claimed by two Israeli brigades (the 10th and 4th), sweeping from the city's northern approaches to meet up with other Israeli forces at French Hill and then tracking further south to block the road to Jericho. That, plus the seizure of Arab Abu Tor that denied Jordan access to Jerusalem from Bethlehem, meant that the Old City was entirely surrounded, save for a weak link at the Mount of Olives.

Since Israeli gains were being accrued at a far faster rate than originally anticipated, in the early hours of June 6 Dayan had second thoughts about widening the conflict with Jordan. In a meeting with Eshkol, the two agreed to authorize the IDF to assume control of the entire West Bank. For the remainder of the day the Israelis took one city after another. In the process, Jordan lost 120 of its 240 tanks. Hussein sent urgent appeals for assistance to both Syria and Saudi Arabia but other than soothing words nothing of substance was forthcoming. Late that night, realizing the futility of offering further resistance, Hussein, with Nasser's concurrence, ordered his army to withdraw to the east bank of the Jordan. Less than two hours later, after learning that the US and Russia had reached an agreement for a UN cease-fire resolution, Hussein had canceled that order.[34] He felt that if only he could hold the approaches to Jericho and the Jordan bridges he would be able to recover much of the West Bank and save the Old City.

In the early hours of June 7, with pressures for a cease-fire mounting, Dayan now chose to conquer the Old City and with Eshkol's concurrence he directed that it be taken forthwith. Israeli Sherman tanks pounded the 12-meter high Lion's Gate, blasting it open. That paved the way for the entry into the Old City of a column of half-tracks followed by infantry. A thousand soldiers participated. Some headed to the

Via Dolorosa, others went in the direction of the Damascus and Jaffa Gates. A company from the Jerusalem Brigade crawled through a small hatch on the Zion Gate to then pass through the Armenian Quarter on their way to the former Jewish quarter. They ended up liaising with paratroopers arriving through the Dung Gate. No more than a hundred Legionnaires, equipped with small arms, had remained. After offering token resistance, they surrendered.

At 10.30 a.m. Gur signaled that "the Temple Mount is in our hands." The Israelis were rapturous. For all Jews, both religious and secular, the occasion represented the consummation of the modern day re-emergence of Jewish sovereignty. Guided by an Arab, Gur and his entourage had found their way to the Western Wall as had many joyful soldiers. Rabbi Shlomo Goren, the chief army chaplain, recited *kaddish* (the mourner's prayer) and sounded a *shofar* (ram's horn). He then pressed Uzi Narkiss, the Central Regional Commander, to "put a hundred kilograms of explosives in the Mosque of Omar [on the Temple Mount] – and that's it, we'll get rid of it once and for all."[35] Narkiss, appalled at Goren's temerity, dismissed him out of hand.

Later in the afternoon, Dayan, flanked by Rabin and Narkiss in what amounted to a carefully choreographed pose, was photographed entering the Old City. So keen was Dayan to hog the limelight, he not only deprived Eshkol of it (by cautioning him not to come to the Old City because of possible residual snipers) but treated Rabin as if he were a bit player in a movie in which only he – Dayan – starred.[36] Having arrived at the wall with much hullabaloo, Dayan scribbled a note and inserted it into one of the wall's crevices. At one point Dayan noticed an Israeli flag fluttering on the Mosque of Omar. The flag was promptly ordered down in keeping with Dayan's conviction that Islamic and Christian holy places should not be encroached upon.

Throughout the remainder of June 7, the IDF consolidated its West Bank gains. Hussein's hopes of maintaining a foothold in that sector proved to be elusive once Nablus and Jericho buckled under. In Nablus a farcical situation arose. Thinking that the Israelis were a contingent from Iraq, the Arabs enthusiastically welcomed them. Once they became the wiser, local troops made a futile bid to repel them before swiftly being quelled. Finally on June 8, Hebron, greeting the Israelis with a sea of white sheets, capitulated.

Plate 9.3 *Israeli paratroopers on reaching the Western Wall*

With Sinai and the West Bank in Israeli hands, the question naturally arose as to what to do about Syria. On June 6, the Syrians made a half-hearted and unsuccessful effort to seize land in the Tel Dan area. Prior to that, they had seriously contemplated a massive invasion of Israel with the intention of overrunning the entire northern finger of the Galilee as a prelude to a drive toward Haifa.[37] As with Egypt, the prospective campaign, named "Victory," was Soviet-designed.[38] It was scheduled for June 6.[39] The plan's existence was revealed by material that subsequently fell into Israeli hands. But having botched their preparations (the bridges over the Jordan were too narrow for their wide Soviet tanks)[40] and having learnt what befell Egypt, the Syrians thought better of it. However, not to be outdone by Egyptian pretensions, they informed Nasser that their forces were rapidly advancing toward Rosh Pina and Safad and that Nazareth was expected to fall the following day.[41] What the Syrians actually settled for was the unrelenting raining down of shells on Jewish settlements in the plain beneath the Golan Heights, damaging some 205 houses and 45 vehicles.[42] Settlers living alongside the border advanced the case for military retribution on a large scale. On June 8, they sent a three-man delegation to confer with Eshkol (who himself had once farmed not far from their kibbutzim). Being receptive to their demands, Eshkol took the unusual step of inviting them to attend a cabinet meeting where they ardently presented their case. But Dayan was not won over. He was worried that if Israel attacked Syria the Russians would intervene. Syria was far more aligned with Russia than was Egypt. It received extensive Soviet military and economic aid. Syrian communists were represented in the government and Russian was the major second language taught in schools. No other country outside the Eastern bloc, save Cuba and Yugoslavia, was more ideologically in tune with Russia than Syria.[43] In addition to the Russian threat, Dayan advanced three other reasons for exercising restraint. Bearing in mind the possibility of Egypt making a comeback (not all of its army was eliminated), he dreaded the prospect of Israel simultaneously becoming ensnared in two separate and potentially messy fronts. Syria, in Dayan's evaluation, would never come to terms with the loss of any of its territory and what is more, he contentiously asserted, there was no need for Israeli settlements to be located so close to the border.[44] Making his point in terms that were the very antithesis of Zionist dogma, Dayan declared: "I prefer to move the settlements ten or twenty miles from the Syrian artillery rather than get caught up in a third front leading to a clash with the Soviets. Thousands of Arabs were relocated as a result of this war; we can relocate several dozen Israelis."[45] Dayan was, however, prepared to approve of a small probe into Syria that was not to exceed 2–3 kilometers in depth. Rabin found that "concession" totally unacceptable, believing that it would yield numerous casualties without altering the strategic balance. The cabinet meeting ended without a vote being taken. Members assumed that the issue would be pursued by Eshkol, Dayan, and Rabin and that another cabinet meeting would be called should the need arise.[46]

Early the next morning (June 9), without consulting Eshkol and bypassing Rabin, Dayan directly instructed David Elazar, the northern commander, that Syria was to be invaded. Outraged at Dayan's seeming contempt for democratic norms and standard procedures, Eshkol called him "a rogue." Dayan had no difficulty in vindicating his behavior. He pointed out that the Egyptians had just accepted an unconditional cease-fire, Israeli intelligence had assessed that Russia would now not intervene unless the Syrian regime was about to collapse, and information had come to hand that Syrian residents were evacuating the Golan Heights, including the main town of Kuneitra. In contradiction to his previous reasoning, Dayan now insisted that, because Syria had declared that it too would abide by the UN cease-fire, Israel had to act immediately to settle scores with its troublesome neighbor.[47] Among other things, Dayan had also informed Elazar that he had grounds for believing that the Syrian army was on the verge of disintegrating. In utter disbelief, Rabin advised Elazar to accept such an assertion with a pinch of salt.[48] Rabin's skepticism was well founded. Shortly beforehand Dayan had asked Yariv to confirm that the Syrian positions were crumbling but Yariv refused to do so.[49]

Toward noon on June 9, Avraham Mendler's 8th Brigade began to assail the series of interconnected Syrian fortifications near the northern frontier. Initial objectives were the villages of Zaura and Sir Al Dib not far from Kfar Szold. The battles were very taxing for the Israelis had, in broad daylight, to surmount steep mine-laden escarpments as well as trenches and barbed-wire enclosures, all protected by concrete machine gun nests and other impenetrable fixtures. In some locations, bulldozers preceded tank columns to clear away mines and fences but most were soon battered and immobilized. The Syrians evinced much fortitude and the fighting was very intense. An Israeli column under Ayre Biro erroneously advanced in the direction of the Syrian fortress at Qala rather than toward Zaura. On realizing his mistake, Biro, with ratification from his superiors, stuck to the path he had taken. Before they knew it, he and his men were up against an immense fusillade that led to Biro being seriously wounded. His replacement Rafael Mokady, a university lecturer in civilian life, was killed within the next few minutes. The baton of command was then passed onto Nataniel Horowitz who, although having sustained a head injury, continued to direct armor that had entered a narrow defile bounded by mines. Horowitz was in a real predicament. Only two of his tanks were still in working order. In desperation, he appealed for air cover and, on being told by Mendler that no planes were available, he replied, "If we don't receive air support at once, it's good-bye, for I don't think we will see each other again."[50] Miraculously, two jets came to his rescue.

Further north, the troops of the Golani Infantry Brigade had overrun Tel Fakhr after a relentless 7-hour battle. A battalion led by Moshe Klein divided into two and charged Tel Fakhr from opposite directions. They dashed into enemy trenches firing at the Syrian defenders at an arm's length distance. In the indescribable turmoil Klein was killed, as were many others. By the day's end the IDF held a 5-mile wide bridgehead in the Zaura region.

Beginning to feel the pinch, the Syrians appealed to the UN for a cease-fire. By contrast the Israelis hesitated. Their UN spokesperson, Gideon Rafael, complained of a Syrian premeditated attack on Israel. So desperate was Syria that it was prepared to settle for an unconditional cease-fire but Russia insisted on appending terms that the US found unacceptable, such as the immediate withdrawal of Israel to the armistice lines. As a result, the Security Council adjourned to reconvene some hours later. In Israel at 8 p.m, the ministerial defense committee met to assess developments. Several members, perturbed by a growing international outcry against Israel's invasion of Syria as well as by mounting casualties, were reluctant to stay the course. Even Dayan wanted to wind down all operations by first light of June 10. But Eshkol was most emphatic that Syria had to be penalized and that the war effort had to continue until at least noon.[51]

Preparations for continued fighting were well advanced. Immediately prior to the invasion, reinforcements drawn from Sinai were so numerous that Israel's road network could not adequately handle the sudden surge of traffic. But by the close of day, all snarls were cleared and the IDF managed to muster eight full brigades for the final showdown. Their assignment was somewhat alleviated by Syria transferring three frontline brigades to the environs of Damascus. An Israeli feint in Lebanon was seen as a prelude to a direct attack on its capital.[52]

During the late night of June 9 and the small hours of the morning of June 10, Mendler's men wrested Wasit and then proceeded to Mansura, meeting with next to no opposition. Awaiting them was a treasure trove of Syrian armaments including tanks in perfectly good order. Moving northward, the Golani Brigade, with little trouble, took possession of Banias. By dawn an Israeli armored column, headed by Peled and approaching from the south, scaled the Golan Heights to challenge from their rear Syrians facing other Israeli units. Assisting Peled were airborne forces that seized control of vital crossroads. Racing against the clock (Israel had officially acceded to a cease-fire), Israeli commanders pursued various courses of action without referring to General Staff.

In overall terms, the situation on the various fronts was still fluid. A quick Israeli conquest in time to placate the UN was not fully assured. However, Syria itself finally handed Israel victory on a plate. It deceitfully declared that Kuneitra had fallen, hoping that such news would induce the UN to compel Israel to uphold, at once, its cease-fire acceptance. What was not foreseen was the effect that such an announcement would have on its own troops, for when they heard it, many became despondent and retreated in a disorderly manner.

By 6.30 that evening, with the Golan Heights in Israel's possession, the Six-Day War came to an end. Russia did not intervene but in the war's closing stage it issued Israel with a strong note of censure, indicating that it was breaking off diplomatic relations with the Jewish state. All its satellites, with the exception of Romania, followed suit. The rupture with Israel was ostensibly caused by the Soviet's reaction to Israel's "aggression" against the Arabs and to its so-called crude violation of the Security Council decision.[53]

In the course of the war, US–Israeli relations were seriously strained by an unfortunate incident. On June 8, the IAF attacked the American vessel *Liberty* sailing in international waters not far from El Arish. The ship was badly damaged and 34 seamen, some of whom were Jews, lost their lives[54] and 171 were wounded. The *Liberty* was a spy ship in the service of the National Security Agency. Equipped with sophisticated listening devices, it was alleged to have been prying on IDF inter-unit field communications. Thus Jews fluent in Hebrew were among the crew.[55] The murky circumstances of the *Liberty*'s presence in close proximity to the Sinai coast fueled much speculation. Some hypothesized that the *Liberty* was deliberately attacked in the full knowledge that it was an American vessel. The Israelis supposedly feared that the intelligence it was gleaning might be passed on to the Egyptians by way of the US competing for influence with the Soviet Union.[56] However, Michael Oren for one, Israel's foremost historian on the Six-Day War, believes that to the contrary, the *Liberty* was more likely tracking the movements of Egyptian troops and their Soviet advisers.[57]

The *Liberty* was first sighted at daybreak on June 8 and recognized as a US navy ship by an Israeli reconnaissance plane. Not having been apprised of its presence, Rabin upbraided the US naval attaché in Tel Aviv, telling him that the US should either acknowledge the *Liberty*'s whereabouts or remove it. (On June 5, Rabin had requested that "the United States either withdraw all its vessels from our shores, or inform us of the exact location of all vessels close to our shores.")[58] Hours later, after the *Liberty* was no longer tracked and was believed to have sailed away, a large explosion shook the beaches of El Arish. Without firmly establishing its source, the IDF jumped to the conclusion that it emanated from an offshore naval bombardment. (It had in fact arisen from an accident within an ammunition dump.) A little later, an unidentified ship was seen heading toward Egypt at top speed. That aroused suspicion. At that time, aside from the *Liberty*, the only foreign vessels in the eastern Mediterranean were Soviet ones.[59] Two Israeli Mirages sent in pursuit of the mysterious vessel were ordered to attack it unless it proved to be an Israeli ship. Having ascertained that the *Liberty* was not part of Israel's war fleet, the Mirages struck it with both regular and napalm-bearing bombs.

Israel has consistently maintained that the attack arose by accident and that two of its three torpedo boats that also approached the *Liberty* mistook it for the Egyptian warship the *El Quseir*. The moment the

Israelis identified the *Liberty* as an American vessel, they ceased fire and did all in their power to rescue and assist the ship's crew, an action that certainly did not suggest any malign or sinister intentions. An official US commission of inquiry failed to arrive at any definitive conclusion and, as far as President Johnson was concerned, the case was closed. Israel had apologized for the mishap and paid an indemnity. Subsequent to the *Liberty* disaster, the US remained a firm and trustworthy supporter of Israel.

After the Six-Day War, many observers and commentators inferred that it essentially arose as a result of a series of miscalculations on the part of all sides. One misjudgment or rash step followed another until there was no longer any scope for backpedalling. That is, the combatants were ineluctably drawn into a conflict that they themselves were not seeking. For instance, had Israel not attacked the Jordanian village of Samu with such ferocity, Jordan would not have taunted Egypt and Nasser would not then have felt pressurized to deploy troops in Sinai.

While neither Israel nor Jordan was keen on going to war, the same cannot be said of Syria. Almost five years earlier, on August 27, 1962, the Syrian ruler Ahram al-Hurani released his plans for the liberation of Palestine. They included the following four major points: an inter-Arab military pact; the removal of the UNEF from Sinai; the blocking of the Straits of Tiran; and a decisive counter-blow to Israel's expected attempt to open the Straits.[60] By contrast, the Israeli government under Eshkol was a very moderate one. As mentioned in the previous chapter, most of its members abhorred war and did all in their power to avoid it. On May 17, as the UNEF's continued presence in Sinai was being put in question, Eshkol emphasized that Israel neither sought war nor anything else for that matter from its neighbors other than the restoration of the status quo ante.[61] As for Egypt, granted that the actual timing of the war was not of its choosing, when it came to the crux of the matter, war was welcomed. That was the view at least held by Salah al Halidi, an eminent Egyptian judge, who subsequently attested: "I can state that Egypt's political leadership called Israel to war. It clearly provoked Israel and forced it into a confrontation."[62]

Aspiring to Arab leadership, Egypt felt the need to be perceived as spearheading the "liberation of Palestine." In the process, it had to compete with premature Syrian efforts to engineer the outbreak of hostilities. The Syrians in their determination to root out Israel kept demanding an *immediate* pan-Arab strike. Its Palestinian protégés headed by Arafat were no less enthusiastic. Fatah and similar guerrilla bands sabotaged Israeli targets not simply to incur the odd amount of damage but with a strategic plan to provide the sparks that would ignite an inferno. Between January 1965 and June 1967, Fatah and allied groups organized 122 raids into Israel.[63] On May 8, 1967, an Arab infiltrator was seized just south of Kiryat Shmona. He was bearing 12 kilograms of explosives with the intention of detonating them amidst a large gathering of Israelis so that his mission would culminate in mass murder.[64] As has so often been the case, that would-be terrorist did not conform to Frantz Fanon's idealized stereotype as espoused in his book, *The Wretched of the Earth*. Far from being a marginalized poverty-stricken dispossessed individual, he was a university graduate with a command of both Hebrew and English and in possession of a false UK passport.

The ultimate consequences of Fatah's activities were not what their leaders had in mind but, of all factors leading to the Six-Day War, they were paramount. In view of the hazardous difficulties in undertaking punitive raids against Fatah operatives and their leaders ensconced in Syria, Israel insisted that neighboring countries used as a springboard for terrorist missions be taken to task. That meant that they were to bear the brunt of Israeli reprisals that so inflamed pan-Arab passion. The way was clearly set for an all-out confrontation and, had the war not occurred in June 1967, it would still have erupted sooner or later.

However, in order for the Arabs merely to have contemplated going to war, they needed a prodigious amount of weaponry. In that regard, the insidious role of the Soviet Union needs to be borne in mind. Not only did Russia inflame the region through its fraudulent claims of detecting an imminent Israeli invasion of Syria but it armed the Arabs to the teeth. As Theodore Draper, the renowned commentator and scholar, observed, it was not necessary for the Soviets to pronounce that they aimed to bring about a third Arab–Israel war, "it was merely necessary for them to arm those Arab states which were proclaiming it as *their* war aim."[65]

As its name suggests, the Six-Day War was a very short one. The Arabs suffered a humiliating defeat. They lost at least 10,000 men,[66] a vast quantity of equipment and large swathes of land. (Israeli-controlled territory more than tripled in size.) The Egyptians' sudden and unexpected reversal of fortune can largely be attributed to the demise of almost all their air power in the opening hours of the conflict. Israel possessed superbly trained pilots who had the advantage of a thorough understanding of the general capabilities of the Mig-21, the lead warplane of Egypt, Syria, and Iraq. In August 1966, a disaffected Iraqi fighter pilot was persuaded to defect to Israel along with his Mig-21. This enabled the IAF to analyze the aircraft's features.[67] Added to that, thanks to the extraordinary competence of Israel's air maintenance crew, planes landing were able to resume flight in an amazingly short span of time.[68]

Considering that Israel's planes were airborne for over 80 percent of the day, it seemed that the country was either endowed with far more aircraft than originally estimated or that it was actively being assisted by foreign states such as the US and UK. This may partially have persuaded Nasser and Hussein to assert that Israel was not acting alone. On June 5, in an intercepted telephone conversation, Nasser and Hussein agreed to release a joint statement claiming that the US and the UK were placing at Israel's disposal fighter-bombers operating from aircraft carriers in the Mediterranean.[69] The fact that Israel's initial air strikes were executed by planes arriving from over the sea lent some credence to such a view. Ironically, at the outbreak of hostilities when that canard was first issued, the US, in the interest of its reputation among the Arabs, imposed an arms embargo on the entire Middle East.[70]

Apart from Israel's superior air force, there were a number of other factors that placed Egypt in particular at certain disadvantages. The transfer and deployment of several Egyptian army divisions into Sinai was undertaken with needless haste. Logistical provisions were haphazard and maintenance work was substandard. There were gross deficiencies in the supply of food, water, fuel, and ammunition to frontline units. In an interview to a Saudi newspaper given on June 27, 1975, the Egyptian General Abdul Gamasi claimed that his country's political leadership had not provided the army sufficient notice to prepare for battle in an orderly manner.[71]

With the officer corps recruited from privileged members of society and the rank and file from the peasantry, the Egyptian army as a whole

lacked social cohesion and a universally shared *esprit de corps* that nega-
tively impacted on its fighting qualities.[72] Many officers promoted on
the basis of nepotism were lacking in competence to rely on their own
resourcefulness or to adapt to changing military imperatives.

In terms of general factors contributing to Israel's success, the
three-week waiting period, from May 14 to June 5, ought also to be
acknowledged. Originally, it was considered as being near disastrous
both in terms of the IDF's and the general population's morale and of
Israel's ability to ward off its enemies. Nowadays, it is widely perceived
as having yielded beneficial results. By August 1969, 63 percent of
Israelis polled likened the waiting period to a responsible act of states-
manship.[73] Just before the outbreak of war, that is, on May 31, Eban
received a telegram from a Jewish friend in America who had close ties
with Johnson and other members of the US administration. In it Eban
was told that had Israel not shown undue restraint, the final outcome
would have been dire.[74] The forbearance exhibited by Israel in face of
the palpable and mounting threat to its existence left a very favorable
impression on the western world and on the USA in particular. It rallied the US media and then members of Congress to its support and
paved the way for Israel to be able to retain the territories it gained in
the absence of the Arabs suing for a viable peace. Of no less significance,
the waiting period provided the IDF with an opportunity to reintegrate
its reservists into their units, to hone their fighting skills, to calibrate
objectives and operational plans, to prepare all weapons and transport
facilities, and to ensure that appropriate logistics were in place.

Though not as high as its adversaries, the price that Israel paid for
the war was exacting. Between 700 and 800 soldiers were killed,[75] of
whom more than 25 percent were officers and NCOs.[76] A disproportionate burden was also borne by the kibbutz movement. Although
kibbutz members constituted only 4 percent of the total population,
they accounted for one in five of all fatalities.[77] The grief of mourning
widows, children, and parents was partially overshadowed by a widespread sense of euphoria. People were relieved that the horrendous
fate that the Arabs had wished upon them did not eventuate. Soon by
their thousands Israelis poured into the Old City and the rest of the
West Bank to be enchanted by the landscape of the Judean hills, the
"authentic Land of Israel." The human traffic flowed in both directions

since Dayan had removed all internal travel restrictions on Arabs in the West Bank and Gaza, allowing them to wander freely throughout Israel. Many went to gaze at their former homes and districts. Others delighted in savoring Israeli delicacies. On June 9, Teddy Kollek, the mayor of the former West Jerusalem who had previously expressed qualms about the wisdom of permitting unrestricted movements of both Arabs and Jews, sent Dayan a telegraph saying, "You were right. Well done. There is a festive air in the city. All the Arabs are in Zion Square and all the Jews are in the bazaars."[78] At that stage a comingling of the two populations was seen in a positive light. Only after many years of increasing Arab violence did the Israeli authorities reluctantly embark on the construction of a security barrier to protect their citizens from deadly terrorist attacks.

For the first time since the state's formation, Israelis felt that they were on the threshold of peace. Gratified by such prospects there was remarkably little gloating over their adversaries' misfortunes and there were certainly no celebratory parades or victory balls. As the writer Shabtai Teveth recalled, "People did not dance in the streets, public houses did not give free drinks to the masses, and lovely young girls did not climb on tanks to kiss the soldiers." Rather, "the very first event was a three days' mourning period."[79] In a speech delivered at the Hebrew University on receiving an honorary doctorate, Rabin remarked that the Jewish people are not habituated to experiencing the joy of conquest and victory. He noted that in addition to the sorrow his men felt at losing their comrades, the terrible price that the enemy paid also touched many of them.[80] What has never been sufficiently appreciated is that in contrast to the Arabs who avidly craved Jewish blood, there was a complete absence within Israel of any *public* or *official* articulation of hatred or contempt toward the Arabs. In all the popular songs sung during the war and in all those that afterward rejoiced in Israel's victory, *not a single one* cast any slurs on the country's enemies.[81] The mood of the day was also exemplified in January 1968 by Eshkol who, on a visit to the US, addressed President Johnson as follows:

Mr President. I have no sense of boastful triumph nor have I entered the struggle for peace in the role of victor. My feeling is one of relief that we were saved from disaster in June and for this I thank God. All my thoughts now are turned toward getting peace with our neighbors – a peace of honor between equals."[82]

The overweening post-war haughtiness that shortly characterized Israeli society was yet to appear.

As for the Egyptians, they were convulsed by the war's outcome. To plunge, in so brief an interval, from buoyant expectations of a quick and decisive victory to the shame and degradation of a thorough routing was insufferable. On June 8, the day that Egypt forfeited its control of Sinai, Amer, Shams ed-din Badran, the minister of war, and other senior officers met with Nasser and Zakaria Muhiedin (Nasser's unpopular deputy). Looking to Nasser as a scapegoat for their ineptitude, they demanded his resignation. In a heated exchange, in which Muhiedin held that the military and civilian hierarchy were equally culpable, Nasser undertook to step down along with Amer and Badran. The next evening he addressed the nation. In announcing that he was handing over power to Muhiedin, he assumed full responsibility for his country's ignominy. Taking his cue from Amer (who had no end of excuses for the country's dismal performance), Nasser attributed Egypt's crushing defeat to a non-existent American and British intervention, suggesting that it was mainly US and UK planes that furthered Israel's victory. In his view "the enemy [Israel] was operating with an air force three times stronger than his normal force." The Egyptians, according to Nasser, were able to ascertain that Israel was assisted by imperialist forces because Israel "covered at one go all military and civilian airfields in the UAR [Egypt]."[83] Therefore foreign forces must have been protecting Israel's "skies against any retaliatory action from our side."[84] His speech ended on an upbeat note, holding out hope that by remaining steadfastly united the Arabs would ultimately triumph over both the forces of imperialism and Israel. It had the desired effect. For if the imperialists had a large hand in defeating Egypt, how could Nasser in all honesty assume personal responsibility for the disaster? Thousands upon thousands of Egyptians converged on the streets in what appeared to be a spontaneous display of grief. But in reality, Nasser's political henchmen in the Arab Socialist Union had taken prior steps to ensure that crowds would come out in force. Well before Nasser went on air, they had mustered their supporters in strength and issued them with previously prepared placards calling upon Nasser to remain in office. Nevertheless many if not most of the demonstrators joined in of their own accord. Ululating and weeping, they reaffirmed their devotion to Nasser whom they regarded as no mere politician but as a national father figure. "Deeply touched" by such an outpouring of popular support, Nasser retracted his resignation. Almost instantly, the wailing masses mutated into deliriously happy revelers. Nasser once again transformed a decisive military debacle into a grand personal triumph.[85] With his hold on power much entrenched and with Amer and Badran having been deceived into resigning, up to one thousand senior officers and generals suspected of personal disloy-alty to Nasser were cashiered. A potential military coup, which so often occurs when dictatorial regimes oversee disastrous defeats, was nipped in the bud. Yet Amer remained determined to unseat Nasser. In late August, while plotting to regain his former command, he was placed under house arrest. On September 15, 1967, it was announced that he had committed suicide but many suspect that he was murdered.[86]

Short-term repercussions resulting from the war resonated over a wide area. In Egypt, 800 Jews were arrested and their property sequestrated. Further afield, in Yemen, Lebanon, Tunisia, Libya, and Morocco, Jews were attacked and their synagogues burnt.[87] Within the West Bank more than 200,000 Arabs uprooted themselves to resettle east of the Jordan. Although some measure of coercion was entailed,[88] the majority left of their own volition. They had many motives for doing so. Thousands of Palestinians working abroad remitted their earnings to their families in the West Bank who in the post-war period could only cash such transfers in East Jordan. Similarly, to earn their liveli-hood, civil servants and soldiers needed to retain direct contact with the Jordanian administration. Some left because they feared retribution for being closely associated with the PLO while others simply did not wish to live under Israeli rule.[89] That most of the refugees fled with-out Israeli prompting is suggested by the fact that only approximately 11,000 availed themselves of an Israeli offer to accept them back by no later than early August 1967.[90] Furthermore, virtually none of the long-term residents of Jerusalem, Ramallah, Nablus, Hebron, and Gaza departed.[91]

Arab states imposing an oil embargo against countries ostensibly aiding Israel found that it rebounded to their own detriment. Except for causing some inconvenience and financial distress to the UK, the embargo had little other foreign impact. By the end of June, Saudi Arabia had lost 11 million pounds in oil royalties and Kuwait reported a marked drop in national income.[92] Not surprisingly, the embargo was soon lifted. Finally, it should be noted that the Egyptians had scuttled boats in the Suez Canal blocking all passage until June 1975.

In Jerusalem on the night of June 10, around 135 houses adjacent to the Western Wall were summarily bulldozed. Without consulting either Dayan or Rabin, Uzi Narkiss took it upon himself to direct the demolitions. The operation was undertaken to allow for a large plaza facing the Western Wall in which a multitude of people could congregate during Jewish festivals and national holidays. Narkiss and others believed that the clearance had to be effected as rapidly as possible in anticipation of international pressures preventing Israel from undertaking structural modifications within the Old City. The Arab residents in the houses in question were allowed no more than an hour or so to vacate their homes and to remove whatever possessions they could carry. An army officer promised them that they would ultimately be rehoused.[93] Four days later, the cabinet authorized the eviction of the Arabs who had moved into the Jewish quarter in 1948 after all the original Jewish residents had been expelled. (About 300 Arab families were involved).[94]

Israelis were virtually unanimous that Jerusalem was be reunited and to remain under Israeli sovereignty in perpetuity. Accordingly, its municipal boundaries were redrawn to incorporate the Old City, Mount Scopus, Sheikh Jarrah, and the suburb of Shuafat up to the airport at Atarot (Kalandia), and on June 28 the Knesset formally annexed East Jerusalem. (In the actual legislation, the word "annexation" was strictly avoided.) All dividing walls were razed to the ground, mines and barbed-wire fences were cleared from what was previously no man's land, municipal services were integrated, and telephone lines were fully interconnected.

Away from Jerusalem, four villages in the vicinity of Latrun were flattened to ensure unhindered and safe traffic along the Jerusalem–Tel Aviv highway. Two other villages in the region of Hebron were also demolished and in Kalkilya, IDF officers acting off their own account expelled the inhabitants and dynamited their houses. The mayor of Kalkilya was ordered onto a jeep and forced to call upon his townsfolk to take leave of their homes. Fearing for the worst, most fled.[95] A little later Dayan and Weizman visited the scene. They were appalled. All the stores were broken into and looted[96] and some 800 housing units were badly damaged.[97] Upset by the sight of Kalkilya's residents squatting in the open air in nearby olive groves, Dayan, at the next cabinet meeting, successfully recommended that their homes be restored and that they be allowed to return to them. Similarly, the Arabs from the two destroyed villages near Hebron were given finance and building materials to assist them in rehabilitating their dwellings.[98]

Within the Israeli government, conflicting views relating to the appropriate management of the country's new wards and territory were bitterly contested, thus impeding effective and decisive policy-making. Had Gahal and Rafi not entered a government of national unity it is quite possible, but by no means certain, that a moderate consensus would have emerged. On June 19, the cabinet did at least resolve, by a vote of 11 to 10, to convey to both Egypt and Syria that in the framework of a peace agreement, Israel was prepared to withdraw to recognized international frontiers. That is, it would vacate all of Sinai (but not the Gaza Strip which was originally within mandated Palestine) and the Golan Heights. The only pre-conditions were unrestricted use of the Suez Canal and the Straits of Tiran, the demilitarization of Sinai and the Golan Heights and no Syrian tampering with Israel's water sources. The offer was transmitted to the US government to be forwarded to the two states in question. Within a matter of days, Egypt and Syria rejected it, demanding instead an unconditional withdrawal.[99] Having been so curtly spurned, Israel began to entertain second thoughts about the disposition of its forces in conquered Syrian territory. By mid-July, heeding military advice that some long-term presence was needed for security purposes, the government began endorsing plans for the establishment of Jewish settlements on the Golan Heights.

Missing from the Israeli overture of June 19 was any mention of the West Bank, the heartland of ancient Jewish kingdoms. In that regard, the government was deadlocked and resorted to the expedient of leaving matters up in the air. If Ben-Gurion had had any say, Israel would have ceded the entire West Bank save for East Jerusalem so as not to become embroiled in a hostile Arab population. In April 1968, he explained his position in an interview with Tom Segev (then a contributor to a student newspaper) thus: "If I have to choose between a small Israel, without territories, but with peace, and a greater Israel without peace, I prefer a small Israel."[100] On another occasion he outlined his way of thinking somewhat more forthrightly by affirming that "historically this country [Palestine] belongs to two races . . . the Arabs drastically outbreed us . . . a Jewish state must at all times maintain within her own borders an unassailable Jewish majority . . . the logic of all this is that to get peace, we *must* return in principle to the pre-1967 borders."[101] Although Ben-Gurion's views were seen by a very small following (including Eban and Shapira) as being eminently sensible, they were widely ridiculed. His detractors claimed that they either reflected jealousy at Eshkol's successes or signs of senility.[102] In addition to Begin's "solution" of simply annexing the entire West Bank, two other divergent mainstream proposals were propagated by Allon and Dayan.

Allon formulated a scheme that became known as the Allon Plan, according to which Israel would indicate a willingness to sue for peace in exchange for returning sections of the West Bank to the local Palestinians or, after that proved to be unattainable, to Jordan. What Allon would not surrender was a large strip of land in the Jordan valley (to serve as a defense buffer along the Jordan River), a very much extended Jerusalem municipal region, and a widened Jerusalem corridor that would include Latrun. The area to be relinquished was to enjoy semi-autonomy and to be economically integrated with Israel. Realizing that his plan was highly contentious, Allon never formally presented it to cabinet for fear of precipitating a coalition crisis leading to a general election in which Dayan, with his newly acquired status as national savior, would have substantially boosted Rafi's electoral prospects. Dayan's approach is outlined somewhat further below.

Three weeks after the war Ya'akov Herzog, Eshkol's private secretary, met with King Hussein in the offices of Dr Emmanuel Herbert, the king's London physician. That meeting, like a previous one in 1963, was conducted in utmost secrecy. Speaking man to man and with mutual respect, Herzog asked of Hussein whether, after all that had happened and in view of the grave consequences of not resolving the ongoing conflict, he was now ready to enter into formal negotiations with Israel. Much to Herzog's regret, even in the seclusion of a private and confidential conversation, the king refused to commit himself.[103] A similar stance was manifested by Palestinian notables. After consulting them, in conjunction with other high-ranking Israelis and with Eshkol's endorsement, Herzog discovered that they were in no frame of mind to countenance any offer that would have gone a long way toward meeting their national aspirations. During a series of talks with such dignitaries, trial balloons were floated. These included the formation of an independent Palestinian state with its capital in the greater Jerusalem area and secure passage between Gaza and the West Bank. (The state was to have been demilitarized and defended by the IDF.) At first, a number of Palestinians seemed to be receptive to at least some of the ideas submitted but they soon had misgivings. Bearing in mind Israel's full withdrawal after the Sinai Campaign, they questioned how long Israel would remain in the newly conquered territories and were therefore fearful of being branded as collaborators.[104]

After the Arabs had failed to defeat Israel on the battlefield, the Soviet Union tried to recoup their losses through the medium of the UN and through big-power machinations. The first shot in the diplomatic war was registered on June 14 in the UN Security Council. Russia called for the condemnation of Israel as an aggressor and for it to withdraw unconditionally to the 1949 armistice lines. Much to Israel's surprise, the Soviet resolution was rejected. Unfazed, Russia arranged for the General Assembly to convene on June 19 in a continuous special emergency session. An hour before its opening, President Johnson publicly enunciated America's newly found principles for resolving the Arab–Israel conflict. They were encapsulated by five points: embracing the recognition of each country's right to full sovereignty, the resolution of the Palestinian refugee problem, unfettered passage in all international waterways, limits to the arms race, and territorial integrity. In his address, Johnson mentioned that peace could not be obtained by restoring the "fragile and often violated armistice."[105] Johnson's position set the stage for the UN to adjudicate with a measure of uncharacteristic even-handedness. That is not to say that Soviet and other delegates refrained from denigrating Israel. Aleksei Kosygin, the Russian prime minister, accused the Jewish state of "acting in a Hitlerist manner." In response to that grotesque comparison, Abba Eban reminded the General Assembly that "Our nation never compromised with Hitler's Germany. Our nation never signed a pact with it as did the USSR in 1939."[106] On July 4 after lengthy debate, a resolution was tabled, sponsored by Yugoslavia, calling for the total withdrawal of Israeli forces without any Arab quid pro quo. Although it was supported by, among others, the Arabs, the communists, Muslim states and France, it failed to secure the necessary two-thirds majority. The Soviet Union then proposed a resolution of its own that was even more censorious of Israel and which demanded the payment of reparations by Israel to the Arabs. It too was rejected. The genocidal ambitions of the Arab world that were openly broadcast on the eve of the war had yielded a welcome albeit fleeting ground swell of sympathy and support for Israel. By July 21, the special session of the General Assembly had run its course.

Three months later, on November 22, 1967, after interminable haggling, the UN Security Council adopted Resolution 242 drafted in the main by Lord Caradon of the UK. By its own definition, the two most important clauses of the resolution were "the withdrawal of Israel armed forces from territories occupied in the recent conflict," and "the termination of all claims or states of belligerency and respect for and acknowledgment of the sovereignty, territorial integrity and political independence of every state in the area and their right to live in peace within secure and recognized boundaries free from threats or acts of force."[107] It is no accident that the first clause refers to a withdrawal "from territories," rather than "from *the* territories." The US in particular as well as other western members realized that the 1949 armistice lines had posed a strategic nightmare to Israel. That being the case, it would have been unconscionable to insist on a complete withdrawal to pre-Six-Day War boundaries. For that reason "the armistice lines," or "the lines of June 4, 1967," were not included in the text.[108] Nevertheless, the USSR and others still insisted on interpreting the resolution as if it called for the withdrawal from "all the territories." This prompted Lord Caradon to remark that such interpretations were invalid for "the resolution meant what it said and not a word more."[109] In like vein, on December 9, 1969, William Rogers, the US secretary of state, reaffirmed that "the Security Council resolution neither endorses nor precludes the armistice lines as the definitive political boundaries."[110]

The Soviet communists and the Arabs had sanctimoniously proclaimed that no country had a right to territory taken by force and therefore Israel had to withdraw to the armistice lines. Leaving aside the hypocrisy of the Soviet Union whose empire was based on conquest, an Israeli retreat to the 1949 armistice lines would have legitimized the 1948 land grabs in Palestine of Jordan, Egypt, and Syria whose reach extended beyond the original international Palestine–Syrian frontier. More to the point, the phrase (in Clause 2) "their right to live in peace within secure and recognized boundaries" implies that final Israel–Arab frontiers were to be subject to negotiation.

Even had Israel accepted that UN Resolution 242 entailed a withdrawal to the 1948 armistice lines, as far as both Egypt and Syria were concerned it would have been beside the point. The day after the resolution was passed, Nasser decreed that "all that taken from us by force can *only* be retrieved by force." Whereas Nureddin al-Attasi, president of Syria, declared that "a popular war is the *only* way to resolve the struggle with Israel and *there is no room for a political solution.*"[111]

Between June and October, the Soviet Union replenished the bulk of Egypt's armaments, including all aircraft lost and most of its tanks. Russian advisers and technicians were sent in large numbers to both Egypt and Syria. Fortified by Soviet support and by the promise of subsidized oil from Saudi Arabia, at an Arab summit, held between August 28 and September 2 in Khartoum, Egypt and Jordan endorsed a resolution ruling out any recognition of, negotiation and peace with Israel.[112] Whatever moderate views were supposedly held behind the scenes[113] (the Israelis were not aware of any), the Khartoum pronouncement was taken as an official indication that there were no medium- to long-term prospects of resolving the Arab–Israeli conflict. The realization of this induced Eshkol to inform the Knesset that "Israel will maintain the situation fixed by the cease-fire agreements and reinforce its position by taking into account its security and development needs."[114] Having forced Israel into a war from which they emerged as the vanquished, the Arabs short-sightedly continued on a path that compounded their losses. As far as they were concerned, should they ever succeed in war they would assume everything but on being defeated they would yield nothing.[115]

In the face of continued Arab intransigence, Dayan argued that there was no point in trying to entice the Arabs with generous peace offers. Dayan believed that the best that could be attained was a reduction in inter-state military tensions and social unrest among the population of the conquered territories. To strengthen Israel's grip on the West Bank, which he regarded as a strategic asset, Dayan advocated that the IDF maintain a permanent military presence on commanding hilltops near densely populated Arab centers. On August 20, the cabinet approved of the establishment of five such bases.

With regard to the Arab inhabitants of the conquered territories, Dayan was prepared to see them only as individuals, never as a collective entity.[116] That did not prevent him from promoting the alleviation of their living conditions. To a large degree, the Arabs were allowed to conduct their affairs with minimal interference. Their freedom also extended to their being able to travel and transport goods across the Jordan River in terms of the much vaunted "open bridges policy." In the summer of 1967, Palestinian farmers reaped bumper crops and had they not been able to dispose of their goods in Jordan they would have suffered substantial income losses. Because all bridges over the Jordan had been destroyed, vehicles had to be hauled across shallow stretches of the river. (It was the dry summer season.) To facilitate easier passage, Israel approached Jordan to arrange for the reconstruction of the bridges. Jordan was amenable to the idea provided it undertook the job by itself. Israel agreed and thus toward winter, two Bailey bridges were installed, one alongside the old Allenby Bridge and the other at Damiya.

Despite realizing a far higher degree of employment and income than they had ever enjoyed in the past, the occupied Arabs, or at least a significant number of them, did not remain passive. After the initial shock of defeat, it did not take long for the PLO and its supporters to resume acts of sabotage and murder. This time, they had direct access to crowded Israeli venues. In October 1967, a viewer at the Zion cinema in Jerusalem noticed a bag under the seat in front of him placed by two dark-skinned women who had left prematurely. He alerted an usher who found that it contained a time bomb. Soon it became the norm for handbags to be checked at the entrances to most public places.[117] During the first year after the Six-Day War, the PLO and its allies carried out 687 acts of terror, causing 175 Israelis to be killed.[118] The IDF responded by blowing up houses providing shelter to known terrorists and by exiling their leaders. But as Dayan pointed out, on no occasion in the wake of grisly PLO acts of violence in Jerusalem and Tel Aviv did the Jewish population "turn on the Arab workers and visitors in their midst."[119]

As opposed to the pre-Six-Day War years, when the international frontier was never more than a short drive away, Israelis began to relish their enhanced territorial space. Just as the world came to recognize Israel's post-1949 borders, many assumed that eventually its post-1967 ones would also be accepted.[120] Overnight as it were, the previously moderate and pacifist religious Mafdal party began to sanctify the acquisition of territory.[121] Rabbi Zvi Kook, head of the Merkaz Harav Yeshiva (seminary) and the spiritual guide to Bnei Akiva, Mafdal's youth movement, intoned that the Jews had returned under divine injunction to their homeland (in the West Bank) from where they would never budge.[122] Many socialist secular Israelis also manifested strong emotional attachments to the West Bank. From such ranks emerged some of the founders of a body established in September 1967 called the Movement for the Complete Land of Israel. Its manifesto declared that just as Jews may not forgo the state of Israel, so may they not forgo the entire Land of Israel. Among the more than fifty signatories inaugurating the movement were Labor stalwarts such as Nathan Alterman and Rachel Ben Zvi, the widow of Israel's second president.

Settlement in the conquered territories, known in those days simply as "the territories," rapidly got off the mark. As early as August 1967 the government authorized the cultivation of land in the Golan Heights and in next to no time a kibbutz, ultimately called Merom Golan, took root there. By the following June it had a membership of 169 people.[123] On the heels of the founding kibbutz came a number of other "holdings." The legal adviser of the Israeli foreign office, Theodore Meron, determined that settlements in the Golan Heights (on which Israel never had any prior claims) violated Chapter 49 Article 4 of the Geneva Convention.[124] The Convention explicitly forbade a conqueror to transfer or allow the transfer of its own citizens onto occupied land. With that in mind, some settlements were first formed in the guise of army bases. Nevertheless, by June 1968 there were already six settlements in the Golan Heights.

The onset of Jewish settlements in the West Bank occurred at the end of September 1967 when a band of young adults left Jerusalem in a motorized convoy to re-establish Kfar Etzion. Kfar Etzion was one of a group of four religious kibbutzim that, on the eve of the War of Independence, were overrun and destroyed by the Arab Legion. A large percentage of the original settlers were massacred. The resurrection of Kfar Etzion, which had full public support, was launched with a festive fanfare. Then in April 1968, Allon, as minister of Labor, permitted Rabbi Levinger and his followers to stay in the Park Hotel (formerly the Hahar al-Khalid Hotel) in Hebron for the duration of Pesah (Passover). Their stopover in Hebron was subject to the condition that they were to leave the city at the conclusion of the festival. However, Rabbi Levinger reneged on the agreement. He hoisted an Israeli flag over the hotel and announced that he and his party had come to stay there permanently. Being in a bit of a quandary and certainly not wishing to dislodge the recalcitrant "visitors," Allon secured Eshkol's agreement to leave them in peace until such time as the government formulated a policy on Jewish settlement in Hebron. As with the Gush Etzion bloc, there had in the past been a Jewish presence in that city. (Hebron, along with Jerusalem, Safad, and Tiberias, had from time immemorial been designated as one of Judaism's four holy cities. In 1929, the religious and predominantly non-Zionist Jews of Hebron were subject to a murderous pogrom that culminated in their eviction from the city.)

For almost all Israelis, the Six-Day War was seen as deliverance, divine or otherwise, from the specter of a second Holocaust. Instead of all doom and gloom, the country was, until the 1973 Yom Kippur War, enjoying a measure of normalcy and economic progress. Immigration and capital inflows increased considerably. The economy moved from recession to boom, giving rise to a labor shortage that continued for the next six years.[125] Israel's relations with the US were distinctly improved and above all, with the demise of Nasserism as the leading ideology of Arab nationalism, it seemed that an Arab military threat had well and truly receded. It was in the early years of the aftermath of the war that, in Eban's assessment, the Arabs had the best chance "of recovering most of their territories."[126] Up to 1973, only around 7,000 Jews were living in the West Bank and Gaza. Had the Arab leaders been willing to come to terms with Israel, a mutually acceptable peace agreement could have been secured.

CONCLUSION

Although Israel emerged from its War of Independence triumphant, it was seemingly very frail at birth. Just two months before the Jewish state arose, that is, on March 19, 1948, Warren Austin, the US ambassador to the UN, informed the UN Security Council that the UN Palestine partition resolution was unworkable and that plans for its implementation ought to be suspended. Austin arrived at that conclusion on the basis of reports emanating from Palestine that indicated that the Yishuv (the Jewish population) was taking a battering and that, by all accounts, it was unlikely to get the better of the Arabs. On March 11, an Arab parked a van loaded with explosives in front of the Jewish Agency's headquarters in Jerusalem. Moments later, a violent blast not only shattered the building but also the Yishuv's fragile self-confidence. On March 26, a Jewish convoy returning from the Gush Etzion (the bloc of four settlements near Hebron) was ambushed. Many men were wiped out and those that survived did so as a result of the British coming to their rescue. Three days later, another Jewish convoy traveling in the Western Galilee was surrounded by Arab bands and in the ensuing battle 42 Jews met their death. Worse to come, on March 30, on the winding ascent to Jerusalem, below the steep wooded slopes of Bab-el Wad, the largest Jewish convoy ever mounted came under the withering fire of Palestinian forces. Dozens of vehicles were destroyed, Jewish casualties were heavy and access to Jerusalem was cut off. As Colonel Lund, a Norwegian member of the UN mission in Palestine saw things, the situation of the Yishuv was "worse than that of Norway in 1940."[1]

As the end of the British mandate drew near, George Marshall, the US secretary of state, who was not at all sanguine about the viability of a Jewish state, cautioned Moshe Sharett (who was acting as the Jewish Agency's foreign representative) against any premature declaration of Jewish independence. In the event of his advice not being heeded, he added, US military assistance could not be assured.[2] (Similar warnings were issued by the US to Israel on the eve of the Six-Day War.) Marshall's gloomy assessment of Israel's chances of survival was to some extent shared by Yigal Yadin, Israel's de facto chief of staff, who put the odds of Israel overcoming the invading Arab armies at no more than 50 percent. Yadin had valid grounds for concern, considering that the invaders were vastly better equipped than the Israelis.

Until the commencement of the first truce on June 11, 1948, the probable outcome of the War of Independence remained unclear. The Israelis basically held the enemy in check but they were stretched to the limit. The four-week lull in fighting enabled them to take delivery of large quantities of weapons, primarily from Czechoslovakia, as well as to enhance and reorganize their forces. By contrast, because of a UN arms embargo (which Israel circumvented), the Arabs and Transjordan in particular were hard pressed to replace their ordnance. Once hostilities resumed, Israel gained the distinct upper hand. It not only thwarted all Arab attempts to subdue it but went on to expand its frontiers beyond those demarcated in the UN partition resolution. As a by-product of the war and through no prior Israeli intentions or scheming, the Jewish state found itself divested of most of the Arabs that had resided in the territory it subsequently controlled. The resulting hundreds of thousands of Palestinian refugees proved to be a permanent and bitter bone of contention between Israel and the entire Arab world. To this day, it remains a stumbling block for a final and comprehensive peace settlement.

For Israel, the war ended well. Despite losing 1 percent of its original Jewish population, the country was largely unscathed. Having attained a measure of self-assurance in its ability to deter future acts of aggression, Israel concentrated its efforts on developing its economy and absorbing a multitude of Jewish immigrants from war-ravaged Europe and from countries in the Middle East and North Africa. Pursuing both objectives within the same time frame was no mean feat. The economy was in a shambles. Food supplies had dwindled drastically as a result of nearly 10 percent of the population being mobilized and of the flight of Arab farmers. Foreign reserves were just about exhausted and the internal tax-raising capacity of the government was, to say the least, rudimentary. To ensure that the population at large had access to basic essentials, a strict system of rationing was imposed.

All the while, migrants came pouring in at uncontrollable rates. Although the disorderly and chaotic ingress of a differentiated mass of impoverished Jews imposed tremendous strains on Israel, not to mention the problems of adjustment and feelings of alienation experienced by many of the migrants themselves, in the long run nearly everyone benefited. Over four years, Israel's Jewish population had doubled. New development towns came into being as did numerous frontier farming villages. From the migrants' point of view, they and their children were ultimately integrated into the general fabric of Israeli society, notwithstanding their initial encounter with discrimination and (especially those from Arab countries), their placement at the lower end of the social scale.

During the latter half of the 1950s and early 1960s, thanks to a massive infusion of foreign capital arising from German reparations payments, US government aid and world Jewry's benevolence, Israel's economy rebounded. Employment, exports, labor productivity and earnings all rose as did general standards of living. Israelis could now confidently aspire to a far better material future.

Unfortunately the same could not be said regarding the state's long-term security. Before the ink of the signatories of the armistice agreements had time to dry, displaced Arabs began illicitly crossing Israel's borders, first in attempts to either resettle in their former villages or salvage their crops but eventually in order to wreak havoc on the Jewish population. With increasing intensity, Israelis were subject to murderous incursions and willful property damage. Acts of sabotage even extended to the blowing up of railway lines. In time, infiltrators were taken under the wing of the Egyptian army stationed in the Gaza Strip. They were organized into a unit of Fedayeen (literally "those who sacrifice themselves") and sent on missions at Egypt's behest. Israel retaliated by attacking villages thought to have provided succor to the terrorists but, in the main, such responses simply led to the escalation of further violence. Matters came to a head when, in September 1955, a Czech–Egyptian arms deal was announced. It soon became clear that Egypt was to be the recipient of very large consignments of updated Soviet weapons which when delivered would decisively tilt the strategic arms balance in its favor. The Israelis were under no doubt that it was Nasser's intention to attack them.

From the IDF's point of view, if Israel were to avoid being badly mauled, it was imperative to initiate a preventive war before Egypt's new fighting potential was fully realized. Inadvertently, by nationalizing the Suez Canal Company in July 1956, Nasser provided Israel with a golden opportunity to proceed with a full frontal onslaught on all Egyptian forces stationed in Sinai. Nasser's bold act had so antagonized Britain and France that within a short while they not only determined to unseat him but had also engaged Israel as a surreptitious ally in their budding campaign to wrest control of the Suez Canal area. After having been fortified with shipments of French weapons, including tanks and aircraft, and having secured a French commitment to help defend Israel's airspace, the IDF went on the offensive at the end of October 1956. With many Egyptian troops having been removed from Sinai in anticipation of a joint Anglo-French invasion, Israel took full possession of the peninsula in a matter of days.

Bowing to inexorable international pressures, particularly from the US and the Soviet Union, the IDF reluctantly withdrew to within its 1949 frontier. Israel did at least secure guarantees from leading maritime powers, including the US, that if its newly gained access through the Straits of Tiran were ever again denied, they would support Israel in its efforts to reassert its shipping rights.

During the next few years, quiet reigned on all of Israel's borders but from 1965 onward, skirmishes occurred with both Syrian and Jordanian troops and/or Palestinian guerrillas operating from Syria and Jordan. In May 1967, the Soviet Union stirred the pot by falsely claiming that Israel was massing 11–13 brigades alongside Syria with a view to invading it. Invoking Egypt's mutual defense treaty with Syria, Nasser promptly poured thousands of troops into Sinai, after which one thing led to another. The United Nations Emergency Force was evicted and, in closing the Straits of Tiran to Israeli shipping, Nasser provided Israel with a casus belli. Jordan committed itself to go to war in Egypt's defense as did Iraq and a number of other Arab countries. As Israel was being encircled by an iron ring of Arab might, the international community, far from honoring its previous undertakings, demonstrated a general lack of willingness to intervene on Israel's behalf. All alone and facing an inevitable Arab blitzkrieg, Israel pre-empted its adversaries by lashing out first. As related in the previous chapter, Egypt, Jordan, and Syria were soundly beaten.

In the aftermath of the Six-Day War, the Israelis were convinced that they had entered a new era of, if not peace, then at least an absence of war. Paradoxically, in early 1948, where the story of this book begins, although the Israelis felt that they were very much endangered, they were far stronger than they had realized. By contrast, immediately after routing their enemies in June 1967 (the closing period of this book), the Israelis felt invincible at a time when they were actually subject to weaknesses that they had not fully appreciated. So confident were Israeli generals of their army's newly revealed might that they talked freely of Israel having become a regional power whose neighbors would never again dare to challenge it. Their self-assurance was in part derived from their having simultaneously beaten three separate states in a matter of days. But it also in part followed from their satisfaction with the strategic implications of Israel's new borders. Previously, when Israel was very much smaller in size, its tortuous frontiers were 985 kilometers in length. Now while occupying a far greater land area, Israel's frontiers became less meandering and, as a result, were only 650 kilometers long. The frontier with Jordan presented a natural obstacle, the River Jordan. Along the new Syrian cease-fire line the IDF was less than an hour's drive from Damascus and from Israeli army observation posts the whole of southern Syria was discernible.[3] The Egyptians were hundreds of kilometers away from Israel proper but best of all the Suez Canal presented itself as the "biggest anti-tank ditch in the world." The way the General Staff actually felt about themselves was captured by Ezer Weizman when stating "we are now strutting about as if each of us were three meters tall, like giants among grasshoppers."[4]

A closer and clear-headed look about them might have shown the

Israelis that there was still reason to be seriously concerned about the country's medium-term security. For one, with the Israeli and Egyptian armies separated merely by the width of the Suez Canal, there was scope for the Egyptians to launch a surprise attack, which they actually did at the commencement of the Yom Kippur War in October 1973. Previously, if Egypt wished to wage war against Israel, it had first to transport its troops across Sinai to Israel's borders, which would have served Israel with a timely warning. But that no longer applied after the Six-Day War. In other words, from Israel's strategic point of view, its new borders with Egypt did not necessarily provide it with any appreciable improvement. Had the Egyptian army not rearmed significantly, then matters might have been different. But the Soviet Union wasted no time in replenishing Egypt's reduced stock of arms. Within one month alone, Russia airlifted to it 70 percent of the weapons that the country had forfeited. Since the weapons in question were state of the art, the Egyptian army was not only regaining its former strength but was about to surpass it. In addition, Russia, by dispatching 10,000 technicians and advisers to Egypt, demonstrated that it intended to play a far more active role in guiding and organizing the Egyptian army. Such factors, combined with an absolute determination by both the Egyptian and Syrian regimes to erase the shame of their defeat, should have given the Israelis grounds for being less complacent. Unfortunately, their firm belief that the Bar Lev line, a series of fortifications built on the eastern bank of the Suez Canal, would suffice to ward off any Egyptian attack was no more realistic than the faith that the French had prior to the Second World War in their series of border fortifications known as the Maginot Line. Apart from the strategic peril that Israel faced, the country was bedeviled by an increased intensity of Palestinian insurgency.

The Palestinian issue in effect rose to center stage as a direct outcome of the Six-Day War. Beforehand, the Palestinians in the West Bank and Gaza were ruled by Jordan and Egypt respectively. Now that they were in practice left to their own devices under Israeli rule, they resorted to outright acts of terrorism as a means of weakening and demoralizing the Israelis. For many years they studiously avoided head-on collisions with the IDF, preferring instead to target civilians both within Israel and abroad. Parallel to that, Israeli religious fundamentalists, supported by ardent secular nationalists, spearheaded the Jewish settler movement that incorporated more and more land into the Jewish state without regard to Palestinian sensibilities. It can legitimately be argued that the settlers exacerbated Palestinian animosity toward Israel. However, as the years went by and successive generations of Palestinians lived under the yoke (benign or otherwise) of an Israeli occupation without any inkling as to why it came about and without appreciating why the PLO's misplaced goal of eliminating Israel guaranteed its continuity, the total absence of Jewish settlements would by no means have made them any less hostile. Extolling violence as the *only* means of furthering their cause, the PLO leadership inadvertently paved the way for the ultimate ascendancy of the Islamic extremists. Such fanatics have to a large extent succeeded in altering the contours of the Arab–Israeli conflict. From a clash of national claims and rights (which conceivably could be resolved by mutual bargaining), the Islamic fascists have elevated their struggle into a jihad in which compromise is inconceivable and a fight to the finish is theologically mandatory. Far from resolving the Jewish state's strategic problems, at best the Six-Day War yielded Israelis with a rather brief security interlude. Alas, it did not take long for many of their newly acquired illusions to be shattered.

Appendix: General Election Results

Results of the January 1949 Election

Mapai (a social democratic party led by Ben-Gurion)	46 seats
Mapam (a Zionist Marxist party)	19 seats
United Religious Front (Agudat Yisrael, Poalei Agudat Yisrael, Hamizrahi and Poalei Hamizrahi)	16 seats
Herut (the political successor to the Irgun)	14 seats
The General Zionists (a conservative party)	7 seats
The Progressives (a liberal party)	5 seats
Union of Mizrahi and Sephardi Jews	4 seats
Communists	4 seats
Democratic Arab List	2 seats
The Sternists (offshoot of Lehi)	1 seat
Wizo (Women Zionists)	1 seat
United Yemenites	1 seat

Results of the July 1951 Election

Mapai	45 seats
General Zionists	20 seats
Mapam	15 seats
Hapoel Hamizrahi (a workers' religious party)	8 seats
Herut	8 seats
Communists	5 seats
Progressives	4 seats
Agudat Yisrael (an ultra-orthodox party)	3 seats
Poalei Ha'aguda (a workers' ultra-orthodox party)	2 seats
Mizrahi (a middle-of-the road religious party)	2 seats
Sephardim	2 seats
Yemenites	1 seats
Three separate Arab lists	5 seats

Results of the July 1955 Election

Mapai	40 seats
Herut	15 seats
General Zionists	13 seats
United Religious Front (the two Hamizrahi parties)	11 seats
Ahdut Ha'avodah	10 seats
Mapam	9 seats
Communists	6 seats
Agudat Yisrael	6 seats
Progressives	5 seats
Three minority lists (associated with Mapai)	5 seats

Results of the July 1959 Election

Mapai	47 seats
Herut	17 seats
Mafdal (National Religious Party)	12 seats
Mapam	9 seats
General Zionist	8 seats
Ahdut Ha'avodah	7 seats
Progressives	6 seats
Agudat Yisrael	6 seats
Pro-Mapai Arab Parties	5 seats
Communists	3 seats

Results of the August 1961 Election

Mapai	42 seats
Liberal Party	17 seats
Herut	17 seats
Mafdal	12 seats
Mapam	9 seats
Ahdut Ha'avodah	8 seats
United Torah (Agudat Yisrael and Poalei Agudat Yisrael)	6 seats
Communists	5 seats
Pro-Mapai Arab Lists	4 seats

Results of the November 1965 Elections

Hama'arah	45 seats
Gahal	26 seats
Mafdal	11 seats
Rafi	10 seats
Mapam	8 seats
Agudat Yisrael	6 seats
Independent Liberals	5 seats
Pro-Mapai Arab Lists	4 seats
Rakah	3 seats
Maki	1 seat
This World-New Force (led by a dissident journalist, Uri Avneri)	1 seat

Notes

Introduction

1 Koestler 1983, p. 4.
2 Reproduced in Eliav 1981, vol. 2, p. 245.
3 As quoted in Shalmon 1981, p. 136.
4 Eliyahu Even-Tov, "In Petach Tikva at the Time of the Ban," in Habbas 1947, p. 183.
5 As quoted in Bein 1970, p. 103.
6 See Bein 1970, p. 105.
7 As quoted in Bein 1970, p. 105.
8 As quoted in Be'eri 1985, p. 119. Italics added.
9 As quoted in Mandel 1976, pp. 47–8. Italics added.
10 Sachar 1990, p. 566.
11 See Wasserstein 1978, p. 131.
12 Bauer 1966, Part Two, p. 26.
13 See Segev 2000, pp. 420–6.
14 See Weizmann 1949, p. 535.
15 Weizmann 1949, p. 535.
16 As quoted in Bregman and El-Tahri 1998, p. 28.

Chapter 1 The War of Independence

1 Kimche, J. and D. 1960, p. 161. Morris 2008, p. 205 puts the Arab invasion troop number at 20,000.

2 Morris 2008, p. 204.

3 Kimche, J. and D. 1960, p. 161 and Morris 2008, p. 88.

4 Luttwak and Horowitz 1975, p. 30.

5 Because of poor maintenance and because a certain amount was withheld in their home countries.

6 For most of the war, Yadin stood in for Ya'acov Dori, the Haganah's chief of staff, who was incapacitated by illness.

7 Tal 2004b, p. 156.

8 Slutsky 1972, p. 1439.

9 Morris 2008, p. 172.

10 Israel Defense Force 1966, p. 166.

11 As quoted in Lorch 1961, p. 152.

12 Bar-Zohar 1975, p. 756.

13 As quoted in Lorch 1961, p. 152.

14 Golan 1974, p. 115.

15 Tal 2004b, p. 253; Morris 2008, p. 254.

16 Bar-Zohar 1975, p. 756.

17 Teveth 1972, p. 142.

18 See Karsh 2008, p. 26.

19 Glubb 1957, p. 258.

20 Glubb 1957, p. 107.

21 Kurzman 1972, p. 403.

22 Kurzman 1972 p. 383.

23 Morris 2008, p. 218.

24 Lorch 1961, p. 180.

25 Glubb 1957, p. 125.

26 Ben-Gurion 1971, p. 180, and Joseph 1960, p. 158.

27 As quoted in Morris 2008, p. 215.

28 Joseph 1960, pp. 143 and 151.

29 Golan 1974, p. 139.

30 Itzchaki 1982, pp. 190–1.

31 Itzchaki 1982, p. 182.

32 Shapira 1996, p. 23.

33 Itzchaki 1982, p. 168.

34 See Hefez and Bloom 2006, p. 7, and Dan 2006, p. 8.

35 Sharon with Chanoff 1989, p. 57.

36 Sharon with Chanoff 1989, p. 58.

37 Sharon with Chanoff 1989, p. 60.

38 Ibid, p. 60.

39 Shapira 1996, p. 25. Beer 1995, p. 43, mentions a figure of 75 killed. Elsewhere far more inflated numbers have been offered. For example, Kurzman 1972, p. 415, reports that 140 perished.

40 Beer 1955, p. 43.

41 Yablonka 1997, p. 46.

42 See Beer 1955, p. 33.

43 So as not to embarrass the American government.

44 See Israel Defense Force 1954, p. 186.

45 See Israel Defense Force 1966, p. 209.

46 Kurzman 1972, p. 424.

47 Tal 2004b, p. 179, refers to "30 odd settlements of the Negev."

48 Larkin 1965, p. 140.

49 Larkin 1965, p. 145.

50 Israel Defense Force 1966, p. 220.

51 Larkin 1965, pp. 213 and 231.

52 Tal 2004b, p. 184.

53 Weizman 1976, p. 67.

54 Tal 2004b, p. 187. Gelber 2006, p. 144, suggests that the Egyptians moved north from Majdal to help Palestinian irregulars and refugees flocking to Yibna (Yibneh). By contrast, Morris 2008, p. 239, thinks that whether the Egyptians were seeking "to advance as far as possible toward Tel Aviv," or merely to reach the northern extreme of the area the UN allocated to the Arabs in Southern Palestine, remains an open-ended question.

55 Israel Defense Force 1966, p. 227.

56 Golan 1974, p. 171.

57 Kurzman 1972, p. 307.

58 Tal 2004b, p. 189.

59 Ben-Gurion, *Israel: A Personal History*, 1971, p. 110.

60 Morris 2008, p. 263.

61 Ben-Gurion, *Israel: A Personal History*, 1971, pp. 155–9.

62 Ben-Gurion, *Israel: A Personal History*, 1971, p. 243.

63 Lorch 1961, p. 255.
64 Begin 1979, p. 159.
65 Begin 1979, p. 167.
66 As quoted in Silver 1984, p. 102. Italics added.
67 Kurzman 1972, p. 472. Kurzman obtained that information in an interview with Faglin.
68 Information relating to the Tubiansky affair has been drawn from Teveth 1996, pp. 1–54.
69 See Teveth 1996, p. 30.
70 Black and Morris 1991, p. 60.
71 Eban 1978, p. 124.
72 Gelber 2001, p. 191.
73 McDonald 1951, p. 20.
74 Named after Dani Mass who in January 1948 led 35 Palmahniks to their death when ambushed while attempting to relieve Gush Etzion.
75 As quoted in Lorch 1961, p. 285.
76 Gelber 2001, p. 161. Kurzman 1972, p. 515, puts the figure at close to 200.
77 Shapira 2004, pp. 370–1.
78 Tal 2004b, p. 311.
79 See Gelber 2006, p. 146.
80 Lorch 1961, p. 290.
81 Tal 2004b, p. 324.
82 Shapira 1996, p. 22. There has been much inaccurate reporting regarding the battles of Latrun. For example, Luttwak and Horowitz (1975, pp. 37–8) erroneously claimed that "more than four hundred new immigrant soldiers serving in the 7th Brigade were killed."
83 Lorch 1961, p. 324.
84 Morris 2008, p. 83.
85 Lorch 1961, p. 327.
86 Israel Defense Force 1966, p. 234, names the settlement in question as Mishmoret but Weizman 1976, p. 69, identifies it as Kfar Vitkin. Both sources concur that the incident followed the bombing of Tulkarem.
87 Lissak 1999, p. 84.

88 Gelber 2001, pp. 43–4.
89 Kurzman 1972, p. 486.
90 McDonald 1951, p. 73.
91 As already mentioned, because West Jerusalem, which was ruled by a military governor, was not yet officially considered part of the state of Israel, the Irgun and Lehi had been allowed to continue to function there.
92 As quoted in Pappe 1988, p. 59.
93 Kurzman 1972, p. 575.
94 As quoted in McDonald 1951, p. 77.
95 Operation Yoav, that originally was to be called Operation Ten Plagues, took the title of the *nom de guerre* of a deceased fighter at Negba.
96 Rabin, *The Rabin Memoirs*, 1979, p. 66.
97 See Pappe 1988, p. 59.
98 Kurzman 1972, p. 579, italics in the original.
99 Shapira 2004, p. 395.
100 Lorch 1961, p. 354.
101 Israel Defense Force 1966, p. 306.
102 Kurzman 1972, pp. 600–1.
103 Gelber 2001, p. 209; Morris 1987, p. 222; Ben-Gurion 1982, vol. 3, p. 807.
104 Shapira 2004, p. 402.
105 See Cohen 1964, p. 415.
106 Israel Defense Force 1966, p. 331.
107 As quoted in Lorch 1961, p. 386.
108 Gelber 2001, p. 213. Tal 2004b, p. 443, puts the death toll at more than seventy.
109 Morris 1987, p. 230.
110 Gelber 2001, pp. 226–7. Other sources indicate that the number killed was thirty. See Morris 1995, p. 55.
111 See Morris 1995, p. 55.
112 As quoted in Shaham 1998, p. 80.
113 See Ben-Gurion, *Israel: A Personal History*, 1971, pp. 178 and 188.
114 As quoted in Segev 1986, p. 26.
115 Shapira 2004, p. 431.

116 Ben-Gurion, *Israel: A Personal History*, 1971, p. 163.

117 Ben-Gurion, *Israel: A Personal History* 1971, p. 252.

118 Rabin, *The Rabin Memoirs*, 1979, p. 24.

119 Lorch 1961, p. 410.

120 Israel Defense Force 1954, p. 107.

121 Israel Defense Force 1954, p. 116.

122 See Bar-Joseph 1987, pp. 144–5.

123 See Bar-Joseph 1987, p. 202.

124 Lorch 1961, p. 40.

125 See for instance, Pappe 1988, pp. 18–19.

126 Tal 2004b, p. 154.

127 See Gelber 2006, p. 124.

128 Morris 2008, p. 212.

129 Morris 2008, p. 189.

130 Pappe 1988, p. 25.

131 Tal 2004b, p. 146.

132 As quoted in Morris 2008, p. 395.

133 See Pappe 1988, p. 74.

134 Tal 2004b, p. 279.

135 Tal 2004b, p. 354.

136 Glubb 1957, p. 152.

137 Karsh 1997, p. 177.

138 Karsh 1997, p. 156.

139 See Ilan 1996, p. 124.

140 Eytan 1958, p. 61.

141 Pappe 1988, p. 188.

142 Bar-Joseph 1987, p. 165.

143 Glubb 1957, p. 258.

144 Gazit 1988, p. 413.

145 Gelber 2001, p. 233.

146 As quoted in Lorch 1961, p. 241.

147 Kimche and Kimche 1960, p. 307.

148 Meinertzhagen 1959, p. 226.

149 As quoted in Ginat 1993, p. 85.

150 Black and Morris 1991, p. 69.

151 Kimche and Kimche 1960, p. 232.

152 Ilan 1996, p. 62.

153 Morris 2008, p. 206.

154 This point was well appreciated by the Arab Legion's commander. See Glubb 1957, p. 95.

155 Gelber 2001, p. 14.

156 As quoted in Bar-Zohar 1975, p. 874.

157 The UN November 1947 resolution allocated 14,900 square kilometers to the incipient Jewish state whereas after the War of Independence it emerged with 20,666 square kilometers.

158 Shapira 2004, p. 305.

159 As quoted in Bar-Joseph 1987, p. 155.

160 Sivan 1991, p. 30.

161 Van Creveld 1998, p. 99.

Chapter 2 The Arab Refugees

1 Gelber 2001, p. 273.

2 Gelber 2001, p. 273.

3 Hurewitz 1950, pp. 319–21. Morris 1993, p. 4, estimates that the number of refugees ranged from 600,000 to 760,000.

4 *Jerusalem Post*, February 11, 2007.

5 As quoted in Gold 2004, p. 55.

6 As quoted in Ben-Gurion 1969, p. 489.

7 Pappe 2006, p. xii.

8 Pappe 2006, p. xii.

9 Flapan 1987, p. 93.

10 As translated by Khalidi 1988, p. 29.

11 Tal 2004b, p. 89.

12 Gelber 2001, p. 98.

13 Morris 2001, p. 256.

14 Pappe 2006, p. xiii.

15 Pappe 2006 (endnotes), p. 263.

16 Ben-Gurion 1954, pp. 530–1.

17 Pappe 2006, p. 95.

18 Pappe 2006, n. 19, p. 272.

19 Pappe 2006, p. 95.

20 Pappe 2006, p. 95.

21 As quoted in Morris 2008, p. 299.

22 Flapan 1987, p. 87. Italics added.

23　See Morrrs 1987, p. 219.

24　Shapira 2004, p. 372.

25　Gelber 2006, p. 213.

26　Gelber 2006, p. 103.

27　Kimche and Kimche 1960, p. 122.

28　See Morris 2008, p. 146.

29　As quoted in Gelber 2006, p. 107.

30　Gelber 2006, p. 104.

31　As quoted in Schechtman 1952, pp. 8–9.

32　Morris 1987, p. 73.

33　Gelber 2006, p. 101.

34　As quoted in Morris 2008, p. 158.

35　As quoted in Morris 2008, p. 409.

36　See Stein 2003, p. 235.

37　As quoted in Karsh 2008, p. 26.

38　Oz 2004, p. 342.

39　Black and Morris 1991, p. 38.

40　Cohen 1964, p. 433.

41　Schechtman 1952, p. 5.

42　Morris 1987, p. 30. Gabbay 1959, p. 66, reports an alternative figure amounting to only 30,000. Morris's estimation is embodied in the text since his study was completed years later when more documents were available.

43　Al-Haj 2004, p. 110. Italics added.

44　Gelber 2006, p. 37.

45　See Teveth 1990, p. 224.

46　See Morris 2001.

47　As quoted in Lorch 1961, pp. 82–3.

48　See Israel Defense Force 1954, pp. 18 and 34.

49　As quoted in Gabbay 1959, p. 92.

50　As quoted in Morris 1987, p. 101.

51　Ben-Gurion 1982, p. 438.

52　Morris 2008, p. 154.

53　Morris 1987, p. 290.

54　Morris 1987, p. 67.

55　See Teveth 1990, p. 223.

56　As quoted in Atiyah 1955, p. 183.

57 Karsh 2002, p. 89.
58 As quoted in Karsh 2008, p. 27.
59 Gabbay 1959, p. 93.
60 Rubinstein 1990, p. 9.
61 Flapan 1987, p. 97. Italics added
62 Flapan 1987, p. 96. Arab sources put the number at 450. See Rubinstein 1990, p. 13.
63 See Gelber 2006, p. 8.
64 As quoted in Gelber 2006, p. 115.
65 As quoted in Morris 2008, p. 162.
66 Yiftah 1948, pp. 460–1.
67 Yiftah 1948, p. 457.
68 As quoted in Gelber 2006, p. 161.
69 Shapira 2004, p. 372.
70 See Tal 2004b, p. 312.
71 See Shapira 2004, pp. 435–6.
72 A dunam is approximately a quarter of an acre.
73 Flapan 1987, p. 107.
74 Segev 1986, pp. 87–90.
75 Morris 1987, p. 191.
76 Joseph 1960, p. 302.
77 Glubb 1957, p. 397.
78 Morris 1993, p. 5.
79 From 1958 UN speech as reproduced in Laqueur 1970, p. 193.
80 See Eytan 1958, p. 112.
81 Ambrose 1984, p. 317.
82 Reproduced in Laqueur and Rubin, 2001, p. 85.
83 Eban 1992, p. 178.
84 Gelber 2001, p. 184.
85 See Harkabi 1967, p. 6.
86 As quoted in Peters 1984, p. 22.
87 As quoted in Peters 1984, p. 23.
88 As quoted in Gabbay 1959, p. 297.
89 As quoted in Katz 1973, p. 31.
90 As quoted in Bodansky 2002, p. 323.
91 Eytan 1958, p. 55.

92 Ariene Kushner, "The First World: Why Does UNRWA Exist?" *Jerusalem Post*, Oct. 27, 2005.
93 Friedman 1990, p. 36.
94 Gold 2004, p. 55.

Chapter 3 The Ingathering of the Exiles

1 Patinkin 1967, p. 21.
2 Ben-Gurion 1969, p. 370.
3 Lissak 1999, p. 12.
4 See Lissak 1999, p. 14.
5 Lissak 1999, p. 18.
6 Lissak 1999, p. 18.
7 Hacohen 2003, p. 54.
8 Hacohen 2003, p. 139.
9 Schechtman 1961, p. 31. Although Operation Magic Carpet officially ended in 1950, Yemenite Jews continued to be conveyed to Israel in the period 1951–4 but the yearly transfer never exceeded 573.
10 Tzur 1997, p. 70.
11 Schechtman 1961 p. 55.
12 As quoted in Hacohen 2003, p. 69.
13 Schechtman 1961, pp. 102–3.
14 Gat 1997, p. 38.
15 Hillel 1987, p. 113.
16 Tzur 1997, p. 72.
17 Hillel 1987, p. 229.
18 Hillel 1987, p. 231.
19 Schechtman 1961, p. 190.
20 Schechtman 1961, p. 134.
21 Schechtman 1961, p. 138.
22 Schechtman 1961, p. 288. (A higher figure is given in Table 3.2 but that also includes migrants from Tunisia and Algeria.)
23 Black and Morris 1991, p. 180.
24 Tzur 1997, p. 59.
25 Schechtman 1961, p. 152.
26 As quoted in Schechtman 1961, pp. 154–5.
27 Schechtman 1961, p. 240.

28 Lewis 1955, pp. 158–9.
29 Schechtman 1961, p. 227.
30 Hacohen 2003, p. 74.
31 Hacohen 2003, p. 77.
32 Hacohen 2003, p. 22.
33 Lissak 1999, p. 57.
34 Hacohen 2003, p. 73.
35 Hacohen 2003, pp. 71–4.
36 Chetrit 2004, p. 74.
37 Bein with Perlman 1982, p. 55.
38 Lissak 1999, p. 22.
39 Bein with Perlman 1982, p. 64.
40 Lissak 1999, p. 25.
41 See Shaham 1998, p. 77.
42 Bar-Zohar 1975, p. 885.
43 Bein with Perlman 1982, p. 61.
44 Hacohen 2003, p. 92.
45 Hacohen 2003, p. 143.
46 Bernstein 1980, p. 9.
47 Bernstein 1980, p. 9.
48 Lissak 1999, p. 77.
49 Hillel 1987, p. 287.
50 Bein with Perlman 1982, p. 60.
51 As quoted in Lissak 1999, p. 75.
52 As quoted in Bernstein 1980, p. 11.
53 Shaham 1998, p. 74.
54 Lissak 1999, p. 33.
55 Bein with Perlman 1982, p. 73.
56 Eisenstadt 1975, p. 108.
57 Bein with Perlman 1982, p. 90 and Lissak 1999, p. 33.
58 As quoted in Chetrit 2004, pp. 88–9.
59 See Cohen in Shapira 2001, p. 109.
60 Halevi and Klinov-Malul 1968, p. 77.
61 As quoted in Eisenstadt 1975, pp. 120–1.
62 As quoted in Meir-Glitzenstein in Shapira 2001, p. 137.
63 As quoted in Lissak 1999, p. 59.
64 As quoted in Lissak 1999, p. 61.

65 As quoted in Selzer 1965, p. 15.

66 Lissak 1999, p. 60.

67 As quoted in Bernstein 1980, p. 32.

68 See Ben-Gurion 1969, p. 391.

69 Tzameret and Yablonka 1997, p. 9.

70 Bar-Moshe as quoted in Lissak 1999, p. 120.

71 As quoted in Bernstein 1980, p. 33.

Chapter 4 Early Social, Economic, and Political Developments

1 Oz 2004, p. 386.

2 Shaham 1998, p. 52.

3 As quoted in Zucker 1973, p. 67.

4 See Ben-Gurion, *Israel: A Personal History*, 1971, p. 555.

5 Ben-Gurion, *Israel: A Personal History*, 1971, p. 554.

6 See Safran 1981, p. 155.

7 See Tzahor 1997, p. 31.

8 Temko 1987, p. 133.

9 As quoted in Shalom 1995, p. 33.

10 Tzahor 1997, p. 33.

11 Tzahor 1997, pp. 3–4.

12 Crossman 1962, p. 331.

13 Crossman 1962, p. 355.

14 As quoted in Marmorstein 1969, p. 150. The stream system was "eliminated" in August 1953 when a new law established a state school system that severed all school ties with political parties or movements. The state school system had two components, a secular one and a religious one, which meant that in practice the only real casualty of the education reform was the Labour Stream. The state religious component had been administered by a council consisting of religious members only. Agudat Yisrael's school functioned outside of the state system. Despite being almost fully state-funded, it imparted education that was alien to Israeli society in general.

15 As quoted in Bar-Zohar 1975, p. 955.

16 Eban 1992, p. 237.

17 See Bar-Zohar 1975, p. 1005.

18 Bar-Zohar 1975, p. 973.

19 In truth Ben-Gurion was won over to the idea of having Lavon as minister of defense by Shimon Peres. See Golan 1982, p. 29.

20 Golan 1982, p. 31.

21 Unless otherwise specified, almost all of the information in this section is derived from Weitz 1995, *The Man Who Was Murdered Twice*.

22 Weitz 1995, *The Man Who Was Murdered Twice*, p. 31.

23 Originally the Jews were supposed to proceed to Spain. I am indebted to Yehuda Feher for that information.

24 Segev 1993, p. 257.

25 Segev 1993, p. 266.

26 Weitz 1995, *The Man Who Was Murdered Twice*, p. 200.

27 As quoted in Weitz 1995, *The Man Who Was Murdered Twice*, p. 133.

28 As quoted in Segev 1993, p. 269.

29 Weitz 1995, *The Man Who Was Murdered Twice*, p. 195.

30 Segev 1993, p. 282.

31 See for instance Segev 1993, p. 273.

32 See Weitz 1995, *The Man Who Was Murdered Twice*, p. 299.

33 Weitz 1995, *The Man Who Was Murdered Twice*, p. 284.

34 Segev 1993, p. 284.

35 As described by Weitz 1995, *The Man Who Was Murdered Twice*, pp. 269–70.

36 Weitz 1995, *The Man Who Was Murdered Twice*, p. 271.

37 Weitz 1995, *The Man Who Was Murdered Twice*, p. 12.

38 As quoted in Weitz 1995, *The Man Who Was Murdered Twice*, p. 325.

39 Weitz 1995, *The Man Who Was Murdered Twice*, p. 333.

40 Weitz 1995, *The Man Who Was Murdered Twice*, p. 334.

41 Bar-Zohar 1975, pp. 926–7.

42 Weitz 1995, *The Man Who Was Murdered Twice*, p. 339.

43 Gross 1997, p. 140.

44 Halevi et al. 1977, p. 130.

45 Gabbay 1990, p. 86.

46 Halevi et al. 1977, p. 130.

47 Ben-Gurion 1969, p. 385.

48 Ben-Gurion, *Israel: A Personal History*, 1971, p. 365.

49 As quoted in Prittie 1969, p. 174.
50 Halevi et al. 1977, p. 132.
51 Halevi et al. 1977, p. 133.
52 Gross 1997, p. 142.
53 Silver 1984, p. 115.
54 As quoted in Segev 1993, p. 202.
55 Barzel 1997, p. 203.
56 Barzel 1997, p. 204.
57 Segev 1993, p. 225.
58 Silver 1984, p. 117.
59 As quoted in Ben-Gurion, *Israel: A Personal History*, 1971, p. 399.
60 Segev 1993, p. 224.
61 Temko 1987, p. 136.
62 Segev 1993, p. 216.
63 Silver 1984, p. 117.
64 Silver 1984, p. 116.
65 As quoted in Temko 1987, p. 139.
66 Bar-Zohar 1975, pp. 924–5.
67 Temko 1987, p. 139.
68 Temko 1987, p. 140.
69 Brecher 1974, p. 67.
70 Silver 1984, p. 119.
71 Tessler 1994, p. 331.
72 As quoted in Brecher 1974, p. 107.
73 Bar-Zohar 1975, p. 925.
74 Sanbar 1990a, p. 12.
75 Gross 1997, p. 143, and Horowitz 1967, p. 37.
76 Gross 1997, p. 143.
77 Horowitz 1967, p. 42.
78 Horowitz 1967, p. 22.
79 Patinkin 1967, p. 32.
80 Roter and Shamai 1990, p. 156.
81 Safran 1981, p. 228.
82 Horowitz 1967, p. 58.
83 A dunam is a quarter acre.
84 Ben-Rafael 1995, p. 269.

85 Bein with Perlman 1982, p. 90.
86 Bein with Perlman 1982, p. 107.
87 Bein with Perlman 1982, p. 108.
88 Efrat 1997, p. 104.
89 As quoted in Bein with Perlman 1982, p. 136.
90 Bein with Perlman 1982, pp. 147–8.
91 Eisenstadt 1975, p. 129.
92 Roter and Shamai 1990, pp. 159–60.
93 Lissak 1999, p. 105.
94 Segev 1993, p. 249.
95 Horowitz 1967, p. 24.
96 Near 1995, p. 251.
97 Near 1995, p. 244.
98 Lieblich 1981, p. 55.
99 Near 1995, p. 257.
100 Ben-Rafael 1995, p. 271.
101 I am indebted to a personal communication from Anita Shapira for this point.
102 Lieblich 1981, p. 132.
103 Lieblich 1981, p. 156.
104 Abramov 1976, p. 255, Zucker 1973, p. 217.
105 Birnbaum 1970, p. 250.
106 Reproduction of proclamation in Cohen 1997, p. 229.
107 As quoted in Marmostein 1969, pp. 119–20.
108 Birnbaum 1970, p. 83.
109 Birnbaum 1970, pp. 103–4.
110 Leibowitz 1992, p. 178.
111 Weizmann 1949, p. 569.
112 Marmorstein 1969, p. 128.
113 As it happens the author is a long-standing member of an orthodox congregation.
114 As quoted in Abramov 1976, p. 169. Italics added.
115 Abramov 1976, p. 216.
116 Non-Jews also have no recourse to civil marriages and have to marry in accordance with Muslim or Christian norms.
117 Marmorstein 1969, p. 114.
118 Cohen 1997, p. 233.

119 Cohen 1997, p. 234.

120 Birnbaum 1970, p. 171.

121 Cohen 1964, p. 418.

122 Hacohen 2003, p. 21.

123 Cohen 1964, p. 484.

124 Ben-Gurion 1969, p. 460.

125 Morris 2001, p. 282.

126 Eytan 1958, p. 95.

127 Morris 1993, p. 321.

128 Eban 1992, p. 236.

129 Bar-On 1994, pp. 133–4.

130 Meinertzhagen 1959, p. 283.

131 Bar-Zohar 1975, p. 913.

132 Sheffer 1996, p. 587.

133 As quoted in Cohen 1964, p. 456.

134 As quoted in Cohen 1964, p. 459.

135 Cohen 1964, p. 458. This obnoxious anti-Israel slur now constitutes an important element of the credo of Noam Chomsky and his radical acolytes.

136 See Silver 1984, p. 115.

137 Sharett 1978, p. 29.

138 Bar-Zohar 1975, p. 1143.

139 Sheffer 1996, p. 798.

140 Cohen 1964, pp. 450–1.

141 Shlaim 2000, p. 56.

142 Sheffer 1996, p. 844.

143 As quoted in Shalom 1995, p. 118.

144 Golani 1998, p. 22.

145 Sheffer 1996, p. 627.

146 Gabbay 1959, p. 445.

147 Sheffer 1996, p. 503.

148 Eytan 1958, p. 73.

149 As quoted in Bar-Zohar 1975, p. 913.

150 Soon after the January 1949 general election, the Knesset was housed in Tel Aviv.

151 As quoted in Bar-Zohar 1975, p. 891.

152 As quoted in Tessler 1994, p. 329.

Chapter 5 The Scourge of Arab Infiltration

1 Peres 1970, p. 12.
2 As quoted in Cohen 1964, p. 460.
3 As quoted in Cohen 1964, p. 461 from Achbar al-Yum 14.5.49.
4 As quoted in Gabbay 1959, p. 425.
5 As quoted in Gabbay 1959, pp. 424–5.
6 As quoted in Ben-Gurion 1969, p. 463.
7 Shalom 1995, p. 17.
8 Ben-Gurion 1969, p. 483; Morris 1993, pp. 97–8.
9 Teveth 1972, p. 203.
10 See Shalom 1995, pp. 154–5.
11 Dayan 1976 (Hebrew edition), p. 110.
12 See Morris 2001, p. 275.
13 Morris 1993, p. 39.
14 Shapira 2004, pp. 448–9; Tal 2004a, p. 75.
15 Morris 1993, pp. 132–3. Reis later half-heartedly regretted such actions.
16 Morris 1993, pp. 157–61.
17 Morris 1993, p. 163.
18 Morris 1993, pp. 167–8.
19 Morris 1993, pp. 168–72.
20 Morris 1993, p. 417.
21 Slater 1991, p. 134.
22 Luttwak and Horowitz 1975, p. 71.
23 Luttwak and Horowitz 1975, p. 101.
24 Dayan 1976 (Hebrew edition), p. 111.
25 Milstein 1985, p. 108.
26 Tal 2004a, p. 77.
27 Shlaim 2000, p. 83.
28 Teveth 1972, p. 204.
29 Glubb 1957, p. 305.
30 Morris 1993, p. 238.
31 Benziman 1985, p. 42.
32 As quoted in Milstein 1985, p. 210.
33 Dayan 1976 (Hebrew edition), p. 114.
34 Creveld 1998, p. 132.
35 Har-Zion 1969, p. 134

36 Luttwak and Horowitz 1975, p. 116.
37 Ya'ari 1975, p. 12.
38 Morris 1993, p. 242.
39 Ya'ari 1975, p. 12.
40 Tal 2004a, p. 76.
41 Morris 1993, p. 244.
42 Bar-Zohar 1975, p. 976.
43 Sharon with Chanoff 1989, p. 89.
44 Tal 2004a, p. 76.
45 Slater 1991, p. 150, and Luttwak and Horowitz 1975, p. 110.
46 Teveth 1972, p. 212.
47 Morris 2001, p. 278.
48 Sharett 1978, p. 44.
49 Sharett 1978, p. 44.
50 Milstein 1985, p. 232.
51 Bar-Zohar 1975 p. 981.
52 Aharonson and Horowitz 1971, p. 79.
53 Sheffer 1996, pp. 655–7.
54 Dayan's assurance that the IDF would cease harming enemy civilians was not *always* carried out to the letter. In March 1955, four young Israeli men crossed into Jordan to undertake an act of vengeance for the murder of a young woman and her male companion who had been illegally hiking in Jordan's Judean desert. The ringleader, Meir Har-Zion of Unit 101 fame who was the late woman's brother, knifed to death four of six young Bedouin falling into the group's hands. A fifth Bedouin was shot to death, while the sixth was released to relate the incident to his tribesmen from whose ranks the murderers of the two Israelis were thought to have arisen. It transpired that Har-Zion's group had received assistance from the army which, with Ariel Sharon's blessing, provided them with transport to the border, food and ammunition, and which also covered their retreat. On their return to Israel, they were detained and questioned but in a matter of weeks they were released with impunity. Sharett felt that the outcome of the affair indicated that Israel was losing its moral compass. However, apart from the Har-Zion incident, in which the army was not *officially* involved, the IDF *generally* took care to ensure that civilian casualties were either

avoided or at least minimized. Nonetheless, as outlined further below, it again failed to do so in April 1956 during an exchange of mortar fire with Egyptian forces.

55 Bar-Zohar 1975, p. 1139.
56 As quoted in Teveth 1972, p. 241.
57 See for example Shalom 1995, p. 161.
58 Morris 2001, p. 279.
59 Morris 1993, p. 83.
60 See Shalom 1995, p. 158.
61 Morris 1993, p. 83.
62 Cohen 1964, p. 494.
63 As quoted in Cohen 1964, p. 236.
64 Ben-Gurion 1969, p. 484.
65 As quoted in Bar-Zohar 1975, p. 1152.
66 Sharon with Chanoff 1989, p. 93.
67 Sharon with Chanoff 1989, p. 95.
68 Sharon with Chanoff 1989, p. 97.
69 Glubb 1957, p. 319.
70 Morris 2001, p. 281.
71 Shlaim 2000, pp. 115–16.
72 Kurzman 1983, p. 378.
73 Sharett 1978, pp. 804–5.
74 See Bar-Zohar 1975, pp. 1127–8.
75 As quoted in Bar-Zohar 1975, p. 1129.
76 Tal 2004a, p. 80.
77 Morris 1993, p. 322.
78 Morris 1993, p. 86.
79 Glubb 1957, pp. 380–1.
80 As quoted in Shlaim 2000, p. 126.
81 As quoted in Eban 1978, p. 183.
82 Bar-Zohar 1975, p. 1138.
83 See Sheffer 1996, pp. 790–2.
84 As quoted in Gabbay 1959, p. 504.
85 As quoted in Ben-Gurion 1969, p. 521.
86 As quoted in Lorch 1961, p. 461.
87 Creveld 1998, p. 136.
88 As quoted in Dayan 1966, p. 6.

89 Cohen 1964, p. 491.
90 All the information in this paragraph is derived from Ye'or 2005, p. 42.
91 Black and Morris 1991, p. 101.
92 Golani 1998, p. 12.
93 Nutting 1972, p. 101. Italics added.
94 Nutting 1972, p. 74.
95 See Sheffer 1996, p. 822.
96 Sheffer 1996, pp. 832 and 834.
97 Sheffer 1996, p. 851.
98 See Glassman 1975, p. 9.
99 Glubb 1957, pp. 377–8.
100 See Bar-Zohar 1975, p. 1149.
101 Bar-Zohar 1975, p. 1167.
102 Bar-Zohar 1975, p. 1167.
103 Glubb 1957, p. 377.
104 Morris 2001, p. 284.
105 Ya'ari 1975, p. 19.
106 Sheffer 1996, p. 824.
107 Brecher 1974, pp. 258–9.
108 Bar-On 1994, p. 48.
109 Morris 1993, p. 360. Slightly different casualty rates were provided in Bar-On 1994, p. 50. That is, seven Israeli deaths and 70 Egyptian ones.
110 Dayan 1976 (Hebrew edition), p. 170.
111 Ben-Gurion 1969, p. 477.
112 Morris 1993, p. 281.
113 As quoted in Ya'ari 1975, p. 23.
114 As quoted in Dayan 1966, p. 150.
115 Bar-On 1994, p. 70.
116 Dayan 1976 (Hebrew edition), p. 194.
117 See Teveth 1957, pp. 29–30.
118 Morris 1993, p. 372.
119 Cohen 1964, p. 492.
120 Bar-Zohar 1975, p. 1169.
121 As quoted in Bar-On 1994, p. 119.
122 Dayan 1976 (Hebrew edition), p. 191.

123 As quoted in Morris 1993, p. 388.

124 Morris 1993, p. 392.

125 Dayan 1976 (Hebrew edition), p. 225.

126 Dayan 1976 (Hebrew edition), p. 200.

127 Cohen 1964, p. 493.

128 Morris 1993, p. 396.

129 Dayan 1976 (Hebrew edition), p. 246.

130 *Ba'Mahaneh*, October 15, 1956.

131 Sharon with Chanoff 1989, p. 139.

132 Dayan 1976 (Hebrew edition), p. 248.

133 Sharon with Chanoff 1989, p. 137.

134 Sharon with Chanoff 1989, p. 140.

135 Dayan 1966, p. 43.

136 Dayan 1966, pp. 51–2; Sharon with Chanoff 1989, pp. 139–40.

137 Slater 1991, p. 186.

138 Bar-Zohar 1975, p. 1126.

139 As quoted in Dayan 1976 (Hebrew edition), p. 208.

Chapter 6 Operation Kadesh: The Sinai Campaign

1 Slater 1991, p. 167; Dayan 1966, p. 4; and Golan 1982, p. 35.

2 Dayan 1966, p. 5.

3 Bar-On 1994, p. 18.

4 As quoted in Bar-On 1994, p. 3.

5 As quoted in Bar-On 1994, p. 40.

6 Creveld 1998, p. 138.

7 Sheffer 1996, p. 863.

8 As quoted in Bar-On 1994, p. 32. The statement was drafted by Evelyn Shuckburgh on behalf of the UK and Francis Russell on behalf on the US. Both were senior foreign affairs bureaucrats.

9 *Haaretz*, January 26, 1956.

10 See Bar-Zohar 1975, p. 1165.

11 As quoted in Bar-On 1994, p. 93.

12 Ambrose 1984, p. 329.

13 Teveth 1972, pp. 253–4.

14 Peres 1970, p. 61.

15 Bar-Zohar 1975, p. 1178.

16 Bar-Zohar 1975, pp. 1198–1200.

17 Rosenthal 1997, p. 190.
18 Kyle 1991, p. 129.
19 As quoted in Druks 1979, p. 59.
20 Kyle 1991, p. 13.
21 Thomas 1967, p. 33.
22 As quoted in Thomas 1967, p. 38.
23 Bar-Zohar 1975, p. 1212.
24 Peres 1995, p. 122.
25 Rafael 1981, p. 54.
26 Teveth 1972, p. 250.
27 Bar-Zohar 1975, p. 1210.
28 Dayan 1976 (Hebrew edition), pp. 222–32.
29 By a strange quirk, the conference was not named after the area in which it was held but rather after the suburb in which the Israelis were staying.
30 Bar-Zohar 1975, p. 1222; and Bar-On 1994, p. 199.
31 Eban 1992, p. 254.
32 Rosenthal 1997, p. 194.
33 Bar-Zohar 1975, pp. 1229–30.
34 Brecher 1974, p. 272.
35 Bar-Zohar 1975, p. 1239.
36 Dayan 1976 (English edition), p. 231.
37 As reported by Brecher 1974, p. 273.
38 Golani 2004, p. 90.
39 Dayan 1976 (Hebrew edition), p. 242.
40 Bar-Zohar 1975 p. 1244. There is possibly some ambiguity here, for Bar-On 1994, p. 242, asserted that there was agreement that the document would highlight Israel's intentions of retaining the Straits of Tiran without explicitly including British and French endorsements. It is conceivable that oral commitments were provided.
41 As quoted in Kyle 1991, p. 67.
42 As quoted in Golani 1998, p. 21.
43 Golani 1998, p. 55.
44 As quoted in Kyle 1991, p. 74.
45 As quoted in Bar-On 1994, p. 207.
46 As quoted in Kyle 1991, p. 149.

47 Kyle 1991, p. 92 and *The Globe and Mail* (Toronto), January 3, 1986, in quoting *The Times* (London).

48 Golani 2004, pp. 103–4.

49 Sharett 1978, p. 54.

50 See Huntington 1997.

51 Shalom 1995, pp. 8–9.

52 As quoted in Shalom 1995, p. 25.

53 As quoted in Sharett 1978, p. 1021.

54 As quoted in Ben-Gurion 1969, p. 525.

55 As quoted in Bar-On 1997.

56 Teveth 1957, p. 21.

57 As reported by Temko 1987, p. 144.

58 Bar-Zohar 1968, pp. 220–1.

59 Bar-Zohar 1975, p. 1260.

60 Morris 2001, p. 291.

61 Slater 1991, p. 194.

62 Creveld 1998, p. 142.

63 Ben-Gurion 1969, pp. 526–7.

64 Kadesh was the final Sinai stopping point of the Israelites on their way to the Promised Land.

65 Milstein 1985, p. 490. At variance with almost all other writers, Dayan avers that only after the second aerial reconnaissance, which he claims was inconclusive, was the designated landing site changed from the west to the east of the Pass. See Dayan 1966, p. 79. The author has difficulty in coming to terms with Dayan's account, especially since he had a personal interest in justifying a decision which even he conceded was less than optimal.

66 Eitan 1991, p. 66.

67 Eitan 1991, p. 67.

68 Kyle 1991, p. 349.

69 Luttwak and Horowitz 1975, p. 147.

70 See Dayan 1976 (Hebrew edition), p. 267.

71 Dayan 1966, p. 117.

72 Dayan 1966, pp. 112–14.

73 Milstein 1985, p. 507.

74 As quoted in Teveth 1957, p. 94.

75 Milstein 1985, p. 506.

76 Milstein 1985, p. 515.
77 Teveth 1957, p. 101.
78 Teveth 1957, pp. 106–7.
79 Meron Rapoport, "In the Valley of Death," *Haaretz*, February 2, 2007.
80 Sharon with Chanoff 1989, p. 149.
81 Teveth 1972, pp. 271–3. Dayan 1976 (English edition), p. 258, reckons on 150 Egyptian fatalities.
82 Slater 1991, p. 201.
83 Dayan 1976 (Hebrew edition), p. 258.
84 Creveld 1998, p. 150.
85 Golani 1998, p. 166.
86 As quoted in Golani 2004, p. 91.
87 Dayan 1966, pp. 132–3.
88 Dayan 1966, pp. 135–7.
89 Teveth 1957, p. 152.
90 Dayan 1966, pp. 147–8.
91 Teveth 1957, p. 160.
92 Dayan 1976 (Hebrew edition), p. 272.
93 Dayan 1976 (English edition), pp. 195–200.
94 Dayan 1976 (English edition), p. 80.
95 Bar-Zohar 1968, p. 228.
96 Kyle 1991, pp. 399–400.
97 Kyle 1991, pp. 399–400.
98 Teveth 1972, p. 257.
99 Morris 2001, p. 290.
100 Bar-On 1997, p. 25.
101 Kyle 1991, pp. 102 and 206.
102 Bar-Zohar 1975, p. 1272.
103 Eban 1978, p. 231.
104 Eban 1978, p. 214. Dulles's previously declared unwillingness to preserve what he termed "temporary armistice borders" obviously applied only to Israel.
105 Eban 1992, p. 273.
106 Bar-Zohar 1975, p. 1270.
107 As quoted in Bar-On 1994, p. 281.
108 Bar-Zohar 1968, pp. 229–32.

109 Meinertzhagen 1959, p. 286.

110 Eban 1978, p. 228.

111 Years later Ben-Gurion expressed regret that he ever delivered such an impetuous and ridiculous speech but, as he confided to his interviewer, it was "because the victory was so swift I became so intoxicated by it." See Eban 1978, p. 230.

112 Morris 2001, p. 299.

113 As quoted in Ben-Gurion 1969, p. 533.

114 Teveth 1957, p. 222.

115 Bar-On 1994, pp. 283–4.

116 Ben-Gurion 1969, p. 544.

117 Eban 1978, p. 229.

118 Bar-On 1994, p. 212.

119 Bar-Zohar 1975, p. 1300.

120 As quoted in Eytan 1958, p. 101.

121 As quoted in Ben-Gurion, *Israel: A Personal History*, 1971, p. 527.

122 Weitz 1995, *The Man Who Was Murdered Twice*, p. 323.

123 As quoted in Weitz 1995, *The Man Who Was Murdered Twice*, p. 323.

124 Dayan 1976 (Hebrew edition), p. 330.

125 As quoted in Meinertzhagen 1959, p. 352.

126 As quoted in Ben-Gurion 1969, p. 535, who in turn sourced the material from *Foreign Affairs*, January 1957.

127 Golani 1998, p. vii.

128 Golani 1998, p. 182.

129 Milstein 1985, p. 561.

130 Kyle 1991, p. 102.

131 Bar-On 1997, p. 24.

132 Slater 1991, p. 207.

133 Shlaim 2000, pp. 183–4.

134 Nutting 1972, p. 192.

135 Peres 1970, p. 15.

136 Eban 1992, p. 260.

137 Luttwak and Horowitz 1975, pp. 126–7.

138 Luttwak and Horowitz 1975, p. 129.

139 Milstein 1985, p. 560.

140 Dayan 1976 (Hebrew edition), p. 187.

141 Shaham 1998, p. 139.
142 As quoted in Rokach 1982, p. 67.
143 Segev 1993, p. 299.
144 Morris 1993, p. 417.
145 From subsequently released documents of the state archives as reported in *Haaretz*, March 28, 2001.
146 As quoted in Jiryis 1969, p. 92.
147 As quoted in Segev 1993, p. 300.
148 As quoted in Jiryis 1969, p. 116.
149 Segev 1993, p. 302.
150 *The Jerusalem Post*, October 30, 1997.

Chapter 7 Interlude Between Wars

1 Bar Zohar 1975, pp. 1443–4.
2 Bar Zohar 1975, p. 1464.
3 Bar Zohar 1975, p. 1447.
4 As quoted in Teveth 1996, p. 67.
5 Bar-Zohar 1975, p. 1020.
6 Dayan 1976 (Hebrew edition), p. 139.
7 Discussed in chapter 1, pp. 38–9.
8 Bar-Zohar 1975, p. 1043.
9 Bar-Zohar 1975, p. 1064.
10 Ben-Gurion, *Israel: A Personal History*, 1971, p. 607.
11 Ben-Gurion 1969, p. 612.
12 Teveth 1996, p. 202.
13 Bar-Zohar 1975, p. 1488.
14 Bar-Zohar 1975, p. 1489.
15 Bar-Zohar 1968, p. 263.
16 Shaham 1998, p. 209.
17 Bar-Zohar 1968, p. 264.
18 Ben-Gurion 1969, p. 639.
19 Shaham 1998, p. 199.
20 As quoted in Ben-Gurion, *Israel: A Personal History*, 1971, p. 639.
21 Shaham 1998, p. 209.
22 As quoted in Bar-Zohar 1975, p. 1546.
23 Bar-Zohar 1975, pp. 1558–9.
24 Halevi with Klinov-Malul 1968, p. 91.

25 Shaham 1998, p. 181.
26 Shaham 1998, p. 181.
27 Shaham 1998, p. 231.
28 Shaham 1998, p. 233.
29 Yablonka 1997, p. 54.
30 Unless otherwise stated, all information relating to Eichmann's capture is derived from Eisenberg et al. 1978, pp. 24–35.
31 Ben-Gurion, *Israel: A Personal History*, 1971, p. 576.
32 Yablonka 2004, p. 15.
33 Segev 1993, p. 325.
34 Ben-Gurion, *Israel: A Personal History*, 1971, p. 576.
35 Unless otherwise stated, all information relating to Eichmann's trial is derived from Segev 1993, pp. 326–66.
36 Segev 1993, p. 336.
37 As reported by Ben-Gurion, *Israel: A Personal History*, 1971, p. 582.
38 Ben-Gurion, *Israel: A Personal History*, 1971, p. 591.
39 Segev 1993, p. 514.
40 Roter and Shamai 1990, p. 163.
41 As quoted in Avineri 1972, p. 14.
42 Ben-Rafael 1982, p. 4.
43 Ben-Rafael 1982, p. 4.
44 Unless otherwise indicated, the information in this section is derived from Chetrit 2004, pp. 101–5.
45 As reported by Chetrit 2004, p. 101.
46 As quoted in Chetrit 2004, p. 105.
47 Tzur 1997, p. 79.
48 Shaham 1998, p. 182.
49 Eisenstadt 1967, p. 309.
50 Landau 1969, p. 3.
51 Greitzer 1997, p. 155.
52 Landau 1969, p. 4.
53 Hacohen 2003, p. 4.
54 As quoted in Sharett 1978, p. 150.
55 See for instance Cohen 1964, p. 509.
56 Cohen 1964, p. 510.
57 Pappe 1995, p. 626.
58 Cohen 1964, p. 525.

59 Calculated from data supplied in Cohen 1964, p. 529.

60 Ozacky-Lazar in Shapira 2001, p. 64.

61 Shaham 1998, p. 59.

62 Lustick 1980, p. 19.

63 Lustick 1980, p. 177.

64 Lustick 1980, pp. 181–2.

65 Lustick 1980, p. 185.

66 Lustick 1980, p. 185.

67 Gross 1997, p. 148.

68 Gross 1997, p. 148.

69 Cohen 1964, p. 531.

70 *Al Hamishmar*, September 3, 1959.

71 Non-Muslims in various Arab countries face similar issues as do non-Christians in certain western countries where the national flag includes a cross or, as in the UK, where the queen is head of the Anglican Church.

72 Ozacky-Lazar in Shapira 2001, p. 63.

73 Jiryis 1969, p. 147.

74 Cohen 1964, pp. 539–40, and Lustick 1980, p. 159.

75 Shaham 1998, pp. 161–2.

76 Shaham 1998, p. 169. Much of the information in this paragraph is derived from this source.

77 Shaham 1998, p. 234.

78 Shaham 1998, p. 188.

79 As quoted in Shlaim 2000, p. 208.

80 Gluska 2004, p. 65.

81 Shaham 1998, p. 214.

82 Sheffer 1996, p. 585.

83 Brecher 1974, p. 204. Gluska 2004, p. 82, claims that the Israel allocation amounted to 38 percent.

84 Unless otherwise indicated, all information relating to Eli Cohen has been derived from Eisenberg et al. 1978, pp. 70–132.

85 Shaham 1998, p. 167.

86 Shaham 1998, p. 186.

87 Shaham 1998, p. 203.

88 Oren 2002, p. 15.

89 Shaham 1998, p. 206.

90 It might be contended that it is illegitimate to include what was in 1948 Transjordan and not Palestine. However, consider the following hypothetical scenario: Suppose that in 1921 when Transjordan was formed, the British also allocated to it the West Bank and Gaza and declared the remaining land to be Palestine. By that logic, Israel by the end of 1948 would have possessed the totality of the Palestinians' homeland.

91 Gilboa 1968, p. 40.

92 Becker 1984, p. 256.

93 Becker 1984, p. 41.

94 Becker 1984, pp. 41–2.

95 Becker 1984, p. 44.

96 Segev 2005, p. 235.

97 Kimche and Bawly 1968, pp. 27–8.

98 Haber 1987, p. 105.

99 As quoted in Segev 2005, p. 165.

100 Oren 2002, p. 32.

101 Dayan 1976, p. 306.

102 Kimche and Bawly 1968, p. 80, reports that no less than forty houses were destroyed. Gluska 2004, p. 162, states that the bottom line was fifty. By contrast, Dayan 1976, p. 306, suggests that no more than ten buildings were dynamited.

103 Segev 2005, p. 167.

104 Shaham 1998, p. 241.

105 Segev 2005, p. 168.

106 Gluska 2004, p. 77.

107 Rafael 1981, p. 82.

108 Ojo 1982, p. 38.

109 Peres 1970, p. 157.

110 Shlaim 2000, p. 213.

Chapter 8 The Lead Up to the Six-Day War

1 As quoted in Gilboa 1968, p. 52.

2 Oren 2002, p. 27.

3 Such was the opinion of Yisrael Lior. See Haber 1987, p. 152.

4 As quoted in Gluska 2004, p. 110.

5 As quoted in Gluska 2004, p. 152.

6 Morris 2001, p. 304.

7 Gluska 2004, p. 153.

8 As quoted in Haber 1987, p. 147.

9 As quoted in Gilboa 1968, p. 56.

10 As quoted in Laqueur 1968, p. 47.

11 Parker 1993, p. 5.

12 Gilboa 1968, p. 56.

13 Gilboa 1968, p. 61.

14 Parker 1993, p. 10.

15 Yariv 1988, p. 19.

16 See for example Dayan 1976 (Hebrew edition), p. 392: (English edition), p. 17.

17 Shaham 1998, p. 249, and Parker 1993, p. 246.

18 Ginor 2003, p. 38, suggests that the message was delivered a day earlier (on May 12) by Semyonov.

19 Parker 1993, p. 27.

20 As quoted in Parker 1993, p. 32.

21 As quoted in Oren 2002, p. 64.

22 Nadav 1981, p. 391.

23 Parker 1993, p. 18.

24 Dayan 1976 (English edition), p. 310.

25 As quoted in Kimche and Bawly 1968, p. 91.

26 Teveth 1972, p. 323. That was not the first occasion that Dayan's assessment of future events was wide of the mark. As noted in chapter 6, just over a year before the 1956 Sinai campaign, Dayan felt that there would be no war with Egypt during the ensuing eight to ten years.

27 Parker 1993, p. 4, and Haber 1987, p. 147.

28 Gluska 2004, p. 147.

29 Nadav 1981, p. 392.

30 Gluska 2004, p. 230.

31 Parker 1993, p. 42.

32 Gilboa 1968, p. 107.

33 Rosenthal 2005, p. 443.

34 Haber 1987, p. 151.

35 Eban 1978, p. 321.

36 Rafael 1981, p. 139.

37 Shaham 1998, p. 252.
38 Dayan 1976 (English edition), p. 305.
39 Haber 1987, p. 153.
40 Gluska 2004, p. 228.
41 Reported in the *Jerusalem Post*, August 23, 2007.
42 Ginor and Remez 2007.
43 As quoted in Shaham 1998, p. 252.
44 Shaham 1998, p. 253.
45 Rosenthal 2005, p. 448.
46 Rabin, *The Rabin Memoirs*, 1979, p. 143.
47 As quoted in Shaham 1998, p. 254.
48 As quoted in Oren 2002, p. 84.
49 As quoted in Parker 1993, p. 61.
50 As quoted in Peres 1970, p. 228.
51 Dayan 1976 (English edition), p. 310.
52 As quoted in Parker 1993, p. 72.
53 Peres 1970, pp. 226–7.
54 Kimche and Bawly 1968, p. 99.
55 Dayan 1976 (English edition), p. 311.
56 Segev 2005, pp. 261–2.
57 Oren 2002, p. 90.
58 Gluska 2004, p. 274.
59 Gluska 2004, p. 271.
60 Gilboa 1968, p. 136.
61 As quoted in Kimche and Bawly 1968, p. 131.
62 Kimche and Bawly 1968, p. 131.
63 Gluska 2004, p. 493, endnote 53.
64 Rosenthal 2005, p. 465.
65 Quandt 2005, p. 33.
66 Quandt 2005, p. 35.
67 Rosenthal 2005, p. 467.
68 As of late, some ex-senior Russian officials have testified that prominent military and political Soviet leaders were avidly anticipating Israel's destruction. For example, according to Vladimir Rezen, in the second half of May 1967, a statement by Marshal Grechko, the Soviet minister of defense, to final-year officer cadets read in part: "the fiftieth year of the Great October Socialist Revolution

(1967) will be the last year of the existence of the State of Israel."
Quoted in Ginor 2003, p. 50.

69 As quoted in Gluska 2004, p. 497, n. 15.

70 Oren 2002, p. 119.

71 Kimche and Bawly1968, p. 161; Segev 2005, p. 276.

72 Oren 2002, pp. 120–1.

73 As quoted in Gluska 2004, p. 235.

74 Haber 1987, p. 192.

75 Oren 2002, p. 123, suggests that a straw vote was taken but Eban claimed that "no vote was taken that evening; that we might have split 9 to 9 is a conjecture based, presumably, on the general tenor of the speeches." See Eban 1978, p. 367. Rabin, who was also present wrote: "Finally, the vote was taken. Nine members in favor, nine against." See Rabin, *The Rabin Memoirs*, 1979, p. 91. By contrast Gilboa 1968, p. 154, wrote "no vote was taken but the participants in the discussion were evenly balanced."

76 Gluska 2004, p. 321.

77 Gluska 2004, p. 323.

78 Rabin, *The Rabin Memoirs*, 1979, p. 92.

79 Haber 1987, p. 194.

80 Gluska 2004, pp. 37–8.

81 As quoted in Segev 2005, p. 313.

82 Segev 2005, p. 112.

83 Segev 2005, p. 329. Peres had claimed that the IDF was not ready for war. See also Gilboa 1968, p. 162.

84 Segev 2005, pp. 291–2.

85 Gilboa 1968, p. 192.

86 Parker 1993, p. 54.

87 As quoted in Dayan 1976 (English edition), p. 314.

88 Gluska 2004, p. 507, n. 4.

89 Dayan 1976, p. 314.

90 Kimche and Bawly 1968, p. 107.

91 As quoted in Gilboa 1968, p. 221.

92 As quoted in Haber 1987, p. 201.

93 On May 24, Begin had personally put that proposition to Eshkol who brushed it aside by noting that two such horses (that is, he and Ben-Gurion) could not possibly pull the same cart.

94 Haber 1987, p. 181.
95 Rabin, *The Rabin Memoirs*, 1979, vol. 1, p. 114.
96 Haber 1987, pp. 44–5.
97 See Oren 2002, photographs prior to p. 143.
98 As quoted in Kimche and Bawly 1968 p. 100.
99 Kimche and Bawly 1968, p. 101. What is not appreciated by many westerners even to this day is that within the Arab world there is a culture of blood lust and revenge that motivates rulers and ruled alike to seek to extirpate their perceived enemies. To some extent this emanates from strongly held beliefs in the sacredness of personal and national honor and that any derogation of it necessitates a violent response. However, not all Arab heads of state are so inclined. Despite all conflicts with him, Israel held a high regard for the integrity of King Hussein and upon his death Israeli flags flew at half-mast. Political and media commentators referred to him as a *mensch* [a decent human being] with a *kafiya*. But alas, Hussein had been one among few exceptions.
100 As quoted in Dayan 1976 (English edition), p. 344.
101 Yoel Marcus, "Truth Serum on the Tip of a Missile," *Haaretz*, June 17, 2003.
102 As quoted in Draper 1967, p. 98.
103 Gluska 2004, p. 27.
104 In the event, the Egyptians did not deploy such weapons, either because their air force could not deliver them or because they feared a resounding Israeli response. See Ze'evi 1988, p. 29.
105 Teveth 1968, p. 28.
106 As quoted in Segev 2005, pp. 289–9.
107 Kimche and Bawly 1968, p. 136.
108 Segev 2005, p. 272.
109 Gleaned from Morris 2001, p. 31, Oren 2002, pp. 168 and 171, and Gluska 2004, p. 75.
110 Gluska 2004, p. 74.
111 Parker 1993, p. 114.
112 Oren 2002, p. 164.
113 As quoted in Oren 2002, p. 81.
114 Rabin, *The Rabin Memoirs*, 1979, p. 76.
115 As quoted in Rabin, *The Rabin Memoirs*, 1979, p. 80.

116 Rosenthal 2005, p. 461.

117 Rosenthal 2005, pp. 461–2.

118 There was a subsequent follow-up to Rabin's one-off breakdown. The incident was hushed up and knowledge of it was confined to a select few. However, in April 1974 when Rabin stood for the premiership in a general election, Weizman, a member of the main opposition party, publicly released information relating to that episode. He did so to show that Rabin was not suitable for high office. A political storm arose in which the issue was bitterly contested. Needless to say, Rabin emerged as the frontrunner.

119 Gluska 2004, p. 408.

120 Teveth 1972, p. 324.

121 Shaham 1998, p. 261.

122 At one point of time, because the Egyptians were mainly entrenched in strongly fortified garrisons in Sinai, Rabin believed that the IDF should concentrate on overrunning the Gaza Strip. This, in his view would either have led to Nasser offering to reopen the Straits of Tiran in exchange for the return of the Gaza Strip or, alternatively, he would have committed the bulk of his army to the retrieving of the Gaza Strip by force. Should the latter eventuality have arisen, Rabin reasoned that the IDF could then have confronted the main body of the enemy in a locality where it lacked the protective cover of its fortresses. However, Dayan took the view that Gaza was not important enough for Nasser to pursue either option, which meant that there was no escaping the need to contest the Egyptians head on where they were in the first place.

123 Teveth 1972, p. 333.

124 As quoted in Gilboa 1968, p. 207.

125 Rosenthal 2005, p. 485.

126 As quoted in Oren 2002, p. 141.

127 Eban 1978, p. 394.

128 Shaham 1998, p. 262.

129 Dayan 1976 (Hebrew edition), p. 426.

130 Gluska 2004, p. 389. Paradoxically, both Amit and Harman counseled further restraint. Since such views were at variance with their findings, they carried no weight. See Haber 1987, pp. 216–17.

131 Quandt 2005, p. 39.

132 Everyone except the two Mapam members voted in favor. The Mapam members explained that they had first to take council with their party's leaders. A short time later, once party approval was obtained, the two Mapam members requested that a positive vote on their behalf be added to the previous cabinet vote tally so that in retrospect the decision was a unanimous one.

133 Gluska 2004, p. 395.

134 Dayan 1976 (Hebrew edition), p. 428.

135 Gluska 2004, p. 14.

136 Ezer Weizman later reminded his fellow officers that "because we had all lived in the shadow of the 1956 Campaign, none of us believed that on conquering territories we would be able to retain them." Gluska 2004, p. 262.

137 *Ma'ariv*, May 12, 1967.

Chapter 9 The Six-Day War and Its Aftermath

1 Rabin, *The Rabin Memoirs*, 1979, p. 98. On the same page Rabin wrote "I often wondered what would have happened if the air battle against Egypt had lasted more than three hours and Syrian and Jordanian planes had attacked Israel while most of our fighters were away over Egypt." In fact, by the outbreak of the war, Israel had 50 Hawk anti-aircraft missile batteries in place. See Glassman 1975, p. 321.

2 Oren 2002, p. 176.

3 Oren 2002, p. 176.

4 Dayan 1976 (English edition), p. 352.

5 Parker 1993, p. 57.

6 The substance of this paragraph is derived from Oren 2002, p. 177.

7 As quoted in Shaham 1998, p. 264.

8 Dayan 1976 (English edition), p. 356.

9 Shaham 1998, p. 265.

10 Segev 2005, p. 363.

11 Oren 2002, p. 199.

12 Dayan 1976 (English edition), p. 360.

13 Oren 2002, p. 212.

14 Oren 2002, p. 181.

15 Oren 2002, p. 203.

16 Dayan 1976 (English edition), p. 363.

17 Morris 2001, p. 320.

18 As quoted in Oren 2002, p. 258.

19 Gilboa 1968, p. 212.

20 Dayan 1976 (English edition), p. 367.

21 Gluska 2004, p. 507, endnote 10.

22 As quoted in Kimche and Bawly 1968, p. 191.

23 Segev 2005, p. 203.

24 As quoted in Gilboa 1968, p. 224.

25 Oren 2002, p. 187.

26 Shlaim 2000, p. 244.

27 Dayan 1976 (Hebrew edition), p. 444.

28 Oren 2002, p. 191.

29 Haber 1987, p. 230.

30 As quoted in Rosenthal 2005, p. 492.

31 Shaham 1998, p. 268.

32 Oren 2002, p. 218.

33 Oren 2002, p. 222. Dayan 1976 (English edition), p. 369, by contrast claimed that 21 were killed.

34 Oren 2002, p. 239.

35 As quoted in Shlaim 2000, p. 245.

36 Segev 2005, pp. 390 and 391. Haber 1987, p. 234, wrote that Dayan did not allow for any glory to be shared with anyone other than himself, not even with Rabin. Narkiss told the writer Dan Kurzman that he believed that it was Dayan's original intention to be photographed alone but that last-moment qualms got the better of him. See Kurzman 1998, p. 226.

37 Kimche and Bawly 1968, p. 86; Gilboa 1968, p. 14.

38 Oren 2002, p. 162.

39 Gilboa 1968, p. 230.

40 Oren 2002, p. 230.

41 Oren 2002, p. 231.

42 Oren 2002, p. 229.

43 Kimche and Bawly 1968, p. 48.

44 One source, Arnan Ezriyahu, suggested that essentially Dayan opposed confronting Syria simply because his rival Yigal Allon was in favor of it. See Gluska 2004, p. 500, endnote 12.

45 As quoted in Oren 2002, p. 276.
46 Gilboa 1968, p. 236.
47 Dayan 1976 (Hebrew edition), p. 475, and Shaham 1998, p. 270.
48 Rosenthal 2005, p. 507.
49 Slater 1991, p. 276.
50 As quoted in Oren 2002, p. 182.
51 Gilboa 1968, pp. 241–2.
52 Oren 2002, pp. 292–3.
53 Dayan 1976 (Hebrew edition), p. 481.
54 Shaham 1998, p. 275.
55 Rabin, *The Rabin Memoirs*, 1979, p. 110.
56 See for instance Loftus and Aarons 1994, pp. 259–86.
57 Oren 2002, p. 142.
58 As quoted in Goodman and Schiff 1984, p. 81.
59 Ginor 2003, p. 49.
60 Gilboa 1968, p. 29.
61 Gluska 2004, p. 226.
62 As quoted in Oren 2002, pp. 310–11.
63 Morris 2001, p. 303.
64 Gluska 2004, p. 236.
65 Draper 1967, p. 31. Italics in the original.
66 Morris 2001, p. 327.
67 Luttwak and Horowitz 1975, p. 219.
68 Kimche and Bawly 1968, pp. 179–80.
69 Dayan 1976 (Hebrew edition), p. 440.
70 Quandt 2005, p. 42. Much to Israel's chagrin, the embargo remained in force until the end of the year.
71 Yariv 1988, p. 21.
72 Kimche and Bawly 1968, p. 168.
73 Eban 1978, p. 375.
74 Gilboa 1968, p. 12.
75 Oren 2002 on p. 304. Morris 2001, p. 327, gives the number as 779, while Shlaim 2000, p. 250, puts it at 983.
76 Kimche and Bawly 1968, p. 173.
77 Perlmutter 1970, p. 74.
78 As quoted in Dayan 1976 (Hebrew edition), p. 494.
79 Teveth 1968, p. 281.

80 Segev 2005, p. 460. Rabin's speech received widespread approbation but in truth it was largely drafted and inspired by Colonel Mordechai Bar-On. On the other hand, it contained nothing that did not conform to Rabin's own notions and way of thinking.

81 Segev 2005, p. 584.

82 As quoted in Oren 2002, p. 317.

83 Laqueur and Rubin 2001, p. 104.

84 Laqueur and Rubin 2001, p. 104. Although Egypt later officially repudiated the charges of Israeli collusion with the West, to this day they are still featured as being factual in Egyptian high school history textbooks. See Podeh 2004, p. 51.

85 Shaham 1998, p. 271.

86 Kimche and Bawly 1968, pp. 268–9.

87 Oren 2002, pp. 306–7.

88 Morris 2001, pp. 327–8.

89 Kimche and Bawly 1968, p. 220.

90 Kimche and Bawly 1968, p. 221.

91 Pryce-Jones 1972, p. 12.

92 Kimche and Bawly 1968, p. 255.

93 Segev 2005, pp. 421–3.

94 Morris 2001, p. 331.

95 Segev 2005, p. 426.

96 Weizman 1975, p. 297.

97 Dayan 1976 (English edition), p. 398.

98 Dayan 1976 (English edition), p. 398.

99 Shlaim 2000, p. 254.

100 Segev 1993, p. 468.

101 As quoted in Kurzman 1983, p. 461. Italics in the original.

102 Shaham 1998, p. 276.

103 Segev 2005, p. 535.

104 Segev 2005, pp. 536–41.

105 Eban 1978, p. 430.

106 Eban 1978, p. 433.

107 As reproduced by Laqueur and Rubin 2001, p. 116.

108 Eban 1978, p. 451.

109 Eban 1978, p. 453.

110 As quoted in Eban 1978, p. 452.

111 As quoted in Gilboa 1968, p. 262. Italics added.
112 Quandt 2005, p. 46.
113 See for instance Shlaim 2000, pp. 258–9.
114 As quoted in Shlaim 2000, p. 259.
115 Draper 1967, p. 10.
116 Eban 1992, p. 465.
117 Segev 2005, pp. 522–3.
118 Segev 2005, p. 617.
119 Dayan 1976 (English edition), p. 406.
120 Shaham 1998, p. 278.
121 Eban 1992, p. 462.
122 Morris 2001 p. 332.
123 Segev 2005, p. 610.
124 Segev 2005, p. 611.
125 Nadav 1981, p. 96.
126 Eban 1992, p. 471.

Conclusion

1 As quoted in Bar-Zohar 1968, p. 104.
2 Benson 1997, p. 133.
3 Shaham 1998, p. 280.
4 As quoted in Shaham 1998, p. 281.

Glossary

Agudat Yisrael A religious, essentially non-Zionist, political party

Ahdut Ha'avodah A leftwing socialist party that ceded from Mapam in 1954

aliyah Immigration to Israel

Ashkenazi A Jew of western origin

Bnei Akivah A religious Zionist youth movement

Gadna A cadet-type teenage military organization

Gahal Conscripts from newly arrived migrants

General Zionists A conservative Zionist party

Hael Hatsfar Border militia

Haganah The Yishuv's defense force

halaha Accepted religious practice

Hama'arah An alignment of Mapai and Ahdut Ha'avodah

Hapoel Mizrahi Religious workers' party

Haredim God-fearing extreme orthodox Jews

Hashomer The Yishuv's defense force that preceded the formation of the Haganah

Hasidim A Jewish religious orthodox sect that believed that one's relation to God should be direct and joyful

Herut A political party subscribing to the Revisionist Zionist platform

Histadrut A general trade union federation that also provides social and economic services

Irgun A dissident military organization based on the principle that the Jewish state should span both sides of the River Jordan

Jewish Agency A World Jewry non-government body committed to the promotion and absorption of Jewish immigrants into Israel. Prior to independence, the Jewish Agency through its various departments (such as land development for example), steered the Yishuv toward sovereignty

Jewish National Fund Fund for the purchase of land and Jewish settlement in Israel

kaddish Mourner's prayer for a parent or child

Keren Hayesod (The Foundation Fund) Fund of the World Zionist Organization

kibbutz (pl. *kibbutzim*) A collective farm based on complete equality

Knesset Israel's parliament

Lehi A dissident Zionist militia dedicated to driving the British from Palestine

ma'abarah (pl. *ma'abarot*) A migrant transition camp

Mafdal The National Religious Party

Mahal Volunteers from abroad

Maki An Israeli communist party with some sympathy for the continued existence of Israel

Mapai A social-democratic labor party

Mapam A Marxist-Zionist party

menorah A seven-branched candelabrum used in the ancient Holy Temple.

Mishmar Hagvul Border patrol or border police

Mizrahi A Jew originating from the Middle East or North Africa

Mizrahi Party A mainstream Jewish orthodox party

moshav (pl. *moshavim*) A settlement with a large degree of private ownership

Mossad Israel's intelligence organization

Neturei Karta An extreme Jewish religious sect opposing the existence of Israel

Palmah Shock troops of the Haganah

Poalei Agudat Yisrael A Workers' Party of Agudat Yisrael

Progressives A very liberal Israeli party

Rafi Israel Workers' List. A party founded by Ben-Gurion in 1965 as a breakaway from Mapai

Rakah An Israeli communist party unsympathetic to the Jewish state

shofar A ram's horn blown for Jewish religious purposes

Talmud A record of rabbinic discourses pertaining to Jewish law

Torah The five books of Moses

Yeshiva A Jewish religious seminary

Yishuv The pre-state Jewish population in Palestine

Zionism The national movement of the Jewish people furthering their sovereignty in their historic homeland, Israel

BIBLIOGRAPHY

Works in English

Abramov, S. Z. 1976. *Perpetual Dilemma: Jewish Religion in the Jewish State*. Cranbury, New Jersey: Associated University Presses.

Abu-Muna, B. 1965. "Spotlight on Arab Students," *New Outlook* (March).

Aharoni, Y. 1991. *The Israeli Economy: Dreams and Realities*. London: Routledge.

Al-Haj, M. 2004. "The Status of the Palestinians in Israel: A Double Periphery in an Ethno-National State," in Dowty 2004.

Allon, Y. 1970. *The Making of Israel's Army*. London: Vallentine-Mitchell.

Almog. O. 2000. *The Sabra: The Creation of the New Jew*. Berkeley: University of California Press.

Ambrose, S. E. 1984. *Eisenhower: The President*, Vol. 2. New York: Simon and Schuster.

Atiyah, E. 1955. *The Arabs: The Origins, Present Conditions, and Prospects of the Arab World*. London: Penguin.

Avineri, S. 1972. "Israel: Two Nations?" *Midstream* 18(4) (March).

Avineri, S. 1981. *The Making of Modern Zionism: The Intellectual Origins of the Jewish State*. New York: Basic Books.

Aykroyd, W. R. 1979. *The Conquest of Famine*. London: Chatto and Windus.

Aynor, H. S. 1986. "Israel Versus Apartheid at the United Nations," *The Jerusalem Journal of International Relations* 8(1).

Badi, J. 1959. *Religion in Israel Today: The Relationship between State and Religion*. New York: Bookman Associates.

Barer, S. 1952. *The Magic Carpet*. London: Secker and Warburg.

Bar-Joseph, U. 1987. *The Best of Enemies: Israel and Transjordan in the War of 1948*. London: Frank Cass.

Barkai, M. 1968. *Written in Battle: The Six-Day War as Told by the Fighters Themselves*. Tel Aviv: Le'Dory.

Bar-On, M. 1994. *The Gates of Gaza: Israel's Road to Suez and Back, 1955–1957*. Basingstoke: Macmillan.

Bar-On, M. 2004. *A Never-Ending Conflict*. Westport: Praeger Press.

Bar-On, M. 2006. "Remembering 1956: Three Days in Sèvres, October 1956," *History Workshop Journal*, Issue 62.

Bar-Siman-Tov, Y. 1988. "Ben-Gurion and Sharett: Conflict Management and Great Power Constraints in Israeli Foreign Policy," *Middle Eastern Studies* 24(3) (July).

Bar-Zohar, M. 1968. *Ben-Gurion: The Armed Prophet*. Englewood Cliffs: Prentice Hall.

Bar-Zohar, M. 1970. *Embassies in Crisis: Diplomats and Demagogues Behind the Six-Day War*. Englewood Cliffs: Prentice Hall.

Bass, Warren. 2003. *Support Any Friend: Kennedy's Middle East and the Making of the US–Israeli Alliance*. New York: Oxford University Press.

Bauer, Y. 1966. "The Arab Revolt of 1936," *New Outlook*, July–August (Part One) and September (Part Two).

Becker, J. 1984. *The PLO: The Rise and Fall of the Palestine Liberation Organization*. London: Weidenfeld and Nicolson.

Begin, M. 1979. *The Revolt*. London: W. H. Allen.

Beit-Hallami, B. 1993. *Original Sins: Reflections on the History of Israel and Zionism*. New York: Olive Branch Press.

Ben-Gurion, D. 1954. *Rebirth and Destiny of Israel*. New York: Philosophical Library.

Ben-Gurion, D. 1971. *Israel: A Personal History*. New York: Funk and Wagnalls.

Ben-Rafael, E. 1982. *The Emergence of Ethnicity: Cultural Groups and Social Conflict in Israel*. Connecticut: Greenwood Press.

Ben-Rafael, E. 1995. *The Kibbutz in the 1950s: A Transformation of Identity*, in Troen and Lucas 1995.

Benson, M. T. 1997. *Harry S. Truman and the Founding of Israel*. Westport: Praeger.

Benziman, U. 1985. *Sharon: An Israeli Caesar*. New York: Adama Books.

Bey, M. R. 1949. "The Story of El Faluje," *The Islamic Review* (July).

Birnbaum, E. 1970. *The Politics of Compromise: State and Religion in Israel*. Cranbury: Associated University Presses.

Black, I. and Morris, B. 1991. *Israel's Secret Wars: The Untold History of Israeli Intelligence*. London: Hamish Hamilton.

Bodansky, Y. 2002. *The High Cost of Peace*. Roseville: Prima.

Bornet, V. D. 1983. *The Presidency of Lyndon B. Johnson*. Lawrence: University Press of Kansas.

Brecher, M. 1974. *Decisions in Israel's Foreign Policy*. London: Oxford University Press.

Bregman, A. and El-Tahri, J. 1998. *Israel and the Arabs*. New York: TV Books.

Childers, E. 1961. "The Other Exodus," *Spectator* (May 12).

Cohen, R. 1988. "Intercultural Communication Between Israel and Egypt: Deterrence Failure before the Six-Day War," *Review of International Studies* 14(1) (January).

Collins, L. and Lapierre, D. 1973. *O Jerusalem*. London: Pam Books.

Cristol, A. J. 2002. *The Liberty Incident: The 1967 Israeli Attack on the US Navy Spy Ship*. Washington: Brassey's.

Crossman, R. 1962 "The Prisoner of Rehovot," in Weisgal and Carmichael 1962.

Dan, U. 2006. *Ariel Sharon: An Intimate Portrait*. New York: Palgrave Macmillan.

Dayan, M. 1966. *Diary of the Sinai Campaign*. London: Weidenfeld and Nicolson.

Dayan, M. 1976. *The Story of My Life*. London: Sphere Books.

Deshen, S. and Shokeid, M. 1974. *The Predicament of Homecoming: Cultural and Social Life of North African Immigrants in Israel*. Ithaca: Cornell University Press.

Dowty, A. 2004. *Critical Issues in Israeli Society*. Westport: Praeger.

Dowty, A. 2005. *Israel/Palestine*. Cambridge: Polity.

Draper, T. 1967. *Israel and World Politics: Roots of the Third Arab–Israeli War*. New York: Viking Press.

Druks, H. 1979. *The US and Israel 1945–1973*. New York: Speller and Sons.

Eban, A. 1962. "Tragedy and Triumph," in Weisgal and Carmichael 1962.

Eban, A. 1978. *An Autobiography*. London: Weidenfeld and Nicolson.

Eban, A. 1992. *Personal Witness: Israel through My Eyes*. New York: Putnam Press.

Eisenberg, D., Dan, U., and Landau, E. 1978. *The Mossad: Israel's Secret Intelligence Service*. New York: Paddington Press.

Eisenstadt, S. N. 1967. *Israeli Society*. London: Weidenfeld and Nicolson.

Eisenstadt, S. N. 1975. *The Absorption of Immigrants*. Westport: Greenwood Press.

Eitan, R. 1991. *A Soldier's Story*. New York: Shapolsky.

Ennes Jr, J. M. 1979. *The Assault on the Liberty: The True Story of the Israeli Attack on an American Intelligence Ship*. New York: Random House.

Eytan, W. 1958. *The First Ten Years: A Diplomatic History of Israel*. London: Weidenfeld and Nicolson.

Flapan, S. 1987. *The Birth of Israel: Myths and Realities*. New York: Pantheon Books.

Friedman, R. I. 1990. "The Palestinian Refugees," *New York Review* (March 29).

Gabbay, R. 1959. *A Political Study of the Arab–Jewish Conflict: The Arab Refugee Problem*. Geneva: Librairie Droz.

Gabbay, Y. 1990. "Israel's Fiscal Policy, 1948–1982," in Sanbar 1990b.

Galidi, G. N. 1990. *Discord in Zion*. Buckhurst Hill: Scorpion.

Gat, M. 1988. "The Connection between the Bombings in Baghdad and the Emigration of the Jews from Iraq: 1950–51," *Middle Eastern Studies* 24(3) (July).

Gat, M. 1997. *The Jewish Exodus from Iraq 1948–1953*. London: Frank Cass.

Gazit, M. 1988. "The Israel–Jordan Peace Negotiations (1949–51): King Abdallah's Lonely Effort," *Journal of Contemporary History* 23(3) (July).

Gelber, Y. 2001. *Palestine 1948: War, Escape and the Emergence of the Palestinian Refugee Problem*. Brighton: Sussex Academic Press.

Gelber, Y. 2006. *Palestine 1948: War, Escape and the Emergence of the Palestinian Refugee Problem*. 2nd edn. Brighton: Sussex Academic Press.

Gilbert, M. 1998. *Israel: A History*. London: Doubleday.

Gilmour, D. 1982. *The Dispossessed*. London: Sidgwick and Jackson.

Ginat, R. 1993. *The Soviet Union and Egypt, 1945–1955*. London: Frank Cass.

Ginor, I. 2003. "The Cold War's Longest Cover-Up: How and Why the USSR Instigated the 1967 War," *Middle East Review of International Affairs* 7(3) (September).

Ginor, I. and Remez, G. 2007. *Foxbats Over Dimona: The Soviets' Nuclear Gamble in the Six-Day War*. New Haven: Yale University Press.,

Givati, H. 1985. *A Hundred Years of Settlement*. Jerusalem: Keter.

Glassman, J. D. 1975. *Arms for the Arabs: The Soviet Union and War in the Middle East*. Baltimore: Johns Hopkins University Press.

Glazer, S. 1980. "The Palestinian Exodus in 1948," *Journal of Palestine Studies* (Summer).

Glubb, J. B. 1957. *A Soldier with the Arabs*. London: Hodder and Stoughton.

Golan, A. 1974. *The War of Independence*. Tel Aviv: Ministry of Defense Publishing House.

Golan, M. 1982. *Shimon Peres: A Biography*. London: Weidenfeld and Nicolson.

Golani, M. 1998. *Israel in Search of a War: The Sinai Campaign, 1955–1956*. Brighton: Sussex Academic Press,

Golani, M. 2004. "The Sinai War, 1956: Three Partners, Three Wars," in Bar-On 2004.

Gold, D. 2004. *Tower of Babble: How the United Nations has Fueled Global Chaos*. New York: Crown Forum.

Goldberg, E. J. (ed.). 1996. *The Social History of Labor in the Middle East*. Boulder: Westview.

Goldman, E. 1964. *Religious Issues in Israel's Political Life*. Jerusalem: World Zionist Organization.

Goodman, H. and Schiff, Z. 1984. "The Attack on the Liberty," *Atlantic Monthly* (September).

Gross, N. 1995. "The Economic Regime during Israel's First Decade." Research Paper 208, Jerusalem: Maurice Falk Institute for Economic Research in Israel.

Hacohen, D. 2003. *Immigrants in Turmoil: Mass Immigration to Israel in the 1950s and After.* Syracuse: Syracuse University Press.

Hadawi, S. 1972. *Crime and No Punishment: Zionist Israeli Terrorism 1939–1972.* Beirut: Near East Ecumenical Bureau of Information and Interpretation.

Hadawi, S. 1991. *Bitter Harvest: A Modern History of Palestine.* New York: Olive Branch Press.

Haidar, A. 1995. *On the Margins: The Arab Population in the Israeli Economy.* New York: St Martin's Press.

Halevi, N. and Klinov-Malul, R. 1968. *The Economic Development of Israel.* New York: Praeger.

Halevi, N., Gross, N., Kleiman, E., and Sarnat, M. 1977. *Banker to an Emerging Nation.* Jerusalem: Shikmona.

Halpern, B. 1961. *The Idea of the Jewish State.* Cambridge: Harvard University Press.

Hammel, E. 1992. *Six Days in June: How Israel Won the 1967 Arab–Israeli War.* New York: Scribner's.

Harari, H. 2005. *A View from the Eye of the Storm.* New York: Regan Books.

Harel, I. 1975. *The House on Garibaldi Street.* New York: Viking Press.

Harkabi, Y. 1972. *Arab Attitudes to Israel.* London: Vallentine-Mitchell.

Hefez, N. and Bloom, G. 2006. *Ariel Sharon: A Life.* New York: Random House.

Hertzberg, A. 1970. *The Zionist Idea.* Westport, Connecticut: Greenwood Press.

Hertzberg, A. 1992. *Jewish Polemics.* New York: Columbia University Press.

Hillel, S. 1987. *Operation Babylon.* New York: Doubleday.

Hirst, D. H. 1984. *The Gun and the Olive Branch.* London: Faber

Horowitz, D. 1967. *The Economics of Israel.* Oxford: Pergamon Press.

Huntington, S, 1997. *The Clash of Civilizations and the Remaking of World Order.* London: Simon and Schuster.

Hurewitz, J. C. 1950. *The Struggle for Palestine.* New York: Norton.

Ilan, A. 1996. *The Origin of the Arab–Israeli Arms Race*. Basingstoke: Macmillan.

Jiryis, S. 1969. *The Arabs in Israel, 1948–1966*. Beirut: The Institute for Palestinian Studies.

Joseph, D. 1960. *The Faithful City: The Siege of Jerusalem 1948*. New York: Simon and Schuster.

Kapeliouk, A. 1987. "New Light on the Israeli–Arab Conflict and the Refugee Problem and its Origins," *Journal of Palestine Studies* (Spring).

Karpin, M. 2006. *The Bomb in the Basement*. New York: Simon and Schuster.

Karsh, E. 1997. *Fabricating Israeli History: The 'New Historians'*. London: Frank Cass.

Karsh, E. 2002. *The Arab–Israeli Conflict: The Palestine War 1948*. Oxford: Osprey.

Karsh, E. 2008. "1948: Israel and the Palestinians," *Commentary* (May).

Katz, S. 1968. *Days of Fire*. London: W. H. Allen.

Katz, S. 1973. *Battleground: Fact and Fantasy in Palestine*. New York: Bantam.

Khalidi, W. 1988. "Plan Dalet: Master Plan for the Conquest of Palestine," *Journal of Palestine Studies* 18(1) (Autumn).

Kimche, D. and Bawly, D. 1968. *The Sandstorm: The Arab–Israeli War of June 1967, Prelude and Aftermath*. London: Secker and Warburg.

Kimche, J. and Kimche, D. 1960. *Both Sides of the Hill: Britain and the Palestine War*. London: Secker and Warburg.

Kleiman, E. 1977. "Israeli Etatisme," *Israel Studies* 2(2).

Kleiman, E. 1986. "Khirbet Khiz'ah and Other Unpleasant Memories," *The Jerusalem Quarterly* 40.

Koestler, A. 1983. *Promise and Fulfilment: Palestine 1917–1949*. London: Macmillan.

Kurzman, D. 1972. *Genesis 1948: The First Arab–Israeli War*. London: Vallentine-Mitchell.

Kurzman, D. 1983. *Ben-Gurion: Prophet of Fire*. New York: Simon and Schuster.

Kurzman, D. 1998. *Soldier of Peace: The Life of Yitzhak Rabin, 1922–1995*. New York: HarperCollins.

Kyle, K. 1991. *Suez*. London: Weidenfeld and Nicolson.

Landau, D. 1993. *Piety and Power*. New York: Hill and Wang.

Landau, J. M. 1969. *The Arabs in Israel*. London: Oxford University Press,

Laqueur, W. 1968. *The Road to Jerusalem: The Origins of the Arab–Israeli Conflict, 1967*. New York: Macmillan.

Laqueur, W. 1970. *The Israel-Arab Reader*. Harmondsworth, Middlesex: Penguin Books.

Laqueur, W. 1989. *A History of Zionism*. New York: Schocken Books.

Laqueur, W. and Rubin, B. 2001. *The Israel–Arab Reader*. 6th edn. New York: Penguin Books.

Larkin, M. 1965. *The Six Days of Yad Mordechai*. Yad Mordechai: Yad Mordechai Museum.

Lehrman, H. 1949. "The Arabs of Israel," *Commentary* (December).

Leibowitz, Y. 1992. *Judaism, Human Values and the Jewish State*. Cambridge, MA: Harvard University Press.

Leonard, L. L. 1949. "The United Nations and Palestine," *International Conciliation* 454 (October).

Leslie, S. C. 1971. *The Rift in Israel's Religious Authority and Secular Democracy*. London: Routledge and Kegan Paul.

Lewis, G. 1955. *Turkey*. New York: Praeger Press.

Lieblich, A. 1981. *Kibbutz Makom: Report from an Israeli Kibbutz*. New York: Pantheon Books.

Loftus, J. and Aarons, M. 1994. *The Secret War against the Jews: How Western Espionage Betrayed the Jewish People*. New York: St Martin's Griffin.

Lorch, N. 1961. *The Edge of the Sword: Israel's War of Independence, 1947–1949*. New York: Putnam.

Lustick, I. 1980. *Arabs in the Jewish State: Israel's Control of a National Minority*. Austin: University of Texas Press.

Luttwak, E. and Horowitz, D. 1975. *The Israeli Army*. London: Allen Lane.

Mandel, N. J. 1976. *The Arabs and Zionism before World War I*. Berkeley: University of California Press.

Marmorstein, E. 1969. *Heaven at Bay: The Jewish Kulturkampf in the Holy Land*. London: Oxford University Press.

Marx, E. 1992. "Palestinian Refugee Camps in the West Bank and the Gaza Strip," *Middle Eastern Studies* (April).

Massad, J. 1996. "Israel's Internal Others: Israel and the Oriental Jews," *Journal of Palestine Studies* 25(4) (Summer).

McDonald, J. G. 1951. *My Mission in Israel: 1948–1951*. London: Victor Gollancz.

Meinertzhagen, R. 1959. *Middle East Diary, 1917–1956*. London: The Cresset Press.

Melman. Y. 1922. *The New Israelis: An Intimate View of a Changing People*. New York: Birch Lane Press.

Miller, A., Miller, J. and Zetouni, S. 2002. *Sharon: Israel's Warrior Politician*. Chicago: Academy Chicago Publishers and Olive Publishers.

Morris, B. 1987. *The Birth of the Palestinian Refugee Problem, 1947–1949*. Cambridge: Cambridge University Press.

Morris, B. 1993. *Israel's Border Wars, 1949–1956: Arab Infiltration, Israeli Retaliation, and the Countdown to the Suez War*. Oxford: Oxford University Press.

Morris, B. 1995. "Falsifying the Record: A Fresh Look at Zionist Documentation of 1948," *Journal of Palestine Studies* (Spring).

Morris, B. 1996. "The Israeli Press and the Qibya Operation, 1953," *Journal of Palestine Studies* 25(4) (Summer).

Morris, B. 2001. *Righteous Victims: A History of the Zionist–Arab Conflict, 1881–2001*. New York: Vintage Books.

Morris, B. 2008. *1948: A History of the First Arab–Israeli War*. New Haven: Yale University Press.

Mutawi, S. A. 1987. *Jordan in the 1967 War*. Cambridge: Cambridge University Press.

Nadav, S. 1981. *Israel, the Embattled Ally*. Cambridge: Belknap Press.

Nasser, G. A. 1959. *The Philosophy of the Revolution*, Buffalo: Smith, Keynes and Marshall Publishers.

Nasser, G. A. and Khalidi, W. 1973. "Nasser's Memoirs of the First Palestine War," *Journal of Palestine Studies* 2(2) (Winter).

Near, H. 1970. *The Seventh Day: Soldiers Talk About the Six-Day War*. London: Andre Deutsch.

Near, H. 1995. "The Crisis in the Kibbutz Movement, 1949–1961," in Troen and Lucas 1995.

Near, H. 1997. *The Kibbutz Movement: A History*. Vol. 2. London: Mitchell and Co.

Nutting, A. 1972. *Nasser*. London: Constable.

O'Brien, C. C. 1986. *The Siege: The Saga of Israel and Zionism*. New York: Simon and Schuster.

Ojo, G. 1982. "Israeli–South African Connections and Afro-Israeli Relations," *International Studies* 21(1) (January–March).

Oren, M. 2002. *Six Days of War: June 1967 and the Making of the Modern Middle East*. New York: Oxford University Press.

Oz, A. 2004. *A Tale of Love and Darkness*. Orlando: Harcourt.

Pappe, I. 1988. *Britain and the Arab–Israeli Conflict, 1948–51*. Basingstoke: Macmillan.

Pappe, I. 1994. *The Making of the Arab–Israeli Conflict 1947–51*. London: Tauris.

Pappe, I. 1995. "An Uneasy Coexistence: Arabs and Jews in the First Decade of Statehood," in Troen and Lucas 1995.

Pappe, I. 2006. *The Ethnic Cleansing of Palestine*. Oxford: Oneworld.

Parker, R. B. 1992. "The June War: Whose Conspiracy?" *Journal of Palestine Studies* 21(4) (Summer).

Parker, R. B. 1993. *The Politics of Miscalculation in the Middle East*. Bloomington: Indiana University Press.

Patinkin, D. 1967. *The Israeli Economy: The First Decade*. Jerusalem: Maurice Falk Institute for Economic Research in Israel.

Peres, S. 1970. *David's Sling*. London: Weidenfeld and Nicolson.

Peres, S. 1995. *Battling for Peace: Memoirs*, ed. David Landau. London: Weidenfeld and Nicolson.

Peretz, D. 1986. *The West Bank: History, Politics, Society and Economy*. Boulder: Westview Press.

Perlmutter, A. 1970. "Assessing the Six-Day War," *Commentary* (January).

Peters, J. 1984. *From Time Immemorial*. New York: Harper and Row.

Podeh, E. 2004. "The Lie That Won't Die: Collusion, 1967," *Middle East Quarterly* 11(1) (Winter).

Porath, Y. 1977. *The Palestinian Arab National Movement: From Riots to Rebellion, 1929–1939*. London: Frank Cass,

Preuss, W. 1965. *The Labour Movement in Israel: Past and Present*. Jerusalem: Rubin Mass.

Prittie, T. 1969. *Eshkol of Israel: The Man and the Nation*. London: Museum Press.

Pryce-Jones, D. 1972. *The Face of Defeat: Palestinian Refugees and Guerrillas*. London: Weidenfeld and Nicolson.

Pryce-Jones, D. 2002. *The Closed Circle: An Interpretation of the Arabs*. Chicago: Ivan R. Dee.

Pryce-Jones, D. 2005. "Jews, Arabs and French Diplomacy: A Special Report," *Commentary* (May).

Quandt, W. B. 2005. *Peace Process: American Diplomacy and the Arab–Israeli Conflict since 1967*. Washington, DC: Brookings Institution Press.

Rabin, Y. 1979. *The Rabin Memoirs*. Boston: Little Brown.

Rabinovitch, I. 1991. *The Road Not Taken: Early Arab–Israeli Negotiations*. New York: Oxford University Press.

Rafael, G. 1981. *Destination Peace: Three Decades of Israeli Foreign Policy: A Personal Memoir*. London: Weidenfeld and Nicolson.

Rejwan, N. 1971. "Arab Intellectuals and Israel," *New Outlook* (August).

Rodinson, M. 1973. *Israel: A Colonial-Settler State?* New York: Monad Press.

Rodinson, M. 1982. *Israel and the Arabs*. New York: Penguin.

Rokach, L. 1982. *Israel's Sacred Terrorism*. Belmont: Association of Arab-American University Graduates.

Rose, P. 1951. *The Siege of Jerusalem*. London: Patmos Publishers.

Roter, R. and Shamai, N. 1990. "Social Policy and the Israeli Economy, 1948–1980," in Sanbar 1990b.

Rubinstein, A. Z. 1984. *The Arab–Israeli Conflict*. New York: Praeger.

Sachar, H. M. 1981. *A History of Israel: From the Rise of Zionism to Our Time*. New York: Alfred Knopf.

Sachar, H. M. 1990. *The Course of Modern Jewish History*. New York: Vintage.

Sacher, H. 1952. *Israel: The Establishment of a State*. London: Weidenfeld and Nicolson.

Safran, N. 1981. *Israel: The Embattled Ally*. Cambridge: Belknap Press.

Sanbar, M. 1990a. "The Political Economy of Israel 1948–1982," in Sanbar 1990b.

Sanbar, M. (ed.). 1990b. *Economic and Social Policy in Israel*. Lanham: University Press of America.

Schechtman, J. 1952. *The Arab Refugee Problem*. New York: Philosophical Library.

Schechtman, J. 1961. *On Wings of Eagles: The Plight, Exodus, and Homecoming of Oriental Jewry*. New York: Thomas Yoseloff.

Segev, T. 1986. *1949: The First Israelis*. New York: The Free Press.

Segev, T. 1993. *The Seventh Million: The Israelis and the Holocaust*. New York: Hill and Wang.

Sela, A. 1992. "Transjordan, Israel and the 1948 War: Myth, Historiography and Reality," *Middle Eastern Studies* 28(4) (October).

Selzer, M. 1965. *The Outcasts of Israel: Communal Tensions in the Jewish State*. Jerusalem: Council of the Sephardic Community.

Shalev, M. 1996. "The Labor Movement in Israel: Ideology and Political Economy," in Goldberg 1996.

Shalmon, J. 1981. "The Bilu Movement," in Eliav 1981, Vol. 1.

Shalom, Z. 1996. "Kennedy, Ben-Gurion and the Dimona Project, 1962–1963," *Israel Studies* 1(1) (Spring).

Shalom, Z. 2002. "Strategy in Debate: Arab Infiltration and Israeli Retaliation Policy in the Early 1950s," *Israel Affairs* 8(3) (Spring).

Shapira, A. 1996. "Historiography and Memory: Latrun, 1948," *Jewish Social Studies* 3(1).

Shapira, A. 2000. "Hirbet Hizah: Between Remembrance and Forgetting," *Jewish Social Studies* (Fall).

Shapira, A and Penslar, D. 2002. *Israeli Historical Revisionism: From Left to Right*. Abingdon: Routledge.

Sharkansky, I. 1987. *The Political Economy of Israel*. New Brunswick: Transaction.

Sharon, A. with Chanoff, D. 1989. *Warrior: The Autobiography of Ariel Sharon*. New York: Simon and Schuster.

Sheffer, G. 1996. *Moshe Sharett: Biography of a Political Moderate*. Oxford: Oxford University Press.

Shemesh, M. 2006. "The Fida'iyyun Organization's Contribution to the Descent to the Six-Day War," *Israel Studies* 11(1).

Shimoni, G. 2003. *Community and Conscience: The Jews in Apartheid South Africa*. Lebanon, NH: University Press of New England,

Shlaim, A. 2000. *The Iron Wall*. New York: Norton.

Sicron, M. 1957. *Immigration to Israel 1948–1953*. Jerusalem: Falk Project for Economic Research in Israel.

Silver, E. 1984. *Begin: A Biography*. London: Weidenfeld and Nicolson.

Sirham, B. 1975. "Palestinian Refugee Camp Life in Lebanon," *Journal of Palestine Studies* (Winter).

Slater, R. 1991. *Warrior Statesman: The Life and Times of Moshe Dayan*. New York: St Martins.

Stein, L. 2003. *The Hope Fulfilled: The Rise of Modern Israel*. Westport: Praeger.

Sternhell, Z. 1998. *The Founding Myths of Israel*. Princeton: Princeton University Press.

Super, A. S. and Lennon, D. 1971. *Absorption of Immigrants*. Jerusalem: Israel Digest.

Sykes, C. 1967. *Crossroads to Israel*. London: The New English Library,

Szereszewski, R. 1968. *Essays on the Structure of the Jewish Economy in Palestine and Israel*. Jerusalem: Maurice Falk Institute for Economic Research.

Tal, D. 2004a. "Israel's Armistice Wars, 1949–1956," in Bar-On 2004.

Tal, D. 2004b. *War in Palestine 1948: Strategy and Diplomacy*. London: Routledge.

Temko, N. 1987. *To Win or to Die: A Personal Portrait of Menachem Begin*. New York: William Morrow and Co.

Tessler, M. 1994. *A History of the Israeli–Palestinian Conflict*. Bloomington: Indiana University Press.

Teveth, T. 1968. *The Tanks of Tammuz*. London: Weidenfeld and Nicolson.

Teveth, S. 1972. *Moshe Dayan*. London: Weidenfeld and Nicolson.

Teveth, S. 1987. *Ben-Gurion: The Burning Ground 1886–1948*. Boston: Houghton Mifflin.

Teveth, S. 1990. "The Palestine Arab Refugee Problem and its Origins," *Middle Eastern Studies* (April).

Teveth, S. 1996. *Ben-Gurion's Spy: the Story of the Political Scandal that Shaped Modern Israel*. New York: Columbia University Press.

Thomas, H. 1967. *The Suez Affair*. London: Weidenfeld and Nicolson.

Troen, S. I. and Lucas, N. (eds). 1995. *Israel: The First Decade of Independence*. New York: State University of New York Press.

Van Creveld, M. 1998. *The Sword and the Olive: A Critical History of the Israeli Defence Force*. New York: PublicAffairs.

Wasserstein, B. 1978. *The British in Palestine: The Mandatory Government and the Arab–Jewish Conflict 1917–1929*. London: Royal Historical Society.

Weintraub, D., Lissak, M., and Azmon, Y. 1969. *Moshava, Kibbutz and Moshav: Patterns of Jewish Rural Settlement and Development in Palestine*. Ithaca: Cornell University Press.

Weisgal, M. W. and Carmichael, J. (eds) 1962. *Chaim Weitzmann*. London: Weidenfeld and Nicolson.

Weitz, Y. 1995a. "Mapai and the 'Kastner Trial,'" in Troen and Lucas 1995.

Weizman, E. 1976. *On Eagle's Wings*. London: Weidenfeld and Nicolson.

Weizmann, C. 1949. *Trial and Error*. London: Hamish Hamilton.

Wheatcroft, G. 1996. *The Controversy of Zion: How Zionism Tried to Resolve the Jewish Question*. London: Sinclair-Stevenson.

Wigoder, G. 1997. *The New Standard Jewish Encyclopedia*. Jerusalem: Massada Press.

Wistrich, R. 1985. *Anti-Zionism as an Expression of Antisemitism in Recent Years*. Jerusalem: Shazar Library, The Hebrew University of Jerusalem.

Wistrich, R. 1990. *Anti-Zionism and Anti-Semitism in the Contemporary World*. Basingstoke: Macmillan.

Yablonka, H. 2004. *The State of Israel vs. Adolf Eichmann*. New York: Schocken.

Ye'or, B. 2005. *Eurabia: The Euro-Arab Axis*. New Jersey: Fairleigh Dickinson.

Zu'bi, A. A. 1958. "Discontent of Arab Youth," *New Outlook* (January).

Zucker, N. L. 1973. *The Coming Crisis in Israel*. Cambridge: MIT Press.

Works in Hebrew

Aharonson, S. and Horowitz, D. 1971. "The Strategy of Controlled Retaliation – The Israeli Example," *State, Government and International Relations* 1(1) (Summer).

Avinom, R. 1968. *Twenty Years of Revival and Independence*. Jerusalem: Defense Office.

Bar-On, M. 1968. *The Six-Day War*. Tel Aviv: Ministry of Defense.

Bar-On, M. 1997. "The Struggle for the Attainments of 1948: Israel's Security Policies," in Tzameret and Yablonka 1997.

Barzel, N. 1997. "Israeli-German Relations: From Policies of Boycott to Complex Connections," in Tzameret and Yablonka 1997.

Bar-Zohar, M. 1975. *Ben-Gurion: A Political Biography*. Tel Aviv: Am Oved.

Beer, I. 1955. "Battles of Latrun," *Ma'Arahot*, No. 6 (November).

Be'eri, E. 1985. *The Beginning of the Israeli–Arab Conflict*. Tel Aviv: Sifriat Poalim.

Bein, A. 1970. *A History of Zionist Settlement: From the Time of Herzl to the Present Age*. Masada: Ramat Gan.

Bein, A. with Perlman, R. 1982. *Immigration and Settlement in the State of Israel*. Jerusalem: Am Oved.

Ben-Gurion, D. 1969. *The Restored State of Israel*. Tel Aviv: Am Oved.

Ben-Gurion, D. 1971. *Memoirs*. Tel Aviv: Am Oved.

Ben-Gurion, D. 1982. *War Diary*. Tel Aviv: Department of Defense.

Bernstein, D. 1980. *The Ma'abarot in the 1950s*. Haifa: University of Haifa.

Chetrit, S. 2004. *The Mizrahi Struggle in Israel: Between Oppression and Liberation Identification and Alternative, 1948–2003*. Tel Aviv: Am Oved.

Cohen, A. 1964. *Israel and the Arab World*. Tel Aviv: Sifriat Hapoalim.

Cohen, A. 1997. "Religion and State: Secularists, Religiously Observant and Extreme God Fearers," in Tzameret and Yablonka 1997.

Dayan, M. 1976. *Milestones: An Autobiography*. Jerusalem: Edanim.

Dinur, B. (ed.).1964. *Book of the History of the Hagana*. Jerusalem: Hasifriya Hatzionit.

Efrat. A. 1997. "Development Towns," in Tzameret and Yablonka 1997.

Eilon, A. 1978. "Operation Crusher," *Ma'Arahot* (March/April).

Eliav, M. 1981. *The First Aliyah*. Vols 1 and 2. Jerusalem: Yad Izhak Ben Zvi.

Even-Shoshan (Rozenstein), Z. 1955. *The History of the Labour Movement in Eretz Yisrael*. Vols 1, 2 & 3. Tel Aviv: Am Oved.

Gilboa, M. 1968. *Six Years–Six Days: Origins and History of the Six-Day War*. Tel Aviv: Am Oved.

Gluska. A. 2004. *Eshkol, Give the Order! The Israeli Defense Force and Government on the Road to the Six-Day War, 1963–1967*. Tel Aviv: Ma'arahot.

Golan, A. 1997. "Settlement in the First Decade of the State of Israel," in Tzameret and Yablonka 1997.

Greitzer, D. 1997. "Ben-Gurion, Mapai and the Arabs of Israel," in Tzameret and Yablonka 1997.

Gross, N. 1997. "Economics of Israel," in Tzameret and Yablonka 1997.

Habbas, B. 1947. *Book of the Second Aliyah*. Tel Aviv: Am Oved.

Haber, E. 1987. *Tomorrow A War Will Break Out*. Tel Aviv: Edanim.

Hacohen, D. 2001. "Population Dispersal and Merging of Diasporas: Incompatible Missions? The Experience of Immigrant Settlements (Moshavim)," in Shapira 2001.

Harkabi, Y. 1967. *Israel's Viewpoints in its Conflicts with the Arabs*. Tel Aviv: Dvir.

Harpaz, Y. 2002. *Through Fire: The Palmah's Fifth Battalion in the War of Independence*. Tel Aviv: Ma'arahot.

Har-Zion, M. 1969. *Chapters of a Diary*. Tel Aviv: Levin-Epstein.

Israel Defense Force. 1954. *In the Eyes of the Enemy: Three Arab Publications on the War of Independence*. Tel Aviv: Ma'arahot.

Israel Defense Force (General Staff: History Branch). 1966. *The History of the War of Independence*. Tel Aviv: Ma'arahot.

Itzchaki, A. 1982. *Latrun*. Jerusalem: Cana.

Lissak, M. 1999. *The Great Immigration in the Years of the 1950s: Failure of the Melting Pot*. Jerusalem: Bialik Institute.

Meir-Glitzenstein, E. 2001. "Class and Ethnicity Concerning the Public Struggle of Iraqi Jews in Beersheba in the early 1950s," in Shapira 2001.

Milstein, U. 1985. *The History of the Israel Paratroopers*. Tel Aviv: Schlagi.

Milstein, U. 1989–1991. *The War of Independence Vols 1–2 1989; Vols 3–4 1991*. Tel Aviv: Zmora Bitan.

Ozacky-Lazar, S. 2001. "The Formation of Jewish–Arab Relations during the First Decade," in Shapira 2001.

Pollack, A. N. 1955. *The Rise of the State of Israel*. Tel Aviv: Sefarim

Rabin, Y. 1979. *Service Notebook*: *Vols 1 and 2*. Tel Aviv: Ma'Ariv.

Rosenthal, Y. 1997. "Israel's Foreign Policy: Between Security and Diplomacy," in Tzameret and Yablonka 1997.

Rosenthal, Y. 2005. *Yitzah Rabin*. Vol. 1, 1922–1967. (Series for the Perpetuation of the Memories of Israel's Presidents and Prime Ministers.) Jerusalem: Israel State Archives.

Rubinstein, D. 1990. *The Fig Tree Embrace*. Jerusalem: Keter.

Segev, T. 2000. *One Palestine Complete*. New York: Metropolitan Books.

Segev, T. 2005. *1967 and the Country had a Change of Face*. Jerusalem: Keter.

Shaham, D. 1998. *Israel – 50 Years*. Tel Aviv: Am Oved.

Shalom, Z. 1995. *David Ben-Gurion: The State of Israel and the Arab World 1949–1956*. Beersheba: Ben Gurion University.

Shapira, A. 2001. (ed.). *A State in Transition: Israeli Society in the Early Decades*. Jerusalem: Zalman Shazar Center.

Shapira, A. 2004. *Igal Alon: Spring of His Life*. Bnei Barak: Kibbutz Hameuhad.

Sharett, M. 1958. *In the Forum of Nations*. Tel Aviv: Am Oved.

Sharett, M. 1978. *Personal Diary*. Tel Aviv: Sifriyat Maariv.

Sivan, E., 1991. *The 1948 Generation: Myth, Profile and Memory*. Israel Defense Forces, Tel Aviv: Ma'arahot.

Slutsky, Y. 1964. "From Defence to Strife," in B. Dinur 1964, Vol. 2.

Slutsky, Y. 1972. "History of the Haganah," in B. Dinur 1964, Vol. 3.

Susser, A. 1999. *Six Days, Thirty Years: New Perspectives on the Six-Day War*. Tel Aviv: Am Oved.

Teveth, S. 1957. *The Sinai Campaign of the Israel Defense Force*. Tel Aviv: Schocken.

Tzahor, Z. 1997. "Early Israeli Electoral Arrangements and the Political Map," in Tzameret and Yablonka 1997.

Tzameret, Z. 1997. "Ten Years of Education," in Tzameret and Yablonka 1997.

Tzameret, Z. and Yablonka, H. (eds) 1997. *The First Decade*. Jerusalem: Yad Yitzah Ben Zvi.

Tzur, Y. 1997. "Immigration from Islamic Countries," in Tzameret and Yablonka 1997.

Weitz, Y. 1995. *The Man Who Was Murdered Twice*. Jerusalem: Keter.

Weitz, Y. 2001. "Separation from the Founding Father: The Withdrawal of Ben Gurion, the Head of Government in 1963," in Shapira 2001.

Weizman, E. 1975. *Go to the Sky, Go to the Land*. Tel Aviv: Ma'Ariv.

Ya'ari, E. 1975. *Egypt and the Fedayeen*. Givat Haviva: Center for Arabic and Afro-Asian Studies.

Yablonka, H. 1997. "Immigrants from Europe and Awareness of the Holocaust," in Tzameret and Yablonka 1997.

Yariv, A. 1988. "The Six Day War – Twenty Years Later," in Ze'vi and Doron 1988.

Yiftah, A. 1948. (pseudonym of S. Gutman) "Lydda Goes into Exile." *Mibifnim* (November).

Ze'evi, R. 1988. "Military Lessons," in Ze'evi and Doron 1988.

Ze'evi, R and Doron, G. (eds). 1988. *Elazar Papers*. Tel Aviv: The Elazar Memorial Association.

INDEX